Communications in Computer and Information Science 1551

More information about this series at https://link.springer.com/bookseries/7899

Edgar Jembere · Aurona J. Gerber ·
Serestina Viriri · Anban Pillay (Eds.)

Artificial Intelligence Research

Second Southern African Conference, SACAIR 2021
Durban, South Africa, December 6–10, 2021
Proceedings

Editors
Edgar Jembere (iD)
University of KwaZulu-Natal
Durban, South Africa

Aurona J. Gerber (iD)
University of Pretoria
Pretoria, South Africa

Serestina Viriri (iD)
University of KwaZulu-Natal
Durban, South Africa

Anban Pillay (iD)
University of KwaZulu-Natal
Durban, South Africa

ISSN 1865-0929   ISSN 1865-0937 (electronic)
Communications in Computer and Information Science
ISBN 978-3-030-95069-9   ISBN 978-3-030-95070-5 (eBook)
https://doi.org/10.1007/978-3-030-95070-5

This Springer imprint is published by the registered company Springer Nature Switzerland AG
The registered company address is: Gewerbestrasse 11, 6330 Cham, Switzerland

Preface

This volume of the Springer CCIS series (CCIS 1551) contains the revised accepted papers of SACAIR 2021, the 2nd Southern African Conference for Artificial Intelligence Research[1].

Message from the Conference Chairs

Dear authors and readers,

It is with great pleasure that we write this foreword to the proceedings of the second Southern African Conference for Artificial Intelligence Research (SACAIR 2021) held online during December 6–10, 2021[2]. The program included an unconference for students on December 6 (a student-driven event for students to interact with each other as well as with sponsors and other possible employers), a day of tutorials on December 7, and the main conference during December 8–10, 2021.

SACAIR 2021 is the second full international conference focussed on Artificial Intelligence hosted by the Centre for AI Research (CAIR), South Africa. The inaugural CAIR conference, the Forum for AI Research (FAIR 2019) was held in Cape Town, South Africa, in December 2019, and SACAIR 2020 was held in February 2021 after being postponed due to the COVID-19 pandemic.

The Centre for AI Research (CAIR)[3] is a South African distributed research network that was established in 2011 with the aim of building world class Artificial Intelligence research capacity in South Africa. CAIR conducts foundational, directed, and applied research into various aspects of AI through its nine research groups based at six universities (the University of Pretoria, the University of KwaZulu-Natal, the University of Cape Town, Stellenbosch University, the University of the Western Cape, and North-West University). Research groups at CAIR include an Adaptive and Cognitive Systems Lab situated at the University of Cape Town, an AI and Cybersecurity research group at the University of the Western Cape, an AI for Development and Innovation group at the University of Pretoria, two Machine Learning groups focused on deep learning at North-West University and the University of Kwa-Zulu Natal, a Knowledge Abstraction and Representation group at Stellenbosch University, an Ethics of AI research group at the University of Pretoria, a Knowledge Representation and Reasoning group at the University of Cape Town, and a Mathematical and Computational Statistics group focused on applied data science at the University of Pretoria.

The theme for SACAIR 2021 was AI for Science, Technology and Society. AI technologies in their current data-driven form have the potential to transform

---

[1] https://sacair.org.za/.

[2] The original plan was to have a hybrid event in Ballito, South Africa, but due to the emergence of the Omicron COVID-19 variant end of November 2021, and the rapid rise in infections, the event was online only.

[3] https://www.cair.org.za/.

our world for the better. However, humans are faced with serious challenges in the context of AI advances in all areas of their lives, as wide apart as employment and labour on the one hand and social companionship on the other. In the context of machine learning applications, these challenges lead to concerns around fairness, structural bias and amplification of existing social stereotypes, privacy, transparency, accountability and responsibility, and trade-offs among all these concerns, especially within the context of security, robustness, and accuracy of AI systems. Furthermore, AI technologies can perform tasks that previously only humans could perform, such as calculating the best treatment for certain illnesses and caring for older persons. In some cases this is a good thing, but in some it challenges human agency and experience, and even political stability, in profound ways. Human notions of morality, of responsibility, and of ethical decision-making are challenged in ways humanity has never before encountered. In addition, children grow up in novel contexts affected by technological manipulation of social narratives and we do not yet know what the impact of this will be. In turn, media and information literacy has become an essential skill, which is just as important as technical skills. Finally, there are also cultural concerns such as the loss of nuances of human languages and expression in the context of NLP, concerns around the ownership of art, and others.

The choice of conference theme was intended to ensure multi-disciplinary contributions that focus both on the technical aspects and the social impact and consequences of AI technologies. In addition, there was a healthy balance between contributions from logic-based AI and those from data-driven AI, as the focus on knowledge representation and reasoning remains an important ingredient of studying and extending human intelligence. In line with the above, it was decided that the conference topics would cover several broad areas of Artificial Intelligence namely Machine Learning, Knowledge Representation and Reasoning, Quantum Artificial Intelligence, Deep Learning, Computer Vision and Image Processing, Philosophy and Ethics of AI, AI in and for Information Systems, and AI in the Humanities and Society. Our keynote speakers were Knut Hinkelmann of FHNW Switzerland, Francesco Petruccione of UKZN, South Africa, and Vincent C. Müller of TU/e, the Netherlands.

We expect this multi- and interdisciplinary conference to grow into the premier AI conference in Southern Africa as it brings together nationally and internationally established and emerging researchers from across various disciplines including Computer Science, Mathematics, Statistics, Informatics, Philosophy, and Law. The conference is also focused on cultivating and establishing a network of talented students working in AI from across Africa.

We sincerely thank the technical program chairs for the hard work on the volume and the editorial duties performed. A thank you to the topic chairs, the local and international panel of reviewers, our keynotes, and the authors and participants for their contributions. Last but not least, our gratitude to the members of the organizing committee, student organizers, and our sponsors without whom this conference would not have been realised.

December 2021   Anban Pillay
                                                                                Aurona Gerber

Message from the Technical Program Chairs

Dear readers,

This volume of the SACAIR proceedings contains the revised accepted papers of SACAIR 2021. We are thankful that our second annual Southern African Conference for Artificial Intelligence Research elicited the support it did during this challenging year with all the uncertainties due to the COVID-19 pandemic.

We received just over 100 abstracts, and after submission and a first round of evaluation, 71 papers were sent out for review to our SACAIR Programme Committee. The SACAIR submissions were solicited according to relevant SACAIR topics. The Program Committee comprised 88 members, 28 of whom were from outside Southern Africa. Each paper was reviewed by at least three members of the Program Committee in a rigorous, double-blind process whereby the following criteria were taken into consideration: Relevance to SACAIR, Significance, Technical Quality, Scholarship, and Presentation (which included quality and clarity of writing). For this SACAIR proceedings volume, 22 full research papers were selected for publication in Springer's CCIS series (which translates to an acceptance rate of 31%). The accepted full research papers per topic are as follows: Deep Learning (5), AI in and for Information Systems (3), Knowledge Representation and Reasoning (2), Machine Learning (6), Philosophy and Ethics of AI (3), AI in the Humanities and Society (1), and Computer Vision and Image Processing (2).

Thank you to all the authors and Program Committee members, and congratulations to the authors whose work was accepted for publication in this proceedings. We wish our readers a fruitful reading experience with these proceedings!

December 2021

Edgar Jembere
Serestina Viriri

Organization

Local Organizing Committee

Anban Pillay (Co-chair)	University of KwaZulu-Natal, South Africa
Aurona Gerber (Co-chair)	University of Pretoria, South Africa
Edgar Jembere (Technical Program Chair)	University of KwaZulu-Natal, South Africa
Serestina Viriri (Technical Program Chair)	University of KwaZulu-Natal, South Africa
Francesco Petruccione	University of KwaZulu-Natal, South Africa
Sibonelo Dlamini	University of KwaZulu-Natal, South Africa
Yüvika Singh	University of KwaZulu-Natal, South Africa
Emile Engelbrecht	Stellenbosch University, South Africa
Renee le Roux	Mongoose Communications & Design, South Africa

Program Committee Chairs

Philosophy and Ethics of AI

Emma Ruttkamp-Bloem	University of Pretoria, South Africa
Vincent Müller	Technical University of Eindhoven, The Netherlands

AI in and for Information Systems

Sunet Eybers	University of Pretoria, South Africa
Knut Hinkelmann	FHNW University of Applied Sciences and Arts Northwestern Switzerland, Switzerland

AI in Humanities and Society

Bethel Mutanga	Mangosuthu Univerisity of Technology, South Africa
Dino Carpentras	University of Limerick, Ireland

Machine Learning

Alta de Waal	University of Pretoria, South Africa
Maria Schuld	Xanadu, South Africa

Knowledge Representation and Reasoning

Thomas Meyer   University of Cape Town, South Africa
Ivan Varzinczak   Université d'Artois, France

Quantum Artificial Intelligence

Daniel Kyungdeock Park   Sungkyunkwan University Seoul, South Korea
Ilya Sinayski   University of KwaZulu-Natal, South Africa

Deep Learning

Deshendran Moodley   University of Cape Town, South Africa
Marelie Davel   North-West University, South Africa

Computer Vision and Image Processing

Mandla Gwetu   University of KwaZulu-Natal, South Africa
Jules-Raymond Tapamo   University of KwaZulu-Natal, South Africa

Program Committee

Amira Abbas   University of KwaZulu-Natal, South Africa
Ritesh Ajoodha   University of the Witwatersrand, South Africa
Kehinde Aruleba   Walter Sisulu University, South Africa
Bubacarr Bah   African Institute for Mathematical Sciences
                                  (AIMS), South Africa
Etienne Barnard   North-West University, South Africa
Sihem Belabbes   LIASD, Université Paris, France
Sonia Berman   University of Cape Town, South Africa
Jacques Beukes   North-West University, South Africa
Willie Brink   Stellenbosch University, South Africa
Arina Britz   Stellenbosch University, South Africa
Jan Buys   University of Cape Town, South Africa
Joan Byamugisha   IBM Research Africa, South Africa
Dino Carpentras   University of Limerick, Ireland
Giovanni Casini   ISTI-CNR, Italy
Colin Chibaya   Sol Plaatje University, South Africa
Olawande Daramola   Cape Peninsula University of Technology,
                                  South Africa
Jérémie Dauphin   University of Luxembourg, Luxembourg
Marelie Davel   North-West University, South Africa
Tanya de Villiers Botha   Stellenbosch University, South Africa
Alta de Waal   University of Pretoria, South Africa
Febe de Wet   Stellenbosch University, South Africa

Tiny Du Toit	North-West University, South Africa
Sunet Eybers	University of Pretoria, South Africa
Inger Fabris-Rotelli	University of Pretoria, South Africa
Sebastian Feld Delft	Delft University of Technology, The Netherlands
Eduardo Fermé	Universidade da Madeira, Portugal
Fred Freitas	Universidade Federal de Pernambuco, Brazil
Anne Gerdes	University of Denmark, Denmark
Mandlenkosi Gwetu	University of KwaZulu-Natal, South Africa
Shohreh Haddadan	University of Luxembourg, Luxembourg
Bertram Haskins	Nelson Mandela University, South Africa
Marie Hattingh	University of Pretoria, South Africa
Knut Hinkelmann	FHNW University of Applied Sciences and Arts Northwestern Switzerland, Switzerland
Omowunmi Isafiade	University of the Western Cape, South Africa
Nobert Jere	Walter Sisulu University, South Africa
Herman Kamper	Stellenbosch University, South Africa
Richard Klein	University of the Witwatersrand, South Africa
Hari Kishan Kondaveeti	VIT-AP University, India
Eduan Kotzé	University of the Free State, South Africa
Jaco Kruger	St Augustine College of South Africa, South Africa
Louise Leenen	University of the Western Cape, South Africa
Guido Löhr	TU Eindhoven, The Netherlands
Patricia Lutu	University of Pretoria, South Africa
Truong-Thanh Ma	CRIL CNRS and University of Artois, France
Zola Mahlaza	University of Cape Town, South Africa
Patrick Marais	University of Cape Town, South Africa
Vukosi Marivate	University of Pretoria, South Africa
Réka Markovich	University of Luxembourg, Luxembourg
Muthoni Masinde	Central University of Technology, South Africa
Jocelyn Mazarura	University of Pretoria, South Africa
Felix McGregor	Saigen, South Africa
Thomas Meyer	University of Cape Town and CAIR, South Africa
Thipe Modipa	University of Limpopo, South Africa
Deshendran Moodley	University of Cape Town, South Africa
Coenraad Mouton	North-West University, South Africa
Vincent C. Müller	Technical University of Eindhoven, The Netherlands/University of Leeds, UK
Murimo Bethel Mutanga	Mangosuthu University of Technology, South Africa
Peeter Müürsepp	Tallinn University, Estonia
Fred Nicolls	University of Cape Town, South Africa

Geoff Nitshcke	University of Cape Town, South Africa
Thambo Nyathi	University of Pretoria, South Africa
Ítalo Oliveira	Free University of Bozen-Bolzano, Italy
Daniel Kyungdeock Park	Sungkyunkwan University, South Korea
Laurent Perrussel	IRIT - Universite de Toulouse, France
Iliana M. Petrova	Inria, France
Laurette Pretorius	University of South Africa, South Africa
Catherine S. Price	University of KwaZulu-Natal, South Africa
Gavin Rens	Katholieke Universiteit Leuven, Belgium
Helen Robertson	University of the Witwatersrand, South Africa
Cleyton Rodrigues	Universidade Federal de Pernambuco, Brazil
Irene Russo	Istituto di Linguistica Computazionale - CNR, Italy
Emma Ruttkamp-Bloem	University of Pretoria, South Africa
Maria Schuld	University of KwaZulu-Natal, South Africa
Giuseppe Sergioli	University of Cagliari, Italy
Jonathan Shock	University of Cape Town, South Africa
Ilya Sinayskiy	NITheP and University of KwaZulu-Natal, South Africa
Riana Steyn	University of Pretoria, South Africa
Umberto Straccia	ISTI-CNR, Italy
Ryan Sweke	University of KwaZulu-Natal, South Africa
Jules-Raymond Tapamo	Univesity of KwaZulu-Natal, South Africa
Tian Theunissen	North-West University, South Africa
Anitta Thomas	UNISA, South Africa
Wiebke Toussaint	Delft University of Technology, The Netherlands
Hossana Twinomurinzi	University of Johannesburg, South Africa
Dustin Van Der Haar	University of Johannesburg, South Africa
Terence Van Zyl	University of Johannesburg, South Africa
Ivan Varzinczak	University of Artois and CNRS, France
Peter-Paul Verbeek	University of Twente, The Netherlands
Philippe Verreault-Julien	Eindhoven University of Technology, The Netherlands
Christopher Wareham	University of the Witwatersrand, South Africa
Bruce Watson	Stellenbosch University, South Africa
Zhihao Wu	UCLA, USA

SACAIR Sponsors

The sponsors of SACAIR 2021, The Journal of Artificial Intelligence, the Centre for AI Research (CAIR), the National Institute for Theoretical and Computational Sciences (NITheCS), and the Discipline of Computer Science in the School of Mathematics, Statistics and Computer Science at the University of KwaZulu-Natal are herewith gratefully acknowledged.

Contents

Knowledge Representation and Reasoning

Machine Learning

Philosophy and Ethics of AI

AI in the Humanities and Society

John Searle's Chinese Room, and Its Predecessor, a Short Story "The Game" by Anatoly Dneprov

Konstantin V. Azarov$^{(\boxtimes)}$

University of Bonn, Regina-Pacis-Weg 3, 53113 Bonn, Germany
konstantin.v.azarov@gmail.com

Abstract. There are two views against the possibility of strong AI. The first is centered around John Searle's well known 1980 skeptical thought experiment, "the Chinese Room." However, there is a second, largely unknown, view, that preceded Searle's. This second view is in Anatoly Dneprov's 1961 short story, "The Game." Both ask: "can computers think?" both answer: "no." Although Searle's experiment received a lot of criticisms, "The Game" did not receive any response. However, if we take into account Dneprov's 'The Game' together with his other works, we will find that Dneprov's argument is developed to a level comparable to Searle's. This paper argues that the radical difference between the two is the perception of the brain. Searle believes that machines can think, but the human brain is the only machine capable of thinking, while Dneprov would not agree. For him, the brain is part of an organism and an organism cannot be regarded as a machine. Therefore, Dneprov's work can be helpful to challenge conceptions of the brain as a machine in the current debates on AI.

Keywords: Searle · Chinese room · Strong AI · Dneprov · Machine-organism distinction

1 Two Thought Experiments

When answering the question "Can digital computers think?" both John Searle, an American philosopher, and Anatoly Dneprov, a Russian editor and writer of Ukrainian descent, answered: "no, they cannot." Searle presented his argument in a thought experiment "The Chinese Room" published in an academic article [1]; and Dneprov presented his argument in the short story "The Game" [2]. Searle's argument has benefited greatly from a vigorous discussion, but, Dneprov's argument has not received any criticism. However, if we take into account Dneprov's "The Game" together with his other works, we find that Dneprov's argument is developed to a similar level of sophistication as Searle's. Even though Dneprov is unknown, he presented the first version of the Dneprov-Searle type thought experiment, and therefore it is logical to analyze his thought experiment first.

In "The Game," Dneprov describes a game where 1,500 willing students are divided into groups that are intended to communicate, interact, and process information in the

© Springer Nature Switzerland AG 2022
E. Jembere et al. (Eds.): SACAIR 2021, CCIS 1551, pp. 3–11, 2022.
https://doi.org/10.1007/978-3-030-95070-5_1

same way as a mainframe computer. In the story, the students are attending a big mathematics conference, and the game, which takes place in a stadium, is the final event of the conference. The 1,500 students are divided into small groups and the story is narrated from the first-person perspective of one of the participating students. Unbeknown to them, each group represents a component of a mainframe computer. The first group functions as the memory unit, the second as the input unit, the third as the output unit, the fourth as the central processing unit, and so on. The whole structure of the mainframe computer is mirrored, and recreated through the interactions between the students. Some groups transmit binary numbers to each other, and other groups manipulate the binary numbers. However, there are students, who find the process boring, and at least one student leaves the game before the end.

The next day Professor Zarubin, the main organizer of the conference, tells the students the results. At first, Zarubin asks the students what did they think they were doing the day before? Some students answer: "it was a Chinese whispers game," others answer: "a check of the reliability of the binary code." Zarubin dismisses all the answers and asks a new question: "who speaks Portuguese?" None of the mathematicians can. Zarubin then reveals that the real purpose of the game was to show that computers can't think. In the game, the students were interacting as components of a digital machine running a program to translate a sentence from Portuguese to Russian. Because somebody left early, the last word of the translation was corrupted, and the result was imperfect. The Portuguese sentence was "os maiores resultados sao produzidos por – pequenos mas continues esforços," and the translation came out as: "the greatest goals are achieved through minor but continuous ekkedt," where "ekkedt" should be translated as "efforts." In this story, the students weren't aware of what they were doing, in a similar way, Dneprov concludes, through Zarubin, that computers cannot be aware of what they are doing.

However, one of the students, Anton Golovin (whom the narrator knows is a "big fan of cybernetics"), tries to argue: "Of course, they were unaware of what were they doing. Nobody believes that neurons can understand what the brain is thinking. The same holds true for computer chips. Only the computer as a whole could be capable of thinking." Zarubin refutes the student: "If so, some entity should have been created at the stadium during the game, some sort of Hegel's Weltgeist" [2], p. 41.

The line of thought in Searle's Chinese room is similar, but later interpretations reveal a striking difference between Searle and Dneprov. In Searle's experiment, somebody (or Searle himself) is locked in a room in China without any knowledge of Chinese. He receives a text in Chinese from the outside, and strictly following a set of instructions in his native language, creates a fluent response in Chinese. In fact, acting in this way, the person in the Chinese room passes Turing's test, and creates the impression of being fluent in Chinese; which, according to Turing, is sufficient proof of intelligence, or of what Searle calls strong AI [1], p. 422. For Searle, computers work in the same way as this Chinese room, and this formal combination of symbols without awareness is similar to the view expressed by Dneprov in "The Game." In the same way as Dneprov's students have no awareness that they are translating Portuguese, and as Searle's man in the Chinese room has no awareness of what he is communicating in Chinese; computers have no awareness of what they are processing.

When compared to Searle's Chinese room, "The Game" has both formal and theoretical disadvantages. There are at least five of these disadvantages as follows: first, "The Game" lacks technical terminology, a task far more demanding than a short story allows. Second, there is no distinction between syntax and semantics that is present in Searle. Third, where Searle's aim is an actual Turing test, Dneprov's "The Game" aims only at the translation of a sentence, which is only a rough analogy of Turing's test. Fourth, Dneprov is not concerned with the complications related to the dualism inherited in a view of the human mind presupposed by the computationalist. Fifth, Dneprov is not interested in the question of whether we need to know how the brain works to create AI, or, on the contrary, if creating AI could explain the mind. Dneprov is also not interested in a set of other minor philosophical questions important to Searle. The great advantage of Dneprov's "The Game" is its simplicity, and it gives the same argument in a more condensed fashion.

"The Game" is a criticism of only a rough analogy of Turing's test, and therefore it doesn't directly undermine the Turing test. Unlike Searle's Chinese room, the computer in "The Game" cannot show rationality in a dialogue. However, the way Dneprov approaches the Turing test in "The Game" has the advantage of commonsensical realism: the principles behind processing a translation of a sentence and the principles behind providing a line in Turing's dialogue are identical. And it is obvious that a computer processing a translation of a sentence is identical in principle to a computer providing a line in a Turing's dialogue.

By comparing Searle and Dneprov's thought experiments, I found a problem with proving the existence of the mind in speaking machines alone, and this issue seems to be overlooked in contemporary debates on AI. If the computational theory is correct, and a program approved by the Turing test possesses AI in a strong sense, i.e. if such a program has a mind, then why don't we ascribe other programs with minds? By proving the existence of the mind in some programs we necessarily create a situation where we need to disprove the existence of minds in other programs. In other words, if Turing and other computationalists are correct, why not view the smartphone as a sapient being, with a mind being tormented in a 'body' lacking conditions necessary for the mind's own happy existence (which may include communication with fellow beings and personal freedoms among others)?

Computationalists may answer this objection by claiming that there is a fundamental difference between speaking and translating; however, humans need awareness when doing both. The only way to acknowledge the lack of awareness behind translating is by ascribing both speaking and translating to a computer that is incapable of self-awareness in any form. A strong analogy for this idea can be drawn when we look at the way we view dogs and humans. In this analogy, dogs can be viewed as computers that don't pass the Turing test and humans as computers that do. Dogs are protected by law because even though they are not sapient, they feel. Additionally, as Searle puts it, "we find it completely natural to ascribe intentionality to members of certain other primate species such as apes and monkeys and to domestic animals such as dogs" [1], p. 421. Of course, it is analogous to human beings, whose intellectual powers we take for granted. Since both species, dogs and humans, are animals, it is assumed that we share some essential characteristics like feelings of pain and happiness, behavior based on decision making, and, judging by how we treat pet dogs in everyday life, humans believe dogs to possess some sort of intentionality. However, the same analogy should hold true for both the programs that pass the Turing test and all the other programs that don't. Machines that can both translate and speak and machines that can only translate are, in many ways, very similar. They have the same processing architecture, and are built on microchips made out of the same silicon.

The Turing's test defender could reply, that he wants to limit the scope to the behavioral field alone. But how is this possible? Will we treat a human being that fails the Turing test as a mindless machine? Another possible defense for the Turing test here is that the aim of the test is not to prove awareness, mind, and other associated things, but only the intellectual capacity of machines. But this begs the question: if we assume not all things in a program can pass the Turing test, then the test is only evaluating a chatbot. And this is definitely not what Turing wanted, when he wrote that just like wheels replace legs in automobiles, the electrical circuits replace "the essential properties" of the nerves [3], p. 117.

One of the main advantages of the Chinese room over "The Game," is that Searle tries to answer a set of objections to his thought experiment, the most common of which he now believes to be "the system reply" [4]. The system reply suggests that although the man in the Chinese room is not aware of what is going on, the system as a whole has this capability. Searle responds by internalizing the room – let us suppose that all the books in the Chinese room, and all the rules have been learned by heart by somebody; in this situation to suppose that there is any strong AI consciousness is to suppose some sub-personality capable of Chinese. However, this is fine with some of Searle's opponents.

It is striking, that the system reply is present in Dneprov's short story. "The big fan of cybernetics," the student Golovin, presented the same objection. Dneprov's form of the thought experiment is even stronger than Searle's in this regard, because there is nothing material in Dneprov's "computer." Searle's answer to the system reply could be more convincing, if instead of interiorization, he had chosen exteriorization. The best way out of the system reply is the way out of the Chinese room. The only entity a system reply can detect in Dneprov is some sort of a ghost of the stadium, which is much less plausible empirically, when compared to the unconscious sub-personality of the man with internalized Chinese room.

2 Machines and Brains

The first major divergence between Searle and Dneprov stems from the fact that Searle, while stressing the biological nature of the mind, believes the brain to be a machine. Thus, he stressed that "[n]o one would suppose that we could produce milk and sugar by running a computer simulation of the formal sequences in lactation and photosynthesis, but where the mind is concerned many people are willing to believe in such a miracle" [1], p. 424. Moreover, according to Searle, mental states are as real as any other biological phenomena, for example, like lactation, photosynthesis, and digestion [1], p. 450, [5], p. 265. But when answering, "can a machine think?" he replied explicitly that "only a machine could think, and only very special kinds of machines, namely brains and machines with internal causal powers equivalent to those of brains" [1], p. 417. In fact, Searle's notion of the machine is broader than a commonsensical idea of it. Later Searle even puts it quite explicitly: in his 1999 article he claims, the idea that the Chinese room denies the possibility of thinking machines is the main misconception related to this thought experiment [4], p. 116.

It is hard to see these two positions (the brain as a machine and thinking as a bio-logical process) as consistent. Are cows "milk-producing machines," and are "plants photosynthesizing machines"? It is obvious that, from the viewpoint of bioethics, there is a difference between a machine, synthesizing milk, and a cow [6]. Cows reproduce, regenerate and every one is unique, it is impossible to turn a cow off. It is impossible to disassemble two "broken" (ill) cows into a single "working" (healthy) cow. This is clear even without mentioning the grim ethical consequences of conflating living organisms and machines which must be mentioned. This line of thought is a natural corollary to the criticism of animal exploitation as formulated by Leo Tolstoy [7] or Ruth Harrison [8]. Globus expresses a concern which is close to mine when he writes about the problem of objectification in Searle and in his opponents [9], p. 389.

The fact that some mechanisms can be detected in biological organisms does not mean that there are any machines there, except for possible artificial augmentation. It constitutes a shortcoming in Searle's approach which seems to be overlooked by all his opponents. Searle mechanized the notion of the brain for it to be comparable to the notion of the computing machine. Already Turing did it by approaching "man as a machine" [3], p. 116. At the same time, Searle wants this brain-machine to have organicist functions, like human self-determination and intentionality. However, for such human features as self-determination and intentionality to really work in an argument against strong AI, they should be defined as they are, as our embodied features. For the sake of brevity, we will not consider here the problem of Searle's notion of intentionality in its entirety. Briefly speaking, the living nature of human intentionality does not receive much atten-tion in the main book by Searle on the subject [5] because Searle's intentionality is not sufficiently embodied. Searle mentioned body in relation to intentionality only 3 times in *Intentionality: An Essay in the Philosophy of Mind*. Moreover, he proposes "dissolu-tion" of the mind-body problem [5], pp. 262–272, which in many aspects detaches the body from intentionality as only a mere function of the body: Searle uses a metaphor of relations such as between the stomach and digestion [5], p. 15. The disconnection between body and intentionality in Searle is especially obvious if to compare Searle's notion with the notion of intentionality by Merleau-Ponty. Of course, Searle himself views his own account as only a "general theory," [5], p. vii, with much further work to do; but then it is exactly the case when the limitation of the general theory encounters a big problem in a case of its particular application. In our case, it is the application to the problem of AI.

From some technocratic perspective, self-determination and intentionality could be easily ascribed to machines, even to very simple ones that cannot pass the Turing test. Some believe that intentionality can be ascribed to the Chinese room, for example Kugel [10]. Antiviral software self-determines to do a full disk check every month, or update itself. One, of course, can say, that it is not the real self-determination, since a program follows not its own purposes, but one given by humans. Antiviral software serves human beings. Dneprov's "fan of cybernetics," the student Golovin, presented an objection: yes, computers are programmed, but we are also programmed; and it is not clear whether humans really "write" these programs for themselves [2], p. 40. Moreover, it is easy to modify a program so that the connection between what I want to do, and what the program "wants to do" will be much harder to distinguish. I'm happy when my program "serves" me, but I can be quite upset when a chess program "beats" me; does such a program have an intent to beat me in chess? For Turing, the answer is yes, if I cannot distinguish it from a human being in a dialog.

Moreover, I can create a thought experiment, in which a program shows independent spontaneity without being appropriate for the Turing test. Let us consider a hypothetical program called "The Writer." It has 4 elements: a random number generator; a big electronic English dictionary, where all words are numbered; text editor with access to one of the online search engines; and a text file. The generator gives the dictionary a random number, and the dictionary sends the text editor a word that corresponds to this number. The text editor then uses this word to do an online search with its search engine, and adds 500 characters from the first entries found by the search engine to the text file in "The Writer." If we add a function to remember used words (and a simple algorithm to use the word next to the used one or a group of used ones) to "The Writer," it will even be able to "develop" its "writing style" in a formal sense. "The Writer" would then be able to perform operations with one particular word in a fraction of a second, and, in some formal sense, this fraction of second can be seen as a period when "The Writer" "has an intention" for that word. "The Writer" shows that self-determination and intentionality (not defined in regard to the machine-organism distinction) are not sufficient to distinguish between real human self-determination and intentionality, and the ones belonging to the program called "The Writer." What is lacking are the crucial elements of any living organism such as unity and uniqueness.

A mechanical connection presupposes simple relations, while organic connections demand a particular harmony of the whole. To accept this, there is no need for introducing any metaphysically demanding conceptions, such as in the early 20th century's Vitalism. All one needs to see is the difference between human intelligence and the computer's combinatorial abilities. Human intelligence comes from the unity and uniqueness of a human being, its biological, cultural and social evolution. Computer "intelligence" is, on the contrary, just a machine, ready to be copied, dissembled, turned off or upgraded.

Of course, this distinction is not a final blow in the debates pro et contra strong AI, but it is a big advantage for the opponents and skeptics of strong AI. There is an old response to it, considered already by Searle in 1980 (to some degree). It is correct that a human-made, non-unique, non-holistic computer lacks this potential, but what if we let computers evolve? What if we create an AI that is capable of evolving on its own with random mutations and posterior selections and choose its best results, so that even the engineers will have trouble explaining how their machines work? Turing suggested something like this when he introduced a notion of "unorganized machine" – a machine with random connections between its elements, which Turing viewed as "the simplest model of a nervous system" [3], p. 113. Globus can be seen as a defender of a close line of thought when, in the context of the debates related to the possibility of the strong AI, he stresses the fact that "the semantic relation is found to be dynamical – a spontaneous, stochastic, self-organizing process" [9], p. 12. Searle seems to be willing to accept such a scenario, when he wrote that "[p]erhaps other physical and chemical processes could produce exactly these effects; perhaps, for example, Martians also have intentionality but their brains are made of different stuff. That is an empirical question" [1], p. 422. However, it is an empirical question only when speculating about extraterrestrial life, but it is not an empirical question with regard to machines. By not acknowledging this explicitly, Searle gives his opponents more than he should. And again the reason is an overly mechanistic view of the brain, which distinguishes Searle from Dneprov.

3 AI of the Evolutionary Programming

Neither Searle nor Dneprov considered evolutionary programming as a way to create strong AI. However, in cases where the brain is duplicated sufficiently in the evolutionary process, Searle seems to accept the possibility of creating a strong AI through evolutionary programming (or through a german way, relying on indeterminacy and selection). Dneprov seems to reject this idea for the reasons presented below. However, before we can begin to consider Dneprov's view, first it is necessary to clarify a particular problem on the premises of evolutionary programming.

If we consider artificial selection towards AI in evolutionary programming in more detail, its proponents miss one more condition: life in general, and humans in particular, are not products of artificial selection. In fact, when comparing the creation of strong AI, ceteris paribus, with the creation of human intelligence, one needs more than some artificially implemented conditions (1) for the random evolution of machines. Instead, one needs to implement (2) the conditions of the random creation of the conditions (1) for the random evolution of the machines. From the current scientific perspective, life didn't originate in artificially set conditions for the creation of life. Nor did human rationality. Furthermore, to try to create computers through establishing random conditions for mutations of the environment in which conditions of computer evolution could (or could not) be established, are definitely too resource-consuming for the computer industry to follow. Moreover, one needs to know everything related to the creation of life and the origin of our intellectual abilities; both subjects are still, to a significant degree, a scientific mystery.

Dneprov actually has another short story that can further illuminate the organism-mechanism aspect of the strong AI problem in his view. In the science fiction short story which is translated as 'Crabs on the Island' [11] (CoI for further references), Dneprov introduced a case of artificial evolution. In CoI Dneprov depicts a scientific-engineering experiment, where the mechanisms (mechanical crabs) are created to reproduce with slight random variations and compete for the metal on an island somewhere in the tropical zone of the ocean. The competition meant to be violent, so that in the end the fastest and the most invulnerable sub-species of the crab-like metal collector will win. The project pursues a broad military goal, to create a means to collect all metal in the enemy territory, and it would be particularly handy if the crabs will also collect the metal which constitutes the tanks and cannons of the enemy. The instance of this artificial selection ends in an utter failure: crabs killed the main engineer for his metal dental prostheses, and destroyed all means of existence of his employee, the narrator of

CoI. Moreover, instead of developing the speed and effectivity, the crabs start to grow in size. In the end, the narrator is rescued unconscious by the expedition's ship which arrived to pick up the results of the experiment. He was lying between the giant tentacles of the last mechanical crab. The crab was dead or dead-like because all the island's metal was collected.

This idea of an artificial evolution fated to fail proliferated in Russian science fiction after Dneprov's story, and even influenced writers in neighbouring countries. It could partly be seen as a form of protest against control over the social processes in the Soviet Union and its satellites. Polish writer Stanisław Lem, more famous because of Tarkovsky's movie based on his novel "Solaris," made his version of Dneprov's story in a novel "Peace on Earth" (Pokój na Ziemi, 1984), where the artificial evolution made a turn opposite to one in CoI: the mechanisms meant to evolve in better and better weapons on the Moon disappeared. The astronauts, who return to collect the results of the experiment of artificial evolution, are shocked by this fact. But in the end the truth is revealed: machines were evolving in more and more miniature models. As a result, the struggle shifted to the nano level and the fighting mechanisms turned into the dust covering the Moon. The nano-machines managed to return to Earth with the Moon expedition and destroy all mechanic potential of humanity, reducing human civilization to the pre-Modern level. Besides the simple moral of the story by Dneprov (and the stories written under Dneprov's influence), where the creation turns against the creator in Mary Shelley's fashion, there is one idea important to the debates regarding strong AI: the analogy between artificial and natural selection should not be overemphasized. They are two different processes and there is no reason to expect the same results.

4 Conclusion

The comparison of Dneprov and Searle's thought experiments gives a new counterargument to the system response to the Chinese room. The best way out of the system response is the way out of the Chinese room, the way given in a backbone of Dneprov's thought experiment, as a story about an outdoor activity. It is better than the way of the internalization of the Chinese room chosen by Searle, because the objection of the sub-personality capable of Chinese in the man with such an internalized Chinese room would be impossible in the externalized variant. Dneprov's thought experiment proceeds outdoors, at the stadium, and only personality the system responder could detect is something as unlikely as a ghost of the stadium.

On a deeper level the comparison shows that the unity of intentionality and of self-determination (in itself and with each other) Searle wants, originates from the organic nature of human beings. Searle perfectly understands it, but he does not follow a necessary corollary: not only are we as a whole unlike machines, all our parts are unlike machines and our evolution is not of a mechanical type. Our brains are not computers, but organs inside of living beings, they are unique, can regenerate and grow with the organism and reproduce with the organism as a whole, unlike any machine; so that any parallel between the human mind and a computer's computational abilities are flawed on both theoretical and ethical levels.

At the same time, Searle goes too far when he equals information processing in computer with processes in "stomachs, thermostats, rainstorms, and hurricanes" [1],

p. 423. He does it as an irony regarding the rules of the discussion he participates in and greatly contributes to. But Searle could do more if, instead, he undermines some of the rules and follows a strict machine-organism distinction, which is shown by the comparison of his own thought experiment and Dneprov's thought experiment, where the latter does have such a distinction in a strong form. Someone with a strong notion of the machine-organism distinction could make a better attack on strong AI by targeting the brain-computer analogy as a sort of a conflation between a machine and a living organ. In this way it is also possible to avoid the ethical dangers of the conflation of organisms with machines, because from the fundamental bioethical view, as given by Leo Tolstoy [7] or Ruth Harrison [8], the former should not be regarded as the latter.

References

1. Searle, J.R.: Minds, brains, and programs. Behav. Brain Sci. **3**(3), 417–457 (1980). https://doi.org/10.1017/S0140525X00005756
2. Dneprov, A.: Igra the game, in Russian. Znanie sila Knowl. Power **5**, 39–41 (1961)
3. Turing, A.: Intelligent Machinery, A Heretical Theory (c.1951). In: Turing, A. (ed.) The Essential Turing. Oxford University Press (2004). https://doi.org/10.1093/oso/9780198250791.003.0018
4. Searle, J.R.: Chinese Room Argument. In: Robert, A.W., Frank, K. (eds.) The MIT Encyclopedia of the Cognitive Sciences, pp. 115–116. The MIT Press, Cambridge, Massachusetts (1999)
5. Searle, J.R.: Intentionality: An Essay in the Philosophy of Mind. Cambridge University Press, Cambridge (1983)
6. Nicholson, D.J.: Organisms ≠ machines. Stud. Hist. Philos. Sci. **44**(4), 669–678 (2013). https://doi.org/10.1016/j.shpsc.2013.05.014
7. Tolstoy, L.: The first step. In: Maude, A. (tr.) Essays and Letters, pp. 53–93. Oxford University Press, London (1911)
8. Harrison, R.: Animal Machines: The New Factory Farming Industry. CABI, Wallingford (2013)
9. Globus, G.G.: Deconstructing the Chinese room. J. Mind Behav. **12**(3), 377–391 (1991)
10. Kugel, P.: The Chinese room is a trick. Behav. Brain Sci. **27**(1), 153–154 (2004). https://doi.org/10.1017/S0140525X04210044
11. Dneprov, A.: Crabs on the Island. In: Strugatsky, A., Strugatsky, B. (eds.) Molecular Cafe: Science-Fiction Stories, pp. 29–58. Mir Publishers, Moscow (1968)

AI in and for Information Systems

The Detection of Conversation Patterns in South African Political Tweets Through Social Network Analysis

Aurona Gerber[1,2]([⊠]) [iD]

[1] University of Pretoria, Pretoria, South Africa
aurona.gerber@up.ac.za
[2] The Center for AI Research (CAIR), Pretoria, South Africa

Abstract. Within complex societies, social communities are distinguishable based on social interactions. The interactions can be between members or communities and can range from simple conversations between family members and friends to complex interactions that represent the flow of money, information, or power. In our modern digital society, social media platforms present unique opportunities to study social networks through social network analysis (SNA). Social media platforms are usually representative of a specific user group, and Twitter, a microblogging platform, is characterised by the fast distribution of news and often provocative opinions, as well as social mobilizing, which makes it popular for political interactions. The nature of Twitter generates a valuable SNA data source for investigating political conversations and communities, and in related research, specific archetypal conversation patterns between communities were identified that allow for unique interpretations of conversations about a topic. This paper reports on a study where social network analysis (SNA) was performed on Twitter data about political events in 2021 in South Africa. The purpose was to determine which distinct conversation patterns could be detected in datasets collected, as well as what could be derived from these patterns given the South African political landscape and perceptions. The results indicate that conversations in the South African political landscape are less polarized than expected. Conversations often manifest broadcast patterns from key influencers in addition to tight crowds or community clusters. Tight crowds or community clusters indicate intense conversation across communities that exhibits diverse opinions and perspectives on a topic. The results may be of value for researchers that aim to understand social media conversations within the South African society.

Keywords: Social network analysis · Twitter networks · Community clusters · Network visualisation · South African politics

1 Introduction

How communities form plays a significant role in understanding society and society interactions [1, 2]. In the past decade, various studies were done on the usage and influence of the internet, technology, and social media in society [3–5]. These studies indicate

© Springer Nature Switzerland AG 2022
E. Jembere et al. (Eds.): SACAIR 2021, CCIS 1551, pp. 15–31, 2022.
https://doi.org/10.1007/978-3-030-95070-5_2

that social media is one of the most important means of communication in our digital society and therefore forms a significant part of what determines the views and opinions of people [6–9]. To study conversations and communities, social network analysis (SNA) emerged as a distinct research field. SNA analyses network structures in social media networks, for instance, networked communities and clusters that are established because of interactions between members. Understanding how online communities form and communicate allows us to interpret the flow of information and opinions, as well as identify notable influencers [10].

Several social media platforms are used for social media interactions, and each of these platforms became representative of a specific means of communication and user profile [11–13]. Twitter, specifically, is a microblogging platform that is characterized by the fast flow of information and opinions, often from notable influencers, as well as social mobilization [14]. These characteristics are particularly valuable when analysing political conversations within a specific society, an important capability given evidence of collective action observed globally that resulted in substantial turmoil due to protest action [15–17]. In South Africa, protest action and unrest that occurred in July 2021 were mainly organized using social media platforms [18, 19], which emphasizes the necessity to understand social media networks, conversations, and communities. In particular, in the aftermath of the looting, alleged instigators were arrested based on their social media activity, specifically using Twitter [20].

Twitter was established in 2006 and is described as a social media platform that is dedicated to the sharing of news and opinions through tweets or microblogs, which are a maximum of 280 characters long [21]. Users can follow other users without mandatory interaction, but can of course reply, retweet, or mention other users or tweets and use hashtags to markup tweets with topics. Twitter is particularly popular for expressing political and controversial opinions and Twitter's APIs, therefore, provide access to a valuable source of conversational data. This study aimed to detect the social network structures and conversation patterns within Twitter datasets surrounding specific political events during 2021 in South Africa.

Understanding the formation and dynamics of politics in social networks can provide useful insights into the interactions and changes in political communities, and might assist in the design of interventions [15, 16]. The remainder of the paper is structured as follows. The next section, Sect. 2, provides a brief background and summary of related work, followed by Sect. 3 discussing the research approach. Section 4 presents the results and findings given the SNA analysis of the datasets, and Sect. 5 concludes.

2 Background and Related Work

This section provides an overview of social networks and social network analysis (SNA), followed by the application of SNA on social media data.

2.1 Social Network Analysis

Social network analysis (SNA) is defined as the analysis of social (media) structures using network and graph theory [22–24]. A set or group of social actors that interact create a complex network that can be studied to gain insight into the relationships between individuals and groups within societies [25]. When studying social networks, the inter-actions and relations between actors are considered, and not the properties of the actors themselves [1, 26]. The identification of clusters, communities, or groups given the inter-actions of actors is an important objective of SNA, and groups are detected by analysing the interactions within a group as well as the interactions between different groups or clusters [8, 27]. Several algorithms exist that assist with the detection of groups or communities in networks, for instance, the Clauset-Newman-Moore algorithm [28, 29]. The algorithm detects communities by greedily optimizing using modularity [28].

The Social Media Research Foundation (SMRF) [30] was established with the dis-tinct purpose of studying social media and uses SNA extensively. One of their research outputs is a network analysis application, NodeXL, that assists with network analysis, as well as social network and content analysis [31, 32]. NodeXL uses data from social media platforms that provide data extraction APIs such as Twitter.

2.2 Archetypical Twitter Conversational Patterns

Using NodeXL from the SMRF to analyse Twitter data, Smith et al. identified six dis-tinct archetypical conversational patterns using network-level metrics namely density, modularity, centralization, and the fraction of isolated users [32–34]. These conversa-tion patterns have specific characteristics that portray the conversations around specific topics, hashtags, or identities, and the patterns are briefly summarised below:

- **The Polarized Crowd** is a conversation pattern where a relatively small number of groups are clearly divided with dense conversations within groups but few interactions between groups. Hashtags are mostly not shared between groups. Such a pattern implies divisive and polarized discussions where groups do not argue but ignore each other. The distinct groups rely on different information sources and do not interact. Several examples of such patterns were detected within the USA, for instance as documented by the seminal work of Adamic and Glance [15] who investigated the political blogosphere of the 2004 U.S. Elections and found a distinct divide between liberal and conservative blogs.
- **The Tight Crowd** pattern is the opposite of the polarized crowd in that the groups are highly interconnected within as well as between groups, and have few isolates. Hash-tags are shared between groups. This pattern implies that participants have interactive conversations, even arguments, and exchange ideas and opinions. Such a pattern could typically be observed when communities form at events or conferences, or when com-munities discuss professional topics or hobbies. Such groups support each other with information flows between members of the group [32, 35].
- **Brand Clusters** is a conversation pattern where groups are fragmented and there are many isolates, which indicates that there are mentions or isolated conversations about well-known brands, topics, services, or celebrities. The groups are small and interconnected, and there is a limited exchange of ideas between members of a group or between groups. Hashtags about the brand are shared between groups. Information about the topic is just passed on [32, 35].
- **Community Clusters** is a conversation pattern that resembles a bazaar with differ-ent stalls characterized by several even-sized groups rather than a crowd of mostly

unconnected nodes [36]. Multiple medium-sized groups or hubs each have their own audience, influencers, and sources of information. Conversations are typically within a group that would entail diverse opinions on a subject with limited exchanges between groups. There are also a fair number of isolates [32, 35].

- *A Broadcast Network* conversation pattern is the first of two distinct hub-and-spoke patterns, which resembles a broadcast information flow typically where news from a media outlet, influencer, or agenda setters is distributed through the network [36]. The nodes are connected to the hub and are not connected, indicating that are no conversations about the topic [32, 35].
- *A Support Network* pattern is also a hub-and-spoke pattern but with outgoing information flows from the hub. This pattern indicates that there are responses from the hub to the spokes, which are typically observable where "customer services for a major business are handled by Twitter service accounts" [35]. This conversation pattern could be detected where an account such as government provides services and support via social media [32, 35].

The archetypal conversation patterns detectable in Twitter data provide a mechanism to understand social media communities and their conversations, and therefore allow a unique opportunity to gain insight into the Twitter data surrounding specific political events during 2021 in South Africa.

3 Research Approach

The research approach adopted for this study is experimental and was based on the method proposed by the SMRF to detect archetypal conversation patterns in Twitter data [33]. The purpose of the study was to determine which distinct conversation patterns could be detected in the datasets collected and what could be derived from these patterns given specific South African political events. These datasets were collected because the specific political events in 2021 evoked a lot of media attention and resulted in significant Twitter activity, which made the datasets ideal candidates for conversation pattern mining. Twitter limits the number of tweets that can be collected, and all the datasets were therefore limited to a maximum of 18 000 tweets. Five datasets were collected namely:

- Dataset 1 (DS1): Tweets using the #PutSouthAfricaFirst hashtag at the beginning of May 2021. The hashtag was key in the political landscape during this time period due to xenophobia discussions [37, 38].
- Datasets 2 and 3 (DS2 and DS3): Two Twitter datasets were collected using the #VoetsekANC hashtag during two time periods, 24 August 2020 and 4 May 2021. The #VoetsekANC hashtag emerged in August 2020 in response to the frustration experienced by South Africans after more than 4 months of lockdown, the ineptitude of the government to handle the pandemic, and the constant emergence of corruption allegations [39–41]. The Twitter community constantly urged each other to use the hashtags on every Friday, the so-called #VoetsekANCFriday.

- Dataset 4 (DS4): Twitter data surrounding the violent protests and looting in Gauteng and KwaZulu-Natal using the hashtag #SouthAfricaIsBurning in the second week of July 2021 [42, 43].
- Dataset 5 (DS5): A dataset collected early August 2021 using the identifiers "@TellUnknown OR @AZANIA_kal", which are Twitter accounts of two alleged instigators of the looting in July 2021 [20, 44].

All the datasets collected for the experiments were imported into the NodeXL application, which allows for representing tweet identities as graph vertices and interactions (that is replies or mentions) as directed edges. There is an edge for each "replies-to" relationship in a tweet, an edge for each "mentions" relationship in a tweet, and a self-loop edge for each tweet that is not a "replies-to" or "mentions". Retweets would create a new vertex.

Initial data wrangling included the removal of duplicates. The detection of groups or communities was done by applying the Clauset-Newman-Moore algorithm [28]. Several graph metrics were calculated for each dataset including the number of vertices, unique edges, and self-loops, and these metrics are summarized in Table 1. The top words, hashtags, and word pairs by frequency of mention were determined for the overall network as well as for each group within each network. The network was visualised using the NodeXL graph visualisation features that included visualising groups and interactions between groups using the Fruchterman-Reingold layout algorithm. The Fruchterman-Reingold algorithm is a force-directed iterative algorithm that results in a layout where edges are relatively similar in length for visualization purposes, but the edge length has no specific meaning [45]. The overall graph metrics of the networks are summarized in Table 1.

Table 1. Graph metrics for the datasets

Graph metric	DS1	DS2	DS3	DS4	DS5
Vertices	1800	2708	915	12924	799
Unique edges	2574	6122	1496	18621	1307
Edges with duplicates	0	3077	402	2634	1144
Total edges	2574	9199	1898	21255	2451
Self-loops	123	746	225	2717	80

For this experiment betweenness centrality was used for determining the top vertices since it possibly indicates more central, and arguably, more influential vertices. The top vertices ranked by betweenness centrality for the datasets are depicted in Table 2.

Table 2. Top vertices for the different datasets ranked by betweenness centrality

DS1 (#PutSAFirst)	DS2 (#VoetsekANC 1)	DS3 (#VoetsekANC 2)
mbuyisenindlozi	cyrilramaphosa	tiamontombonina
lerato_pillay	myanc	king78190744
thabe_mudzu	54battalion	sipho_nkosi
peezyjr	vivimpikashe	thokozaninala
hermajestynhla	unathi_kwaza	johnbis75624915

DS4 (#SAIsBurning)	DS5 (Instigators)
miss_zoe101	tellunknown
thearielcohen	azania_kal
nosihlemkhwana2	naomicampbell
cyrilramaphosa	ntsikimazwai
tjrmakhetha	gentlements

4 Results and Findings

In this section, the results of the analysis of each of the datasets are discussed, as well as what could be derived from the detected conversation patterns.

4.1 Dataset 1 - #PutSouthAfricaFirst

The dataset was collected from 1 800 Twitter users whose recent tweets contained "#PutSouthAfricaFirst", or who were replied to or were mentioned in those tweets. The hashtag emerged as representative of the xenophobic discussions that urged South Africans to "take their country back" and "get rid of foreigners" [37, 38]. The network was obtained from Twitter on Tuesday, 04 May 2021 but the tweets in the network were tweeted over the previous 7-day period.

This graph depicted in Fig. 1 is a good example of a Broadcast conversation pattern, which is dominated by a hub-and-spoke structure with many spokes directed towards the hub [33]. This is depicted by Group 1 on the left of Fig. 1. The hub is usually an influencer and the spoke vertices do not interact and therefore only link to the hub. Isolates indicate that the message has an impact beyond the hub, and some groups also exist that discuss the message between themselves (for example, Group 2 on the top right of Fig. 1).

The hub vertex in this graph is *mbuyisenindlozi,* (refer to Table 2 as well, which lists the top vertices) who posted the tweet that was reacted upon to creating the spokes:

> "If there was a new Covid-19 variant in Zimbabwe the border would have been long closed. The #PutSouthAfricaFirst brigade would be trending daily. But because it's India, no one said nyenye SA First. Why? It's only SA firs when it's African people- bloody self-hating hypocrites"

As is typical with the Broadcast pattern, the top hashtags are repeated in the bigger groups and this denotes the repeating of the hub's message and information (see the hashtags in Table 3).

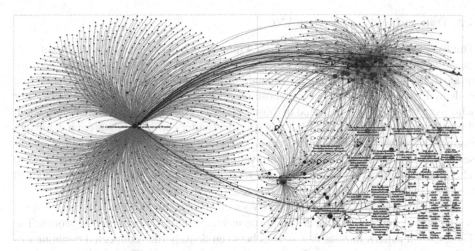

Fig. 1. Conversation pattern for dataset 1, a broadcast pattern.

The Broadcast conversation pattern detected is contrary to the perceptions at the time since the sentiment was that there is a large community that discusses the xenophobic topics surrounding the #PutSouthAfricaFirst hashtags [37, 38]. However, the Twitter conversation pattern indicates that there was mainly a single influencer whose message is reacted upon but very limited interaction or discussion on the topic.

Table 3. Top hashtags[1] by frequency of mention for the largest groups in dataset 1.

Top hashtags I entire graph	Top hashtags G1	Top hashtags G2	Top hashtags G3
putsouthafricafirst	putsouthafricafirst	putsouthafricafirst	putsouthafricafirst
putsouthafricafirst freedomday	ymornings putsouthafricafirst backtoschool girlstalkza jobseekerssa	putsouthafricafirst freedomday	putsouthafricafirst freedomday
putsouthafricafirst foreignersmustleavesa wewantourcountryback	vote putsouthafricafirst	putsouthafricafirst foreignersmustleavesa wewantourcountryback	putsouthafricafirst foreignersmustleavesa wewantourcountryback
localelections2021 voetsekeff putsouthafricafirst		voetsekanc voetseksamedia putsouthafricafirst	voetsekanc voetseksamedia putsouthafricafirst
voetsekanc voetseksamedia putsouthafricafirst		ramaphosa fikilembalula putsouthafricafirst	wewantourcountryback putsouthafricafirst

---

[1] The hashtag lists are depicted exactly as they appear in the tweets with the same capitalisations. Twitter users aims to use similar hashtag lists when the mention, reply or retweet.

4.2   Dataset 2 and 3 - # VoetsekANC

The #VoetsekANC hashtag emerged after 4 months in lockdown in response frustration experienced by South Africans after more exposure about corruption as well as the ineptitude of the government to handle the pandemic [39–41]. The first dataset was therefore collected from 2708 Twitter users whose recent tweets contained "#VoetsekANC", or who were replied to or mentioned in those tweets. However, what was interesting about the "#VoetsekANC" hashtag is that this specific Twitter community started a campaign urging Twitter users to use the hashtag on every Friday, including the so called #VoetsekANCFriday hashtag. This was the motivation for collecting the second dataset as well. The dataset was obtained from Twitter on Tuesday on 24 August 2020 and contained the tweets that were tweeted from 31 July to 24 August 2020.

The conversation pattern of the first #VoetsekANC dataset detected is a Tight Crowd with relatively few groups that are highly connected within and between the groups. The Tight Crowd pattern implies discussions between densely interconnected communities and individuals, and there are few isolates in such a pattern. This pattern means that communities share and provide mutual support through social media even though slightly different perspectives allow the detection of groups using the Clauset-Newman-Moore algorithm [28].

As is typical with the Tight Crowd, hashtags are shared across groups and within the network (see Table 4), and some groups may depict a hub-and-spoke structure such as the group at the top right in Fig. 2. A Tight Crowd pattern is usually observable when participants share a common interest and a common orientation.

The detected Tight Crowd conversation pattern in the dataset is somewhat surprising since the general perception is that the South African political landscape seldom converges around a specific topic [46, 47]. In the case of the initial #VoetsekANC conversation though, the Twitter communities united, shared, and supported each other, resulting in the Tight Crowd pattern, an observation shared by similar research [48].

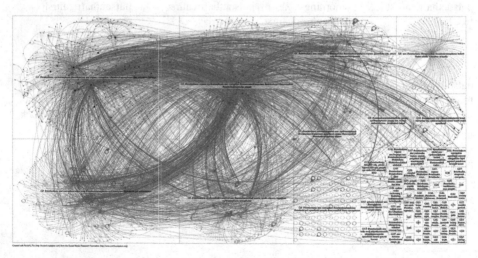

Fig. 2. The conversation pattern for #VoetsekANC end of August 2020.

Table 4. Top hashtags by frequency of mention for the largest groups in dataset 2

Top hashtags I entire graph	Top hashtags G1	Top hashtags G2	Top hashtags G3
voetsekanc	voetsekanc	voetsekanc	voetsekanc
voetsekanc voetsekcyril	myfokcyril voetsekanc	voetsekanc voetsekcyril	voetsekanc voetsekcyril
voetsekanc voetsekramaphosa	voetsekramaphosa voetsekanc	voetsekanc voetsekramaphosa	voetsekanc removeancfrompower
voetsekanc ancmustfall voetsekramaphosa	voetsekanc voetsekramaphosa	voetsekanc voetsekanc	ancmustfall voetsekanc voetsekcyril
voetsekanc removeancfrompower	voetsekanc removeancfrompower	redcard voetsekanc	voetsekanc voetsekramaphosa

The second #VoetsekANC dataset collected was eight months later and there were fewer vertices namely only 915 Twitter users whose recent tweets contained "VoetsekANC VoetsekEFF", or who were replied to or mentioned in those tweets in the week preceding 4 May 2021. Whilst some aspects of the pattern still resemble a Tight Crowd, there were many indicators that this pattern could better be classified as a Community Cluster. In a Community Cluster, popular topics develop evenly sized sub-groups that sometimes depict a few hub-and-spoke structures each with its own audience often centered around an influencer. Community Cluster patterns are often difficult to distinguish from the Tight Crowd or Brand Cluster patterns. However, what distinguishes a Community Cluster is that it should be possible to detect multiple conversations with an own audience, i.e., hub-and-spoke structures within groups. In Fig. 3 it is possible to distinguish such structures within most of the groups, and this structure is indicative of diverse angles on a subject given different audiences each with its own influencers. Community Clusters also have fewer interactions between groups than the Tight Crowd, but more than Brand Cluster. Furthermore, the groups are medium-sized, i.e. smaller than in the Tight Crowd but bigger than in a Brand Cluster. The groups are somewhat more interconnected than found in Brand Clusters and there are fewer isolates. The pattern overall indicates different opinions and perspectives given a specific topic. The hashtags are still shared across groups and within the network as before, with variations and repetitions of #voetsekanc and #voetsekeff appearing in all groups as top hashtags.

The second #VoetsekANC dataset depicting a Community Cluster implies that the Twitter communities surrounding the hashtag matured into established, separated and more isolated groups than before, each with its own audience and discussions. There are still some detectable discussions between groups, but much fewer than before, and there are relatively few isolates distinguishing this pattern from the Brand Cluster that would have smaller, less connected groups and more isolates. The implication is that even though the #VoetsekANC hashtag became established after months, it still does

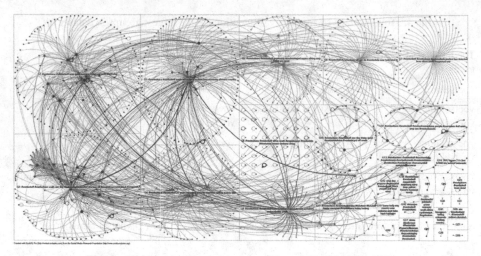

Fig. 3. The conversation pattern for #VoetsekANC in May 2021

not depict a brand conversation pattern given the Twitter datasets. #VoetsekANC is kept alive by several communities that are often centered around an influencer (detectable by a hub-and-spoke structure within a group, see for instance the groups at the top right of Fig. 3).

4.3 Dataset 4 - #SouthAfricaIsBurning

Dataset 4 is the largest dataset reported upon in this study and it was collected in the smallest timeframe. This indicates that there was intense Twitter activity about the violent protests and looting in Gauteng and KwaZulu-Natal using the hashtag #SouthAfricaIs-Burning. The dataset was collected from Twitter 8:21 UTC the morning of Wednesday, 14 July 2021 and it contains 12 924 Twitter users whose recent tweets contained "#SouthAfricaIsBurning", or who were replied to or mentioned in those tweets. The tweets in the network were tweeted over the 3-h, 40-min period preceding 08:21 UTC.

As discussed before, a Community Cluster is characterized by groups of people on Twitter that form networks with several evenly sized sub-groups and the conversation pattern depicted in Fig. 4 is an example of a Community Cluster. The top hashtags are repeated across groups (Table 5), but with slight variations as each group forms its own community with conversations. The hub-and-spoke structure is also detected within several groups, which is also a defining characteristic of the Community Cluster pattern, especially given newsworthy events where news agencies would distribute news that is reacted upon.

The Community Cluster pattern is not unexpected as the unrest would naturally lead to communities forming that need to interact, share news and support each other. The specific Community Cluster pattern of Fig. 4 depicts a noticeable number of interactions between groups, which is not typical of a Community Cluster but rather that of a Tight

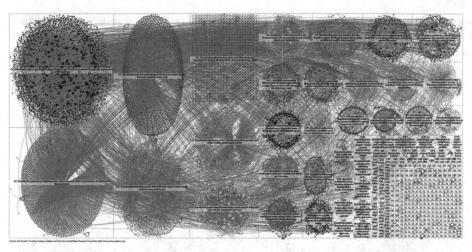

Fig. 4. The conversation pattern for #SouthAfricaIsBurning of 14 July 2021

Crowd. In this case, it might be due to the topic because news about the unrest would be distributed quickly between groups given the nature of Twitter, and even though groups have their own communities, breaking news would be shared between groups.

Table 5. Top hashtags by frequency of mention for the largest groups in dataset 4

Top hashtags I entire graph	Top hashtags G1	Top hashtags G2	Top hashtags G3
southafricaisburning	southafricaisburning	southafricaisburning	Southafricaisburning
southafricaisburning maponyamall soweto	southafricaisburning maponyamall soweto	ancnecleaks southafricaisburning	maponyamall Soweto
reallyramaphosa southafricaisburning	looting jubjub indians mihlali durban duduzilezuma sandton southafricaisburning	duduzilezuma southafricaisburning	southafricaisburning
ancnecleaks	southafricaisburning southafricashutdown sandton mallofafrica	southafricaisburning durban juliusmalema ancnecleaks	maponyamall southafricaisburning malema southafricaisburning mihlali

4.4   Dataset 5 – Instigators @TellUnknown OR @AZANIA_kal

The last dataset, Dataset 5, was collected early August 2021 using the identifiers "@TellUnknown OR @AZANIA_kal", which are the Twitter accounts of two alleged instigators of the looting in July 2021 [20, 44]. The dataset is different from the previous sets that used hashtags to collect the Twitter data, because the identifiers of two users were used to extract the dataset. These users are two alleged instigators identified by an investigation into the July 14 unrest [44]. The data collected was of 799 Twitter users whose recent tweets contained "@TelUnknown OR @AZANIA_kal", or who were replied to or mentioned in those tweets, extracted from Twitter on Tuesday, 03 August 2021 at 14:13 UTC and contained tweets from the 7-day period preceding 3 August.

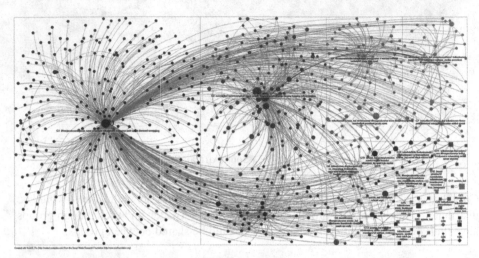

Fig. 5. The conversation pattern for instigators @TellUnknown OR @AZANIA_kal of August 2021

The conversation pattern detected is a Broadcast pattern, which is not surprising given the allegations that these accounts were instigators of the violence and unrest. The top vertices for Dataset 5 depicted in Table 2 indicate that these accounts are the hubs of Group 1 (on the left in Fig. 5) and Group 2 (in the middle top of Fig. 5). Group 2 from @AZANIA_kal (see Fig. 6) also depict a hub-and-spoke structure, but this account depicts many interactions with Group 1, suggesting a dependency on the information distributed to its followers. Normally there are some groups within a Broadcast pattern that depict internal conversations and discussion, however, in Fig. 5 there are limited interactions within groups. Most groups depict a hub-and-spoke structure with vertices that only link to the hub.

The top hashtags that are repeated across the groups such as #FreeJacobZuma are also representative of the Twitter community that supported the unrest (Table 6).

Detecting such a strong and distinct Broadcast pattern from the Twitter dataset collected about the two instigator accounts supports the observation that these two accounts are influencers and therefore typically instigators of unrest as suspected.

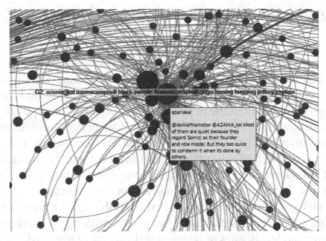

Fig. 6. The hub of group 2: identified @AZANIA_kal

Table 6. Top hashtags by frequency of mention for the largest groups in Dataset 5

Top hashtags I entire graph	Top hashtags G1	Top hashtags G2	Top Hashtags G3
Freejacobzuma	freejacobzuma	naomicampbell	freejacobzuma
Naomicampbell	Freepresidentzuma	Freejacobzuma	freejacobzuma freeikekhumalo
Freepresidentzuma	Racistbanksmustfall	Freezumanow	Freepresidentzuma naomicampbell
Racistbanksmustfall	freejacobzuma freeikekhumalo	Freepresidentzuma	Freejacobzuma
freejacobzuma freeikekhumalo	freejacobzuma ngizwemchunu bbnaija covid19sa cyrilramaphosa sandton	freezumanow freepresidentzuma cyrilramaphosa zizikodwa	freejacobzuma ancnec

5 Conclusion

Social media platforms are at present the most significant mechanism people use to communicate and express opinions. Fortunately, social media platforms also allow researchers to capture data and analyse this data to understand networks or community structures formed by the interactions. Twitter specifically, is a microblogging platform characterized by the fast flow of tweets that express information and opinions, and it became a well-used platform for the expression of political sentiments, or even mobilizing people politically. Twitter users can retweet a tweet, reply on a tweet, or mention a tweeter, and these interactions, as well as the tweets, can be mined to detect how communities organize online, as well as conversation patterns between users and groups.

This paper reports on a study that executed several experiments using a social network analysis (SNA) tool called NodeXL on Twitter datasets collected about political events during 2021 in South Africa. The purpose was to determine which distinct conversation patterns could be detected in data sets collected and what could be derived from these patterns given the South African political landscape and perceptions. The resulting graphs constructed from the datasets resemble distinct conversations patterns with specific characteristics that provide insight into the Twitter communities and conversations. The datasets collected about #PutSouthAfricaFirst and two instigator accounts expose typical Broadcast patterns meaning that the conversation is dominated by an influencer and that there are very limited discussions or conversations between users and groups. The Tight Crowd pattern extracted from the initial #VoetsekANC dataset shows surprising solidarity between users and groups with many interactions, discussions, and support and few isolates or people that do not participate in discussions. Later Twitter datasets about #VoetsekANC, as well as the unrest with hashtag #SAIsBurning, show the Community Cluster patterns, which means that sub-communities formed, each with significant discussions as well as influencers within each group, but also detectable interactions between groups.

In summary, the results indicate that conversation patterns could be detected from the Twitter datasets and that the conversations provide insight into understanding the political landscape within South Africa. Political conversations are less polarized than expected, and the conversations often manifest broadcast patterns from key influencers. In addition, conversation patterns often depict tight crowds or community clusters that reflect intense conversations across communities, and these patterns imply diverse opinions and perspectives on a topic.

Further research may incorporate relevant theory to assist with insights into the reasons why these conversation patterns develop. The results may be of value for researchers that aim to understand social media conversations within the South African society.

References

1. Fu, X., Jar-Der, L., Boos, M.: Social Network Analysis: Interdisciplinary Approaches and Case Studies. CRC Press, Boca Raton (2017). https://doi.org/10.1201/9781315369594
2. Scott, J., Carrington, P.J. (eds.): The SAGE Handbook of Social Network Analysis. SAGE, London (2011)
3. Hanna, R., Rohm, A., Crittenden, V.L.: We're all connected: the power of the social media ecosystem. Bus. Horiz. **54**, 265–273 (2011). https://doi.org/10.1016/j.bushor.2011.01.007
4. Perrin, A.: Social media usage: 2005–2015. Pew Research Center (2015). https://www.sec retintelligenceservice.org/wp-content/uploads/2016/02/PI_2015-10-08_Social-Networking-Usage-2005-2015_FINAL.pdf
5. Kaplan, A.M., Haenlein, M.: Users of the world, unite! The challenges and opportunities of Social Media. Bus. Horiz. **53**, 59–68 (2010). https://doi.org/10.1016/j.bushor.2009.09.003
6. Schivinski, B., Dabrowski, D.: The effect of social media communication on consumer perceptions of brands. J. Market. Commun. **22**, 189–214 (2016). https://doi.org/10.1080/135 27266.2013.871323

7. Wellman, B. (ed.): Networks in the Global Village: Life in Contemporary Communities. Westview Press, Boulder (1999)
8. Khan, G.F.: Seven Layers of Social Media Analytics: Mining Business Insights from Social Media Text, Actions, Networks, Hyperlinks, Apps, Search Engine, and Location Data. CreateSpace Independent Publishing Platform, Leipzig (2015)
9. Tichy, N.M.: Social network analysis for organizations. Acad. Manage. Rev. **4**, 507–519 (1979)
10. Kietzmann, J.H., Hermkens, K., McCarthy, I.P., Silvestre, B.S.: Social media? Get serious! Understanding the functional building blocks of social media. Bus. Horiz. **54**, 241–251 (2011). https://doi.org/10.1016/j.bushor.2011.01.005
11. Green, S., Perrin, A.: Social media update 2016. Pew Research Center (2016)
12. Weller, K.: Trying to understand social media users and usage: the forgotten features of social media platforms. Online Inf. Rev. **40**, 256–264 (2016). https://doi.org/10.1108/OIR-09-2015-0299
13. The Evolution of Social Media: How Did It Begin and Where Could It Go Next? https://online.maryville.edu/blog/evolution-social-media/. Accessed 07 Sept 2021
14. Walton, J.: Twitter vs. Facebook vs. Instagram: What's the Difference? (2021). https://www.investopedia.com/articles/markets/100215/twitter-vs-facebook-vs-instagram-who-target-audience.asp
15. Adamic, L.A., Glance, N.: The Political Blogosphere and the 2004 U.S. Election: Divided They Blog. 8 (2005)
16. Bennett, W.L.: The personalization of politics: political identity, social media, and changing patterns of participation. Ann. Am. Acad. Polit. Soc. Sci. **644**, 20–39 (2012). https://doi.org/10.1177/0002716212451428
17. Trottier, D.: Social Media, Politics and the State: Protests, Revolutions, Riots, Crime and Policing in the Age of Facebook, Twitter and YouTube. Routledge (2014). https://doi.org/10.4324/9781315764832
18. Allen, K.: Social media, riots and consequences (2021). https://issafrica.org/iss-today/social-media-riots-and-consequences
19. Karombo, T.: South Africa goes after social media as it cracks down on looting and protests. https://qz.com/africa/2033328/south-africa-to-monitor-social-media-as-protests-rock-the-country/. Accessed 07 Sept 2021
20. Makhafola, G.: #UnrestSA: Two more alleged instigators arrested, including one who ran popular Twitter account (2021). https://www.news24.com/news24/southafrica/news/unrestsa-two-more-alleged-instigators-arrested-including-one-who-ran-popular-twitter-account-20210829
21. Twitter. https://twitter.com/home. Accessed 20 June 2020
22. Kane, G.C., Alavi, M., Labianca, G. (Joe), Borgatti, S.P.: What's different about social media networks? A framework and research agenda. MISQ. **38**, 274–304 (2014). https://doi.org/10.25300/MISQ/2014/38.1.13
23. Wasserman, S., Faust, K.: Social Network Analysis: Methods and Applications. Cambridge University Press, Cambridge (1994)
24. Borgatti, S.P., Everett, M.G.: Notions of position in social network analysis. Sociol. Methodol. **22**, 1 (1992). https://doi.org/10.2307/270991
25. Hansen, D.L., et al.: Do You know the way to SNA? A process model for analyzing and visualizing social media data. In: International Conference on Social Informatics, p. 10. IEEE (2012)
26. Rainie, H., Wellman, B.: Networked: The New Social Operating System. MIT Press, Cambridge (2012)

27. Rodrigues, E.M., Milic-Frayling, N., Smith, M., Shneiderman, B., Hansen, D.: Group-in-a-box layout for multi-faceted analysis of communities. In: 2011 IEEE Third International Conference on Privacy, Security, Risk and Trust and 2011 IEEE Third International Conference on Social Computing, pp. 354–361. IEEE, Boston (2011). https://doi.org/10.1109/PASSAT/SocialCom.2011.139

28. Clauset, A., Newman, M.E.J., Moore, C.: Finding community structure in very large networks. Phys. Rev. E **70** (2004). https://doi.org/10.1103/PhysRevE.70.066111

29. Woma, J.: Comparisons of Community Detection Algorithms in the YouTube Network. Stanford University, Stanford (2019)

30. Social Media Research Foundation. https://www.smrfoundation.org/. Accessed 30 June 2020

31. Fay, D.: NodeXL: Network Overview, Discovery and Exploration in Excel. https://www.microsoft.com/en-us/research/project/nodexl-network-overview-discovery-and-exploration-in-excel/. Accessed 30 June 2020

32. Hansen, D.L., Schneiderman, B., Smith, M.A.: Analyzing Social Media Networks with NodeXL: Insights from a Connected World. Morgan Kaufmann, Burlington (2011)

33. Smith, M., Rainie, L., Shneiderman, B., Himelboim, I.: Conversational Archetypes: Six Conversation and Group Network Structures in Twitter. https://www.pewresearch.org/internet/2014/02/20/part-2-conversational-archetypes-six-conversation-and-group-network-structures-in-twitter/. Accessed 08 Sept 2021

34. Himelboim, I., Smith, M.A., Rainie, L., Shneiderman, B., Espina, C.: Classifying twitter topic-networks using social network analysis. Soc. Media Soc. **3**, 205630511769154 (2017). https://doi.org/10.1177/2056305117691545

35. Smith, M.A., Rainie, L., Shneiderman, B., Himelboim, I.: Mapping Twitter Topic Networks: From Polarized Crowds to Community Clusters. https://www.pewinternet.org/2014/02/20/mapping-twitter-topic-networks-from-polarized-crowds-to-community-clusters/. Accessed 19 Sept 2019

36. Smith, M.A., Rainie, L., Shneiderman, B., Himelboim, I.: Part 2: Conversational Archetypes: Six Conversation and Group Network Structures in Twitter. https://www.pewresearch.org/internet/2014/02/20/part-2-conversational-archetypes-six-conversation-and-group-network-structures-in-twitter/. Accessed 02 Aug 2021

37. Ndwandwe, Z.: The myth of South African nationality. https://africasacountry.com/2020/10/the-myth-of-south-african-nationality. Accessed 01 Sept 2021

38. Seemela, M.: "#PutSouthAfricaFirst shouldn't be used to hate anybody," says Cassper. https://www.timeslive.co.za/tshisa-live/tshisa-live/2020-10-19-putsouthafricafirst-shouldnt-be-used-to-hate-anybody-says-cassper/. Accessed 01 Sept 2021

39. Tabane, R.: ANALYSIS | Will the governing party ride out the 'Voetsek, ANC' storm? https://www.news24.com/citypress/politics/analysis-will-the-governing-party-ride-out-the-voetsek-anc-storm-20200827-2. Accessed 20 Sept 2021

40. Lindeque, B.: #VoetsekANC has been trending for over a week now... and this response. https://www.goodthingsguy.com/opinion/voetsekanc-has-been-trending-for-over-a-week-now-and-this-response-is-pretty-funny/. Accessed 20 Sept 2021

41. Haffajee, F.: Covid-19 – The 150 Days report (Part 1): Fix South Africa or fix the ANC – Ramaphosa can't do both. https://www.dailymaverick.co.za/article/2020-08-10-fix-south-africa-or-fix-the-anc-ramaphosa-cant-do-both/. Accessed 20 Sept 2021

42. IOL Reporter: LIVE UPDATES: #SouthAfricaIsBurning – Shock as widespread looting rages on. https://www.msn.com/en-xl/africa/other/live-updates-southafricaisburning-shock-as-widespread-looting-rages-on/ar-AAM8uI3. Accessed 20 Sept 2021

43. Lechman, A.: Ramaphosa's words falls on deaf ears as looting continued in SA - Sunday World. https://sundayworld.co.za/breaking-news/ramaphosas-words-falls-on-deaf-ears-as-looting-continued-in-sa/. Accessed 20 Sept 2021

44. Mokoka, M.: Meet the Instigators: The Twitter accounts of the RET Forces Network that Incited Violence and Demanded Zuma's Release. Centre for Analytics and Behavioural Change (2021)
45. Fruchterman, T.M.J., Reingold, E.M.: Graph drawing by force-directed placement. Softw. Pract. Exper. **21**, 1129–1164 (1991). https://doi.org/10.1002/spe.4380211102
46. Maré, G.: Race, democracy and opposition in South African politics: as other a way as possible. Democratization **8**, 85–102 (2001). https://doi.org/10.1080/714000182
47. Seekings, J.: The continuing salience of race: discrimination and diversity in South Africa. J. Contemp. Afr. Stud. **26**, 1–25 (2008). https://doi.org/10.1080/02589000701782612
48. Ndlovu, N.: 'A nation that laughs together, stays together': deconstructing humour on twitter during the national lockdown in South Africa. In: Mpofu, S. (ed.) Digital Humour in the Covid-19 Pandemic, pp. 191–212. Springer, Cham (2021). https://doi.org/10.1007/978-3-030-79279-4_9

The Application of Artificial Intelligence (AI) and Internet of Things (IoT) in Agriculture: A Systematic Literature Review

C. L. de Abreu and J. P. van Deventer$^{(\boxtimes)}$ (iD)

Department of Informatics, University of Pretoria, Pretoria, South Africa
phil.vandeventer@up.ac.za

Abstract. The World Resource Institute estimates that by 2050 there will be a shortfall between food being produced and the amount needed to feed an estimated 10 billion people. With the quantity of available arable land on the decline, the scarcity of water and limiting factors and growing challenges such as soil quality, pest and weed infestations, it is increasingly important that innovative approaches to food production are implemented to optimise agricultural practices. This paper presents a systematic literature review aimed at exploring the use of Artificial Intelligence (AI) and the Internet of Things (IoT) in agriculture. A total of 50 articles were identified and analysed according to the PRISMA approach to understanding the current applications, challenges, and future benefits of AI and IoT in agriculture and how it has the potential to reduce resource wastage and assist in feeding the world's growing population. Based on the data, it is expected that this review will serve as a reference to supplement the reader's knowledge of AI and IoT in the agricultural industry.

Keywords: Artificial Intelligence · Internet of Things · Agriculture 4.0 · Smart sensors · Precision farming · Systematic literature review

1 Introduction

The World Resource Institute (WRI) estimates that by 2050 there will be a significant shortfall between the food being produced and the amount needed to feed an estimated 10 billion people [1]. Around 30.7% of the world's population is directly engaged on 2781 million hectares of agricultural land [2]. With the quantity of available arable land on the decline and limited by factors such as water resources, not to mention growing challenges such as soil quality, pest and weed infestations, it is important that innovative approaches to food production are implemented to optimise agricultural practices without an increase in resource consumption.

According to Dharmaraj *et al.* [3], the application of Artificial Intelligence (AI) in the agricultural sector could assist in improving agricultural processes and outcomes thereby optimising agricultural practices. Using Internet of Things (IoT) devices such as smart sensors and drones, data can be captured which, combined with AI techniques such

© Springer Nature Switzerland AG 2022
E. Jembere et al. (Eds.): SACAIR 2021, CCIS 1551, pp. 32–46, 2022.
https://doi.org/10.1007/978-3-030-95070-5_3

as image recognition and neural networks, has the potential to enhance food security and optimise agricultural practices thereby improving yields and minimising waste.

Not only will these technologies benefit the primary aspects of agriculture, but they may further improve and refine the way agricultural products are monitored, stored, and distributed. Using big data and predictive modelling, yield prediction is made possible which would allow farmers to understand what quantity of crops to sow in real-time. By detecting, predicting, and modelling possible problems with crop yields and agricultural outcomes one would be able to manage yield more efficiently, which, as an added benefit, would improve agricultural profit margins [4]. This echoes throughout the food production value chain, allowing distributors to anticipate and respond to a predicted yield quantity allowing consumers to obtain fresh produce through just-in-time delivery methods and strategies.

Technologies available in the market, and under research and development will be included in this systematic literature review (SLR). It will address the challenges faced by the agricultural sector and how the use of AI and IoT assist in overcoming these challenges.

2 Research Method

This SLR intends to explore, analyse, and provide insight into research focussed on AI and IoT and how they are applied in assisting in overcoming the challenges in feeding the world's growing population. The SLR follows the principles laid out in the Preferred Reporting Items for Systematic Reviews and Meta-Analyses (PRISMA) approach [5] and was additionally informed by Pollock et al. [6] and Nowell et al. [7]. To stay more current, reputable peer-reviewed sources dating from 2015 to 2020 were used in this SLR.

The cut-off date of 2020 was chosen to allow for a more stable review process. The following section will briefly cover the research question, search terms, selection criteria, source selection, PRISMA approach, quality assessment and data extraction details.

2.1 Research Question

To structure this paper, a high-level question was formulated namely *"How are AI and IoT technologies being applied in Agriculture?"* The main objective of this SLR is to present how current emerging technologies are being utilised and how technologies of the near future are being researched and tested to aid in the quest in support of food security. By answering this research question the authors plan to present how technology can play a role in potentially reducing world hunger and hope that it will induce others into contributing additional research.

2.2 Search Terms and Source Selection

To obtain data focussing on the main constructs of this SLR, several search strings (Table 1) related to how AI and IoT are applied in overcoming agricultural challenges were used to retrieve material from peer-reviewed academic journals and conference

Table 1. Search strings for data retrieval during exploratory identification

Search terms	Approx. results[a]
"Artificial Intelligence" AND "Agriculture"	89 900
"Internet of Things" AND "Agriculture"	35 900
"Machine learning" AND "Agriculture"	96 100
"Smart sensors" AND "Agriculture"	5 060
"Agriculture 4.0"	960
"Smart farming"	8 350
"Precision agriculture"	104 000
"Artificial Intelligence in agriculture" OR "Internet of Things in agriculture"	2 180
"Smart sensors in agriculture" OR "Machine learning in agriculture"	219

[a]Preliminary exploratory results of exploratory searches as obtained from Google Scholar on 2020/04/25 to refine and finalise search terms applied to main data sources.

proceedings. The material was sourced from the (1) Agriculture Science Database, (2) Science Direct, (3) IEEE Xplore and (4) Google Scholar.

All the terms related directly to the research question stated in Sect. 2.1 and due to the volume of results returned from the combinations of terms, no additional terms or variations in terminology were required. To limit the study to concepts relevant to this SLR, papers were filtered based on inclusion and exclusion criteria (Table 2).

Table 2. Filtering criteria

Inclusion criteria	Exclusion criteria
• Studies published in English • Studies published in IT-related journals/conference proceedings, except those published in non-IT resources which mentioned the systematic review's keywords were included • Studies that directly answer the research question	• Studies published before 2015 • Publications where only the abstract but not the full text was available • Studies whose findings were unclear and ambiguous • Duplicate papers • Non-academic sources and sources that do not have an identifiable empirical nature

Papers and conference proceedings related to precision irrigation, disease control, weed management, yield prediction, agricultural supply chain and logistics, livestock farming as well as other smart farming applications were considered.

2.3 Source Collection and Extraction

Data extraction (source collection and evaluation) was conducted by applying the keywords listed in Table 1 to the 4 stipulated sources namely the (1) Agriculture Science

Database, (2) Science Direct, (3) IEEE Xplore and (4) Google Scholar. The results of the searches were compared to the inclusion and exclusion criteria. After scrubbing duplicates, an initial total of 3636 sources was analysed and compared. If sources did not meet the inclusion criteria, they were excluded from the review. As can be seen in Fig. 1, after the identification and eligibility screening, a total of 50 papers were included for further analysis.

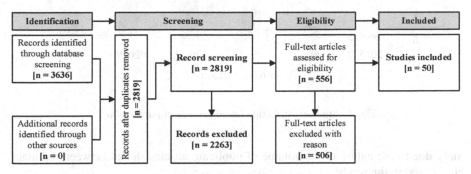

Fig. 1. PRISMA flow diagram

3   Results

A total of 50 empirical sources[1] remained after running through the PRISMA process. The following section details the results of this study.

3.1   General Findings

As mentioned, 50 articles dating from 2015 to 2020 were gathered and used in this review. The distribution of when these articles were published can be seen in Fig. 2. It is interesting to note that of these 50 articles, 17 were published in 2019 while only one article published in 2015 could be included in this SLR. This could be an indication of an increase in overall importance and interest in this topic due to the pressing issues and concerns related to agriculture and population growth.

First, we will provide a simple overview of the total results of the selected pool of articles, after which a more detailed theme-based discussion will be presented. Please note that, when the pool of articles was compiled, articles were pooled together to ensure duplicates were appropriately scrubbed from the data sources to focus only on the core articles to be used for further analysis.

A total of 2819 duplicate records were shared between the article sources, and it would have provided an inconsistent view of where what article or source originated from. Subsequently, it was decided not to present the total articles per data source as it would have presented an extremely skewed view of where what source originated from

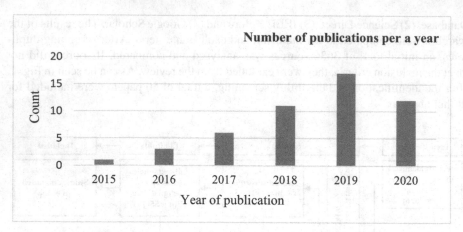

Fig. 2. Studies distribution based on year of publication

simply due to the nature of the volume of duplicate articles shared between the main sources used in this study.

Nine main concepts which all go hand-in-hand with the topics discussed in this paper were identified for each of the academic sources listed in the bibliography and references. Figure 3 shows the distribution of these main topics under consideration.

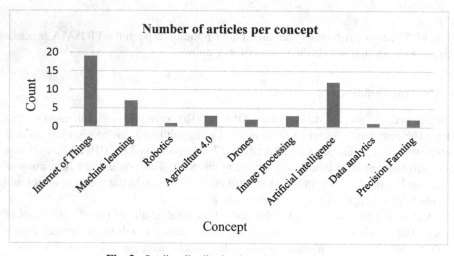

Fig. 3. Studies distribution based on main concepts

---

[1] Analysed papers may be viewed at - https://bit.ly/3o2qOCx.

4 Discussion

Based on the analysis of the identified articles, the following major themes were identified namely, *Irrigation and Soil Control; Weeds and Pest Management; Disease Detection and Remediation; Yield Prediction; Management and Analysis; Agricultural Supply Chain and Logistics* and finally a general category of *Other Smart Farming Applications.* These themes will be systematically discussed in the following sections.

4.1 Irrigation and Soil Control

According to National Geographic, only around 2.5% of the world's water is fresh with only 0.007% of this 2.5% available to sustain nearly 8 billion people [8]. The agricultural industry is one of the top consumers of water and accounts for around 70% of all freshwater consumption [8]. With the access to freshwater limited, it is of great importance that we utilise any tools at our disposal to preserve this resource.

One such technology that is redefining the way farmers tend to and water crops are IoT and the application of smart sensors. By incorporating temperature, moisture, and humidity sensors in and around soil, farmers obtain a real-time accurate reading of the status of a particular crop. Integrating this information with a supporting system capable of analysing and comprehending the results allow for crops to be irrigated without the assistance of human intervention, intuition, and best judgement [9]. Studies such as [10–13] demonstrated how the implementation of IoT sensors can improve irrigation and optimise water consumption. All these studies found a cost reduction to yield ratios and provided clear evidence that the application of smart sensors could assist with optimal soil hydration levels and reduced water consumption.

Above and beyond the aforementioned, the combined application of smart sensors and AI can predict future water consumption and possible weather patterns. For example, Agarwal *et al.* [14] developed a model where a structure with a series of shutters was placed over crops and through IoT sensors and intelligent decision-making was able to collect rainwater, irrigate crops and store surplus water in a tank to be used during droughts. The use of AI coupled with multispectral image sensors is also helpful in the prediction of drought-tolerant crop varieties, with research conducted by Adhiwibawa *et al.* [15] developing an artificial neural network capable of predicting a drought-tolerant variety of soybean with an accuracy of 80%.

Another important resource related to soil and water quality is the application of fertilizers such as Nitrogen, Phosphorous and Potassium. As stated by Higgins *et al.* [16], *"The loss of phosphorus and nitrogen from fields and farmyards through leaching and overland flow has contributed to the eutrophication of freshwater bodies. Greenhouse gas emissions such as nitrous oxide and methane from fertiliser and animal manure applications are a major problem, as is ammonia from cattle housing and land spreading. Improving the precision and efficiency of soil nutrient management can play an important role in minimising nutrient surpluses."* By incorporating pH and other sensors into smart farming systems, farmers minimise the effort of calculating the quantities of fertiliser thereby reducing wastage.

Although minimising wastages is beneficial and profitable to the farmer, one of the greatest waste reductions is the pollution and eutrophication of water. When incorporating the information generated by sensors that are constantly monitoring soil characteristics, the farmer can anticipate which seed will fulfil their requirements and will be ideal for planting. For example, research conducted by Higgins *et al.* [16] and Ananthi *et al.* [17] on the application of smart sensors on soil monitoring found that efficient soil testing provided a potential benefit to farmers by increased yields, reduced operating costs, improved crop maturity and higher tolerance to disease and pest damage. Although additional research is necessary, both studies show that there are potential economic as well as environmental benefits to be gained through the implementation of monitoring soil status with smart sensors.

4.2 Weeds and Pest Management

According to Partel *et al.* [18], the USA spends around $26 billion on herbicides each year and farmers dedicate around 65% of their total expenditure towards herbicides. Aside from irrigation and fertilizer, herbicides and pesticides contribute the most towards a farmer's expenses. In general, conventional spraying techniques apply herbicides and pesticides consistently over a field without considering the dispersal of weeds and pests. This results in using too much of these chemicals which may pollute land and water. Pests may also become resistant to herbicides and pesticides due to overexposure.

A major technology changing the detection and management of weeds and pests is the use of Unmanned Aerial Vehicles (UAVs) or more specifically drones. With the decreasing price of drone technology, it is possible to observe crops easily from an aerial perspective. Using image processing as well as different temporal, spatial and spectral scales, drones along with supporting AI could accurately recognise objects in images collected and can assist in estimating the area of various crops [19]. Gašparović *et al.* [20] and Ampatzidis *et al.* [21] both conducted studies on the analysis of AI classifications on agricultural data obtained from UAVs. Gašparović *et al.* [20] for example found that an AI object classification could detect weeds up to 87.1% of the time whilst, Ampatzidis *et al.* [21] although not directly related to weed detection, was able to detect citrus trees surrounded by other vegetation with an error rate of only 2.3%. Additional research is necessary, but this provides evidence that areas infected with weeds or various pests can be zoned separately from crops for corrective action to be taken. Existing drone technology could be used to detect weeds allowing for targeted spraying regiments [22, 23].

Additionally, IoT sensors (smart cameras and acoustic sensors) can assist in detecting insects and other pests such as rodents [24]. By merging AI and robotics, a model proposed by Partel *et al.* [18] used machine vision, a smart sprayer system and an all-terrain vehicle to detect, single out and spray weeds in real-time with an overall accuracy of 78%. A mechanical variant of weed control proposed by Knoll *et al.* [25] could manually remove weeds in real-time with accuracy rates of over 98% thereby significantly reducing herbicide and pesticide usage. By adopting these technologies, the farmer will ensure that the most efficient and minimal amounts of both pesticides and herbicides are applied to the definite problematic areas identified.

4.3 Disease Detection and Remediation

Plant diseases destroy around 10% of all food produced [26]. With 820 million malnourished people in 2019, it is abundantly clear that each possible source of nutrition is utilised as efficiently and effectively as possible [26]. IoT sensors can monitor plants' soil quality thereby avoiding simple soil quality-based plant diseases. Additionally, AI in concert with IoT can predict where soil quality could lead to plant destroying diseases and prevent the diseases before they occur [27]. By monitoring leaves as well as soil quality through IoT sensors tied into AI predictive modelling, plant diseases can be detected before they can either develop or spread. Work done by Ahmed et al. [28] found that AI in unison with IoT could accurately predict where plant diseases would develop with slightly over 97% accuracy allowing farmers to respond appropriately in negating the diseases. Research conducted by Changmai et al. [29] used IoT sensors as applied to a hydroponic lettuce farm to monitor nutrient levels, automatically adjusting nutrient solutions which yielded lettuce which on average was around 36.59% heavier with 17.2% more leaf, and 13.9% larger stem diameter. Plants were hardier with greater disease resistance. Similarly, Alipio et al. [30] studied the effect of using exact inference in a Bayesian Network also for a smart hydroponics lettuce farm. The study found that the crop produced using the automatic control was 66.67% higher than that of the manual control which implies that the use of exact inference in a Bayesian Network aids in producing higher quality crops. Though hydroponics based, a similar approach could be adapted and applied to crops being grown in the field. This is demonstrated by the development of a similar field-based system which was able to produce an increase of 14.2% and 17.9% in the weight and size of arugula leaves, respectively [31]. The aforementioned studies show that soil quality and general plant nutrient levels can be improved resulting in better crop yields which on average are more resilient and more resistant to plant-based disease.

The detection of diseases among farm animals is exceptionally crucial as the diseases often can be fatal to farm animals. Common causes of these diseases include bacteria, parasites, viruses, nutritional deficiencies, fungi, and chemical poisons.

By installing ambient sensors inside barns, coops and other housing areas, the overall climate can be monitored which would allow for the detection and estimation of animal stress levels. Hazardous gas sensors can also be installed in and around these areas to detect and notify the farmer if, for example, levels of hydrogen sulphide, ammonia, or methane approach danger zones. This idea and approach were extended by making use of a group of "cattle sensors" which included an array of different biometric devices such as thermometers, pulsometers, respiration monitors, accelerometers, and gyroscopes as well as location sensors attached to individual cows through a form of a collar [32, 33]. These devices enabled the farmer to detect various indications of illness such as fevers and high heart rates which could potentially assist in diagnosing a particular condition before it becomes serious and assist in ensuring that the correct treatment is applied [32, 33].

For example, monitoring sheep posture is a known indicator of sheep health. A study aimed at monitoring sheep posture, while grazing in vineyards [34] had a global accuracy of above 91% assisting in early interventions preventing costly treatment or even loss of livestock [34]. Similarly, the use of smart sensors and AI can be applied to the case of fish farming and aquaculture. Making use of submerged cameras and computer vision allows fish tracking focussing on properties such as movement, skin health, fish size, reaction to chemicals and sea-lice infestation levels. It was found that sensors such as acoustic telemetry could be used to monitor fish physiology such as heart rate which provided a good indication of general health and health conditions [35]. Although this method is costly and requires additional research, it can assist in detecting, diagnosing, and preventing the spread of diseases among fish populations.

4.4   Yield Prediction, Management and Analysis

The ability to forecast and analyse crop yields as well as animal production before and even during an agricultural cycle greatly reduces the amount of business risk taken on by farmers. With an increase in the amount of data becoming readily available due to smart sensors, Filippi *et al.* [36] indicated that with AI *"there is an opportunity to explore the value of combining data over multiple fields/farms and years into one dataset"* [36]. For example, Abdelghafour *et al.* [37] used a combination of image sources to detect and count grape bunches at early fruiting stages with an average reliability of 75% thereby estimating final yield before harvest. This supports the idea that intelligent forecasting models can be used to identify yield volumes influencing investment in such things as labour and equipment required before harvesting.

Forecasting models can further be used to bolster yield output. Research on an analytics framework that integrated machine learning with the selection of soybeans for targeted farms and farming practices found that an average farmer can improve their yield by around 9% by making use of the optimised results presented by this framework [38]. Similarly, Cunha *et al.* [39] also developed a machine learning model for pre-season soybean and maize yield forecasting without the need for Normalized Difference Vegetation Index data. The results obtained indicate that farmers and agriculture stakeholders can benefit from the useful information with significantly fewer data requirements or significant data points. Deciding on a crop's maturity and the ideal time to harvest is also a factor that could increase yield and minimise waste. Part of the research conducted by Bhojwani *et al.* [40] proposed a system that assesses the maturity level of a particular crop and identifies the ideal time for harvest which *"will lead to an increased crop production and will reduce the amount of crop failure compared to traditional methods"*. When considering yield, one needs to consider livestock yield production as well. For example, da Rosa Righi *et al.* [41] completed work on the utilisation of IoT to perform automated feeding of individual cows leading to better milk production. Combining this with statistical models, production per cow was predicted with a 94.3% accuracy rate. In the case of an abnormality, such as a large drop in the predicted output, and alternative nutritional plans can be individualised for each cow to improve their milk production indicating that IoT along with predictive modelling can improve output level whilst simultaneously reducing time and resources used to identify and diagnose concerns.

4.5   Agricultural Supply Chain and Logistics

Agricultural goods and fresh produce are a challenge from both a supply chain and logistics perspective. According to Verdouw *et al.* [42], *"a virtual object can alert supply chain participants on e.g., food safety incidents, temperature deviations or food quality problems*" through something like IoT sensors. One agricultural task in the supply chain rapidly being automated is that of harvesting [43, 44]. For example, using AI, image recognition and robotics, ripe tomatoes could accurately be identified 84% of the time with a robotic arm picking accuracy of 89% [43]. Altaheri *et al.* [44] achieved accuracies of 99.01%, 97.25%, and 98.59% for the prediction of date fruit type, maturity, and harvesting decision classification respectively. Additional research is necessary, particularly in relating the image recognition techniques linked with robotics, however, both studies show that AI can assist in augmenting the harvesting process improving supply chain efficiency. Once produce has been harvested, a key process in the agricultural supply chain is sorting and grading. Farhadi *et al.* [45] and Abbas *et al.* [46] studied sorting and grading. Farhadi *et al.* [45] focussed on using a neural network to classify hazelnuts and achieved an accuracy of between 89.3% and 96.1%, for big/small, hollow, or damaged hazelnuts while Abbas *et al.* [46] used image processing to detect imperfections in apples. The aforementioned does show that sorting and grading can be supported by different forms of AI intervention.

AI has the potential to enhance the supply chain by automating tasks, minimising human error, and improving overall consistency. For example, Alifah *et al.* [47] proposed and presented an IoT model to improve efficiencies in the agricultural supply chain that integrates the supply chain of agricultural products, consisting of farmers through to retailers to enable the real-time tracking and effective control of rice. This could support the general distribution of rice potentially reducing loss through veracious forms of loss such as rot or rodents.

Additionally, Ali Mohammadi *et al.* [48] used neural networks to determine the postharvest life of kiwifruit based on nutrient concentrations to predict shelf-life being able to predict fruit quality and firmness up to 180 days after harvest. Additional research is required however it is clear that AI and IoT can improve the general supply chain thereby reducing food wastage – especially towards the end of the supply chain. Although smart agricultural supply chains can address important farming goals, poor management can harm safety, quality, quantity, and the wastage of products [49]. IoT and its practical adoption across food supply chains are still emerging but the literature suggests that as the technology matures, it can facilitate visibility, safety, intelligence and automate workflows to deliver quicker decisions [50].

4.6 Other Smart Farming Applications

It is estimated that one-third of all food that is consumed by humans is from the direct result of pollination carrier agents such as bees, butterflies, moths, and birds. At present almost, all crops are pollinated naturally, but the population of these natural pollinators is rapidly declining. Conserving the population of these animals is a priority however research on automated pollination techniques is ongoing to support pollinators. For example, Chen *et al.* [51] conducted AI research relating to the use of robotic micro air vehicle pollinators to support farming practices with AI controlling movement in the air, path planning, identification and recognition of flowers ensuring that flowers are pollinated. This field of study is still in its early stages however results are promising.

Another area of interest is competitive farming practice. Work done by Bhakta *et al.* [53] focussed on consumer behaviour allowing farmers to predict consumers' interest in produce before choosing what to plant or what to focus on producing. Over the years, humans have strived to better the nature of animal husbandry, but the unpredictable nature and movement of animals have always been a factor that is difficult to control. The implementation of smart sensors supports the real-time locations of animals to support basic administrative tasks such as auditing and tracking animals requiring less labour-intensive interventions. For example, Ren *et al.* [54] studied the use of agricultural robotics in poultry production significantly reduces the number of floor eggs and improved the health and productivity of hens. The study found that there are still many challenges that need to be addressed in robotizing agricultural tasks specifically in poultry production but with additional research, IoT sensors in conjunction with AI and robotics can benefit animal husbandry.

Although the use of IoT and the adoption of precision agriculture can greatly improve the overall yield and farming practices of farmers extensive research is still required in developing areas of interest to have a more tangible impact on not only large-scale farms in developed countries but also for small-scale farms in developing countries [54]. Since the successful adoption of precision agriculture not only depends on the implementation of these technologies on commercial farms, the focus needs to be placed on how these technologies are accessible to developing countries and rural areas. A more efficient network and computing solution for rural areas with better more reliable energy supplies, reduced network delay, throughput and performance is required. This allows areas with poorer connectivity and higher bandwidth restrictions to better access the benefits of precision agriculture through reduced network latency [55]. This would assist in developing small-scale farmers to have access to advances in precession farming resources with the potential of improving yield and potentially improving general agricultural outcomes [55].

5 Conclusion

The large-scale implementation of IoT sensors and applications of AI are considered two of the major technologies driving businesses and organisations into what is termed "Industry 4.0". This SLR evaluated the use of IoT for collecting data applicable to the agriculture industry and the application of AI algorithms being applied to this data to drive decision-making and improve automation. Most of the research tasks conducted in the literature presented positive results but indicated that these technologies are still emerging and that extensive research and advancements are required to reap the true value and intended purposes of these technologies. From the SLR, various conclusions can be drawn. Firstly, the use of smart sensors to discern factors such as temperature, moisture, humidity, visual information and chemical concentration readings, biological attributes (such as heart rates, respiration, movement) as well as geographic positioning is almost always used in conjunction with some sort of AI technology. It is evident from the review that the implementation of these IoT sensors and the application of AI techniques to this sensed data provides an innovative and scalable solution to most of the current problems experienced in the agricultural industry.

The wide-scale adoption of these technologies has the potential to automate and optimise common and often resource-intensive agricultural processes. By allowing data to be gathered in real-time and processed by AI that is constantly learning and analysing the trends of this data, the ideal consumption of resources such as water, pesticides, feed, and chemicals being used in crops and livestock farming can be determined and applied. This echoes throughout the agricultural environment where soil quality is maintained, diseases are minimised and the health of both animals and crops are enhanced. By allowing these tasks to be automated by these technologies, costs are reduced, and yield is improved in the long run. By presenting these findings, it is evident to see that with additional research and testing, the progression of precision agriculture is moving the industry towards supporting global food security and can assist in helping to preserve resources while combatting the imminent water crisis.

This review is subjected to the limitations of only including relevant articles published in English between 2015 and 2020. The use of keywords and databases were chosen to obtain the literature may also limit the study as key findings may not have been selected due to incorrect keyword indexing. Nonetheless, this review has provided an outline of research trends and available solutions assisting with the current challenges faced by the agricultural sector and has presented findings on how the use of both AI and IoT technologies may be applied to assist and overcome certain challenges.

Based on the AI and IoT applied in concert does indeed have the potential of supporting agriculture and agriculture optimisation, food production, food distribution as well the optimisation of scarce and dwindling resources. Further research and support for further research are however required.

References

1. Ranganathan, J., Waite, R., Searchinger, T., Hanson, C.: How to sustainably feed 10 billion people by 2050, in 21 charts (2018)
2. Bannerjee, G., Sarkar, U., Das, S., Ghosh, I.: Artificial intelligence in agriculture: a literature survey. Int. J. Sci. Res. Comput. Sci. Appl. Manage. Stud. 7(3), 1–6 (2018)
3. Dharmaraj, V., Vijayanand, C.: Artificial intelligence (AI) in agriculture. Int. J. Curr. Microbiol. App. Sci 7(12), 2122–2128 (2018)
4. Chlingaryan, A., Sukkarieh, S., Whelan, B.: Machine learning approaches for crop yield prediction and nitrogen status estimation in precision agriculture: a review. Comput. Electron. Agric. 151, 61–69 (2018)
5. Moher, D., Liberati, A., Tetzlaff, J., Altman, D.G., PRISMA Group: Preferred reporting items for systematic reviews and meta-analyses: the PRISMA statement. PLoS Med. 6(7), e1000097 (2009)
6. Pollock, A., Berge, E.: How to do a systematic review. Int. J. Stroke 13(2), 138–156 (2018)
7. Nowell, L.S., Norris, J.M., White, D.E., Moules, N.J.: Thematic analysis: striving to meet the trustworthiness criteria. Int. J. Qual. Methods 16(1), 1–13 (2017)
8. Crisis, F., Young, G., Blair, J.P.: Freshwater Crisis. National Geographic (2014)
9. AlZu'bi, S., Hawashin, B., Mujahed, M., Jararweh, Y., Gupta, B.B.: An efficient employment of internet of multimedia things in smart and future agriculture. Multimedia Tools Appl. Int. J. 78(20), 29581–605 (2019)

10. Giri, A., Dutta, S., Neogy, S.: Enabling agricultural automation to optimize utilization of water, fertilizer and insecticides by implementing Internet of Things (IoT). Paper presented at the 2016 International Conference on Information Technology (InCITe) - The Next Generation IT Summit on the Theme - Internet of Things: Connect your Worlds (2016)

11. Al-Ali, A.R., Al Nabulsi, A., Mukhopadhyay, S., Awal, M.S., Fernandes, S., Ailabouni, K.: IoT-solar energy powered smart farm irrigation system. J. Electron. Sci. Technol. **17**(4): 100017 (2019)

12. Abbasi, M., Yaghmaee, M.H., Rahnama, F.: Internet of Things in agriculture: a survey. Paper presented at the 2019 3rd International Conference on Internet of Things and Applications (IoT) (2019)

13. Abioye, E.A., et al.: A review on monitoring and advanced control strategies for precision irrigation. Comput. Electron. Agric. **173**, 105441 (2020)

14. Agarwal, A.V., Kumar, S.: Unsupervised data responsive based monitoring of fields. Paper presented at the 2017 International Conference on Inventive Computing and Informatics (ICICI) (2017)

15. Adhiwibawa, M.A.S., Setiawan, Y.E., Setiawan, Y., Prilianti, K.R., Brotosudarmo, T.H.P.: Application of simple multispectral image sensor and artificial intelligence for predicting of drought tolerant variety of soybean. Proc. Chem. **14**, 246–255 (2015)

16. Higgins, S., Schellberg, J., Bailey, J.S.: Improving productivity and increasing the efficiency of soil nutrient management on grassland farms in the UK and Ireland using precision agriculture technology. Eur. J. Agron. **106**, 67–74 (2019)

17. Ananthi, N., Divya, J., Divya, M., Janani, V.: IoT based smart soil monitoring system for agricultural production. Paper presented at the 2017 IEEE Technological Innovations in ICT for Agriculture and Rural Development (TIAR), 7–8 April 2017 (2017)

18. Partel, V., Charan Kakarla, S., Ampatzidis, Y.: Development and evaluation of a low-cost and smart technology for precision weed management utilizing Artificial Intelligence. Comput. Electron. Agric. **157**, 339–350 (2019)

19. Agarwal, A., Singh, A.K., Kumar, S., Singh, D.: Critical analysis of classification techniques for precision agriculture monitoring using satellite and drone. Paper presented at the 2018 IEEE 13th International Conference on Industrial and Information Systems (ICIIS), 1–2 December (2018)

20. Gašparović, M., Zrinjski, M., Barković, Đ., Radočaj, D.: An automatic method for weed mapping in oat fields based on UAV imagery. Comput. Electron. Agric. **173**, 105385 (2020)

21. Ampatzidis, Y., Partel, V., Costa, L.: Agroview: cloud-based application to process, analyze and visualize UAV-collected data for precision agriculture applications utilizing Artificial Intelligence. Comput. Electron. Agric. **174**, 105457 (2020)

22. Boursianis, A.D., et al.: Internet of things (IoT) and agricultural unmanned aerial vehicles (UAVs) in smart farming: a comprehensive review. Internet of Things. (2020)

23. Eli-Chukwu, N.C.: Applications of artificial intelligence in agriculture: a review. Eng. Technol. Appl. Sci. Res. **9**(4), 77–83 (2019)

24. Bayrakdar, M.E.A.: Smart insect pest detection technique with qualified underground wireless sensor nodes for precision agriculture. IEEE Sens. J. **19**(22), 10892–10897 (2019)

25. Knoll, F.J., Czymmek, V., Poczihoski, S., Holtorf, T., Hussmann, S.: Improving efficiency of organic farming by using a deep learning classification approach. Comput. Electron. Agric. **153**, 347–356 (2018)

26. Ale, L., Sheta, A., Li, L., Wang, Y., Zhang, N.: Deep learning based plant disease detection for smart agriculture. Paper presented at the 2019 IEEE Globecom Workshops (GC Workshop) (2019)

27. Abhijith, H.V., Jain, D.A., Athreya Rao, U.A.: Intelligent agriculture mechanism using internet of things. Paper presented at the 2017 International Conference on Advances in Computing, Communications and Informatics (ICACCI), 13–16 September (2017)

28. Ahmed, K., Shahidi, T.R., Alam, S.M.I., Momen, S.: Rice leaf disease detection using machine learning techniques. Paper presented at the 2019 International Conference on Sustainable Technologies for Industry 4.0 (STI) (2019)

29. Changmai, T., Gertphol, S., Chulak, P.: Smart hydroponic lettuce farm using internet of things. Paper presented at the 2018 10th International Conference on Knowledge and Smart Technology (KST) (2018)

30. Alipio, M.I., Dela Cruz, A.E.M., Doria, J.D.A., Fruto, R.M.S.: A smart hydroponics farming system using exact inference in Bayesian network. Paper presented at the 2017 IEEE 6th Global Conference on Consumer Electronics (GCCE), 24–27 October (2017)

31. dos Santos, U.J.L., Pessin, G., da Costa, C.A., da Rosa Righi, R.: Agriprediction: a proactive internet of things model to anticipate problems and improve production in agricultural crops. Comput. Electron. Agric. **161**, 202–13 (2019)

32. Alonso, R.S., Sittón-Candanedo, I., García, Ó., Prieto, J., Rodríguez-González, S.: An intelligent Edge-IoT platform for monitoring livestock and crops in a dairy farming scenario. Ad Hoc Netw. **98**, 102047 (2020)

33. Gokul, V., Tadepalli, S.: Implementation of smart infrastructure and non-invasive wearable for real time tracking and early identification of diseases in cattle farming using IoT. Paper presented at the 2017 International Conference on I-SMAC (IoT in Social, Mobile, Analytics and Cloud) (I-SMAC), 10–11 February (2017)

34. Nóbrega, L., Gonçalves, P., Antunes, M., Corujo, D.: Assessing sheep behavior through low-power microcontrollers in smart agriculture scenarios. Comput. Electron. Agric. **173**, 105444 (2020)

35. Føre, M., et al.: Precision fish farming: a new framework to improve production in aquaculture. Biosys. Eng. **173**, 176–193 (2018)

36. Filippi, P., et al.: An approach to forecasting grain crop yield using multi-layered, multi-farm data sets and machine learning. Precision Agric. **20**(5), 1015–1029 (2019)

37. Abdelghafour, F., Keresztes, B., Germain, C., Da Costa, J.P.: Potential of on-board colour imaging for in-field detection and counting of grape bunches at early fruiting stages. Adv. Animal Biosci. **8**(2), 505–509 (2017)

38. Sundaramoorthy, D., Dong, L.: Machine-learning-based simulation for estimating parameters in portfolio optimization: empirical application to soybean variety selection (2019). Available at SSRN 3412648

39. Cunha, R.L.F., Silva, B., Netto, M.A.S.: A scalable machine learning system for pre-season agriculture yield forecast. Paper presented at the 2018 IEEE 14th International Conference on e-Science (e-Science), 29 October–1 November (2018)

40. Bhojwani, Y., Singh, R., Reddy, R., Perumal, B.: Crop selection and IoT based monitoring system for precision agriculture. Paper presented at the 2020 International Conference on Emerging Trends in Information Technology and Engineering (ic-ETITE) (2020)

41. da Rosa Righi, R., Goldschmidt, G., Kunst, R., Deon, C., André da Costa, C.: Towards combining data prediction and Internet of Things to manage milk production on dairy cows. Comput. Electron. Agric. **169**, 105156 (2020)

42. Verdouw, C.N., Wolfert, J., Beulens, A.J.M., Rialland, A.: Virtualization of food supply chains with the Internet of Things. J. Food Eng. **176**, 128–136 (2016)

43. Horng, G., Liu, M., Chen, C.: The smart image recognition mechanism for crop harvesting system in intelligent agriculture. IEEE Sens. J. **20**(5), 2766–2781 (2020)

44. Altaheri, H., Alsulaiman, M., Muhammad, G.: Date fruit classification for robotic harvesting in a natural environment using deep learning. IEEE Access **7**, 117115 (2019)

45. Farhadi, M., Abbaspour-Gilandeh, Y., Mahmoudi, A., Joe Mari, M.: An integrated system of artificial intelligence and signal processing techniques for the sorting and grading of nuts. Appl. Sci. **10**(9), 3315 (2020)
46. Abbas, H.M.T., Shakoor, U., Khan, M.J., Ahmed, M., Khurshid, K.: Automated sorting and grading of agricultural products based on image processing. Paper presented at the 2019 8th International Conference on Information and Communication Technologies (ICICT), 16–17 November (2019)
47. Alifah, S., Gunawan, G., Taufik, M.: Smart monitoring of rice logistic employing internet of things network. Paper presented at the 2018 2nd Borneo International Conference on Applied Mathematics and Engineering (BICAME), 10–11 December (2018)
48. AliMohammadi, T., Ahmadi, A., Gómez, P.A., Maghoumi, M.: Using artificial neural network in determining postharvest LIFE of kiwifruit. J. Sci. Food Agric. **99**(13), 5918–5925 (2019)
49. Mario, L., Hernandez, J.E., Díaz, M.E.A., Panetto, H., Kacprzyk, J.: Agri-food 4.0: a survey of the supply chains and technologies for the future agriculture. Comput. Ind. **117**, 103187 (2020)
50. Nukala, R., Panduru, K., Shields, A., Riordan, D., Doody, P., Walsh, J.: Internet of things: a review from 'farm to fork'. Paper presented at the 2016 27th Irish Signals and Systems Conference (ISSC), 21–22 June (2016)
51. Chen, Y., Li, Y.: intelligent autonomous pollination for future farming - a micro air vehicle conceptual framework with artificial intelligence and human-in-the-loop. IEEE Access **7**, 119706–119717 (2019)
52. Pham, X., Stack, M.: How data analytics is transforming agriculture. Bus. Horiz. **61**(1), 125–133 (2018)
53. Ishita, B., Phadikar, S., Majumder, K.: State-of-the-art technologies in precision agriculture: a systematic review. J. Sci. Food Agric. **99**(11), 4878–4878 (2019). (In English)
54. Ren, G., Lin, T., Ying, Y., Chowdhary, G., Ting, K.C.: Agricultural robotics research applicable to poultry production: a review. Comput. Electron. Agric. **169**, 105216 (2020)
55. Ahmed, N., De, D., Hussain, I.: Internet of Things (IoT) for smart precision agriculture and farming in rural areas. IEEE Internet Things J. **5**(6), 4890–4899 (2018)

A Data Analytics Organisation's Perspective on Trust and AI Adoption

Danie Smit[1]([✉])[iD], Sunet Eybers[1][iD], and Jarod Smith[2][iD]

[1] Department of Informatics, University of Pretoria, Pretoria, South Africa
d5mit@pm.me
[2] Department of Statistics, University of Pretoria, Pretoria, South Africa

Abstract. Artificial Intelligence (AI) has the ability to self-learn, act autonomously and exhibits anthropomorphised characteristics. As a result, it is a powerful technology for organisations, but the implementation of AI, can lead to ethical and trust-related concerns. In an organisational context, trust has been identified as a significant barrier to adopting AI. Previous research has indicated that fairness, accountability and transparency, the so-called FAT factors together with explainability, can potentially influence trust in AI. The Technology-Organisation-Environment (TOE) framework is applied as a theoretical lens whilst considering the context of AI in organisations and their environment. The research question, supported by six hypotheses, is: To what extent do FAT factors and explainability influence trust in AI and consequently AI adoption? In order to answer the research question, the TOE framework, together with online surveys involving analytics experts and AI specialists at a leading automotive company, are analysed. This paper's focus extends previous literature's findings that FAT influences trust and makes a theoretical contribution by confirming the indirect relationship between FAT, explainability, trust and adoption of AI in organisations. What makes our research finding of practical importance is not the finding that FAT and explainability leads to trust in AI, but rather the understanding that FAT and explainability will lead to a higher level of adoption in AI in organisations.

Keywords: Technology adoption ·
Technology-Organisation-Environment (TOE) · Socio-technical · FAT
factors · Trust · AI adoption

1 Introduction

Turing's revolutionary work between 1937 and 1952 laid the foundation for artificial intelligence (AI) [17]. Since then, there have been several advances in both AI and its supporting technologies. As a result, AI is becoming increasingly relevant to organisations and how they conduct business [21]. Broad adoption of AI is seen in its use for loan application evaluations, weather predictions, speech, and image recognition. Not surprisingly, large organisations consider AI

E. Jembere et al. (Eds.): SACAIR 2021, CCIS 1551, pp. 47–60, 2022.
https://doi.org/10.1007/978-3-030-95070-5_4

the most significant new disruptive technology [10]. One example is how tech giants Google and Tesla are disrupting the automotive industry by using deep learning in self-driving cars [41].

Despite the technological advances, such as speech recognition, virtual agents and deep learning platforms, many organisations are only beginning to utilise the full potential of AI [38]. Organisations not embracing these technologies will lose out on a chance to enhance their organisational performance significantly [27]. Even when organisations realise the need to adopt AI and subsequently try to increase adoption, most AI projects remain in the pre-implementation phase as part of prototypes, with relatively few deployed into production environments [10].

The low production implementation rate of AI solutions can be attributed to various reasons, such as user resistance [32], problems integrating with existing technologies, change in business processes, skills shortages and substantial data engineering requirements [10]. A lack of trust in AI has been highlighted as one of the most significant barriers to adoption [23]. The need for trust takes several forms, including trusting the quality of data [22], trusting the organisation's AI capabilities [38], trusting that the AI system will perform or behave as intended and trusting that the AI's values align with the organisation's values [35].

Previous research has indicated that fair, accountable and transparent factors (the so-called FAT factors) can potentially increase trust in AI [40]. This paper's focus extends these findings and applies the Technology-Organisation-Environment framework (TOE) to explain the role of the FAT factors and explainability as critical enablers of adopting AI in organisations.

The TOE framework is a theoretical framework that explains technology adoption at an organizational level analysis. It describes how the technological context, organisational context, influences adopting and implementing technological innovations. [14]. The TOE framework is appropriate as it caters for external stimuli directly influencing AI adoption and allows researchers to focus on higher-level attributes. The framework therefore provides a theoretical lens for this study while considering the context of AI in organisations.

The research question is: *To what extent do FAT factors and explainability influence trust and AI adoption?* The research question accompanies the following hypotheses within an organisational context:

H_1: There is a positive association between perceived fairness and trust in AI

H_2: There is a positive association between perceived accountability and trust in AI

H_3: There is a positive association between perceived transparency and trust in AI

H_4: There is a positive association between perceived FAT factors and trust in AI

H_5: There is a positive association between perceived explainability and trust in AI

H_6: There is a positive association between trust in AI and the adoption of AI

The rest of this paper is structured as follows: Sect. 2 contains the literature review on the adoption of AI in organisations, with the focus on how FAT factors and explainability can lead to trust and how trust supports AI adoption. Section 3 explains the research landscape of this study. The research model and approach are described in Sect. 4, followed by the research context, results and interpretation in Sect. 5. Lastly, Sect. 6 contains recommendations and conclusions.

2   Literature Review

The literature review covers the adoption of AI in organisations, with the focus on how FAT factors together with explainability influence the trust and adoption of AI within an organisation.

First, the adoption of new technologies and its relationship with trust is discussed. Second, the influence of FAT and explainability on trust is considered. Lastly, the construct of AI and its implementation in an organisational context is covered. Each one of the constructs explained in this section contributes to the research landscape.

2.1   Trust and AI Adoption

Previous studies focusing on information systems have highlighted the significant role that trust plays in the adoption of new technologies [37]. Generally, trust is built when actions can be predicted. When it comes to AI, actions are often difficult to predict due to AI's ability to self-learn and function autonomously.

The European Commission's High-level Expert Group on AI (HLEG) proposes three main categories of trust in AI, namely trust in technology; trust in the technical designers and organisations developing the system; and trust in the socio-technical systems involved in the AI's life cycle [36]. For each one of the categories, two main trust paradigms exist, namely cognitive and emotional trust [20, 37]. Trust conceptualised as a cognitive construct involves the rational evaluation of the situation and whether the trustees will uphold the trust placed in them [36]. In contrast, irrational factors such as emotions and mood influence emotional-based trust, where the trustor places confidence in the goodwill of the trustee [36, 37]. Ryan [36] argues that cognitive and emotional trust can be assigned to the designers and organisations that develop AI systems. Cognitive and emotional trust can also be assigned to the socio-technical systems in which AI technologies exist. Furthermore, Ryan [36] argues that trust should not trivially be given to the AI technology itself, as it diverts responsibility from those developing it.

2.2   FAT Factors, Explainability and Trust in an Organisational Context

Previous research has indicated that fair, accountable and transparent factors (the so-called FAT factors) can increase trust in AI [40]. Current literature on

FAT in AI systems range from purely technical aspects such as the algorithms that can enhance FAT [6] to softer issues such as the user's emotional trust influenced by the AI's system transparency and explainability [40]. We introduce FAT and explainability and its relationship with trust in order to create the necessary literature building blocks required to confirm that FAT and explainability will lead to a higher level of adoption in AI on organisations.

Fairness: Even though fairness is generally understood as the lack of discrimination or bias in decisions, there are different interpretations of what is fair. For instance, Lepri et al. [25] elaborates upon group fairness compared to individual fairness. There are also different approaches to determining fairness. For example, O'Neil [30] makes the argument that instead of focusing on a single metric to determine a decision maker's fairness, one should rather identify the stakeholders affected and weighing their relative harms. When AI utilises good quality data supplied as part of a data-driven organisation, AI has the potential to make objective and fair decisions. AI has the potential to be fairer than humans who may be influenced by prejudice [37]. As such, going back to Ryan, this potential for objectiveness and predictability can lead to cognitive trust [36], however when an application is perceived as unfair, it might lead to emotional distrust [37].

Accountability: The allocation concept of accountability between individuals and technology is not new. However, Martin [28] highlights that as AI systems can make decisions autonomously and enable automation, delegation of accountability to technology is happening faster. Agerfalk [3] elaborates that accountability is becoming critical when information systems make decisions that impact people. Organisations need to ensure accountability in decision-making algorithms, which includes clarity on who is responsible for decisions, accepting responsibility and being able to explain and justify decisions taken by AI systems [25]. Furthermore, Martin [28] argues that when algorithms produce biased answers or mistakes, these need to be managed. Organisations and the individuals who develop AI solutions are making critical moral decisions. Mistakes may be unintentional, but ignoring them is unethical and detrimental to trust [28]. Therefore, the implementation of proper governance processes is key to prevent and deal with errors that can lead to cognitive and emotional distrust.

Transparency: The increasing complexities in AI lead to a lack of transparency [40]. It is often not clear to technical experts how these systems work internally and how they arrive at a particular decision outcome [37]. Furthermore, there is a danger that AI decision-making approaches treat the algorithmic process and output as both inevitable and final, where it cannot be questioned, and mistakes are left ungoverned [28]. Barredo [6] states that transparency concerns the requirement to describe, inspect and reproduce the mechanisms through which AI systems make decisions. Felzmann et al. [19] argue that transparency also includes the openness and communication of both the data being analysed and the mechanisms underlying the models. Shin [40] explains that it is the lack of transparency in AI that hinders understanding and negatively influences trust [40].

Explainability: Adadi and Berrada [2] state that explainability entails being able to describe the rationale or logic behind the decisions to stakeholders. Explainability is closely related to transparency. However, Elton [18] argues that even when transparency is ensured, due to the complexity of AI technologies and data it is trained on, AI actions or decisions can still be very difficult to interpret. The vast amount of data and the complexity of AI (neuronal networks beyond the complexity of the human brain), may lead to results and algorithms/methods that one can explain in principle, but the human mind may no longer be able to cope with this amount of data and the complexity. As a result, humans (the consumer) need to trust the outcome of AI applications. In an attempt to address this Bruhn and Anderer [11] explain that trust-building means accepting the opaqueness. One should shift focus to testing and checking outputs so that AI's inherent lack of transparency can be cushioned. Similarly, Asatiani [7] argues that to build trust, even if the model performs well, it may need a human gatekeeper. Interestingly, Elton [18] states that although the human brain is a "black box", we are able to trust each other.

2.3 Organisational Maturity

Organisations are often measured and subsequently categorised based on the extent of their adoption of data analytics and AI capabilities. This is referred to as data-driven maturity levels. The maturity level concept is not the specific focus of this paper but is relevant as it can influence the adoption of AI and is part of the context within which the adoption of AI will occur. Rogers' diffusion of innovation theory [33] reminds us that it is not only the innovation characteristics that play a role in adoption, but that there are different levels of adoption among organisations and that they should be treated differently. The data analytics and AI maturity levels explained by Davenport and Harris [13] range from "analytically impaired" (limited adoption) to organisations having reached "analytical nirvana" (high adoption rate). Organisations that have successfully adopted AI technologies and benefit from these implementations have reached an advanced state of data-drivenness [13,24].

3 Research Landscape

The adoption of AI in organisations is a multi-faceted topic. In the following section, we explain this paper's research landscape including the theoretical lens as depicted in Fig. 1.

Even though AI's technical capabilities are at the core of what AI offers, the implementation in organisations is not limited to the technical elements

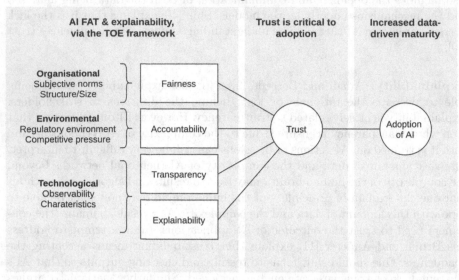

Fig. 1. Constructs of the research landscape

but requires a more holistic approach. We utilise Tornatzky's [14] Technical-Organisation-Environment (TOE) framework as the theoretical lens for this study. The TOE framework explains technology adoption in organisations from a high-level organisational perspective. The TOE framework is appropriate for this study as it caters for external stimuli directly influencing AI adoption and allows researchers to focus on higher-level attributes instead of detailed behaviours of individuals in the organisation. As this study has a high-level organisational view on FAT and explainability, the TOE framework is used to place these constructs in this study's context. For the scope of this study, fairness is viewed from an organisational context, as fairness within an organisation is measured against the organisation's subjective norms. Accountability is viewed from an environmental context, where a regulatory environment insists that accountability in the organisation is set in place. Transparency and explainability are viewed from a technological context, where the characteristics of the technology should allow for observability. Finally, a lack of trust in AI is perceived as a barrier to adoption that must be overcome. This is not the only contextual view one can have on FAT and explainability, however, this is the scope of this research.

There are many contributing factors to the adoption of AI in organisations. However, as mentioned in the opening parts of the paper, this paper focuses on trust as an enabler to AI adoption and the context of becoming more data-driven. Moreover, a lack of trust is a barrier to adoption. Achieving a more mature level of data-driven organisational maturity is the high-level context of this study. A data-driven organisation is an organisation that uses analytical tools and abilities, that creates a culture to integrate and foster analytical expertise and acts on observed data to achieve benefits [1,4,15,42,44]. Considering the definition of a data-driven organisation, when applying the TOE framework and looking at higher-level attributes, the organisational context includes aspects such as organisational culture, availability of skills, and characteristics such as size, structure [16] and subjective norms [8]. The technological context refers to all the technologies relevant to the organisation, including both the technologies already in use and technology innovations that are currently not implemented [43]. The technological context includes aspects such as complexity of the technology, technical characteristics, compatibility with other technologies and, general observability of how the technology functions [31], whilst the environmental context is the environment in which the organisation exists such as industry structure, service providers, regulatory environment [16], competitors, customers, partners and government pressures [12].

4   Research Model and Approach

4.1   Research Context

The organisation involved in the study is a leading international automotive manufacturer that currently employs more than 100 000 employees across more than 15 countries. The organisation has an analytics and AI competence centre where this research took place. This research forms part of a larger study focusing on how to transform an organisation to become more data-driven. The case study explores the relationship between the FAT factors, explainability, trust and AI adoption, according to the view of technical specialists or software product owners. It is assumed that, through the confirmation and communication of the relationship between the factors and AI adoption, the chances of successful AI adoption would increase in the analytics competence centre involved in the study and result in an increased data-driven maturity.

From an organisational context, the main task of the analytics competence centre is to deliver software products to the large automotive manufacturer based in Europe. The centre currently employs approximately 330 data analytics consultants located in the economic hub of South Africa, namely Gauteng. In terms of subjective norms, the competence centre is part of the larger organisation that instils strong organisational values amongst employees. These values are responsibility, appreciation, transparency, trust and openness, which align with the FAT principles. From a technological context, the consultants are experts in analytics, working in different teams using data warehouses and data lakes as well as data engineering with a diverse focus from descriptive reporting to predictive analytics. From an environmental context, in terms of the regulatory environment, the competence centre adheres to international standards such as ISO 9001 and follows a well-defined agile working model [39] employing specific tools to ensure that teams follow protocol in terms of bespoke application reliability and security. Given the agile working model that the organisation follows, products owners (the main research participants) are responsible for achieving the value of software products delivered in scrum teams.

4.2 Research Approach

Based on the research landscape and the context where FAT, explainability, trust and adoption are at the centre, the research model provides an overview of the various hypotheses that will be tested within an organisational context. These include:

H_1: There is a positive association between perceived fairness and trust in AI

H_2: There is a positive association between perceived accountability and trust in AI

H_3: There is a positive association between perceived transparency and trust in AI

H_4: There is a positive association between perceived FAT factors and trust in AI

H_5: There is a positive association between perceived explainability and trust in AI

H_6: There is a positive association between trust in AI and the adoption of AI

In order to test the various hypotheses, the proposed manifest variables are defined as "perceived_fairness", "perceived_accountability", "perceived_trans parency", "perceived_fat" (which is the combination of fairness, accountability and transparency), "perceived_explainability", "ai_trust_to_adoption" and "ai_lack_trust_ low_adoption". The proposed latent factors (variables that are not directly observed but are rather inferred) are identified as "trust" and "adoption". The relationships between the manifest variables and latent factors together with the hypotheses are graphical depicted in Fig. 2. H6 represents both "ai_trust_to_adoption" and "ai_lack_trust_ low_adoption", however it was kept separate during the analysis as a cross-check.

For this study, quantitative data was collected through the online distribution of surveys using purposive sampling (only technical specialists in a leading manufacturing organisation involved in AI projects were included). The surveys focused on each one of the FAT factors namely, fairness, accountability and transparency and additionally on explainability. A total of 313 surveys were distributed, of which 133 were completed, yielding a response rate of 42%. Each hypothesis was supported by a question in the survey. The data were analysed using structural equation modelling (SEM) as the underlying statistical methodology. SEM is used as it allows one to analyse structural relationships between manifest variables and latent constructs. A four-phase approach, similar to Mulaik and Millsap [29] was employed with the objective of confirming the research model and corresponding hypotheses. That is, first the reliability and validity of the survey's Likert measurements (manifest or observed variables) were investigated using multi-collinearity and Cronbach alpha assessments, respectively. Second, a principal component analysis (PCA) was performed to identify the optimal number of latent factors that account for sufficient variability within the survey data. Third, an exploratory factor analysis using varimax rotation (EFA) followed by a two correlated factor confirmatory factor

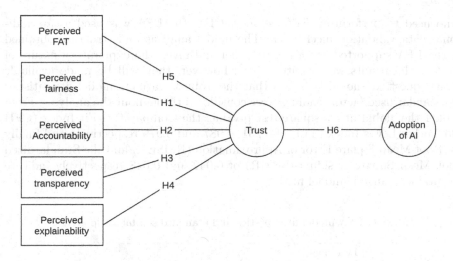

Fig. 2. Research model and hypotheses

analysis (CFA) similar to the approach of Anderson et al. [5] were used to ensure the manifest variables are associated with the latent factors as hypothesised.

Finally, the SEM is used to assess the structural relation between the latent factors in the CFA. In other words, the SEM measures the association (if any) between trust and the adoption of AI.

5   Results and Interpretation

The study was limited to one company, however the analytics specialists and AI experts that provided the raw data for this study are closer to the "engine room" than non experts. The focus of the data analysis was to determine the relationship between AI adoption and the FAT factors together with explainability (the statistical variables) within the context of the analytics competence centre.

It should be noted that the multivariate normality assumption of the manifest variables was moderately violated. To address this violation, diagonally weighted least squares (WLSMV), designed for ordinal data, was used as the estimation method instead of the robust maximum likelihood (MLR) estimation [26]. All analyses were performed using the *lavaan* package in R [34].

Following the statistical methodology outlined in Sect. 4.2, the correlation structure of the data suggested no immediate concerns for large ($r \geq 0.85$) bivariate correlations. Furthermore, the Cronbach aplha values for the manifest groupings: group 1 = {perceived_transparency, perceived_accountability and perceived_explainability }, group 2 = {perceived_fairness and perceived_fat} and group 3 = {ai_trust_to_adoption and ai_lack_trust_low_adoption} of 0.61, 0.657 and 0.672 for groups 1 to 3, respectively, suggested an acceptable level of reliability. Although this study has an a priori model and Awang [9] mentions there is no need to perform an EFA before a CFA, the EFA was used as an additional data validation mechanism. The model analysis and structure obtained by the EFA supported the a priori model and given the exploratory nature of the test the results were omitted here, however, they will be made available upon request. It should be noted that the 'robust' variants model fit statistics and standardised factor loadings were considered throughout the analyses. From Table 1 the global fit chi-square test p-value; the Comparative Fit Index (CFI) and Tucker-Lewis Index (TLI) of 0.251, 0.987 and 0.979 respectively and finally the Root Mean Square Error of Approximation (RMSEA) and the Standardized Root Mean Square Residual (SRMR) of 0.042 and 0.048 respectively indicate acceptable/plausible model fit.

Table 1. CFA model fit statistics and standardised factor loadings.

Loadings		
	Factor 1	Factor 2
ai_transparency_to_trust	0.422	
ai_accountability_to_trust	0.712	
ai_fairness_to_trust	0.696	
ai_trust_to_adoption		0.698
ai_fat_to_trust	0.712	
ai_lack_trust_low_adoption		0.725
ai_must_be_trans_expl	0.628	
Latent factor covariance		
Estimate	0.783	
Model fit statistics		
Chi-square and (p-value)	15.971 (0.251)	
CFI	0.987	
TLI	0.979	
RMSEA	0.042	
SRMR	0.048	

Recall that the CFA assessed the validity of the hypothesized model structure. The SEM was tested by estimating the associations between the latent factors. Not surprisingly, the standardised factor loadings were identical to those of the CFA model, due to the identical model estimation technique, and the latent factor regression coefficient was given by 0.78 suggesting that Trust in AI is positively associated with the Adoption of AI, such that a one-unit increase in trust leads to a 0.78 increase in AI adoption within an organisation. The path analysis SEM diagram is given in Fig. 3.

Consistent with the literature review and the theoretical underpinnings, out of the survey, we identified measured variables as accountability, fairness, trans-

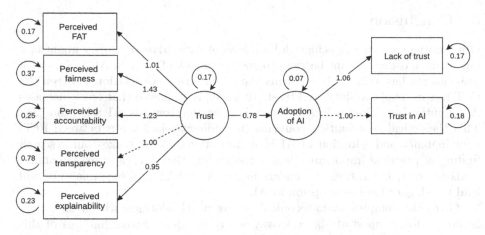

Fig. 3. The SEM path analysis diagram highlighting the associations between the latent factors 'trust in AI' and 'Adoption of AI', respectively.

parency, explainability, the link between FAT factors and trust, the link between the lack of trust with low adoption and the link between trust and adoption. The two latent variables are trust in AI and adoption of AI. The relationship between FAT AI and AI adoption that it leads to trust is confirmed by the SEM as seen in Fig. 3. It is also confirmed that trust in AI will lead to a higher level of adoption in AI, compared to a lack of trust.

The SEM diagram supports the claim that FAT AI considerations by organisations will lead to more trust in AI and remove the lack of trust, which is one of the main barriers to the adoption of AI. The concept of trust not only played a role in to remove barriers to adoption, but trust was also confirmed as an enabler of adoption in AI.

An interesting observation that emerged from our analyses of the data was that even though fairness, accountability, transparency and explainability were all significant (p-value < 0.05) manifest variables, accountability accounted for more of the explained variation within the data. In other words, the standardised factor loading, in Table 1, of the accountability manifest variable of 0.712 was higher than 0.422 and 0.696 standardised factor loadings of the fairness and transparency manifest variables, respectively.

Another informative observation was that the manifest variable associated with a lack of trust would lead to low adoption of AI had the highest standardised factor loading of 0.725. Therefore, it is essential for organisations striving to increase their data-driven maturity and implement AI to educate their product owners about the vital role of trust in the acceptance of AI.

There is a strong association between the FAT factors, explainability, trust and AI organisational adoption. The hypotheses within an organisational context are strongly supported and confirm our hypotheses (H1–H6).

6   Conclusion

Organisations striving to achieve a high-level of data-driven maturity might face one of the most significant barriers to success: a lack of trust in AI. In line with previous studies, this study confirms there is a strong association between the FAT factors, explainability, and trust [19,37,40] and showed that trust increases AI adoption and that a lack of trust is a barrier towards AI adoption [23]. This theoretical contribution confirms the indirect relationship between FAT, explainability and adoption of AI in organisations. What makes our research finding of practical importance is not the finding that FAT and explainability leads to trust, but rather the understanding that FAT and explainability will lead to a higher level of adoption in AI.

Given the complex socio-technical nature of AI adoption within an organisation, a follow-up study is underway where the quantitative findings of this study together with qualitative data from explanatory focus groups will be used to gain a deeper understanding of the constructs identified in the research.

References

1. van der Aalst, W.M.P., Bichler, M., Heinzl, A.: Responsible data science. IEEE Sig. Process. Mag. **59**(5), 311–313 (2017)
2. Adadi, A., Berrada, M.: Peeking inside the black-box: a survey on explainable artificial intelligence (XAI). IEEE Access **6**, 52138–52160 (2018)
3. Ågerfalk, P.: Artificial intelligence as digital agency. Eur. J. Inf. Syst. **29**(1), 1–8 (2020)
4. Anderson, C.: Creating a Data-Driven Organisation, 1st edn. O'Reilly, Oxford (2015)
5. Anderson, J., Kellogg, J., Gerbing, D.: Structural equation modeling in practice: a review and recommended two-step approach. Psychol. Bull. **103**(3), 411–423 (1988)
6. Arrieta, A., et al.: Explainable artificial intelligence (XAI): concepts, taxonomies, opportunities and challenges toward responsible AI. Inf. Fusion **58**, 82–115 (2020)
7. Asatiani, A., Malo, P., Nagbøl, P., Penttinen, E., Rinta-Kahila, T., Salovaara, A.: Challenges of explaining the behavior of black-box AI systems. MIS Q. Executive **19**(4), 259–278 (2020)
8. Awa, H., Ojiabo, O., Orokor, L.: Integrated technology-organization-environment (TOE) taxonomies for technology adoption. J. Enterp. Inf. Manag. **30**(6), 893–921 (2017)
9. Awang, Z.: A handbook on structural equation modeling using AMOS, pp. 83–102. Universiti Technologi MARA Press, Malaysia (2012)
10. Benbya, H., Davenport, T., Pachidi, S.: Artificial intelligence in organizations: current state and future opportunities. MIS Q. Executive **19**(4) (2020)
11. Bruhn, J., Anderer, M.: Implementing artificial intelligence in organizations and the special role of trust. In: Osburg, T., Heinecke, S. (eds.) Media Trust in a Digital World, pp. 191–205. Springer, Cham (2019). https://doi.org/10.1007/978-3-030-30774-5_14
12. Chen, Y., Yin, Y., Browne, G., Li, D.: Adoption of building information modeling in Chinese construction industry: the technology-organization-environment framework. Eng. Constr. Archit. Manag. **26**(9), 1878–1898 (2019)

13. Davenport, T., Harris, J.: Competing on Analytics: The New Science of Winning. Harvard Business School Press, Boston (2007)
14. Drazin, R.: The processes of technological innovation. J. Technol. Transf. **16**(1), 45–46 (1991)
15. Dubois, D., Hájek, P., Prade, H.: Knowledge-driven versus data-driven logics. J. Logic Lang. Inf. **9**(1), 65–89 (2000)
16. Dwivedi, Y., Wade, M., Schneberger, S.: Information Systems Theory. Explaining and Predicting Our Digital Society, vol. 1. Springer, New York (2012). https://doi.org/10.1007/978-1-4419-6108-2
17. Efimov, A.: Post-turing methodology: breaking the wall on the way to artificial general intelligence. In: Goertzel, B., Panov, A.I., Potapov, A., Yampolskiy, R. (eds.) AGI 2020. LNCS (LNAI), vol. 12177, pp. 83–94. Springer, Cham (2020). https://doi.org/10.1007/978-3-030-52152-3_9
18. Elton, D.C.: Self-explaining AI as an alternative to interpretable AI. In: Goertzel, B., Panov, A.I., Potapov, A., Yampolskiy, R. (eds.) AGI 2020. LNCS (LNAI), vol. 12177, pp. 95–106. Springer, Cham (2020). https://doi.org/10.1007/978-3-030-52152-3_10
19. Felzmann, H., Fosch-Villaronga, E., Lutz, C.: Towards transparency by design for artificial intelligence. Sci. Eng. Ethics **26**(6), 3333–3361 (2020)
20. Gillath, O., Ai, T., Branicky, M., Keshmiri, S., Davison, R., Spaulding, R.: Attachment and trust in artificial intelligence. Comput. Hum. Behav. **115**, 106607 (2021)
21. Gomes, C.: Computational sustainability: computing for a better world and a sustainable future. Commun. ACM **62**(9), 56–65 (2019)
22. Grover, V., Chiang, R., Liang, T., Zhang, D.: Creating strategic business value from big data analytics: a research framework. J. Manag. Inf. Syst. **35**(2), 388–423 (2018)
23. Herschel, G., et al.: Predicts 2018: analytics and BI strategy (2018)
24. Johnson, D., Muzellec, L., Sihi, D., Zahay, D.: The marketing organization's journey to become data-driven. J. Res. Interact. Mark. **13**(2) (2019)
25. Lepri, B., Oliver, N., Letouzé, E., Pentland, A., Vinck, P.: Fair, transparent, and accountable algorithmic decision-making processes. Philos. Technol. **31**(4), 611–627 (2018)
26. Li, C.-H.: Confirmatory factor analysis with ordinal data: comparing robust maximum likelihood and diagonally weighted least squares. Behav. Res. Methods **48**(3), 936–949 (2015). https://doi.org/10.3758/s13428-015-0619-7
27. Manyika, J., Chui, M., Lund, S., Ramaswamy, S.: What's now and next in analytics, AI, and automation. McKinsey Global Institute, pp. 1–12 (2017)
28. Martin, K.: Designing ethical algorithms. MIS Q. Executive **18**(2), 129–142 (2019)
29. Mulaik, S., Millsap, R.: Doing the four-step right. Struct. Eqn. Model. **7**(1), 36–73 (2000)
30. O'Neil, C.: Weapons of Math Destruction: How Big Data Increases Inequality and Threatens Democracy. Crown Books, New York (2016)
31. Ramdani, B., Kawalek, P., Lorenzo, O.: Predicting SMEs' adoption of enterprise systems. J. Enterp. Inf. Manag. **22**(1), 10–24 (2009)
32. Reis, L., Maier, C., Mattke, J., Creutzenberg, M., Weitzel, T.: Addressing user resistance would have prevented a healthcare AI project failure. MIS Q. Executive **19**(4), 279–296 (2020)
33. Rogers, E.: Diffusion of Innovations, 4th edn. The Free Press, New York (1995)
34. Rosseel, Y.: Lavaan: an R package for structural equation modeling and more. version 0.5-12 (BETA). J. Stat. Softw. **48**(2), 1–36 (2012)

35. Russell, S.: Human Compatible: Artificial Intelligence and the Problem of Control. Penguin Publishing Group, New York (2019)
36. Ryan, M.: In AI we trust: ethics, artificial intelligence, and reliability. Sci. Eng. Ethics **26**(5), 2749–2767 (2020)
37. Salam, A., Pervez, S., Nahar, S.: Trust in AI and intelligent systems: central core of the design of intelligent systems. In: AMCIS 2021 Proceedings (2021)
38. Schlegel, K., Herschel, G., Logan, D., Laney, D., Judah, S., Logan, V.: Break through the four barriers blocking your full data and analytics potential - keynote insights. Gartner (2018)
39. Schwaber, K., Sutherland, J.: Scrum guide v7. Gartner, pp. 133–152 (2015)
40. Shin, D.: The effects of explainability and causability on perception, trust, and acceptance: implications for explainable AI. Int. J. Hum. Comput. Stud. **146**, 102551 (2021)
41. Simoudis, E.: The Big Data Opportunity in our Driverless Future. Corporate Innovators, Menlo Park (2017)
42. Someh, I., Wixom, B.: Data-driven transformation at Microsoft (2017)
43. Tushman, M., Nadler, D.: Organizing for innovation. Calif. Manag. Rev. **28**(3), 74–92 (1986)
44. Zolnowski, A., Anke, J., Gudat, J.: Towards a cost-benefit-analysis of data-driven business models. In: International Conference on Wirtschaftsinformatik, vol. 13, pp. 181–195 (2017)

Computer Vision and Image Processing

Improving Pose Estimation Through Contextual Activity Fusion

David Poulton$^{(\boxtimes)}$ and Richard Klein

School of Computer Science and Applied Mathematics,
University of the Witwatersrand, Johannesburg, South Africa
1662476@students.wits.ac.za, richard.klein@wits.ac.za

Abstract. This research presents the idea of activity fusion into existing pose estimation architectures to enhance their predictive ability. This is motivated by the rise in higher level concepts found in modern machine learning architectures, and the belief that activity context is a useful piece of information for the problem of pose estimation. To analyse this concept we take an existing deep learning architecture and augment it with an additional 1×1 convolution to fuse activity information into the model. We perform evaluation and comparison on a common pose estimation dataset, and show a performance improvement over our baseline model, especially in uncommon poses and on typically difficult joints. Additionally, we perform an ablative analysis to indicate that the performance improvement does in fact draw from the activity information.

Keywords: Pose estimation · Computer vision · Fully convolutional neural networks · Context fusion

1 Introduction

Human Pose Estimation (HPE) is a widely studied field of Machine Learning focused on finding the joint positions of humans in an image. Pose estimation is a problem with various applications, such as allowing sensor-free capture for animation tracking, easily accessible human kinematics analysis, and advanced biometric security systems, amongst others.

Initially researchers developed models which functioned through the use of hand crafted features, which yielded some success, however the incredible complexity of the problem limited the viability of such methods. Some examples of pose estimation annotations can be seen in Fig. 1, composed of the predictions of our final model on images randomly selected from the test set.

Over time, since the inception of neural networks, and specifically Convolutional Neural Networks (CNNs), models began to shift towards fully learned knowledge without the need for human crafted features or prior information. CNNs enabled models to effectively handle image data due to the nature of their design, which suited HPE and propelled model accuracies and speeds, with networks becoming larger and more carefully structured. Architectures such as

© Springer Nature Switzerland AG 2022
E. Jembere et al. (Eds.): SACAIR 2021, CCIS 1551, pp. 63–76, 2022.
https://doi.org/10.1007/978-3-030-95070-5_5

DeepPose [17] and Stacked Hourglass [10] were forerunners of deep learning for HPE.

The more complex structures that fell under deep learning began enabling models to capture higher level concepts such as whole objects and bodies, above local features or individual limbs [12,16,17], improving their accuracies. This indicates that modern architectures are capable of utilising these concepts, and designing them with this in mind can yield high performing models. Following on from that, we predict that the use of contextual information within pose estimators can further improve performance.

In humans, different activities generally tend to contain markedly different poses, and in turn different poses tend to be found more amongst certain activities, and so we choose activity as our contextual information of choice. Our goal here is to determine whether knowing an image contains a certain activity can drive the model to certain biases that improve its ability to estimate poses. For example, knowing an image comes from a rugby game may inform a pose estimator that it will likely encounter more running, diving, and kicking, rather than sitting.

However, we also need to consider how images are categorised to activities, which is not straightforward. Using one set of activities may be more reasonable conceptually, where using another may better segment poses but be less useful. For example, using "Playing soccer" is more practical than decomposing it into "Running", "Kicking", and "Tackling", even though the latter decomposition may better separate the poses we expect to see.

Using higher level activities means we could apply our research to improve tracking in situations such as sports games, where 3D replays are becoming common and controllers can set a single flag for the entire game. Setting a high level activity for CGI and animation motion tracking can also be advantageous, as actors often role-play an activity in a lab environment that does not visually convey the surrounding context, whereas a lower level activity may better improve individual movement clips.

Regardless, finding an effective way to fuse this activity information into the current deep learning networks available is not a trivial design choice due to the complex nature of modern architectures. Above that, where to provide this information to models requires some thought as well. We hope to address at least some of these concerns through this research.

The remainder of the paper is structured as follows: Sect. 2 explores some of the existing work in the field of pose estimation, as well as related concepts of context fusion in imagery. Section 3 then covers the architectural design choices for the research. Section 4 provides detail on how our chosen models were trained, followed by the results thereof in Sect. 5, including an ablative analysis of our method. We then provide some concepts for future work in Sect. 6, followed by our conclusion in Sect. 7.

Fig. 1. Some annotated examples from the test set, indicating the complexity of the problem, and the large variety of poses the model is capable of handling. The effect of having the target in the center of the image can also be noticed in images where there are several people, even in close proximity. Images are from the MPII dataset [2].

2 Related Work

Early models of HPE utilised largely parts based models [13,21], which were successful at the time but fall well short of the accuracies enjoyed by modern deep learning networks, and are not well suited to higher level conceptual learning.

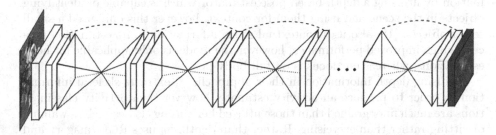

Fig. 2. A visualisation of the original Stacked Hourglass architecture, taken from [10].

Modern networks are far better suited to the task, and fall largely into one of two categories, namely regression based or heatmap based models. DeepPose [17] was a forerunning regression based model. It utilised a holistic method to determine initial pose estimates, and then followed up with a series of cascading CNNs to refine predictions on a per-joint basis.

On the other hand, models such as the Stacked Hourglass model [10] utilise heatmaps entirely for joint predictions. The Hourglass model takes advantage of contractions and expansions, as well as residuals, to find a good balance between holistic, global features, and smaller, localised details in images. Wei et al. [19] developed a similar concept of a repeated sequence of sub-CNN modules which each produce a heatmap that is passed on to the next module, inspired by DeepPose [17]. This structure also displayed improvements in the ability of the model to capture both global and local contextual pose information.

Some approaches also utilised model-based learning to restrict pose estimates to realistic spaces. [14] implemented a bone-based representation that allowed for learning of skeletal structure, rather than directly predicting joint positions. They also adapted their loss functions to account for errors specific to joints, and errors caused by misalignment of bones between the root and current joint. Both these alterations successfully increased accuracy over model-free methods seen before. [4] utilises a model-based generative architecture to try improve out-of-distribution poses, enhancing the model's ability to generalise, rather than focus on more accurate predictions for known distributions.

Rather than using repeated stages of differing refinements, [5] attempts to ensure realistic poses by utilising a GAN system, where adversaries are used to determine how reasonable the generated pose and confidence maps are. An ablative study indicates the GAN structure is indeed contributory to accuracy improvements. [3] also utilises a GAN network to augment inputs and make them easier to predict on, yielding the best performance achieved on the MPII dataset.

As for the concept of activity fusion, it appears that the available literature is relatively sparse. [11] explores the concept of semantic and contextual information by utilising a depth-based pose estimator which is capable of identifying objects in the scene and using them for context, however this only used a small set of objects. [18] also uses contextual scene information in its estimation process which improved performance, however the model is only applicable for head estimations, whereas our focus is on full body poses.

Utilising depth information in their approach, [8] extracts skeletal information in order to produce an activity estimate, however their activity classifications are much finer grained than those utilised here, using classes such as walking or sitting rather than exercising. Rather than depth, [6] uses RGB imagery and extracts poses to be used for broader activity estimates, which is more relevant to the topic, and indicates there is a possible relationship of significance between pose and activity.

[9] explores a similar concept of utilising contextual information around an image, however in their use case it is applied to road image segmentation rather than human poses. Their approach still yielded favourable results, and is encouraging for our concept.

3   Architecture

The utilised architecture was based off of the Stacked Hourglass model [10] with some added layers for the activity fusion. The Stacked Hourglass model was selected because of its high base accuracy, inherently flexible modular design, and balance at finding global and local pose cues. It also maintains the same shape of features throughout the majority of the model, specifically $64 \times 64 \times 256$, making testing various fusion sites more straightforward.

Because the Hourglass network is already designed with capturing global context in mind, it was also of interest to see if explicitly providing the context would have a significant impact, or if the model itself was already capable of extracting the context in some sense.

We use the final version of the Stacked Hourglass model initially presented in the original paper [10] as our baseline, composed of eight glasses, and utilising intermediate supervision for training. A rough visualisation of the original network can be seen in Fig. 2.

Our baseline model still makes use of the initial down-convolution segment of the network, as well as the intermediate bottlenecks and final remapping convolutions, and regularisation and frequent batch normalisation. We then had three sets of models, each composed of an ablative model and a contextual model. The ablative models were the same as our baseline, however with a single extra one-by-one convolution inserted at a specific point in the network. The contextual model involved stacking the activity tensor on top of the existing tensor in the model at the point, followed by a one-by-one convolution, yielding the so called fused image that is then propagated normally through the remainder of the network.

We make use of the one-by-one convolution in order to correct the number of layers in the tensor after we have stacked our activity onto the previous output. Throughout the majority of the network there are 256 channels in the output of the layers, and so stacking our 21 channel activity tensor brings the tensor to 277 channels. In order to minimise the changes needed to the network, we then convolve the tensor back down to 256 layers. This method also ideally allows the convolution to learn an effective mapping to merge our context into the tensor, without having to rely on the existing layers in the network. A diagram of this context block can be seen in Fig. 4, compared to the original hourglass block in Fig. 3.

We utilise both an ablative and contextual version to verify that any possible changes in the accuracy of the model are due to the impact of our activity fusion, rather than the increase in the size of the model over the baseline. Any increase in size or alteration to the flow of the network may be significant enough to noticeably improve the network's ability to learn features, regardless of whether we provide activity context or not. Only testing our contextual augmentations would not reveal the source of improvement. This means we need to test both the contextual augmentation, as well as an ablative version without the activity, to determine if any accuracy changes are resultant from the one-by-one convolution itself, from the contextual information, or from both. If our contextual augmentation outperforms our ablative model, we can have confidence that the improvement is owing to the context itself.

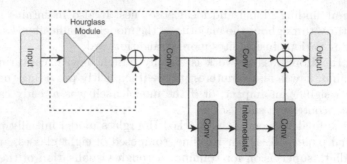

Fig. 3. The original hourglass block format. The input to the module comes from previous layer of the network, and the block produces output for the next block as well as an intermediate heatmap prediction.

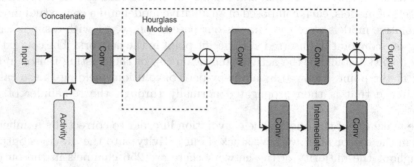

Fig. 4. The context hourglass block used for our fusions. The input to the module comes from the stacking of the activity tensor and the previous layer in the regular network. The ablative version leaves out the activity tensor stacking.

For simplicity we refer to the three different augmented networks as A-, B-, and C-Form, lettered from left-to-right according to their injection points, as can be seen in Fig. 5. A-Form has the fusion before the first hourglass, B-Form before the fourth, and C-Form before the eighth. Their matching ablative models are referred to as A-, B-, and C-Form Ablative. Each line in the figure indicates a position where we tested our augmentation. Note that only a single fusion point was used at a time for each model.

The decision of how to fuse the activity was made difficult by the convolutional nature of the network, which stopped us from simply concatenating on a one-hot encoded vector to our input. To get around this our context took the form of a one-hot encoded activity tensor of size $64 \times 64 \times 21$, where 21 is the number of activities present in the dataset, and 64×64 is the shape of the image features as they move through the network.

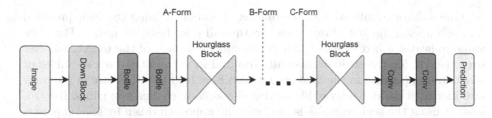

Fig. 5. The augmented network, with lines indicating the three tested fusion points. The input to the fusion modules come from the activity tensor and the previous layer before the insertion point.

4 Training

Training was performed in a similar manner to that of the original Stacked Hourglass paper [10], expanded on below. Our training made use of the MPII Human Pose dataset [1] only, as it is the only one with activity annotations. The MPII dataset provides approximately 25k images (2.5k of which are withheld as their own hidden test set), leaving 22.5k images for use. Of those, approximately 18k (80%) were used for training, with the remaining split evenly between a validation and test set of 2.25k (10%) each.

Our training, validation, and test sets were generated by taking the available data points and randomly allocating them each in the ratios above to a subset. We ensured that the representation of categories was proportionate between all the subsets, in other words "Running" made up an approximately equal percentage of the training, validation, and test sets. Once a suitable split was found we kept the segmentation consistent throughout all further runs of our experiments.

The dataset provides a 2D ground-truth pose with joint visibility flags, an approximate scale, and an approximate center position, among other data not relevant to our analysis, for each person within an image. Images also have an activity classification which is used for our context, which many other datasets do not provide, making MPII particularly valuable. While MPII provides fine grained activity sub-classifications, we did not use them as our context tensors would become intractably large, and many of the sub-classifications had few or no samples. Instead we made use of the 21 higher level activity categories that the dataset was divided into. The full list of activities can be seen in either Fig. 6, or the MPII dataset browser [2].

Because images can contain more than one person, we follow the method of the original paper [10] by cropping the image around the center of the target so the model knows which person to estimate on, The images are cropped based on the provided scale and the provided center coordinates of the target, and the crop is then scaled to 256×256. Cropped images also undergo some additional rotation (in $[-30, 30]$) and scaling (in $[0.75, 1.25]$) to provide augmentation to the dataset.

One issue encountered with the dataset was that utilising the scale provided for each person did not always result in the full pose being in frame. The scale value indicates a box of width 200 px around the center of the target, however even using 1.5× the scale occasionally resulted in extremities such as ankles or wrists not appearing in the final crop, which may lead to a decrease in accuracy and increases the difficulty of identifying the already challenging joints. Regardless, utilising the scale value as-is has been the approach taken by several papers that utilise the MPII dataset [3, 10, 15, 20], and so we follow the same approach.

The cropping and augmentation can also result in black pixels appearing in the final image provided to the network, as black background pixels can be included from outside the bounds of the image. Obviously this is not very realistic, however the complex networks are likely capable of learning to ignore this anomaly. As a possible alternative, mirror padding could be used when cropping, however, again, the simple background inclusion is the approach taken by several papers [3, 10, 15, 20], and so we use the same method.

The baseline model was provided with images cropped around the center of the person with small random rotations and scaling modifications, and a heatmap was generated for each joint of the target pose as ground-truth for the model. The augmented models were provided both with the image crop, and the one-hot encoded tensor for the activity representation.

All models were trained with an MSE loss function over the ground-truth heatmap and predicted heatmap set. The model makes heavy use of batch normalisation [7] to improve training speed and performance. This allowed us to use a relatively high learning rate of 2.5^{-4} with the RMSprop optimiser, taken from the original Stacked Hourglass paper [10]. We utilised our validation set to select the best model as that with the lowest validation loss at any point of training.

Training of the models took approximately three days using an RTX3080 and a batch size of 8, which was the largest we could achieve given the complexity of the network. This meant a prediction time of 60ms per image. This was for both our baseline model and our augmented model set, indicating that our context pipeline has a negligible overhead. Every model was trained and evaluated three times from newly initialised weights, and the final results are taken as the average of all three runs to reduce the impact of training variance.

5   Results

While it does not imply an increase or decrease in accuracy, it should be noted that results were evaluated using our own withheld test set comprised of the released annotations, not the official MPII test set. This is due to the now publicly available test set not having associated activities, and attempts at getting the activity annotations from the original authors of the dataset being unsuccessful. We utilised the common PCKh@0.5 metric, which represents the percentage of correct keypoints, where a correct keypoint is defined as being within a threshold, specifically half the normalised distance between the top of the neck and the top of the head, of the ground-truth keypoint.

5.1   Evaluation

Our final total accuracy for the best model, the C-Form model, was 90.3%, an improvement of 2.7% points over our baseline model's performance of 87.6%. The contextual information was particularly impactful on some conventionally difficult joints such as ankles, knees, and wrists, where the contextual model improved over the baseline by 7.6%, 3.3%, and 1.5% respectively. The accuracies of the different models can be seen in Table 1.

Table 1. Joint and total accuracies of different networks when run on our own test set. PCK is PCK@0.5

Model	Head	Neck	Tors	Pelv	Shld	Elbw	Wrst	Hip	Knee	Ankl	PCK
Baseline	91.6	97.2	98.0	92.7	93.5	91.1	88.7	88.7	83.2	55.9	87.6
A-Form	93.5	**98.1**	99.1	93.7	95.3	92.1	90.1	90.8	86.0	58.8	89.4
A-Form Abl.	92.8	97.7	98.8	94.2	94.6	91.7	89.9	90.6	86.4	60.9	89.3
B-Form	**94.0**	97.9	**99.3**	94.5	95.1	92.4	90.1	91.3	**86.9**	63.3	90.0
B-Form Abl.	92.2	**98.1**	99.0	94.2	95.0	92.5	89.9	90.7	**86.9**	60.8	89.5
C-Form	93.7	98.0	99.2	**95.3**	**96.0**	**92.7**	**90.2**	91.7	86.5	**63.5**	**90.3**
C-Form Abl.	92.4	96.1	97.1	94.1	93.2	88.0	85.2	88.4	78.8	56.8	86.2

In terms of per-activity accuracies, our C-Form model showed noticeable improvements on most activities, faring better in activities with more data points. The average activity improvement was 2.5%. The apparent variance in improvements per activity is likely due to the nature of the activities and their compilations. For example, our model saw the largest improvement in the "Water Activities" classification of 6.3%, where the poses are very different from those found in other activities, with some subjects being in unusual stances, obscured in scuba gear, or even upside down. A comparison on this activity between the Baseline and C-Form model can be seen in Fig. 7. The "Miscellaneous" and "Bicycling" classifications on the other hand showed minimal improvement, likely due to the relatively random grouping, and already common poses that require minimal context, respectively. The different per-activity accuracies can be seen in Fig. 6.

Our C-Form model also shows consistent improvement over the baseline when evaluating at varying PCKh thresholds, having a higher accuracy at every value. This indicates that the performance improvement is actually caused by overall better predictions, rather than by chance that a set of keypoints moved within the threshold distance only for a specific value. This can be seen in Fig. 8.

This indicates that our method of activity fusion may very well be useful if our activities are structured well enough to segment very different poses and cluster similar ones. Naturally this is in itself a challenging task, but nevertheless means there may be room for improvement.

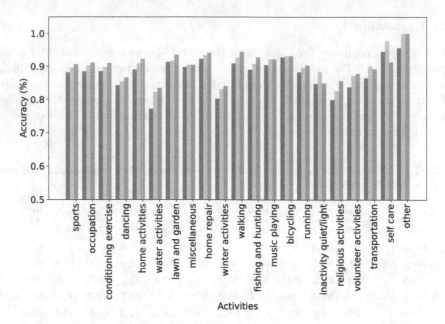

Fig. 6. The different activity accuracies for our baseline (blue), B-Form Ablative (orange), and best augmented model, the C-Form model (green). Activities are sorted left to right by the number of images in the test set, ranging from 600+ (leftmost) to fewer than 10 (rightmost). (Color figure online)

Fig. 7. Images from our test set showcasing how the C-Form model (bottom) is better capable of handling the relatively uncommon poses that fall under the "Water Activities" classification, compared to the Baseline model (top).

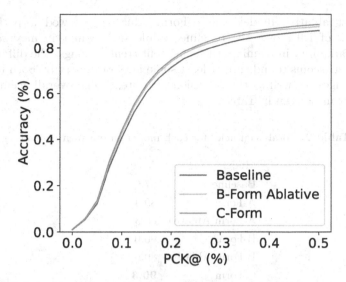

Fig. 8. The different accuracies when varying PCKh thresholds for our baseline, best ablative model, and best contextual model

Interestingly, our results indicate some level of sensitivity of the method to the fusion position. Our ablative models experienced a sharp decline in performance towards the end of the model, with the C-Form actually performing worse than our baseline. Alternatively, our contextual models performed progressively better with fusions towards the end of the model. Only providing context at the beginning of the network may be too early to enable the model to effectively utilise the information for the final predictions, with the signal from the context having diminished by the time it reaches the later hourglasses.

In comparison to state of the art methods, our model seems to perform slightly below the state of the art accuracies reported on the MPII test set [2]. Again, this is not an entirely useful comparison however, as our research was unable to make use of the official test set, and so our true test result is unknown. Nevertheless, the intent of the research was to indicate the usefulness of activity fusion, which was apparent in our noticeable accuracy improvements.

5.2   Ablative Experiments

All of our contextual models fairly significantly outperformed the baseline model in their overall accuracy, however we needed to perform an ablative test to ensure the contextual information itself is actually contributory to our results.

Our testing indicated that adding the additional one-by-one convolutions does, in some cases, increase the performance of the network, namely the A-Form Ablative and B-Form Ablative models. However, performance degrades in the C-Form Ablative model, and so clearly the increase in the C-Form contextual model's accuracy is not only attributable to the additional convolution.

The best ablative model, the B-Form Ablative, showed a performance improvement of 1.9% over the baseline. While such a margin may simply be caused by variability in training, the consistent trend amongst the different augmentation sets seems to indicate at least some level of impact by both the architectural changes, as well as the provision of context. The overall accuracies for each model can be seen in Table 2.

Table 2. Total accuracies for each model on our own test set.

Model	Accuracy
Baseline	87.6
A-Form	89.4
A-Form Ablative	89.3
B-Form	90.0
B-Form Ablative	89.5
C-Form	**90.3**
C-Form Ablative	86.2

It should be noted that the C-Form Ablative model also consistently performed worse than the baseline model, which is unusual as the model could simply learn an identity mapping and have no effect on our predictions. This drop in accuracy could possibly be due to the degrading of gradients during back-propagation, as the Stacked Hourglass makes extensive use of residuals, and adding extra convolutions without skip layers may hinder this.

6   Future Work

While we have explored the basic concept of activity fusion in this report, there are already numerous apparent avenues to continue analysing in various domains.

In terms of the model utilised, this paper focused on a relatively conceptually simple deep learning model, however in the future we could rather make use of even newer state-of-the-art performers. Additionally we could design our own network centered around the concept of activity fusion.

We can also perform more rigorous testing of our results, performing crossfold validation to account for the official test set not being usable, which would eliminate the concern of random variance. Furthermore we could analyse how our activity affects the features our model learns and makes use of, should it have a significant impact.

Exploring more methods of encoding and fusing our context would also be useful, as we only focused on straightforward one-hot encoding with concatenation and a 1×1 convolution to fuse the information. Alternatives could involve using auto-encoders before providing the input to the network, or other latent space methodologies. We could also investigate different methods of fusing involving a more thorough merging strategy rather than just a single convolution layer.

Finally we could explore the usefulness of context in other deep learning fields. While pose estimation seems like a useful field for context provision, there may be many others, such as image segmentation, or translation systems.

7 Conclusion

In this paper we explored the concept of fusing contextual activity information into the existing Stacked Hourglass model. We show that even with rudimentary organising of images into activities, and using straightforward fusing methods, our method is capable of providing performance gains over a baseline model. Above this our method introduced no significant overhead into the training or prediction process.

Our method was capable of improving accuracy on typically difficult joints, and is especially useful in activity classifications where poses are unusual in comparison to the available training data. We also provide various avenues for further exploration, and are hopeful that context fusion is a viable addition to improving deep learning models in the field and beyond.

Acknowledgments. We acknowledge the Centre for High Performance Computing (CHPC), South Africa, for providing computational resources to this research project. Additionally, this work is based on research supported in part by the National Research Foundation of South Africa (Grant Numbers: 118075 and 117808).

References

1. Andriluka, M., Pishchulin, L., Gehler, P., Schiele, B.: 2D human pose estimation: New benchmark and state of the art analysis. In: IEEE Conference on Computer Vision and Pattern Recognition (CVPR), June 2014
2. Andriluka, M., Pishchulin, L., Gehler, P., Schiele, B.: MPII Human Pose Dataset Results (2014). http://human-pose.mpi-inf.mpg.de/#results. 01 Nov 2020
3. Bin, Y., et al.: Adversarial semantic data augmentation for human pose estimation. In: Vedaldi, A., Bischof, H., Brox, T., Frahm, J.-M. (eds.) ECCV 2020. LNCS, vol. 12364, pp. 606–622. Springer, Cham (2020). https://doi.org/10.1007/978-3-030-58529-7_36
4. Bourached, A., Griffiths, R.-R., Gray, R., Jha, A., Nachev, P.: Generative model-enhanced human motion prediction. arXiv preprint arXiv:2010.11699 (2020)
5. Chen, Y., Shen, C., Wei, X.-S., Liu, L., Yang, J.: Adversarial posenet: a structure-aware convolutional network for human pose estimation. In: Proceedings of the IEEE International Conference on Computer Vision, pp. 1212–1221 (2017)
6. Gowda, S.N.: Human activity recognition using combinatorial deep belief networks. In: The IEEE Conference on Computer Vision and Pattern Recognition (CVPR) Workshops, July 2017
7. Ioffe, S., Szegedy, C.: Batch normalization: accelerating deep network training by reducing internal covariate shift. arXiv preprint arXiv:1502.03167 (2015)

8. Jalal, A., Kim, Y.-H., Kim, Y.-J., Kamal, S., Kim, D.: Robust human activity recognition from depth video using spatiotemporal multi-fused features. Pattern Recogn. **61**, 295–308 (2017)
9. Lan, M., Zhang, Y., Zhang, L., Bo, D.: Global context based automatic road segmentation via dilated convolutional neural network. Inf. Sci. **535**, 156–171 (2020)
10. Newell, A., Yang, K., Deng, J.: Stacked hourglass networks for human pose estimation. In: Leibe, B., Matas, J., Sebe, N., Welling, M. (eds.) ECCV 2016. LNCS, vol. 9912, pp. 483–499. Springer, Cham (2016). https://doi.org/10.1007/978-3-319-46484-8_29
11. Rafi, U., Gall, J., Leibe, B.: A semantic occlusion model for human pose estimation from a single depth image. In: Proceedings of the IEEE Conference on Computer Vision and Pattern Recognition Workshops, pp. 67–74 (2015)
12. Rafi, U., Leibe, B., Gall, J., Kostrikov, I.: An efficient convolutional network for human pose estimation. BMVC **1**, 2 (2016)
13. Shakhnarovich, G., Viola, P., Darrell, T.: Fast pose estimation with parameter-sensitive hashing, p. 750. IEEE (2003)
14. Sun, X., Shang, J., Liang, S., Wei, Y.: Compositional human pose regression. In: Proceedings of the IEEE International Conference on Computer Vision, pp. 2602–2611 (2017)
15. Tang, Z., Peng, X., Geng, S., Wu, L., Zhang, S., Metaxas, D.: Quantized densely connected u-nets for efficient landmark localization. In: Proceedings of the European Conference on Computer Vision (ECCV), pp. 339–354 (2018)
16. Tompson, J., Goroshin, R., Jain, A., LeCun, Y., Bregler, C.: Efficient object localization using convolutional networks. In: Proceedings of the IEEE Conference on Computer Vision and Pattern Recognition, pp. 648–656 (2015)
17. Toshev, A., Szegedy, C.: DeepPose: human pose estimation via deep neural networks. In Proceedings of the IEEE Conference on Computer Vision and Pattern Recognition, pp. 1653–1660 (2014)
18. Vu, T.-H., Osokin, A., Laptev, I.: Context-aware CNNs for person head detection. In: The IEEE International Conference on Computer Vision (ICCV), December 2015
19. Wei, S.-E., Ramakrishna, V., Kanade, T., Sheikh, Y.: Convolutional pose machines. In: Proceedings of the IEEE conference on Computer Vision and Pattern Recognition, pp. 4724–4732 (2016)
20. Yang, W., Li, S., Ouyang, W., Li, H., Wang, X.: Learning feature pyramids for human pose estimation. In proceedings of the IEEE International Conference on Computer Vision, pp. 1281–1290 (2017)
21. Yang, Y., Ramanan, D.: Articulated pose estimation with flexible mixtures-of-parts. In: CVPR, vol. 2011, pp. 1385–1392 (2011)

Improving the Performance of Image Captioning Models Trained on Small Datasets

Mikkel du Plessis and Willie Brink[✉]

Stellenbosch University, Stellenbosch, South Africa
wbrink@sun.ac.za

Abstract. Recent work in image captioning seems to be driven by increasingly large amounts of training data, and requires considerable computing power for training. We propose and investigate a number of adjustments to state-of-the-art approaches, with an aim to train a performant image captioning model in under two hours on a single consumer-level GPU using only a few thousand images. Firstly, we address the issue of sparse object and scene representation in a small dataset by combining visual attention regions at various levels of granularity. Secondly, we suppress semantically unlikely caption candidates through the introduction of language model rescoring during inference. Thirdly, in order to increase vocabulary and expressiveness, we propose an augmentation of the set of training captions through the use of a paraphrase generator. State-of-the-art performance on the Flickr8k test set is achieved, across a number of evaluation metrics. The proposed model also attains competitive test scores compared to existing models trained on a much larger dataset. The findings of this paper can inspire solutions to other vision-and-language tasks where labelled data is scarce.

Keywords: Image captioning · Deep learning · Low-data regime

1 Introduction

Image captioning is the task of creating a short natural language expression to describe the visual content of a given image (as illustrated in Fig. 1). An image captioning model should in concept learn to identify salient objects within an image, determine relationships between different objects, form an understanding of the image as a whole, and then generate a sensible and semantically correct phrase. In order to generalise well, current state-of-the-art models require large amounts of diverse training data (samples of image-caption pairs) as well as considerable computing power for training. Oscar [1], for example, was pre-trained on 6 million image-caption pairs, and fine-tuned on the Microsoft COCO dataset [2] which has 328,000 images. Training this model required 22 days on eight Tesla V100 GPUs, with VRAM usage peaking at 168 GB. Of course, in some domains

© Springer Nature Switzerland AG 2022
E. Jembere et al. (Eds.): SACAIR 2021, CCIS 1551, pp. 77–91, 2022.
https://doi.org/10.1007/978-3-030-95070-5_6

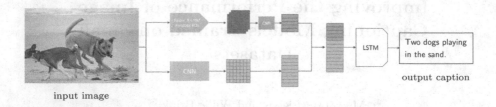

Fig. 1. The task of an image captioning model is to generate a short natural language description of a given input image. Detail of our proposed model is given in Fig. 2.

access to these amounts of labelled data and computing resources can be challenging. A question arises: can comparable performance be achieved by models trained on much smaller datasets?

In this paper we focus specifically on models that can be trained on a single consumer-level GPU in under 2 h, using only a few thousand images. We make use of the Flickr8k dataset [3], and investigate various strategies that may improve performance compared to existing work.

We implement the seminal work of Xu et al. [4] as a base model. They introduced the idea of an encoder-decoder architecture within the context of image captioning, with a transparent attention mechanism that enables the model to focus on appropriate parts of the image while generating a caption. Attention also provides a level of explainability, and gives the user a means to evaluate a model's understanding of objects, interactions, and the scene as a whole.

We propose the following ideas, and explore their ability to improve performance of image captioning models trained on small datasets:

1. A significant challenge in image captioning is the sparse representation of objects and scenes within a limited set of examples. By extracting attention regions at various levels of granularity, we aim to present the caption generator (the decoder) with encodings of the image that carry richer information and context.
2. The expressiveness of the caption generator is learned from a limited set of human-annotated captions in the training set, and a model trained on a small dataset might struggle to generate semantically correct captions. We therefore introduce a language model during inference, to rescore caption candidates in a beam-search scheme and suppress semantically unlikely instances.
3. As mentioned in the previous point, a small dataset may not encapsulate the diversity of a particular language to a sufficient degree, thus restricting the vocabulary and expressiveness of the model. As a potential remedy we augment the training captions by means of a paraphrase generator.

It is shown experimentally that by implementing these ideas, state-of-the-art performance can be achieved on the Flickr8k test set, across a number of evaluation metrics. Additionally, our final model is able to yield competitive results compared to models from the literature trained on substantially more data.

2   Related Work

Like many problems in modern computer vision, image captioning has been approached predominantly with variants of deep neural networks. One of the first models to utilise a neural network [5] uses a multimodal language network that jointly learns an image-text representation. The model can generate descriptions of images, and retrieve images given a natural language query. This work was followed by the first encoder-decoder architecture [6], where an encoder learns a joint image-text representation and a neural language decoder generates a description. Mao et al. [7] replaced the feed-forward neural language model with a recurrent one. A dynamically sized context vector is used, as opposed to a fixed context window, allowing the decoder access to all previously generated words in the description. Vinyals et al. [8] used an LSTM as decoder, and their model presents the image only at the first step of the decoder instead of every step in the output word sequence.

The above-mentioned works all represent an input image as a single static feature vector from the last layer of a pre-trained convolutional neural network. More recent work attempts a more dynamic multi-vector representation of the image. Xu et al. [4] pioneered this approach, by using the feature maps from early layers in a pre-trained CNN as a set of feature vectors, and feeding those to an attention mechanism for information aggregation. We will adopt this architecture as a base model. The model of Xu et al. [4] considers a uniform grid over the input image, that does not adapt to the content of the image. To address this limitation, object-level attention regions have been proposed [9,10] to enable the encoding of more fine-grained information.

When training data is limited, the use of object-level attention regions may not be sufficient for a model to adequately learn about the many appearance variations of objects and salient regions. In an effort to remedy this, we propose a combination of object-level attention regions and multi-layer feature map attention regions. The former typically provides fine-grained image representation, while the latter might be more coarse-grained. Through a combination of the two, we construct a richer representation of the image that could lead to improved caption generation.

A further challenge in image captioning is the potentially low diversity within the set of sample captions in a typical training dataset. To address this, Atliha and Šešok [11] proposed using the bidirectional Transformer-based language model BERT [12] to predict randomly masked out words in a sentence, thereby providing synonyms for the masked out words. The training set of captions is thereby expanded, and diversity is increased. We will investigate a similar idea, but instead of just substituting synonymous words, we train a paraphrase generator to rephrase entire sentences (i.e. to provide synonyms for words and to restructure the sentence).

An overwhelming trend in improving the performance of general-purpose image captioning models is to increase the amount of training data and, consequently, the computing resources required for training. Conversely, little work has been done on image captioning with limited training data and resources.

Park et al. [13] proposed a model for chest X-ray report generation in an abnormality detection pipeline. They trained this model on about 7,500 X-ray images, and used a coarse-grained attention mechanism similar to that of Xu et al. [4] on uniformly sized feature map abstractions. Their output domain is rather narrow, whereas our aim is to train a general-purpose image captioning model on a small dataset and compare it to models trained on much larger datasets.

3   Implementation

This section gives details of our proposed model. Firstly, we describe the architecture of the base encoder-decoder model. Secondly, we describe how a joint embedding is created through a concatenation of high-level attention regions from early convolutional layers of a pre-trained CNN, and low-level attention regions from either the bounding boxes of an object detection module or the pixel-level masks of an object segmentation module. Thirdly, we describe our decoder's beam search procedure for language model suppression of semantically unlikely caption candidates. Finally, we describe our approach to caption data augmentation through a paraphrase generator.

3.1   Base Model

Our base model is an encoder-decoder with attention, that jointly learns to align word-to-region mappings in order to generate a descriptive caption for an input image. A basic approach would be to encode the image as a single fixed-sized vector, to serve as a static representation of the image during decoding (caption generation). We make use of an attention mechanism first proposed by Dzmitry et al. [14] for neural machine translation, and adapted for image captioning by Xu et al. [4]. It has been shown that the addition of attention leads to significantly improved performance over the basic encoder-decoder approach. The model encodes the input image as a sequence of vectors, instead of a single vector, and adaptively selects subsets of these vectors during decoding.

The encoder takes an image as input and produces n vectors $\{\mathbf{a}_1, \ldots, \mathbf{a}_n\}$, where each is d-dimensional and corresponds to an attention region of the image. We explore two approaches to find these vectors for a given image, as explained in Sect. 3.2.

For the decoder we make use of an LSTM network [15] that produces a word at every time step t of the caption generation process. The prediction of a next word is conditioned on a context vector $\mathbf{z}_t$, the previous hidden state $\mathbf{h}_{t-1}$, and previously generated words. The context vector can be a dynamic representation of the image at time t, and in our case is produced by the attention mechanism. This mechanism takes as input the feature vectors $\mathbf{a}_i$ from the encoder and provides a weight $\alpha_{t,i}$ for each, as follows:

$$\alpha_{t,i} = \frac{\exp(e_{t,i})}{\sum_{j=1}^{n} \exp(e_{t,j})}, \quad \text{with} \ \ e_{t,i} = f_{att}(\mathbf{a}_i, \mathbf{h}_{t-1}) . \tag{1}$$

In the above equation, f_{att} is a multi-layer perceptron conditioned on the previous hidden state $\mathbf{h}_{t-1}$. The weights $\alpha_{t,i}$ are used to create a context vector for time step t:

$$\mathbf{z}_t = \sum_{i=1}^{n} \alpha_{t,i}\mathbf{a}_i \ . \tag{2}$$

The emphasis placed on each attention region is therefore dependent on the sequence of words generated thus far, and informs the LSTM decoder what image content to focus on when generating the next word.

3.2   Multi-level Attention Regions

The soft attention model of Xu et al. [4] makes use of high-level image abstractions from convolutional layers in a pre-trained CNN. This leads to rectangular attention regions of predetermined size, that cannot adapt to the appearance of objects within a particular image. In an attempt to provide richer context to the LSTM decoder, we consider attention regions that contain whole objects and other salient image regions. Two ways of extracting such regions from an image are investigated: bounding boxes from the Faster R-CNN object detection model [16], and pixel-level masks from the Panoptic FCN segmentation model [17].

Due to a potential representation sparseness when considering only object-level attention regions, we propose a joint embedding of these low-level regions and the high-level attention regions from the convolutional layers of a pre-trained CNN. We therefore increase the number of feature vectors produced by the encoder (the $\mathbf{a}_i$ vectors in Sect. 3.1), for a richer representation of the image. Figure 2 provides a detailed schematic of the proposed model, with the two levels of attention regions that are concatenated and fed to the LSTM decoder.

For high-level attention regions (HLAR), we feed the image through the convolution block of a pre-trained ResNet-152. An early convolutional layer produces a feature map of size $(14, 14, 2048)$ which we flatten to $(196, 2048)$. For

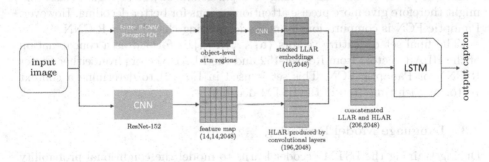

Fig. 2. Pipeline of our image captioning model. The encoder learns a joint embedding of high-level attention regions (HLAR) from ResNet-152 layers, and low-level attention regions (LLAR) from either the bounding boxes of Faster R-CNN or the segmentation masks from Panoptic FCN. This is fed to an LSTM decoder for caption generation.

Fig. 3. Faster R-CNN object detection [16] or Panoptic FCN image segmentation [17] can guide attention regions. The former produces bounding boxes around objects (left), and the latter a pixel-level mask around objects and salient image regions (right).

low-level attention regions (LLAR), we use either a Faster R-CNN model or a Panoptic FCN model. Example outputs of these models are shown in Fig. 3.

Faster R-CNN [16] detects objects in two stages. The first stage outputs object proposals through the refinement of bounding boxes at multiple scales and aspect ratios, and an assignment of class-agnostic objectness scores. Top scoring proposals form input to the second stage, where region-of-interest pooling extracts small feature maps for the classification and further refinement of each bounding box. We take the output from a pre-trained Faster R-CNN model and perform non-maximal suppression on each detected object. We crop out the top 10 bounding boxes (based on their Faster R-CNN classification confidence scores), and feed each one through a pre-trained ResNet-152 network with the final softmax layer removed. This yields 10 feature vectors, each being 2048-dimensional. Panoptic FCN [17] is an efficient fully convolutional network for pixel-level segmentation of an image into foreground objects and background regions. It outputs a mask for each object and region. We overlay each mask on the original image and crop out the tight bounding box. Similar to the above, we feed crops of the 10 highest-scoring objects or regions through ResNet-152 with the softmax layer removed.

Note that the bounding boxes produced by Faster R-CNN are likely to contain irrelevant background pixels. The pixel-level masks from Panoptic FCN blank out pixels that do not belong to a particular object or region class, and might therefore give more precise attention regions for better decoding. However, Panoptic FCN is computationally more demanding than Faster R-CNN.

The final set of feature vectors $\{a_1, \ldots, a_{206}\}$ is formed as a concatenation of the HLAR vectors from ResNet-152 and the LLAR vectors from either Faster R-CNN or Panoptic FCN. This set is used in Eq. (2) to determine a context vector at each time step in the LSTM decoder.

3.3   Language Model Rescoring

During training the LSTM decoder learns to model the conditional probability distribution over the next word given a sequence of already generated words, and a small training set may limit the decoder's abilities for expressiveness and semanticity. For this reason, we propose the incorporation of a pre-trained language model in the decoder.

In the basic LSTM formulation, words are picked greedily by taking at every time step the most likely word from the softmax output probabilities. Instead, we implement a beam search scheme which expands on all possible versions of the caption. The k most likely expansions are stored at every time step, where k is a hyperparameter that controls the number of beams of parallel searches through the sequence of probabilities. The search process may halt separately for each candidate sequence by reaching either a maximum length, the end-of-sequence token, or a threshold likelihood. We penalise a candidate only when the end token is reached, since the semantic legitimacy of an incomplete sentence is hard to assess.

Our aim is to keep computational requirements low, and therefore make use of GPT-2 [18]. It is a network with 1.5 billion parameters (orders of magnitude fewer than its successor GPT-3), trained on 40 GB of Internet text. It uses roughly 3.4 GB of memory and takes less than a second to evaluate a given sentence. The semantic legitimacy of a sentence $S = \{w_1, \ldots, w_m\}$ is linked to the probability of the words w_i occurring in a certain order. Autoregressive language models like GPT-2 define the perplexity of S in terms of the negative log-likelihood of each word conditioned on its predecessors in the sequence:

$$\mathrm{ppl}(S) = \exp\left(-\frac{1}{m}\sum_{i=1}^{m}\log p(w_i|w_1, \ldots, w_{i-1})\right). \tag{3}$$

The likelihood function $p(w_i|w_{1:i-1})$ is learned by the language model during training. We note that perplexity is always positive, and that lower values imply higher model confidence in the semantic legitimacy of S.

During beam search, partially generated captions are scored by their cumulative log-likelihood up to the current time step in the LSTM. We penalise the score of a completed caption candidate by subtracting λ times its GPT-2 perplexity, where λ is a hyperparameter (through cross-validation we found $\lambda = 1$ to work well). This suppresses the scores of semantically unlikely candidates, and increases the quality of output captions. We emphasise that rescoring happens only at test time, and does not have any effect on training resources.

3.4   Caption Data Augmentation

The Flickr8k dataset [3] contains 8,000 images, with 5 human-annotated captions for each. As a means of increasing diversity in the set of training captions, we propose a simple data augmentation strategy. We make use of the Text-To-Text Transfer Transformer (T5) framework [19] and train a T5 model specifically as a paraphrase generator using the PAWS dataset [20], which consists of sentence pairs (paraphrases) with low lexical overlap. Different versions of the Flickr8k captions can thus be generated, as illustrated in Fig. 4. In doing so, vocabulary and structure diversity in the training captions are increased, which may lead to a more expressive model.

Original captions from dataset	Paraphrased captions
A child in a pink dress is climbing up a set of stairs in an entry way.	A child dressed in a pink dress climbing a set of stairs in an entry way.
A girl going into a wooden building.	A girl walking into a wooden building.
A little girl climbing into a wooden playhouse.	A girl climbs into a wood playhouse.
A little girl climbing the stairs to her playhouse.	A little girl climbs the stairs to a playhouse.
A little girl in a pink dress going into a wooden cabin.	A little girl dressed in a pink dress is going into a wooden cabin.

Fig. 4. An image from the Flickr8k training set along with the human annotated captions (left column) and augmented captions achieved through paraphrasing (right column).

4   Experiments

In this section we describe the dataset and metrics to quantitatively evaluate the components of our model. We compare our full model with a number of existing models from the literature, when trained on the same dataset and when trained on a much larger dataset. The section ends with a brief qualitative analysis.

4.1   Dataset and Evaluation Metrics

Our models are trained and evaluated on the Flickr8k dataset [3]. It consists of 8,000 images, with 5 human-annotated captions for each, and is relatively small compared to the more widely used MS COCO [2] which contains about 328,000 images. Flickr8k has a standardised training-validation-test split with 6,000, 1,000 and 1,000 images in each set respectively.

For model evaluation we make use of standard image captioning metrics, namely BLEU [21], METEOR [22] and CIDEr-D [23]. The BLEU-n score measures the similarity between reference and generated sentences as the geometric mean of n-gram precision scores, with a penalty for short sentences. BLEU is widely used but has its limitations [24], and additional metrics should be considered. METEOR is the harmonic mean of precision and recall of uni-gram matches between the reference and generated sentence, and may accept synonyms and paraphrases. CIDEr-D measures similarity to a set of references using co-occurrence statistics of n-grams, where $n = 1, 2, 3, 4$. Common n-grams are inversely weighted and a cosine similarity is computed. All metrics except for CIDEr-D range from 0 to 1, with 1 indicating a perfect match. In theory CIDEr-D can reach a maximum of 10, but due to its strictness scores are generally also between 0 and 1. We will print all scores as percentages.

We compare a generated caption to each of the 5 human-annotated captions and take an average of the 5 scores in the case of BLEU, and a maximum in the case of METEOR and CIDEr-D. Due to the non-standardised use of metrics in the context of image caption evaluation [25], we verified our code with that of cited work [4, 5, 8].

4.2 Quantitative Analysis

Table 1 shows the performance on the Flickr8k test set of our model's components as an ablation study, as well as the full model, compared to models from the literature. Missing values mean that those particular metrics were not reported in the cited papers. Our base model is a re-implementation of the soft attention approach of Xu et al. [4]. We measure the effects of incorporating object-level attention regions into this base model, using Faster R-CNN and Panoptic FCN separately. We also measure the effects of applying language model (LM) rescoring during inference in the base model, as well as caption data augmentation (again on the base model, without any of the other components). Our full model consists of the base model with additional attention regions from Panoptic FCN, language model rescoring during inference, and caption data augmentation.

The inclusion of object-level attention regions brings improvement across all metrics, and indicates that a richer representation of the input image at multiple granularities can be beneficial. The segmentation masks from Panoptic FCN lead to slightly better results over the bounding boxes from Faster R-CNN, probably due to the masks disregarding background information on a finer scale. It may be noted that the additional attention regions lead to the best CIDEr-D scores, across all versions of our model. Incorporating language model rescoring during beam search inference, and augmenting the training set of captions with a paraphrase generator, both lead to marginal improvements over the base model. These relatively small increases in performance may need to be weighed against

Table 1. Versions of our model compared to models from the literature. All models were trained on the Flickr8k training set and evaluated on the Flickr8k test set. BL-n, MTR and CDR are short for the BLEU-n, METEOR and CIDEr-D evaluation metrics.

Model	BL-1	BL-2	BL-3	BL-4	MTR	CDR
Google NIC [8]	63.0	41.0	27.0	–	–	–
Log bilinear [5]	65.6	42.4	27.7	17.7	17.3	–
Soft attention [4]	67.0	44.8	29.9	19.5	18.9	–
Hard attention [4]	67.0	45.7	31.4	21.3	20.3	–
Our base model	66.3	44.2	28.7	20.6	18.6	48.6
Attn: faster R-CNN	66.5	46.4	32.4	22.4	22.5	**53.5**
Attn: panoptic FCN	67.1	47.2	33.2	23.2	22.6	**53.5**
LM rescoring	66.8	46.5	32.3	22.4	22.3	51.6
Caption augmentation	66.7	46.2	32.2	22.1	22.5	50.9
Our full model	**68.6**	**48.5**	**34.7**	**24.5**	**23.2**	49.2

the additional computational requirements. With the full model combining the base with high- and low-level attention regions, language model rescoring and caption augmentation, increases of 1.6 to 3.3% points over published results are achieved. Based on current trends in the image captioning literature, these increases are certainly not insignificant.

The use of a small dataset in training a deep neural network can easily lead to overfitting and poor generalisation. For this reason we made use of various regularisation strategies including dropout, small batch sizes, early stopping based on validation BLEU scores, and caption data augmentation. To get a sense of whether overfitting is present in our full model trained on Flickr8k, we plot in Fig. 5 the BLEU, METEOR and CIDEr-D scores achieved by the trained model on the training set and on the test set. A slight tendency to overfitting can be observed, but it does not seem severe. The difference in CIDEr-D scores seems large, but relative to the maximum for that metric (10, or 1000%) it is actually also quite small.

Next we compare the performance of our full model trained on 6,000 images from Flickr8k to models from the literature trained on MS COCO which has over 165,000 images in its training set. Results are given in Table 2, where all models are evaluated against the Flickr8k test set. We observe that our full model performs on average within 1.6% of the best model (Hard attention). All models in Table 2 except ours were trained with over 25 times more data than our model. With this in mind, the drop in performance can be deemed small and we achieved our objective of obtaining competitive results.

Table 3 shows the training times required by the variations of our model on the Flickr8k training set, with a single consumer-level GPU (specifically a GTX 1070 Ti). The language model rescoring variant is not included in this table since it does not affect training. It may be observed that, out of all the

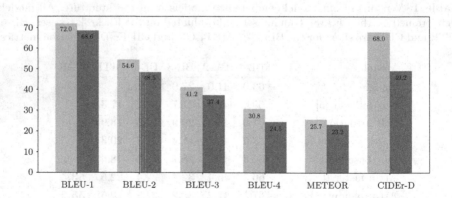

Fig. 5. Evaluation scores that our full model trained on the Flickr8k training set achieves on the Flickr8k training set (blue) and the Flickr8k test set (orange). (Color figure online)

Table 2. Our model trained on the Flickr8k training set (6,000 images) compared to models from the literature trained on the MS COCO training set (165,482 images). All models are evaluated on the Flickr8k test set.

Model	BL-1	BL-2	BL-3	BL-4	MTR	CDR
Google NIC [8]	66.6	46.1	32.9	24.6	–	–
Log bilinear [5]	70.8	48.9	34.4	24.3	20.0	–
Soft attention [4]	70.7	49.2	34.4	24.3	23.9	–
Hard attention [4]	71.8	50.4	35.7	25.0	23.0	–
Our full model	68.6	48.5	34.7	24.5	23.2	49.2

Table 3. Training times required by versions of our model, using the Flickr8k training set and running on a GTX 1070 Ti GPU.

Model	Training time
Our base model	1 h 01 min 01 s
Attn: faster R-CNN	1 h 14 min 41 s
Attn: panoptic FCN	1 h 23 min 32 s
Caption augmentation	1 h 10 min 25 s
Our full model	1 h 51 min 25 s

individual components, the low-level attention regions from Panoptic FCN leads to the highest increase in training time. However, this component also gives the greatest increase in performance over the base model (as shown in Table 1). Note that all versions of our model, including the full one, trains in under 2 h on a single GPU.

4.3 Qualitative Analysis

We visualise in Fig. 6 the attention mechanism as the decoder of our full model generates a caption for a sample image from the Flickr8k test set. At each step of caption generation the LSTM is fed a context vector, hidden state, and the previously generated word. The context vector consists of a weighted sum of attention maps, which in this case stem from a Panoptic FCN segmentation of the input image. We visualise these visual contexts, for an idea of which regions the model deems important while generating words. The weighted attention maps do align to some degree with human intuition. For example, in generating the word dogs the model focuses mostly on pixels belonging to the dogs and ignores all other regions. Similarly, when generating the word water the emphasis is mostly on the water region. Note that this ability is learned from image-caption pairs. The model does not receive any region-specific labels during training.

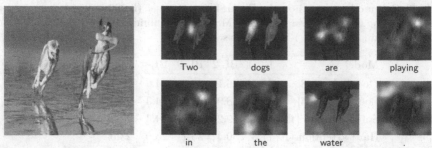

Fig. 6. A visualisation of the weighted average attention maps considered by our full model during caption generation, for a sample image from the Flickr8k test set.

Fig. 7. Examples of captions generated by our full model for Flickr8k test images. Ground truth captions are shown in grey. Generated captions with high and low BLEU scores are shown in green and red, respectively. (Color figure online)

Contrary to conventional attention mechanisms, our model is able to associate entire objects and sub-object regions to words. Visual information is considered at different levels of granularity, thus avoiding the trade-off between focusing solely on coarse regions and focusing solely on finer regions. Our model can focus on the entire water surface when predicting the word water, and on smaller regions such as the dog's mouth when predicting the word playing.

Figure 7 provides examples of captions generated by our full model. Based on BLEU scores, captions in the top row are "good" while those in the bottom row are "bad". Some of the bad examples (e.g. bottom right) are subjectively accurate, highlighting an inherent limitation in the quantitative evaluation of machine generated text against human-annotated labels.

5 Conclusion

This paper considered the challenge of training an effective image captioning model on a small dataset and limited hardware resources. We found that by exploiting the modularity of the encoder-decoder architecture, and leveraging off-the-shelf models pre-trained for other tasks, we could increase the performance of a baseline attention model by Xu et al. [4]. Firstly, we showed that by representing image attention regions at multiple levels of granularity, richer context could be provided to the decoder. Secondly, we showed that by using a pre-trained language model to suppress semantically unlikely caption candidates in a beam search scheme during inference, better quality captions could be produced. Thirdly, we managed to improve the vocabulary and expressiveness of the model by augmenting training captions with the aid of a paraphrase generator. A combination of all these three ideas led to state-of-the-art results on the Flickr8k dataset, and competitive results compared to models trained on much larger datasets.

Further improvements in terms of training time and memory requirements are possible through the use of mixed precision training [26], which could in turn enable better hyperparameter tuning. In future we also aim to investigate the use of Transformers within an encoder-decoder architecture, and find a meaningful way in which to compare our resource-efficient model with even bigger models like Oscar [1]. Finally, it should be noted that our comparison in Table 2 has its limitations, since the models were trained on samples from (possibly) different data distributions. A fairer comparison might be to train our model on a carefully extracted subset of MS COCO.

References

1. Li, X., et al.: OSCAR: object-semantics aligned pre-training for vision-language tasks. In: Vedaldi, A., Bischof, H., Brox, T., Frahm, J.-M. (eds.) ECCV 2020. LNCS, vol. 12375, pp. 121–137. Springer, Cham (2020). https://doi.org/10.1007/978-3-030-58577-8_8
2. Lin, T.-Y., et al.: Microsoft COCO: common objects in context. In: Fleet, D., Pajdla, T., Schiele, B., Tuytelaars, T. (eds.) ECCV 2014. LNCS, vol. 8693, pp. 740–755. Springer, Cham (2014). https://doi.org/10.1007/978-3-319-10602-1_48
3. Hodosh, M., Young, P., Hockenmaier, J.: Framing image description as a ranking task: data, models and evaluation metrics. J. Artif. Intell. Res. **47**, 853–899 (2013)
4. Xu, K., et al.: Show, attend and tell: neural image caption generation with visual attention. In: Proceedings of Machine Learning Research, vol. 37, pp. 2048–2057 (2015)

5. Kiros, R., Salakhutdinov R., Zemel, R.: Multimodal neural language models. In: International Conference on Machine Learning (2014)
6. Kiros, R., Salakhutdinov, R., Zemel, R.: Unifying visual-semantic embeddings with multimodal neural language models. arXiv preprint arXiv:1411.2539 (2014)
7. Mao, J., Xu, W., Yang, Y., Wang, J., Yuille, A.: Deep captioning with multimodal recurrent neural networks (m-RNN). In: International Conference on Machine Learning (2015)
8. Vinyals, O., Toshev, A., Bengio, S., Erhan, D.: Show and tell: a neural image caption generator. In: IEEE Conference on Computer Vision and Pattern Recognition (2015)
9. Cai, W., Xiong, Z., Sun, X., Rosin, P., Jin, L., Peng, X.: Panoptic segmentation-based attention for image captioning. Appl. Sci. **10** (2020). Art. 391
10. Anderson, P., et al.: Bottom-up and top-down attention for image captioning and VQA. In: IEEE Conference on Computer Vision and Pattern Recognition (2018)
11. Atliha, V., Šešok, D.: Text augmentation using BERT for image captioning. Appl. Sci. **10** (2020). Art. 5978
12. Devlin, J., Chang, M., Lee, K., Toutanova, K.: BERT: pre-training of deep bidirectional transformers for language understanding. In: Conference of the North American Chapter of the Association for Computational Linguistics (2019)
13. Park, H., Kim, K., Yoon, J., Park, S., Choi, L.: Feature difference makes sense: a medical image captioning model exploiting feature difference and tag information. In: Meeting of the Association for Computational Linguistics: Student Research Workshop (2020)
14. Dzmitry, D., Cho, K., Bengio, Y.: Neural machine translation by jointly learning to align and translate. In: International Conference on Learning Representations (2015)
15. Hochreiter, S., Schmidhuber, J.: Long short-term memory. Neural Comput. **9**, 1735–1780 (1997)
16. Ren, S., He, K., Girshick, R.B., Sun, J.: Faster R-CNN: towards real-time object detection with region proposal networks. In: Conference on Neural Information Processing Systems (2015)
17. Li, Y., et al.: Fully convolutional networks for panoptic segmentation. In: IEEE Conference on Computer Vision and Pattern Recognition (2021)
18. Radford, A., Wu, J., Child, R., Luan, D., Amodei, D., Sutskever, I.: Language models are unsupervised multitask learners. Technical report, OpenAI (2019)
19. Raffel, C., et al.: Exploring the limits of transfer learning with a unified text-to-text Transformer. J. Mach. Learn. Res. **21**, 1–67 (2020)
20. Zhang, Y., Baldridge, J., He, L.: PAWS: paraphrase adversaries from word scrambling. In: Conference of the North American Chapter of the Association for Computational Linguistics (2019)
21. Papineni, K., Roukos, S., Ward, T., Zhu, W.: BLEU: a method for automatic evaluation of machine translation. In: Annual Meeting on Association for Computational Linguistics (2002)
22. Banerjee, S., Lavie, A.: METEOR: an automatic metric for MT evaluation with improved correlation with human judgments. In: ACL Workshop on Intrinsic and Extrinsic Evaluation Measures for Machine Translation and/or Summarization (2005)
23. Vedantam, R., Lawrence, C., Parikh, D.: CIDEr: consensus-based image description evaluation. In: IEEE Conference on Computer Vision and Pattern Recognition (2015)

24. Mathur, N., Baldwin, B., Cohn, T.: Tangled up in BLEU: reevaluating the evaluation of automatic machine translation evaluation metrics. In: Meeting of the Association for Computational Linguistics (2020)
25. Marie, B., Fujita, A., Rubino., R.: Scientific credibility of machine translation research: a meta-evaluation of 769 papers. In: Meeting of the Association for Computational Linguistics (2021)
26. Micikevicius, P., et al.: Mixed precision training. In: International Conference on Learning Representations (2017)

Deep Learning

Exploring Graph Neural Networks for Stock Market Prediction on the JSE

Kialan Pillay[1,2]([✉]) [iD] and Deshendran Moodley[1,2] [iD]

[1] University of Cape Town, 18 University Avenue, Rondebosch,
Cape Town 7700, South Africa
pllkia010@myuct.ac.za, deshen@cs.uct.ac.za
[2] Centre for Artificial Intelligence Research, 18 University Avenue, Rondebosch,
Cape Town 7700, South Africa

Abstract. Stock markets are dynamic systems that exhibit complex intra-share and inter-share temporal dependencies. Spatial-temporal graph neural networks (ST-GNN) are emerging DNN architectures that have yielded high performance for flow prediction in dynamic systems with complex spatial and temporal dependencies such as city traffic networks. In this research, we apply three state-of-the-art ST-GNN architectures, i.e. Graph WaveNet, MTGNN and StemGNN, to predict the closing price of shares listed on the Johannesburg Stock Exchange (JSE) and attempt to capture complex inter-share dependencies. The results show that ST-GNN architectures, specifically Graph WaveNet, produce superior performance relative to an LSTM and are potentially capable of capturing complex intra-share and inter-share temporal dependencies in the JSE. We found that Graph WaveNet outperforms the other approaches over short-term and medium-term horizons. This work is one of the first studies to apply these ST-GNNs to share price prediction.

Keywords: Graph neural networks · Correlation matrix · Johannesburg Stock Exchange · Price prediction

1 Introduction

Several deep neural network (DNN) architectures have emerged recently to model complex and dynamic systems [1–3]. Examples of such systems are traffic flow (congestion) in a city, weather and stock markets. Typical characteristics are high frequency and noisy observations from multiple sensors with complex and often latent temporal dependencies. The prominent approaches incorporate a graph neural network (GNN) to capture spatial and inter-variable dependencies [2,4]. Each variable is typically represented as a node in a graph that captures the intra-variable dynamics of the variable, whilst the inter-variable dynamics are captured by weighted edges that reflect the strength of the dependencies between variables [2].

Thus a variable (node) has strong connections (links) to variables that are affected by changes in its values and weaker links to variables that are not

© Springer Nature Switzerland AG 2022
E. Jembere et al. (Eds.): SACAIR 2021, CCIS 1551, pp. 95–110, 2022.
https://doi.org/10.1007/978-3-030-95070-5_7

affected by changes in its values. In this way, a node captures local dynamics (intra-variable), while the overall graph structure captures the global (inter-variable) dynamics of the system. The prevalent application is predicting traffic flow at different points in a city traffic network. The inter-variable dependencies for this case are spatial relations between traffic flow at different points in the network. These approaches are referred to as spatial-temporal GNNs (ST-GNNs) [2]. One of the challenges with ST-GNNs is that the spatial dependencies can be dynamic.

Typically the traffic network topology is supplied as prior knowledge encoded as an adjacency matrix in the GNN. Early GNN approaches used a static graph structure provided as prior knowledge before training. However, spatial dependencies in dynamic systems can change and evolve. Graph WaveNet (GWN) [2] was amongst the first to include a dynamic adjacency matrix that learnt and adapted evolving spatial dependencies. A more recent emergent proposal is Spectral-Temporal Graph Neural Network (StemGNN) [5]. StemGNN differs from GWN as it is a purely data-driven approach and requires no prior knowledge about dependencies. It incorporates intra-variable and inter-variable dependencies jointly in the spectral domain and is designed to automatically learn multivariate spatial and non-spatial dependencies across time.

StemGNN was found to outperform GWN on nine benchmark datasets representing problems in the traffic, energy and health domains. However, none of the tested datasets related to the financial domain. Specifically, StemGNN and GWN were not applied to share price prediction in a stock market. StemGNN was not evaluated against MTGNN [6], an evolution of the GWN architecture which yields better performance than GWN on traffic flow prediction. Stock markets are complex, highly dynamic and often erratic systems that are difficult to predict. Recent ST-GNNs, like MTGNN, StemGNN and Graph WaveNet have shown to be highly effective in predicting dynamic and erratic systems, in the traffic, energy and health domains and may well also be highly effective for stock market prediction.

In this paper, we evaluate and compare three state-of-the-art ST-GNN approaches, i.e. StemGNN, GWN and MTGNN, for share price prediction on the Johannesburg Stock Exchange (JSE). We formulate the share price prediction as a multivariate spatial-temporal graph using daily closing share prices and attempt to capture the inter-share dependencies. We compare the prediction performance of the ST-GNN techniques using different input windows sizes and prediction horizons and compare the prediction performance against simple baseline models. We also evaluate the impact of including prior knowledge about inter-share dependencies. In Sect. 2 we review ST-GNN approaches and their applications, then present our experimental design in Sect. 3 and the results in Sect. 4. We provide a discussion and findings in Sect. 5 and describe the limitations and possibilities for future exploration in Sect. 6.

2 Background and Related Work

2.1 Problem Formulation

A time series is a sequence of real-valued observations ordered in time. Formally, a univariate time series is a set of random variables $\{X_t, t \in T\}$, where $T = \{1, 2, ..., M\}$. A multivariate time series $\mathbf{X} \in \mathbb{R}^{N \times M}$ is defined as a set of N univariate series.

Mathematically, a graph is a pair $G = (V, E)$, where V denotes the set of nodes and E the set of edges $e = (v, u)$. A feature vector X_v is associated with each node $v \in V$. The neighborhood of a node is defined as $N(v) = \{v \in V \mid (v, u) \in E\}$. The adjacency matrix $\mathbf{A} \in \mathbb{R}^{N \times N}$ is a mathematical representation of a graph G, with $A_{ij} > 0$ for $(v_i, v_j) \in E$, $A_{ij} = 0$ for $(v_i, v_j) \notin E$ and N denotes the number of nodes.

The prediction problem is formulated as a multivariate spatial-temporal graph, where each node v represents a stock in the market. The feature vector X_v corresponds to a univariate times series representing an individual share's daily closing prices. Node edges are weighted and represent the strength of any latent inter-share dependencies over a given time interval.

Node degree is the number of connected node edges. *Betweenness centrality* is a measure of a node's occurrence frequency on the pair-wise geodesic.

Multivariate single-step forecasting is the task of predicting the value of a single future set of daily share prices (node values) in a spatial-temporal graph conditional on the historical observations. Let $\mathbf{z_t} \in \mathbb{R}^N$ denote a N-dimensional variable at time t. Given $\mathbf{X} = \{\mathbf{z_1}, \mathbf{z_2}, ..., \mathbf{z_t}\}$, the aim is to predict the single-step-ahead vector of node values $\mathbf{Y} = \{\hat{z}_{t+1}\}$.

Multivariate multi-step forecasting is the task of predicting a sequence of daily share price values conditional on the historical observations. Given observed values $\mathbf{X} = \{\mathbf{z_1}, \mathbf{z_2}, ..., \mathbf{z_t}\}$, the aim is to predict the sequence $\mathbf{Y} = \{\hat{z}_{t+1}, \hat{z}_{t+2}, ..., \hat{z}_{t+H}\}$, where H is the next H time-steps, termed the prediction horizon.

2.2 Deep Neural Network Price Prediction

The majority of recent research investigating financial time series forecasting has focused on recurrent neural network (RNN) or Long short-term memory (LSTM) models [7,8]. In their review, Sezer et al. [8] also identified the increased prevalence of hybrid models that combine RNNs with an LSTM or RNNs combined with convolutional neural networks (CNN). In an applied portfolio management context, Ta et al. [9] and Wang et al. [10] apply an LSTM to identify investable financial securities based on the forecasted price, using a composite of price and fundamental data. Building on this methodology, Ma et al. [11] diverge by testing the predictive performance of DNNs using only historical raw price data. Ensemble or hybrid models have also been explored and are shown to perform better than standalone models [12]. DNNs have been used for both single- [13] and multi-step [14–16] forecasting tasks. However, multi-step forecasting tasks involve additional complexity due to error accumulation. Error accumulation is the propagation of past error into future predictions [17], thereby decreasing predictive accuracy.

2.3 Spatial-Temporal Graph Neural Networks

Spatial-temporal GNNs are explicitly designed to model spatial and temporal dependencies in a system [2]. Spatial and temporal components extract underlying patterns from the data in the corresponding domains. The spatial relations are reflected by the graph structure, with dynamic node-level inputs exhibiting one-dimensional temporal dependencies [1,2]. Spatial-temporal graph convolutional networks [3,18] are CNN-based architectures frequently applied to spatial-temporal graph modelling tasks. However, Wu et al. [6] state that previously introduced spatial-temporal GNNs are not suitable for modelling multivariate time series due to two distinct factors: unavailability of prior information and the sub-optimality of the predefined graph. Prior knowledge of the spatial dependencies is further assumed, and the models rely on a predefined static graph structure for training. This approach is unsuitable for stock market systems with complex dependencies and latent structure. Graph WaveNet (GWN) [2], MTGNN [6] and Spectral-Temporal Graph Neural Network (StemGNN) [5] are architectures that overcome the aforementioned limitations.

A graph convolution [7] component is used in all three techniques to extract spatial structure. However, in contrast to GWN and MTGNN, StemGNN extracts dependencies in the spectral domain. Both GWN and MTGNN utilise a temporal convolution network component to learn temporal dependencies within the time series.

GWN, MTGNN and StemGNN are all able to adaptively learn the graph structure without the provision of prior knowledge, i.e. providing an initial graph structure that specifies known dependencies. Both MTGNN and GWN outperforms other spatial-temporal GNNs that are initialised with fixed graph structures. However, GWN's performance declines without prior structural information. A notable limitation of StemGNN is that in its explicit focus on a purely data-driven approach, it fails to accommodate available prior knowledge, whilst GWN and MTGNN are flexible and accept prior knowledge by initialising the adjacency matrix.

GWN, MTGNN and StemGNN have achieved state-of-the-art performance for single-step and multi-step forecasting task performance on the evaluated datasets. Whilst MTGNN and StemGNN have been tested across diverse domains applications and are intended for general multivariate problems, GWN is only evaluated on traffic flow datasets. None of the techniques have been applied to stock market prediction. However, MTGNN has been evaluated on a foreign exchange rate time series data set. Both MTGNN and StemGNN were shown to outperform GWN on the traffic flow datasets. Notably, MTGNN was not one of the techniques compared to StemGNN [5], so its relative performance is unknown.

2.4   Graph Neural Networks for Stock Market Prediction

Whilst the ST-GNNs mentioned above have not explicitly been applied to stock market prediction there have been some isolated studies that have explored graph neural networks for capturing external information. Li et al. [19] propose an LSTM Relational Graph Convolutional Network (LSTM-RGCN) to explore the impact of overnight news on the opening prices of shares listed on the Tokyo Stock Exchange (TSE). The RGCN component extracts spatial dependencies, whilst an LSTM functions as a news text encoder and dynamic information propagation mechanism between RGCN layers. In their graph structure, each stock is a node, and the stock nodes are connected by the pair-wise inter-share correlations filtered by a threshold.

The authors formulate the problem as a movement classification problem instead of a price prediction problem. While LSTM-RGCN outperforms the selected baseline models, it produces a relatively poor classification accuracy rate of 57.53% compared to a random model that achieved 50.55%. Their proposed LSTM-RGCN focuses on the representation and impact of overnight news on the overnight share price movement and not multi-step price prediction.

Matsunaga et al. [20] explore known inter-company relationships for stock prediction on the Japanese Nikkei 225. They incorporate prior knowledge of supplier relations between companies in a knowledge graph and combine GCNs and an LSTM layer to form a Temporal Graph Convolution. Both studies propose and evaluate architectures customised for their applications and do not provide any performance comparisons with ST-GNN approaches. Sawhney et al. [21] propose a similar custom GCN+LSTM framework but construct a predefined stock market hypergraph that reflects complex dependencies instead of a simple graph. However, the authors formulate the problem as a ranking problem. Furthermore, the hypergraph is static and requires expert domain knowledge for its construction, which restricts its application.

3   Experimental Design

In this research, we evaluate and compare the performance of three state-of-the-art ST-GNN approaches, GWN [2], MTGNN [6], and StemGNN [5] for single-step and multi-step prediction of the daily close prices of shares in the Top 40 Index on the Johannesburg Stock Exchange (JSE). Our objective was to capture the latent and dynamic dependencies between different shares on the JSE and evaluate the impact of this on price prediction. To effectively compare the three ST-GNN models, we followed the original experimental setups and configuration settings specified by the authors as closely as possible.

To apply ST-GNN approaches, we formulate the problem as a flow problem, where a daily price movement in certain shares triggers a chain of daily price movements in other shares over several days. Our objective was to discover complex, non-linear latent dependency chains between different shares in the market. Both GWN and MTGNN allow for the specification of an initial adjacency matrix. Inspired by the approach taken by Li et al. [19] we use a correlation matrix to encode pair-wise dependencies to prime the adjacency matrices of GWN and MTGNN. The correlation matrix (Fig. 3) is calculated using the last available historical daily close prices of the 30 companies in the training set and initialises the adjacency matrix of GWN and MTGNN before training. The static correlation matrix represents pair-wise linear dependencies between shares in the market and serves as an initial starting point for representing more complex non-linear dependency chains. We thus adopt a purely data-driven approach and do not incorporate any additional prior knowledge like external news events [19] or supplier relations between companies [20].

3.1   GNN Models

The configuration details of the three ST-GNNs are briefly described below.

Graph WaveNet. GWN is a hybrid architecture for spatial-temporal graph modelling. The GWN architecture consists of temporal convolution (Gated TCN) and graph convolution (GCN) modules. The GCN module contains a self-adaptive adjacency matrix that requires no prior information. The Gated TCN module comprises one-dimensional convolutions that extract long-range temporal dependencies [22]. The GCN module extracts node-level dependencies using neighbourhood feature aggregation. The model outputs the predicted sequence over the entire prediction horizon H instead of iteratively generating H conditioned predictions. Following the authors' [2] adjacency matrix configuration results, we evaluate a double transition matrix plus adaptive adjacency matrix using the structural information initialisation against the adaptive-only adjacency matrix.

MTGNN. MTGNN is a hybrid architecture designed with an explicit focus on multivariate time series forecasting. MTGNN accommodates unavailable prior information through a self-adaptive adjacency matrix, although the structure is not updated during training. A distinct graph learning layer that extracts the adjacency matrix. The GCN module utilises a neighbourhood aggregation strategy [23] to learn node-level spatial dependencies, and the TCN module extracts temporal dependencies. The model is trained using a curriculum learning strategy that splits the input into subgroups. Curriculum learning locates optimal local minima by training the algorithm on a single-step forecasting task first and subsequently increases the prediction horizon at each iteration [6]. We evaluate a predefined static graph structure against the adaptive-only adjacency matrix.

StemGNN. StemGNN is a hybrid architecture for multivariate time series forecasting that captures inter-series correlations and temporal dependencies in the spectral domain. The spectral GCN component analogously extracts dependencies in the spectral rather than spatial domain. Spectral-Temporal GNN models are trained on the spectral representation of the graph [24]. A graph signal x is transformed into the spectral domain by a Fourier transform $\mathcal{F}$, a convolution operator is applied to the spectral signal, and the inverse Fourier transform $\mathcal{F}^{-1}$ is applied to transform the signal into its original representation [24]. StemGNN includes a latent correlation layer to automatically learn inter-series correlations without a predefined structure to extract an adjacency matrix. For our evaluation, StemGNN is not initialised with the correlation matrix.

3.2 Data

The performances of the models are compared on daily close price data for FTSE/JSE Top 40 Index constituent shares from 18 May 2009 to 20 July 2021. The Top 40 Index contains the 40 largest JSE-listed companies by market capitalisation. Market capitalisation is the current value of all outstanding shares. Companies listed after 2012 are excluded such that sufficient training data is available. The final dataset consisted of 30 nodes (stocks) and 3146 samples. For GWN and MTGNN, the data is further pre-processed following Wu et al. [2] and Wu et al. [6] to generate input-output sequences before training. This is performed as an in-processing step for StemGNN. The data is standardised using Z-score normalisation that removes the mean and rescales to unit variance. The dataset is split in chronological order to preserve temporal dependencies with 60% for training, 20% for validation and 20% for testing (2019–2021).

3.3 Implementation

All three ST-GNNs were implemented in PyTorch, based on the authors' implementations. Each experiment is conducted on an Apple MacBook Pro with an Intel(R) Core(TM) i5-8257U CPU @ 1.4 GHz. For an accurate comparative evaluation, we follow Cao et al. [5] and train the GNN and LSTM models using RMSProp optimiser and Mean Squared Error loss function for 50 epochs. The initial learning rate is set to 0.001 with a decay and dropout rate of 0.05. All other hyperparameters are configured as reported by the authors [2,5,6], who adopt a single configuration for all tested datasets. Hyperparameter tuning was not conducted to assess the out-of-the-box generalisability. We also selected the same error metrics to evaluate out-of-sample performance, i.e. Mean Absolute Percentage Error (MAPE), Mean Absolute Error (MAE), and Root Mean Squared Error (RMSE). For multi-step forecasting, these metrics are averaged over H steps corresponding to the prediction horizon and all nodes. Each experiment is evaluated over five different training/test runs and the denormalised mean metric value on the test set is reported.

3.4 Baseline

Several baseline models were implemented and tested for comparison. A grid search was conducted to tune the hyperparameters and locate the optimal configuration.

The first is an LSTM with $l = 2$ hidden layers and $N = 500$ hidden layer nodes. The last LSTM layer is connected to a fully connected neural network layer and outputs a forecast over the prediction horizon for a single node, in contrast to the GNN models that produce multi-node predictions for the entire horizon in a single run. The LSTM is trained independently for each node, and the mean metric value is reported.

For single-step forecasting, a Huber regressor ($\epsilon = 1, \alpha = 0.0001$), Ridge regressor ($\alpha = 1$), SVR ($C = 10, \epsilon = 0.03$) and last-value model are selected in addition to the LSTM model to produce baseline performance results. For any time series $X = \{x_1, x_2, x_3, ...x_t\}$, a last-value model outputs the last sequential observation x_t as the forecasted series value x_{t+1}. The baseline models are implemented using the PyTorch and sklearn machine learning libraries.

4 Results

4.1 Single-Step Forecasting

Table 1 shows the performance of GWN, MTGNN and StemGNN and the baseline models on a single-step forecasting task for 30-, 60- and 120-day input window sizes. Regular trading days for the Johannesburg Stock Exchange are Monday through Friday, and thus the selected input window sizes correspond to 6, 12 and 24 trading weeks.

Table 1. Single-step forecasting test set performance comparison of GNNs and baseline models

	30-day window			60-day window			120-day window		
	MAPE	MAE	RMSE	MAPE	MAE	RMSE	MAPE	MAE	RMSE
Last-value	12.56	1096.77	1672.06	12.98	1062.39	1459.65	12.92	1082.40	1493.29
Huber	12.83	**771.57**	**1129.51**	12.82	**804.25**	**1161.12**	13.46	905.29	1291.06
Ridge	12.18	801.95	1161.86	13.08	817.01	1178.17	12.45	**858.87**	**1230.04**
SVR	32.45	1396.30	2305.08	42.58	1824.44	2966.35	91.52	2602.45	3947.69
LSTM	27.96	2449.67	3431.34	29.07	2602.87	3409.67	43.69	3135.29	3977.02
Graph WaveNet	10.44	3072.72	8496.79	24.35	5432.03	15325.71	32.90	7603.66	20206.61
MTGNN	**6.76**	1478.92	3511.12	**9.06**	1953.99	4871.51	**10.62**	2472.13	6857.16
StemGNN	18.01	8415.90	21715.64	23.62	9329.78	21636.29	23.25	9249.32	21583.35

The results illustrate that MTGNN outperforms GWN and StemGNN by a substantial margin across all metrics for all window sizes. In addition, the choice of input window size affects performance, with performance degrading for larger window sizes. The degradation is more pronounced for GWN. Whilst GWN outperforms StemGNN for a 30-day window, the results indicate a sharp decline in GWN's performance as the window size is doubled from 30 to 60.

MTGNN is by far the best performing model using a 30-day input window amongst both the ST-GNNs and the baseline models. It achieves an approximately 3% lower MAPE compared to the next best ST-GNN, GWN, and a 5% lower MAPE score compared to the best baseline model, i.e. Ridge regressor.

4.2 Multi-step Forecasting

Table 2 compares the performance of GWN, MTGNN and StemGNN and baseline LSTM on a multi-step forecasting task for 20-, 40- and 60-day window sizes and 5-, 10- and 20-day close price prediction horizons.

Table 2. Multi-step forecasting test set performance comparison of GNNs and baseline LSTM model across different window sizes

20-day window	5-day horizon			10-day horizon			20-day horizon		
	MAPE	MAE	RMSE	MAPE	MAE	RMSE	MAPE	MAE	RMSE
LSTM	47.74	3168.03	**4411.10**	53.65	3729.25	**5157.98**	70.02	4928.60	**6656.45**
Graph WaveNet	**17.87**	**2554.10**	6430.45	**17.27**	**2716.00**	6819.69	**12.17**	**3147.66**	8852.29
MTGNN	216.97	29217.75	54875.26	258.05	31484.04	54808.86	232.43	32251.45	63249.00
StemGNN	24.96	10327.52	24464.46	26.64	10907.52	25375.75	30.92	11992.33	27384.19
40-day window									
LSTM	45.96	3207.62	**4363.04**	53.72	3712.97	**5037.78**	71.10	5224.54	**6676.38**
Graph WaveNet	**12.44**	**3960.92**	11642.37	**15.35**	**4370.69**	12882.04	25.69	**5022.74**	13472.62
MTGNN	122.63	19905.99	42729.60	152.71	23566.66	49893.09	182.12	29028.59	62179.24
StemGNN	19.78	8640.64	21504.16	19.94	85f76.14	21305.53	**21.97**	9287.20	22693.34
60-day window									
LSTM	46.39	**3241.21**	**4204.87**	56.91	**3916.42**	**5053.54**	65.50	**4563.63**	**5884.99**
Graph WaveNet	25.82	5535.79	15284.90	26.23	5792.11	16287.67	28.82	5998.07	16441.86
MTGNN	269.24	32627.72	59139.12	324.88	34788.54	54687.03	269.80	30684.99	51937.85
StemGNN	**23.10**	9198.82	21732.27	**25.55**	10797.06	26811.51	**23.51**	9604.94	22622.16
Best model	Graph WaveNet			Graph WaveNet			Graph WaveNet		
Best MAPE	12.44%			15.35%			12.17%		

When comparing MAPE scores, GWN significantly outperforms MTGNN, StemGNN and the LSTM for the tested hyperparameters. Whilst MTGNN was the best performer on a single-step forecasting task, it fared very poorly on multi-step forecasts. Even though StemGNN's performance is much closer to GWN's performance than MTGNN, there is still a substantial and clear performance overall difference between the two approaches.

Interestingly, increasing the prediction horizon does not always result in performance degradation. For example, the best overall prediction performance of GWN is on 20-day forecasts and not on 5-day forecasts. This result could be because GWN captures longer-term dependencies more accurately than StemGNN.

All techniques yield the best 5-day and 10-day predictions on a 40-day input window, with GWN producing the best performance of 12.44% and 15.35% respectively. For 20-day predictions, GWN also yields the best overall performance (12.17%) but on a 20-day input window. However, StemGNN outperforms GWN on 60-day window sizes. The results do not demonstrate a clear relation between window size and prediction error.

StemGNN demonstrates inferior performance on the shortest window size, producing superior MAPE scores with a 40-day input window. An outlier is its performance for a 40-day window and 20-day horizon, where it outperforms

GWN and MTGNN as measured by MAPE. Furthermore, StemGNN's performance is relatively stable as the prediction horizon increases for both 40- and 60-day input windows across all metrics for the tested horizons.

4.3   Correlation Matrix Impact

We then tested the impact of prior knowledge, i.e. the inclusion of a static correlation matrix on multi-step prediction performance. Table 3 shows the performance of GWN and MTGNN on the 5- and 10-day multi-step forecasting task for 20- and 40-day input window sizes, with and without the inclusion of the correlation matrix to initialise the GWN and MTGNN adjacency matrices.

Table 3. Multi-step forecasting test set performance comparison of GWN and MTGNN with predefined adjacency matrix across different window sizes

20-day window	Adjacency matrix	5-day horizon			10-day horizon		
		MAPE	MAE	RMSE	MAPE	MAE	RMSE
Graph WaveNet	Adaptive-only	17.87	**2554.10**	**6430.45**	17.27	**2716.00**	6819.69
Graph WaveNet	Forward-backward-adaptive	**15.80**	3237.76	9103.10	**16.59**	3348.49	9104.82
MTGNN	Adaptive-only	216.97	29217.75	54875.26	258.05	31484.04	54808.86
MTGNN	Predefined	214.05	28885.62	54690.14	237.09	30302.03	55173.77
40-day window							
Graph WaveNet	Adaptive-only	**12.44**	**3960.92**	**11642.37**	**15.35**	**4370.69**	**12882.04**
Graph WaveNet	Forward-backward-adaptive	22.25	5150.09	14683.01	20.43	5089.13	14254.43
MTGNN	Adaptive-only	122.63	19905.99	42729.60	152.71	23566.66	49893.09
MTGNN	Predefined	118.53	20303.73	44546.03	192.05	26726.98	52491.44
Best model		**Graph WaveNet Adaptive**			**Graph WaveNet Adaptive**		
Best MAPE		**12.44%**			**15.35%**		

The MAPE scores indicate that the provision of initial structural information does not improve predictive performance. For a 20-day window, the GWN with the forward-backward-adaptive adjacency matrix obtains a marginally higher MAPE score. However, doubling the window size significantly degrades the GWN performance when initialised with the correlation matrix. This may be attributed to the temporal divergence between the longer input sequence length and the shorter-term dependencies captured by the correlation matrix.

The impact of prior information on MTGNN is inconclusive. There is a substantial performance improvement when using a 40-day horizon. The predefined MTGNN configuration yields the best 5-day predictions with a 40-day input window, while the best 10-day predictions are produced by the adaptive-only MTGNN with a 40-day input window.

4.4   Inter-share Dependency Analysis

We then compared the inter-share dependencies and graph structure produced by the three ST-GNNs. GWN and MTGNN extract a graph structure (Fig. 4 in the

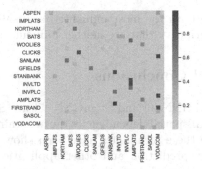

Fig. 1. GWN adaptive adjacency matrix (20-day window, multi-step horizon)

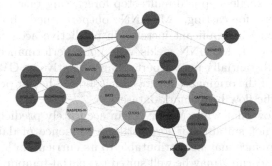

Fig. 2. GWN adaptive graph (20-day window, multi-step horizon)

appendix) that is highly dissimilar to that represented by the correlation matrix (Fig. 3 in the Appendix). Comparing the adaptive adjacency matrices, GWN extracts a sparse graphical structure, in contrast to the dense graph learnt by MTGNN. There are no identifiable commonalities between the two matrices, nor is one matrix a more fine-grained representation of the extracted dependencies. In contrast to GWN and MTGNN, StemGNN appears to elevate intra- rather than inter-node correlations. StemGNN learns only trivial positive correlations (self-correlation) and extracts weak negative correlations between other pairs (Fig. 4).

Node colour is a gradient scale of node degree, whilst node size illustrates betweenness centrality. Figure 2 illustrates that there are multiple nodes with a relatively high degree which is indicative of salient stocks. For GWN, there are fewer highly connected stocks as expected, with the analysis indicating that Anglo American Platinum, Capitec, and AngloGold Ashanti are the dominant stocks. Furthermore, the GWN graph contains few influential nodes, with Anglo American Platinum, Capitec, and AngloGold Ashanti providing maximal influence through strategic placement. The number of identified communities (two) corresponds with the bi-clustering (Fig. 3 in the appendix) performed on the correlation matrix, which finds two compact clusters of highly correlated stocks. The correlation network (Fig. 5) illustrates that Discovery, Remgro and

AngloGold Ashanti are both the most influential and salient stocks. There are several nodes on the periphery that are neither influential nor important.

5   Discussion and Conclusions

Graph WaveNet [2], MTGNN [6] and StemGNN [5] are ST-GNN architectures that can adaptively learn spatial dependencies during training without requiring prior knowledge. While these techniques have been shown to outperform other methods for traffic flow prediction and other applications in the energy and health domains, it is unclear whether they can achieve similar performance for stock market prediction. This study evaluated and compared GWN, MTGNN and StemGNN for single-step and multi-step forecasting tasks on the JSE.

For single-step forecasting, MTGNN outperformed both GWN and StemGNN, achieving a significant increase in predictive accuracy across varying windows. However, MTGNN yields very poor performance for multi-step forecasting and substantially poorer performance relative to GWN. This differs from the findings of the original study [6] which showed better performance than GWN on two traffic flow benchmark datasets.

Our results show that while MTGNN can accurately predict a single future share price, it is not suitable for forecasting a sequence of daily close prices. MTGNN's performance may be attributable to its curriculum learning strategy. While curriculum learning may be well suited to spatial-temporal flow problems where the next point can be a suitable starting point for identifying a trajectory, inter-share dependencies in the stock market exhibit complex relationships which can pan out erratically over multiple time steps.

For multi-step forecasting tasks, GWN is the clear winner. It achieved the highest predictive accuracy over all the tested window sizes and horizon lengths. The size of the input window had a substantial impact on performance. All techniques produced the best performance over a 40-day input window. This window corresponds to the previous two-months daily close prices and is potentially the optimal input sequence length for latent inter-share temporal effects to unfold within the JSE. However, GWN with a 20-day input window and prediction horizon produced the highest performance overall, marginally higher than that produced with a 40-day input window and 5-day horizon configuration. This result is an interesting phenomenon and requires further exploration.

Even though StemGNN yielded adequate results compared to MTGNN, MAPE scores were approximately 10% lower than those reported on the Electricity, ECG and Solar datasets [5], and in almost all cases it was outperformed by GWN. Similarly, comparing the best GWN performance score to the metrics reported for traffic flow forecasting, we find that the approximately 10% decrease in MAPE is realistic given the dynamic and erratic intra- and inter-share dependencies exhibited within a stock market and the inherent complexity in extracting and representing these dependencies.

Based on the results of the correlation matrix experiment, we found that the *a priori* inclusion of multivariate correlations produced a negligible impact on model predictive accuracy. While GWN appears to have performed well without prior structural information, this requires further exploration, e.g. the sector and industry groupings for each share may contain important structural information.

Our results demonstrate that ST-GNN models outperform the baseline LSTM model on multi-step predictions. Furthermore, GWN, an older approach, outperformed the more recent MTGNN and StemGNN models for multi-step prediction. This differs from the findings in other domains where MTGNN outperformed GWN [6], and StemGNN outperformed GWN [5]. GWN has a high potential for predicting future daily close price values over short- and medium-term prediction horizons, but this requires further investigation. Furthermore, this study found that certain ST-GNNs have broader applicability to a range of complex systems, especially those without explicit spatial dependencies. In this study, the graph is used to represent and learn the internal dynamics of the Johannesburg Stock Exchange. The extracted GWN adaptive graph produces an approximate representation of inter-share dependencies in the JSE Top 40 Index. This work provides a foundation for future investigation of ST-GNNs for real-world applications of share price forecasting.

6   Limitations and Future Work

The results of this work present several opportunities for further investigation. The selected models were evaluated on a single dataset. Obtaining empirical results on data from different stock exchanges allows for a broader assessment of model generalisability and identifying potential commonalities and discrepancies in market dynamics. The methodology was restricted to evaluating ST-GNNs using only the original hyperparameter configurations. Future research can include hyperparameter tuning for JSE stock market data which may yield higher predictive performance. In addition, testing prior structural information sources other than a correlation matrix, or feature combinations thereof, presents an avenue for future study. The hypergraph proposed by Sawhney et al. [21] is a promising starting point.

Acknowledgements. This research is wholly funded by the National Research Foundation (Grant Number MND200411512622).

Appendix

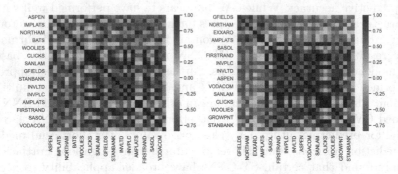

Fig. 3. FTSE/JSE Top 40 Index static correlation and bi-clustered correlation matrices

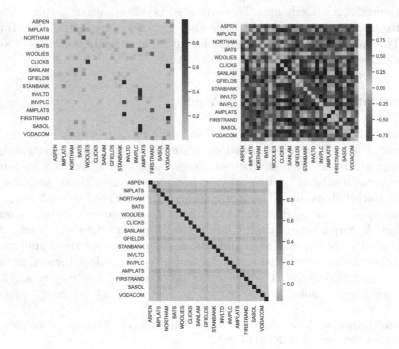

Fig. 4. GWN, MTGNN and StemGNN adaptive adjacency matrices (20-day window, multi-step horizon)

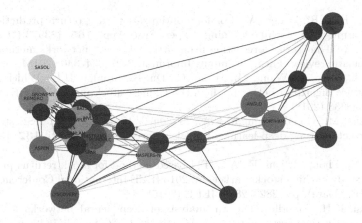

Fig. 5. FTSE/JSE Top 40 Index correlation graph

References

1. Wu, Z., Pan, S., Chen, F., Long, G., Zhang, C., Philip, S.Y.: A comprehensive survey on graph neural networks. IEEE Trans. Neural Netw. Learn. Syst. **32**(1), 4–24 (2020)
2. Wu, Z., Pan, S., Long, G., Jiang, J., Zhang, C.: Graph WaveNet for deep spatial-temporal graph modeling. In: Proceedings of the 28th International Joint Conference on Artificial Intelligence, IJCAI-2019, pp. 1907–1913. International Joint Conferences on Artificial Intelligence Organization (2019)
3. Song, C., Lin, Y., Guo, S., Wan, H.: Spatial-temporal synchronous graph convolutional networks: a new framework for spatial-temporal network data forecasting. In: Proceedings of the AAAI Conference on Artificial Intelligence, vol. 34, pp. 914–921 (2020)
4. Li, Y., Yu, R., Shahabi, C., Liu, Y.: Diffusion convolutional recurrent neural network: data-driven traffic forecasting. In: 6th International Conference on Learning Representations, ICLR 2018 (2018)
5. Cao, D., et al.: Spectral temporal graph neural network for multivariate time-series forecasting (2021)
6. Wu, Z., Pan, S., Long, G., Jiang, J., Chang, X., Zhang, C.: Connecting the dots: multivariate time series forecasting with graph neural networks. In: Proceedings of the 26th ACM SIGKDD International Conference on Knowledge Discovery & Data Mining, pp. 753–763 (2020)
7. Ismail Fawaz, H., Forestier, G., Weber, J., Idoumghar, L., Muller, P.-A.: Deep learning for time series classification: a review. Data Min. Knowl. Discov. **33**(4), 917–963 (2019). https://doi.org/10.1007/s10618-019-00619-1
8. Sezer, O.B., Gudelek, M.U., Ozbayoglu, A.M.: Financial time series forecasting with deep learning: a systematic literature review: 2005–2019. Appl. Soft Comput. **90**, 106181 (2020)
9. Ta, V.D., Liu, C.M., Tadesse, D.A.: Portfolio optimization-based stock prediction using long-short term memory network in quantitative trading. Appl. Sci. **10**(2), 437 (2020)
10. Wang, W., Li, W., Zhang, N., Liu, K.: Portfolio formation with preselection using deep learning from long-term financial data. Expert Syst. Appl. **143**, 113042 (2020)

11. Ma, Y., Han, R., Wang, W.: Portfolio optimization with return prediction using deep learning and machine learning. Expert Syst. Appl. **165**, 113973 (2021)
12. Tealab, A.: Time series forecasting using artificial neural networks methodologies: a systematic review. Future Comput. Inform. J. **3**(2), 334–340 (2018)
13. Chen, L., Qiao, Z., Wang, M., Wang, C., Du, R., Stanley, H.E.: Which artificial intelligence algorithm better predicts the Chinese stock market? IEEE Access **6**, 48625–48633 (2018)
14. Hiransha, M., Gopalakrishnan, E.A., Menon, V.K., Soman, K.: NSE stock market prediction using deep-learning models. Procedia Comput. Sci. **132**, 1351–1362 (2018)
15. Chen, K., Zhou, Y., Dai, F.: A LSTM-based method for stock returns prediction: a case study of china stock market. In: 2015 IEEE International Conference on Big Data (Big Data), pp. 2823–2824. IEEE (2015)
16. Kouassi, K.H., Moodley, D.: An analysis of deep neural networks for predicting trends in time series data. In: SACAIR 2021. CCIS, vol. 1342, pp. 119–140. Springer, Cham (2020). https://doi.org/10.1007/978-3-030-66151-9_8
17. Cheng, H., Tan, P.-N., Gao, J., Scripps, J.: Multistep-ahead time series prediction. In: Ng, W.-K., Kitsuregawa, M., Li, J., Chang, K. (eds.) PAKDD 2006. LNCS (LNAI), vol. 3918, pp. 765–774. Springer, Heidelberg (2006). https://doi.org/10.1007/11731139_89
18. Yu, B., Yin, H., Zhu, Z.: Spatio-temporal graph convolutional networks: a deep learning framework for traffic forecasting. In: Proceedings of the 27th International Joint Conference on Artificial Intelligence, IJCAI-2018, pp. 3634–3640. International Joint Conferences on Artificial Intelligence Organization (2018)
19. Li, W., Bao, R., Harimoto, K., Chen, D., Xu, J., Su, Q.: Modeling the stock relation with graph network for overnight stock movement prediction. In: Proceedings of the 29th International Joint Conference on Artificial Intelligence, IJCAI-2020, pp. 4541–4547. International Joint Conferences on Artificial Intelligence Organization (2020)
20. Matsunaga, D., Suzumura, T., Takahashi, T.: Exploring graph neural networks for stock market predictions with rolling window analysis (2019)
21. Sawhney, R., Agarwal, S., Wadhwa, A., Derr, T., Shah, R.R.: Stock selection via spatiotemporal hypergraph attention network: a learning to rank approach, vol. 35, pp. 497–504 (2021)
22. van den Oord, A., et al.: WaveNet: a generative model for raw audio. In: The 9th ISCA Speech Synthesis Workshop, p. 125. ISCA (2016)
23. Xu, K., Hu, W., Leskovec, J., Jegelka, S.: How powerful are graph neural networks? In: 7th International Conference on Learning Representations, ICLR 2019 (2019)
24. Zhou, J., et al.: Graph neural networks: a review of methods and applications. AI Open **1**, 57–81 (2020)

Multi-style Training for South African Call Centre Audio

Walter Heymans[1,2(✉)], Marelie H. Davel[1,2], and Charl van Heerden[3]

[1] Faculty of Engineering, North-West University, Potchefstroom, South Africa
[2] CAIR, Pretoria, South Africa
[3] Saigen, Cape Town, South Africa
charl@saigen.co.za
http://engineering.nwu.ac.za/must

Abstract. Mismatched data is a challenging problem for automatic speech recognition (ASR) systems. One of the most common techniques used to address mismatched data is multi-style training (MTR), a form of data augmentation that attempts to transform the training data to be more representative of the testing data; and to learn robust representations applicable to different conditions. This task can be very challenging if the test conditions are unknown. We explore the impact of different MTR styles on system performance when testing conditions are different from training conditions in the context of deep neural network hidden Markov model (DNN-HMM) ASR systems. A controlled environment is created using the LibriSpeech corpus, where we isolate the effect of different MTR styles on final system performance. We find that noise perturbation and encoding (including downsampling) are the most effective techniques to improve a system on noisy, encoded audio; with significant improvements observed if the training/testing mismatch is large. We evaluate our findings on a South African call centre dataset that contains noisy, WAV49-encoded audio: MTR provides consistent improvements on this set, but these improvements are very small, given the smaller than expected mismatch observed.

Keywords: Automatic speech recognition · Multi-style training · Call centre audio · WAV49 encoding

1 Introduction

Automatic speech recognition (ASR) has been an active field of research since the 1970s and is still being developed and improved today [1–3]. The word error rate (WER), a typical measure of performance for ASR systems, has been significantly reduced over the last few decades. Main factors that contributed to this improvement were recent developments in deep learning, increased computational power of modern computers, specifically graphical processing units, and large amounts of collected data [4].

© Springer Nature Switzerland AG 2022
E. Jembere et al. (Eds.): SACAIR 2021, CCIS 1551, pp. 111–124, 2022.
https://doi.org/10.1007/978-3-030-95070-5_8

ASR systems tend to perform more poorly when there is a large mismatch between training and testing data. Factors that contribute to this mismatch include various forms of background noise, microphone distortion, different recording environments, encoding noise, people that speak in different speaking styles and accents, etc. It is difficult for an ASR system to generalise to new audio with different conditions if no attempt is made during training to handle such variability in the data.

A popular technique to address mismatch in audio for ASR is multi-style training (MTR) [5–10]. MTR aims to transform the training data to be more representative of the testing data and to learn robust representations of the training data. A new training dataset is created from the existing set by adding a series of MTR styles using data augmentation. These can include: changing the speed and volume [5], speech style [6] or sampling rate [7]; adding time and frequency distortions [9] or background noise; and simulating reverberation [10]. The styles are typically chosen without knowledge of the testing conditions, and must still be able to handle a wide variety of mismatch. In addition, the number of styles that are added must be taken into consideration, because the computational cost of training an ASR system increases significantly with each style that is added.

In this work, we analyse the effects of MTR in a controlled environment using the LibriSpeech corpus [11]. Speed, volume and noise perturbation are added to clean training data and evaluated on WAV49-encoded development and test sets. We show the performance gain as a result of individual and combined MTR styles. This provides a practical approach to improve ASR systems efficiently on WAV49-encoded audio, often used in South African call centres.

Section 2 gives a brief overview of related work in the field of MTR for deep neural network (DNN) based speech recognition. In Sect. 3, we introduce the call centre dataset and how we created a controlled environment using the LibriSpeech corpus. Our experimental setup is explained in Sect. 4 and the results are presented in Sect. 5. Finally, the key findings are discussed in Sect. 6.

2   Related Work

We are not aware of any studies that investigate MTR for DNN-based call centre ASR. There are studies that investigate the effects of different perturbation levels, but none of them focus on call centre audio. The perturbation types used in these studies include additive noise and room impulse responses [8], speed [5] and volume [12].

Doulaty et al. investigated a method to automatically identify noise perturbation levels in a target set of utterances [8]. They used a 'voice-search' dataset for their experiments. A noisy test set was created by perturbing a clean set with different perturbation styles including additive background noise and room impulse responses using different signal-to-noise ratios (SNRs). MTR was used to train a number of multi-layer perceptron (MLP) models, each with different perturbation levels. The MTR model that was trained on data with the closest matched conditions was then used to evaluate the target utterance. Their study revealed that accurately matched noise perturbation levels results in better ASR performance. This showed the importance of selecting conditions for MTR that are matched to that of the test set.

Speed perturbation is a common technique that is applied widely in MTR setups. Ko et al. [5] investigated making two copies of the original dataset, one slowed down by 10% and another made 10% faster. An average relative improvement of 4.3% was observed across 4 different tasks, with a relative improvement of 6.7% on Switchboard [13], a conversational telephone corpus. The improvement on the full LibriSpeech corpus [11] was 3.2% and only 0.32% relatively on the ASpIRE corpus [14]. The authors attribute this small improvement on the ASpIRE corpus to simulated reverberation that was already applied to the training data.

Gokay and Yalcin investigated the effects of speed and volume perturbation in a low-resource 10 h Turkish dataset of natural speech from a professional speaker [12]. They used an end-to-end ASR system based on Deep Speech 2 [15]. Adding speed and volume perturbation, individually and together improved their WER by between 8.2% and 12.9% relatively. They also added 10 h of new training data without MTR and the improvement was 26.3% relatively, much better than any MTR technique they used. The effect of MTR was amplified because their original training dataset was very small. As more matched data is added, the improvements of MTR (speed and volume perturbation in this case) should become less apparent, because the training data itself can include more conditions.

Our work focuses on having a single model instead of multiple MTR models each trained with different conditions. We apply different perturbation styles (additive noise, speed and volume) to clean training data in a controlled environment to analyse the effect of each method on DNN-based ASR using the LibriSpeech corpus (encoded using WAV49 encoding). The findings are applied to a proprietary South African call centre dataset that is WAV49 encoded.

3   Data

We use two datasets: our final aim is to use MTR to determine how much we can improve the performance of an ASR system on mismatched call centre data, but first experiment with individual styles in a controlled environment. An overview of the call centre dataset is given in Sect. 3.1; and in Sect. 3.2 we explain how the controlled environment is set up using the LibriSpeech corpus.

3.1   South African Call Centre Dataset

Call centres handle very large amounts of data on a daily basis. Typically, all calls are recorded and stored for future reference, legal purposes and call centre speech analytics. Due to the large number of calls, the recordings are often compressed for longer term storage. This can decrease the required storage space by up to twenty times. Although compression is beneficial for storage requirements, it is a challenging problem for ASR systems. We use a proprietary South African call centre dataset, referred to from here as the SACC corpus. All data in the SACC corpus consists of narrow-band single channel recordings. The corpus is mostly South African English, but there are occasional non-English words from other official South African languages. Utterances with mostly non-English speech have been removed from the corpus. Table 1 shows the datasets in the SACC corpus after mostly non-English utterances were removed. There are 48.8 h of training data that were originally not encoded, with an encoded version created using Sox[1]. The training, development and test sets were created from the same set by dividing the corpus into three parts. A 1.2 h held-out test set that was recorded and processed by the call centre at a later stage is also available for final testing. Calls are compressed in three steps, namely, lowering the sampling rate, combining dual channel audio to a single channel, and encoding the audio with WAV49 encoding.

Sampling Rate: Most high quality ASR systems work with wide-band audio that is sampled at 16 kHz. All data in the SACC corpus is narrow-band (8 kHz). Narrow-band audio has less frequency information available than wide-band, which tends to hurt ASR systems slightly. The significance of the performance difference is dependent on the type of data.

Channel Combination: Telephone calls usually have two channels, one for the call center agent and one for the client (person who called or is being called). Two audio channels use twice as much storage space as a single channel, which is why they are combined to form only one channel. This creates three problems for an ASR system: (1) noise from both channels are present in the new signal, (2) overlapping speech and (3) speaker confusion. All of these factors contribute to decreased speech recognition performance.

WAV49 Encoding: Compressing audio with a codec can reduce the storage space significantly, but also keep most of the original audio quality. There are many different compression methods, such as: Free Lossless Audio Codec (FLAC), MPEG Audio Layer III (MP3), Advanced Audio Coding (AAC), Ogg Vorbis, Speex and Opus [16]. The SACC corpus is WAV49-encoded: a full-rate GSM 06.10 codec with a compression ratio of 10:1 is applied to the audio file [17]. It is then saved in a WAV file format resulting in a WAV49-encoded file [18].

3.2 LibriSpeech Corpus with WAV49 Encoding

The LibriSpeech corpus contains 1 000 h of English audiobook recordings sampled at 16 kHz [11]. It is a freely available public dataset that is used as a benchmark for many state-of-the-art ASR models [9,19]. The dataset contains

---

[1] http://sox.sourceforge.net.

Table 1. SACC corpus subsets with sampling rate, encoding and total duration.

Dataset	Sampling rate	Encoding	Hours
train	8 kHz	–	48.8
train-e	8 kHz	WAV49	48.8
dev	8 kHz	–	7.1
dev-e	8 kHz	WAV49	7.1
test	8 kHz	–	6.2
test-e	8 kHz	WAV49	6.2
held-out test	8 kHz	WAV49	1.2

about 460 h of clean training data, 500 h of noisy training data, two development and two test sets (one clean and one noisy each). There are also four different language models included ranging from a small tri-gram to a large unpruned 4-gram language model.

We use the LibriSpeech corpus to create a controlled environment for MTR experiments. The corpus is well suited for this, since a large portion of the corpus has been labeled as "clean", meaning that the recordings do not have much noise. Using these clean audio recordings, noise and encoding can easily be added to simulate call centre audio conditions.

We use the 100 h subset of the LibriSpeech corpus for training data and the small tri-gram (tg-small) language model for faster decoding and making the comparison of different acoustic models more efficient. To simulate call centre conditions, we add background noise to the clean development (*dev-clean*) and test (*test-clean*) sets using the QUT-NOISE corpus [20] with a signal-to-noise ratio (SNR) of 5 dB. For our training data, we add noise using the Musan noise corpus [21] to create an artificial mismatch in noise conditions. An artificial mismatch is created between training and test data, because the noise corpus used to create the test set has different types of noise than the corpus used to perturb the training data. For both noise corpora, we randomly add a noise file to each utterance for the total duration of the utterance. We also encode these sets with WAV49 encoding and reduce their sampling rate to 8 kHz using Sox.

Table 2 shows the training datasets we use for MTR. Different combinations are used to see the combined performance impact on the development set. Speed and volume perturbation was applied to the training data with a change of 10% and 20% respectively. The speed was either increased or decreased with equal probability - approximately half of the utterances have a slower speed compared to the original set and the other half have a faster speed. Volume is handled in a similar way. Table 3 shows the development and test sets that are created from the *dev-clean* and *test-clean* subsets, in a similar manner as the training set but with fewer conditions.

Table 2. Multi-style training datasets created using the 100 h clean LibriSpeech subset (*train-clean-100*).

Dataset name	Encoding	Noise corpus	SNR	Speed	Volume
train-clean	–	–	–	–	–
train-clean-8k	–	–	–	–	–
train-clean-e	WAV49	–	–	–	–
train-noisy-e-5	WAV49	QUT	5	–	–
train-clean-e-s	WAV49	–	–	10%	–
train-clean-e-v	WAV49	–	–	–	20%
train-clean-e-sv	WAV49	–	–	10%	20%
train-musan-e-5	WAV49	Musan	5	–	–
train-musan-e-10	WAV49	Musan	10	–	–
train-musan-e-15	WAV49	Musan	15	–	–
train-musan-e-20	WAV49	Musan	20	–	–
train-musan-e-15-s	WAV49	Musan	15	10%	–
train-musan-e-15-v	WAV49	Musan	15	–	20%
train-musan-e-15-sv	WAV49	Musan	15	10%	20%

Table 3. Development and test datasets created using the LibriSpeech *dev-clean* and *test-clean* sets.

Dataset name	Source dataset	Encoding	Noise corpus	SNR	Hours
dev-clean-e	dev-clean	WAV49	–	–	5.4
dev-noisy-e-5	dev-clean	WAV49	QUT	5	5.4
test-noisy-e-5	test-clean	WAV49	QUT	5	5.4

4   Experimental Setup

We use the Pytorch-Kaldi[2] ASR toolkit to train a context-dependant deep neural network hidden Markov model (CD-DNN-HMM) ASR system [22]. We use the toolkit's default training setup with the standard scoring scripts for the LibriSpeech corpus. Everything in our setup is the same as theirs, except that we additionally optimise four selected hyperparameters (batch size, learning rate, language model weight and word insertion penalty).

We use the default MLP acoustic model for the LibriSpeech corpus. The acoustic model is a 5 hidden-layer network with 1 024 hidden units per layer. All hidden layers use rectified linear unit (ReLU) activation functions with batch normalisation and dropout with probability of 0.15. The output layer does not use batch normalisation or dropout and has a softmax activation function. We use feature-space maximum likelihood linear regression (fMLLR) input features

---

[2] Available at: https://github.com/mravanelli/pytorch-kaldi.

with a temporal context window of 11 frames [23]. Our model trained on the *train-clean-100* subset of the LibriSpeech corpus achieved similar results to public baselines (9.2% vs 9.6% WER on test-clean) [22].

All networks are trained with the stochastic gradient descent (SGD) optimiser and a learning rate scheduler that halves the learning rate when the relative improvement[3] on the development set is less than 0.001. The acoustic model is trained with the negative log-likelihood loss function to predict HMM state probabilities. The batch size and learning rate are optimised on the development set using a grid search. We found that these two hyperparameters have the largest effect on WER. The language model weight and word insertion penalty that gave the lowest WER on the development set are used for the final systems. All other hyperparameters are kept fixed. All networks are trained for 24 epochs; at this point all networks have converged. Each network is trained with three different random initialisation seeds. We report on the average WER and WER standard error across seeds.

5 Analysis

In this section, we first investigate the effect of sampling rate differences between training and testing data on the LibriSpeech corpus (Sect. 5.1). This is done to see how much of the performance is lost due to WAV49 encoding and how much is due to the difference in sampling rate. Then we create a controlled environment using the LibriSpeech corpus to isolate the effects that different styles in an MTR setup has on system performance (Sect. 5.2). Noise, speed and volume perturbation are applied to a clean training set to measure how much each of these techniques can improve the WER on the noise-perturbed test set. We also look at how larger networks can benefit MTR setups (Sect. 5.3). Finally, the findings in the controlled experiment are applied to the SACC corpus (Sect. 5.4).

5.1 Sampling Rate Differences on the LibriSpeech Corpus

Two sets of networks are trained on the *train-clean* and *train-clean-e* datasets using 16 kHz and 8 kHz audio, respectively. Encoded data, which was previously downsampled during the encoding stage, was now upsampled to 16 kHz using Sox to train a 16 kHz model. We also downsampled the clean training and development sets to 8 kHz to measure the performance difference caused by WAV49 encoding when unencoded narrow-band audio is used for training.

The WER results are shown in Table 4. All data in the top section is used at 16 kHz (training and development sets); while the data in the bottom section is used at 8 kHz. The *train-clean* model performed the best on the *dev-clean* set for both frequencies. Evaluating the clean 16 kHz model (*train-clean*, 16 kHz) on the encoded development set drastically increased the WER to 19.32%. By downsampling the clean training data (*train-clean*, 8 kHz), the result improved

---

[3] Senone error rate is used to measure performance after each training epoch.

by 40.1% relative WER to 11.44%. This network, trained only using unencoded data, performed only slightly worse than the *train-clean-e* model (11.44% vs 11.21% WER). The large difference in WER can be reduced significantly by downsampling unencoded training data. Encoding the training data only gave a slight improvement over the 8 kHz *train-clean* model of 2.0% relative WER.

We observe that most of the mismatch is a result of the difference in sampling rate and not due to encoding. The improvement achieved when downsampling unencoded training data was 40.1% relative WER and only 2.0% when encoding the training set.

Table 4. WER results of models with different sampling rates on *dev-clean* and *dev-clean-e*. Average WER (%) and standard error is shown over 3 seeds.

Train set	Sampling rate	dev-clean	dev-clean-e
Wide-band			
train-clean	16 kHz	**8.88 ± 0.10**	19.32 ± 0.11
train-clean-e	16 kHz[a]	10.71 ± 0.05	**11.02 ± 0.03**
Narrow-band			
train-clean	8 kHz	10.29 ± 0.03	11.44 ± 0.04
train-clean-e	8 kHz	10.76 ± 0.02	11.21 ± 0.03

[a]Up-sampled from 8 kHz.

5.2   Multi-style Training on the LibriSpeech Corpus

In this experiment, we analyse the effect of different MTR styles on a set with mismatched noise conditions. Different combinations of noise, speed and volume perturbation are used for training data. Table 5 shows the WER results on the development set (*dev-noisy-e-5*). Information about the training datasets used by each model is shown in Table 2. All data, except for the 8 kHz *train-clean-8k* set is upsampled to 16 kHz using Sox. The upsampling process used does not attempt to interpolate values in order to add high frequency information that was lost during downsampling. Only the existing lower frequency components are retained.

Similar to the results in Sect. 5.1, downsampling the clean training data improved the WER, although the improvement is much less than before. Adding WAV49 encoding to the training data improved the relative WER of the *train-clean-8k* model by 15.6%, much more than observed in Sect. 5.1.

Speed and volume perturbation were applied to the clean encoded training data. Different combinations of datasets were evaluated. A small improvement in WER (0.8% relative) was observed when using only speed perturbation. None of the other combinations resulted in a notable improvement; the *train-clean-e-v* and *train-clean-e-sv* networks performed worse than without perturbation. This may be because the training data already captures a large range of speed and

Table 5. WER on development set (*dev-noisy-e-5*) using training datasets with different styles. Average WER (%) and standard error is shown over 3 seeds.

Model	Datasets	Size	Dev WER
Variations of clean set			
train-clean	train-clean	1	36.46 ± 0.14
train-clean-8k[a]	train-clean @ 8 kHz	1	33.23 ± 0.21
train-clean-e	train-clean-e	1	**28.06 ± 0.03**
Speed and volume			
train-clean-e-s	train-clean-e + s	2	**27.83 ± 0.02**
train-clean-e-v	train-clean-e + v	2	28.21 ± 0.07
train-clean-e-sv	train-clean-e + sv	2	28.25 ± 0.10
train-clean-e-s-v	train-clean-e + s + v	3	28.04 ± 0.13
Noise			
train-musan-e-5	train-musan-e-5	1	29.29 ± 0.34
train-musan-e-10	train-musan-e-10	1	27.29 ± 0.12
train-musan-e-15	train-musan-e-15	1	**23.30 ± 0.06**
train-musan-e-20	train-musan-e-20	1	26.64 ± 0.09
Speed, volume and noise			
train-musan-e-15-s	train-musan-e-15 + s	2	24.09 ± 0.05
train-musan-e-15-v	train-musan-e-15 + v	2	23.97 ± 0.11
train-musan-e-15-sv	train-musan-e-15 + sv	2	24.34 ± 0.02
train-musan-e-15-s-v	train-musan-e-15 + s + v	3	**23.80 ± 0.09**
train-musan-e-15-s-v-sv	train-musan-e-15 + s + v + sv	4	23.89 ± 0.08
Matched noise			
train-noisy-e-5	train-noisy-e-5	1	**19.75 ± 0.04**

[a]Training and test data is used at 8 kHz.

volumes, or that the development set does not vary much in terms of speed and volume.

Noise perturbation was applied to clean training data using four different SNR values and the sets were encoded afterwards. The performance with the 15 dB network was much better than the rest (12.5% to 20.4% relative WER), despite the fact that the development set used an SNR of 5 dB. The different noise corpora, QUT-NOISE vs Musan, can explain the difference. Energy in the noise files are distributed differently, so the SNR values are not directly comparable. The *train-musan-e-15* model performed 17.0% relatively better than the *train-clean-e* model. This emphasises how important matched training and test conditions are. It is very important to use the correct SNR for noise perturbation, because it has a large influence on system performance.

We used the best noise-perturbed training dataset and added speed and volume perturbation. The WER when using speed and volume perturbation in any

Table 6. WER on test set (*test-noisy-e-5*) using training datasets with different styles. Average WER (%) and standard error is shown over 3 seeds.

Model	Datasets	Size	Test WER
Variations of clean set			
train-clean	train-clean	1	36.92 ± 0.18
train-clean-e	train-clean-e	1	29.16 ± 0.12
Speed and volume			
train-clean-e-s	train-clean-e + s	3	28.61 ± 0.11
Noise			
train-musan-e-15	train-musan-e-15	1	**24.54 ± 0.22**
Speed, volume and noise			
train-musan-e-15-s-v	train-musan-e-15 + s + v	3	24.87 ± 0.08
Matched noise			
train-noisy-e-5	train-noisy-e-5	1	**20.48 ± 0.03**

combination did not improve the result compared to using only additive noise. A similar phenomenon was observed in [5] on the ASpIRE corpus, where they only observed an absolute WER improvement of 0.1%. We further investigate this in Sect. 5.3.

Finally, we trained a network using a noise-matched training dataset, *train-noisy-e-5* that also uses the QUT-NOISE corpus. The WER for this model is 17.0% relatively better than the best MTR model. This shows that MTR has many shortcomings when test conditions are significantly different from the training set, because the dataset with matched conditions significantly outperformed MTR. When encountering unseen environments on a new test set, most systems will probably struggle to do well.

Up to this point, all results were reported on the development set. Table 6 shows the WERs on the test set (*test-noisy-e-5*) using six selected models that performed the best in each category on the development set. The results on the test set are very similar to those on the development set. The best MTR model of all the combinations tested, is the one that used only noise perturbation using the SNR value that performed the best on the development set. The difference in WER between the best MTR model and the *train-clean* model is 33.5% relative. MTR can clearly reduce the WER significantly if the conditions are properly chosen, but MTR still performed 16.5% worse than the *train-noisy-e-5* model with matched conditions.

5.3 Multi-style Training Using Larger Networks on the LibriSpeech Corpus

By adding speed and volume perturbation, you also add more training data. It is possible that the network with only 1 024 hidden units is too small to capture the larger data distribution. Increasing the network capacity should help the models using more training datasets generalise better and possibly give an advantage to the speed and volume perturbation networks.

Using the same training and optimisation protocol described in Sect. 4, we train three networks with 2 048 hidden units per layer instead of 1 024. The average WERs are shown in Table 7 over three seeds for both network sizes; the dimensions of the hidden layers are shown in brackets. The performance of all models improved, but the model using speed and volume perturbation improved more than the model only using noise perturbation. The larger capacity benefits the model with more training data, but also the model using only encoded training data. The difference between the small and large network for the *train-musan-e-15* model is almost negligible.

Table 7. WER on development (*dev-noisy-e-5*) and test set (*test-noise-e-5*) using MLP acoustic models with 2 048 hidden units per layer. Average WER (%) and standard error is shown over 3 seeds.

Model	Size	Dev WER	Test WER
Encoded			
train-clean-e (1 024×5)	1	28.06 ± 0.03	29.16 ± 0.12
train-clean-e (2 048×5)	1	26.82 ± 0.08	27.74 ± 0.14
Noise			
train-musan-e-15 (1 024×5)	1	23.30 ± 0.06	24.54 ± 0.22
train-musan-e-15 (2 048×5)	1	23.15 ± 0.10	24.55 ± 0.04
Speed, volume and noise			
train-musan-e-15-s-v (1 024×5)	3	23.80 ± 0.09	24.87 ± 0.08
train-musan-e-15-s-v (2 048×5)	3	**22.81 ± 0.06**	**24.34 ± 0.08**

This experiment confirmed the hypothesis that the MTR models required more capacity to outperform the noise-perturbed network. There is however an increased computational cost when doubling the number of hidden units on top of the three times more training data. This becomes an important trade-off to consider if computational resources are limited.

5.4 Multi-style Training on the SACC Corpus

We now evaluate our findings on the SACC corpus described in Sect. 3.1 to determine if MTR is useful to improve a baseline system in a South African call centre environment. A baseline DNN acoustic model is trained using fMLLR features and 8 kHz unencoded training data using the protocol described in Sect. 4. Another network is trained using only a single set of WAV49-encoded training data. For MTR, we use normal and encoded training data, and apply speed perturbation to the encoded training data only. We did not include volume

Table 8. WER results on dev/test sets for the SACC corpus. Average WER (%) is shown over 3 seeds.

Model	dev	dev-e	test	test-e	held-out test
train	28.41	28.91	33.14	33.43	41.90
train-e	28.40	28.63	33.36	33.04	41.80
MTR	**27.98**	**28.19**	**32.77**	**32.46**	**41.42**

perturbation, because the experiment on the LibriSpeech corpus did not show a consistent improvement when using it. The unencoded training data is included, because we want to jointly perform well on both encoded and unencoded testing data. We did not add any noise, because the training data was already noisy and came from the same call centre as our development and test sets. The results on the development and test sets are shown in Table 8.

The model that used only the encoded training set performed better on encoded test sets, but similar to the baseline model on the *dev* set and worse on the *test* set. The MTR model performed the best across all five datasets with relative WER improvements of between 1.1% and 2.9%.

Since the training data is well matched with the testing data (both sets contain noisy narrow-band audio, the only difference is encoding), MTR does not provide large improvements. It does not hurt performance, and small consistent improvements are possible, but the real advantage of MTR is only observed if there is a significant mismatch.

6 Conclusion

MTR can have a very positive effect on ASR performance, given that the styles are chosen appropriately. Speed and volume perturbation can slightly reduce WER in some scenarios, but are computationally much more expensive. When using a system on narrow-band test sets, training with narrow-band audio is absolutely necessary.

The two styles that gave the best improvement on the WAV49 encoded LibriSpeech corpus was: (1) encoding training data (2) and noise perturbation if there is no noise in the training set. However, if the SNR of the added noise is completely different to the test conditions, it can hurt the system. The best MTR setup outperformed the clean baseline on the test set by 33.5% relative WER, but still performed worse than the noise-matched model by 16.5%.

Only two MTR styles were used on the SACC corpus (encoding and speed perturbation), since the recordings already contained noise and were narrow-band. The relative WER improvement on the test sets were limited, ranging from 1.1% to 2.9% when using MTR. The improvements of MTR are small on this corpus, which we attribute to the training and test data being well matched.

With proper network capacity, MTR does not hurt system performance, even when the data is very well matched. Consistent small improvements are observed in matched datasets, with very large improvements achieved on mismatched datasets.

Acknowledgement. The authors acknowledge the Centre for High Performance Computing (CHPC), South Africa, for providing computational resources used in this research.

References

1. Baker, J.: The DRAGON system - an overview. IEEE Trans. Acoust. Speech Signal Process. **23**(1), 24–29 (1975)
2. Jelinek, F., Bahl, L., Mercer, R.: Design of a linguistic statistical decoder for the recognition of continuous speech. IEEE Trans. Inf. Theory **21**(3), 250–256 (1975)
3. Nassif, A.B., Shahin, I., Attili, I., Azzeh, M., Shaalan, K.: Speech recognition using deep neural networks: a systematic review. IEEE Access **7**, 19143–19165 (2019)
4. Lu, X., Li, S., Fujimoto, M.: Automatic speech recognition. In: Kidawara, Y., Sumita, E., Kawai, H. (eds.) Speech-to-Speech Translation. SCS, pp. 21–38. Springer, Singapore (2020). https://doi.org/10.1007/978-981-15-0595-9_2
5. Ko, T., Peddinti, V., Povey, D., Khudanpur, S.: Audio augmentation for speech recognition. In: Proceedings of INTERSPEECH, pp. 3586–3589. International Speech Communication Association (2015)
6. Lippmann, R., Martin, E., Paul, D.: Multi-style training for robust isolated-word speech recognition. In: 1987 IEEE International Conference on Acoustics, Speech, and Signal Processing, vol. 12, pp. 705–708. IEEE (1987)
7. Li, J., Yu, D., Huang, J.-T., Gong, Y.: Improving wideband speech recognition using mixed-bandwidth training data in CD-DNN-HMM. In: 2012 IEEE Spoken Language Technology Workshop (SLT), pp. 131–136. IEEE (2012)
8. Doulaty, M., Rose, R., Siohan, O.: Automatic optimization of data perturbation distributions for multi-style training in speech recognition. In: 2016 IEEE Spoken Language Technology Workshop (SLT), pp. 21–27. IEEE (2016)
9. Park, D.S., et al.: SpecAugment: a simple data augmentation method for automatic speech recognition. In: Proceedings of INTERSPEECH, pp. 2613–2617. International Speech Communication Association (2019)
10. Szöke, I., Skácel, M., Mošner, L., Paliesek, J., Černocky, J.H.: Building and evaluation of a real room impulse response dataset. IEEE J. Sel. Topics Signal Process. **13**(4), 863–876 (2019)
11. Panayotov, V., Chen, G., Povey, D., Khudanpur, S.: LibriSpeech: an ASR corpus based on public domain audio books. In: 2015 IEEE International Conference on Acoustics, Speech and Signal Processing, pp. 5206–5210. IEEE (2015)
12. Gokay, R., Yalcin, H.: Improving low resource Turkish speech recognition with data augmentation and TTS. In: International Multi-Conference on Systems, Signals & Devices (SSD), pp. 357–360. IEEE (2019)
13. Godfrey, J.J., Holliman, E.C., McDaniel, J.: SWITCHBOARD: telephone speech corpus for research and development. In: 1992 IEEE International Conference on Acoustics, Speech and Signal Processing, vol. 1, pp. 517–520. IEEE (1992)
14. Harper, M.: The automatic speech recognition in reverberant environments (ASpIRE) challenge. In: 2015 IEEE Workshop on Automatic Speech Recognition and Understanding, pp. 547–554. IEEE (2015)

15. Amodei, D., et al.: Deep speech 2: end-to-end speech recognition in English and Mandarin. In: International Conference on Machine Learning, pp. 173–182. PMLR (2016)
16. Siegert, I., Lotz, A.F., Duong, L.L., Wendemuth, A.: Measuring the impact of audio compression on the spectral quality of speech data. Studientexte zur Sprachkommunikation: Elektronische Sprachsignalverarbeitung 2016, pp. 229–236 (2016)
17. EN ETSI. 300 961 v7. 0.2: Digital cellular telecommunications system (Phase 2+); Full rate speech; Transcoding (GSM 06.10 version 7.0. 2 Release 1998) (1999)
18. Van Meggelen, J., Bryant, R., Madsen, L.: Asterisk: The Definitive Guide: Open Source Telephony for the Enterprise. O'Reilly Media, Sebastopol (2019)
19. Xu, Q., et al.: Self-training and pre-training are complementary for speech recognition. In: 2021 IEEE International Conference on Acoustics, Speech and Signal Processing, pp. 3030–3034. IEEE (2021)
20. Dean, D., Sridharan, S., Vogt, R., Mason, M.: The QUT-NOISE-TIMIT corpus for evaluation of voice activity detection algorithms. In: Proceedings of INTERSPEECH, pp. 3110–3113. International Speech Communication Association (2010)
21. Snyder, D., Chen, G., Povey, D.: MUSAN: a music, speech, and noise corpus (2015). arXiv:1510.08484v1
22. Ravanelli, M., Parcollet, T., Bengio, Y.: The Pytorch-Kaldi speech recognition toolkit. In: 2019 IEEE International Conference on Acoustics, Speech and Signal Processing, pp. 6465–6469. IEEE (2019)
23. Gales, M.J.F.: Maximum likelihood linear transformations for HMM-based speech recognition. Comput. Speech Lang. **12**(2), 75–98 (1998)

Canonical and Surface Morphological Segmentation for Nguni Languages

Tumi Moeng, Sheldon Reay, Aaron Daniels, and Jan Buys[✉]

Department of Computer Science, University of Cape Town, Cape Town, South Africa
{MNGTUM007,RYXSHE002,DNLAAR001}@myuct.ac.za, jbuys@cs.uct.ac.za

Abstract. Morphological Segmentation involves decomposing words into morphemes, the smallest meaning-bearing units of language. This is an important NLP task for morphologically-rich agglutinative languages such as the Southern African Nguni language group. In this paper, we investigate supervised and unsupervised models for two variants of morphological segmentation: canonical and surface segmentation. We train sequence-to-sequence models for canonical segmentation, where the underlying morphemes may not be equal to the surface form of the word, and Conditional Random Fields (CRF) for surface segmentation. Transformers outperform LSTMs with attention on canonical segmentation, obtaining an average F1 score of 72.5% across 4 languages. Feature-based CRFs outperform bidirectional LSTM-CRFs to obtain an average of 97.1% F1 on surface segmentation. In the unsupervised setting, an entropy-based approach using a character-level LSTM language model fails to outperform a Morfessor baseline, while on some of the languages neither approach performs much better than a random baseline. We hope that the high accuracy of the supervised segmentation models will help to facilitate the development of better NLP tools for Nguni languages.

Keywords: Natural language processing · Morphology · Nguni languages · Conditional random fields · Sequence to sequence models · Unsupervised learning

1 Introduction

Morphological Segmentation is the task of separating words into their composite *morphemes*, which are the smallest meaning-bearing units of a language [16]. This task is particularly important when applied to *agglutinative* languages, which have words that are composed of aggregating morphemes, generally without making significant alterations to the spelling of the morphemes. Obtaining these morphemes enables analysis that can be applied to further Natural Language Processing (NLP) tasks [5]. For example, breaking a word down to its composite morphemes before translation, or generating those morphemes one at a time, could lead to more accurate translation, especially in a low-resource scenario where limited training data is available. Morphological analysis could

© Springer Nature Switzerland AG 2022
E. Jembere et al. (Eds.): SACAIR 2021, CCIS 1551, pp. 125–139, 2022.
https://doi.org/10.1007/978-3-030-95070-5_9

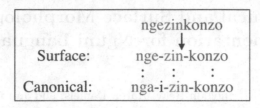

Fig. 1. An isiZulu word with its canonical and surface segmentations.

also be used in the development of tools that could benefit language learners and assist linguists researching these languages.

In this paper, we develop models for morphological segmentation for the Nguni languages, a group of low-resource Southern African languages. We train supervised and unsupervised models for isiNdebele, isiXhosa, isiZulu and siSwati, which are all official languages of South Africa. Morphological segmentation is particularly applicable to Nguni languages because they are agglutinative and written conjunctively [22]. The only previous work we are aware of based on the datasets we use is a rule-based approach [7], which our supervised models outperform substantially. Another work [3] trained a semi-Markov CRF for isiZulu segmentation, but used a different corpus [20].

We investigate supervised sequence-to-sequence models [1,21,23] as well as Conditional Random Fields (CRFs) [11] including neural CRFs [12,13] for segmentation. For sequence-to-sequence models we interpret the process of transforming a word into its segmented form as a character-level sequence transduction problem, which has previously been shown to be effective when applied to other languages [17]. Sequence-to-sequence models are able to deal with input and output sequences of differing lengths, and subsequently to handle *canonical* segmentation, where a morpheme may not be equal to the segment of the word that it corresponds as written [9]. The CRFs on the other hand are suitable for *surface* segmentation, where the morphemes are a pure segmentation of the orthography of the word. Figure 1 shows an example of a word with its canonical and surface segmentations.

Canonical segmentation results show that the bidirectional LSTM with attention outperforms the LSTM without attention, while the Transformer leads to the best performance on all languages, with an average F1 of 72.5%. For surface segmentation, the feature-based CRF obtains an average F1 score of 97.1% across the 4 languages, compared to 94.8% for the Bi-LSTM CRF.

We also implemented an unsupervised entropy-based approach to morphological surface segmentation, based on character-based LSTM language models in the forward and backward directions. We experimented with different entropy-based objective functions for segmentation, but none outperformed the Morfessor baseline. For some of the languages, neither approach perform much better than a random baseline. The code of all our models is available at https://github.com/DarkPr0digy/MORPH_SEGMENT.

2 Background: Morphological Segmentation

2.1 Nguni Languages

The Nguni language group consists of number of languages spoken in Southern Africa. isiZulu, isiXhosa, (Southern) isiNdebele and siSwati are all official languages of South Africa and constitute the majority of Nguni speakers (along with Zimbabwean Northern Ndebele). These languages are closely related to one another, with siSwati being a bit further apart from the rest, and Ndebele's vocabulary being influenced more by the neighbouring Sotho-Tswana languages. All of these languages can be described as low-resource [7]. The Nguni languages are agglutinative and are written conjunctively, meaning that words can be made up of many morphemes written unseparated [22].[1] The meaning of a word is a function of all its morphemes. Therefore extracting the morphemes is essential for syntactic analysis and various forms of further text processing of these languages.

Here is an example of agglutination in isiZulu [2]:

- -phind-a: "repeat"
- -phind-*is*-a: "cause to repeat"
- -phind-*el*-*el*-a: "repeat again and again"

2.2 Morphological Segmentation

We distinguish two ways in which a word w can be segmented, *surface segmentation* and *canonical segmentation* [4]:

- **Surface segmentation:** w is segmented into a sequence of substrings, which when concatenated will result in w.
- **Canonical segmentation:** w is analyzed as a sequence of canonical morphemes representing the underlying forms of the morphemes, which may differ from their orthographic manifestation.

The canonical segments correspond to the underlying morphemes used by linguists, and may be more informative for downstream analysis than pure surface segmentation [4].

2.3 Data

The morphological annotations used in this paper come from the Annotated Text Corpora from the National Center for Human Technology (NCHLT) [7].[2] We use the isiNdebele, isiXhosa, isiZulu and siSwati corpora that are annotated with canonical morphological segmentations. The morphemes are also labelled with

---

[1] Tho Sotho Tswana languages, tho othor major South African language group, are written *disjunctively*: morphemes are generally written as separate words, despite the languages being agglutinative.

[2] Datasets are available at https://repo.sadilar.org/handle/20.500.12185/7.

Table 1. Sizes of the morphological segmentation datasets (number of words) after preprocessing.

Language	Train	Dev	Test
isiZulu	17 778	1 777	3 298
isiXhosa	16 879	1 688	3 004
isiNdebele	12 929	1 119	2 553
siSwati	13 278	1 080	1 347

their grammatical functions, but in this paper we only consider the segmentation task and not the labelling task.

The original annotation for the isiZulu word *ngezinkonzo* is as follows, where the morpheme labels are given in square brackets:

`[RelConc]-nga[NPre]-i[NPrePre]-zin[BPre]-konzo[NStem]`

The data consists of annotated running text. We process the data to extract a set of annotated words. In our setup words are segmented independent of their context as an orthographic word has multiple morphological analyses relatively rarely. We exclude punctuation, numbers, and words that are unsegmented in the annotations (as many of them are actually unannotated or are loan words). The data is given with a training and test split. We ensure that there is no overlap between the training and test sets by removing all words appearing in both texts from the training data. This ensures that we are evaluating the ability of the models to generalize to unseen words. We split a development set from the training set in the same manner: The size of the dev set is 10% of the training set before removing overlapping words. The processed dataset sizes are given in Table 1.

2.4   Generating Surface Segmentations

We map the canonical segmentation annotations heuristically to corresponding surface segmentations. We first check if the de-segmented canonical form is the same as the orthographic word, in which case the canonical and surface segmentations are equivalent. Otherwise, we compute the sequence of minimal edit operations from the de-segmented canonical form to the orthographic word, based on the Levenshtein distance between the forms. The operations are constrained so that each character in the input word corresponds to a character in the de-segmented canonical form. For example, in Fig. 1, the edit operations are to delete the single-character morpheme "i" and to replace the first "a" with "e". Finally, the sequence of edit operations is processed to align the canonical segments to the surface segments. This enables detecting the deletion of canonical segments, and mapping the morpheme boundaries in the canonical form to the orthography to create the surface segmentation.

We computed a number of statistics to determine the efficacy of the method for obtaining surface segmentations. On average over all four languages, 45% of the words' canonical segmentations differ from their surface segmentations. Of all the edit operations, 38.83% of the operations were replacement operations, and the remaining 61.17% were deletion operations. Finally, of all the segments generated in the surface form, 60.26% of the segments are equal to the corresponding morpheme in the canonical form.

2.5   Evaluation

The segmentation models are evaluated using precision, recall and F1 score of the morphemes identified for each word, compared to those in the annotated segmentation. We follow [4] in treating the segmentation as a set of morphemes for evaluation purposes and computing the micro-F1 over the test set. This contrast to the traditional approach to evaluating morphological segmentation with morpheme boundary identification accuracy. That method is not applicable to canonical segmentation, and we believe that basing the evaluation directly on morpheme identification is a better reflection of accuracy on this task.

3   Canonical Segmentation with Sequence-to-Sequence Models

We apply a Recurrent Neural Network (RNN) encoder-decoder model with attention [1] as well as an encoder-decoder Transformer model [23] to the task of canonical morphological segmentation. The task is formulated as transducing the given word's character sequence to an output character sequence consisting of the canonical form of the word together with the segment boundaries.

3.1   BiLSTM with Attention

In an RNN-based encoder-decoder [21] the encoder is an RNN which processes the input sequence x sequentially, updating the hidden state of the RNN after reading each input element. The decoder is another RNN which uses the final encoder hidden state as its initial hidden state to generate the output sequence. At each time step the previous output generated by the decoder is fed back into the RNN, which then produces the next output symbol, until a complete output sequence has been generated. We use RNNs with Long-Short-Term-Memory (LSTM) cells [8] to avoid vanishing or exploding gradients.

The encoder can be extended to be bidirectional [18], encoding the sequence using separate forward and backward LSTMs. For each input element x_j, the encoder produces hidden layers $\overrightarrow{h_j}$ and $\overleftarrow{h_j}$ using a bidirectional RNN. The concatenation of these, h_j, can be seen as a contextual representation of x_j.

To overcome the limitations of using a single fixed context vector to encode the entire input sequence, an attention mechanism can be used, which enables the model to dynamically determine which parts of the input to focus on as the sequence is traversed [1]. The attention mechanism computes an alignment score e_{ij} between the input at position j and the output at position i, using a feed-forward network a,

$$e_{ij} = a(s_{i-1}, h_j), \tag{1}$$

where s_{i-1} is the output from the previous decoder step and h_j is the encoder representation at time step j. The alignment scores are normalized with the softmax function, and the context vector c_i at decoder time step i is computed as a weighted average of the encoder representations h_j:

$$c_i = \sum_{j=1}^{T_x} \text{softmax}_j(e_{ij}) h_j. \tag{2}$$

The decoder is therefore using the attention mechanism to dynamically calculate a context vector representation of the input sequence rather than using the (fixed) final encoder hidden state.

3.2 Transformer

The Transformer is a sequence model which does not use recurrence and is instead based on the concept of self-attention [23]. In the encoder-decoder framework, the transformer encoder uses multi-headed attention to calculate self-attention over the input sequence. The decoder uses two multi-headed attention blocks, over itself and over the encoder. Masking is used to prevent the first block from calculating self-attention over decoder positions which follow the current sequence position. A Transformer block consists of alternating multi-headed self-attention and feed-forward layers. Self-attention can be calculated in parallel, increasing computational efficiency. Due to the lack of recurrence, positional embeddings are used to encode the order of sequence elements in the encoder and the decoder.

3.3 Experimental Setup

The biLSTM with attention was implemented by adapting an existing PyTorch codebase to support character-level transduction and a bidirectional encoder.[3] The Transformer was implemented in the same code base. As the model generates an output segmentation, it generates "-" to indicate a morpheme boundary. As a baseline we use an encoder-decoder without attention. One model is trained (independently) for each language.

Based on hyperparameter tuning, the batch size was set at 32 or 64 for both the Transformer and the biLSTM with Attention models. The best learning rates were 0.0001 for the biLSTM with attention, and 0.0005 for the Transformer. The hidden dimension for both models was set at 256, and dropout was applied with a rate of 0.3. The biLSTM with attention used 2 layers. Adam [10] was found to be a better optimizer than Stochastic Gradient Descent for both models.

---

[3] https://github.com/bentrevett/pytorch-seq2seq.

Table 2. Canonical segmentation results. The Precision (P), Recall (R) and F1 Scores (F1) are given as percentages. The top line for each model reports the average over the 4 languages. For the rule-based systems we report the upper bound on accuracy among the possible segmentations produced. The Transformer performs best across all languages and metrics.

Model	P	R	F1
Rule-based	60.26	43.97	50.72
isiZulu	63.21	47.95	54.42
isiXhosa	59.85	48.88	53.81
isiNdebele	65.81	43.29	52.22
siSwati	52.16	35.76	42.43
LSTM	64.78	56.92	60.59
isiZulu	68.72	60.25	64.20
isiXhosa	65.94	57.44	61.40
isiNdebele	61.90	53.89	57.61
siSwati	62.54	56.10	59.15
BiLSTM+Att	68.25	62.81	65.41
isiZulu	68.58	62.45	65.37
isiXhosa	70.06	62.86	66.26
isiNdebele	64.90	59.67	62.18
siSwati	69.45	66.25	67.82
Transformer	75.58	69.76	**72.54**
isiZulu	77.34	71.04	**74.06**
isiXhosa	75.76	68.36	**71.87**
isiNdebele	73.14	66.67	**69.76**
siSwati	76.07	72.96	**74.48**

In order to compare with previous work, we ran the NCHLT rule-based segmenters [7], which used the same (original) training corpus for model development, on our test set.[4] The systems produce a set of multiple possible segmentations for some words; we compute an upper bound on performance by choosing the highest-scoring segmentation where multiple options are given.

3.4 Results

Table 2 shows the canonical segmentation performance of each model on each language. Previous work [7] reported F1 scores of 82% to 85% for the NCHLT rule-based model on the Nguni languages. However, they do not fully explain their experimental setup and if or how they disambiguate between multiple system

---

[4] Available at https://repo.sadilar.org/handle/20.500.12185/7/discover?filtertype=ty pe\&filter_relational_operator=equals\&filter=Modules.

Table 3. Sample model outputs for canonical segmentation, compared to the target (reference) segmentation.

Model	Output
Baseline	na-u-kuenza
BiLSTM+Attention	na-u-ku-enza
Transformer	na-u-ku-enz-a
Target	**na-u-ku-enz-a**

outputs. The rule-based systems perform substantially worse than any of our models, despite the fact that we are reporting an upper bound on its performance. The gap is narrower on precision than on recall. The rule-based system has higher precision than the LSTM-based model on isiNdebele, but everywhere else our models perform better. The rule-based systems produce canonical segmentations, but they produce segmentations matching the surface form for 92.7% of words in the test set (averaged over the 4 languages), while in the gold annotations only 73.6% have segmentations whose morphemes are equal to their surface forms.

The BiLSTM+Attention model performs better than the encoder-decoder LSTM for all four languages, with an average increase in F1 Score by 4.82%. siSwati, which had an average word length of 7 in the dataset (compared to 9 for the other three languages), achieved the highest increase out of all four languages with an increase of 8.67%.

The Transformer model showed the best results across all languages and metrics. It outperformed the baseline LSTM model by 11.95%, and the BiLSTM+Attention model by 7.13%. The F1 score for isiZulu improved by 9.7% points from 65.37% to 74.06%. This shows the model's ability to learn features within the low resource language. The Transformer performed well within the low resource environment, and more data would likely improve its performance even further. The Transformer's performance was also the most consistent across languages: Its F1 scores have the lowest standard deviation among the three models. The Transformer results shows that relying solely on attention is a feasible approach for morphological segmentation. Table 3 shows sample outputs from all three models compared to the target output.

Figure 2 shows two of the eight encoder-to-decoder attention heads of the Transformer model. The attention matrices show that the attention mechanism is able to align input segments to the correct corresponding output morphemes; this can be seen consistently across attention heads.

The results show that in a low-resource setting the models are able to learn and extract features from the languages at a satisfactory level. Nevertheless, the size of the datasets offers the best explanation of why the models didn't achieve higher accuracies. isiNdebele has the smallest training set, as well as the lowest performance across all the models. siSwati also has a smaller dataset, but the words are shorter and consequently there are less segments, which makes the problem simpler. Consequently, the attention-based models' highest performance

 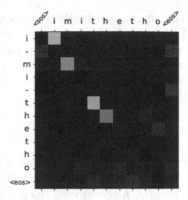

Fig. 2. Attention distributions of two of the Transformer's attention heads.

is on the siSwati dataset. In contrast, the rule-based model and the baseline LSTM perform relatively worse on siSwati.

4   Surface Segmentation with Conditional Random Fields

4.1   CRFs

Conditional Random Fields (CRFs) are a class of discriminative, globally normalized, probabilistic sequence labelling models [11]. We apply traditional feature-based (log-linear) CRFs as well as neural CRFs based on bidirectional LSTMs to the task of surface morphological segmentation. A CRF takes a sequence X as input and estimates the probability distribution $p(Y|X)$, where Y is a sequence of the same length as X. Every label y_i in Y corresponds to an input token x_i.

For morphological segmentation, the input is the word, represented as a character sequence, and the output is a label sequence encoding the segmentation. The possible labels are B, M, E, and S, representing, respectively, whether the character is the start of a new morpheme, a part of the current morpheme, the end of the current morpheme, or a single length morpheme.

A CRF computes a feature score $s(X, y_i, y_{i+1})$ for each position i. That is, it scores every possible assignment of a pair of labels in adjacent positions, so that the label probabilities are correlated with each other and not independent. The total unnormalized score that the CRF assigns to a given label sequence Y is

$$S(X, Y) = \sum_{i=0}^{n-1} s(X, y_i, y_{i+1}).$$ (3)

The probability can then be computed by normalizing the score over $Y^{|X|}$, the set of all possible label sequences of the same length as X:

$$p(Y|X) = \frac{e^{S(X,Y)}}{\sum_{\widetilde{Y} \in Y^{|X|}} e^{S(X,\widetilde{Y})}}.$$ (4)

The summation needs to be computed efficiently during training: This can be done using dynamic programming with the forward algorithm. During testing, the model makes use of a related dynamic programming algorithm, Viterbi Algorithm, to calculate the highest scoring label sequence for a given input. The run-time of the dynamic program is quadratic in the number of possible labels (but here that is a small set).

4.2   BiLSTM CRFs

A traditional CRF is a log-linear model with a large number of manually-designed sparse, usually binary-valued, features. The model learns a weight for each feature. Alternatively, the scoring function can also be parameterized using neural networks, which can learn the features instead. We use a bidirectional LSTM [8] to encode the input sequence. Our BiLSTM CRF follows that of previous work on neural sequence labelling [12,13].

To implement the CRF scoring function, the BiLSTM output is represented as an n by k matrix P, where n is the number of words in the sequence and k is the number of labels in the label alphabet. Each element R_{ij} represents the (unnormalized) score of assigning label $y_i = j$ (as an index into the label vocabulary) to x_i. The CRF score is defined as

$$s\left(X, y_i, y_{i+1}\right) = R_{i,y_i} + A_{y_i,y_{i+1}}, \tag{5}$$

where A is a learned square matrix of dimension $L + 2$, where L is the number of labels in the label alphabet, and the 2 added labels represent the start and the end of the sequence [12].

4.3   Implementation

Our implementation of the feature-based CRF uses the `sklearn-crfsuite` library.[5] The features used are character n-grams with n in the range 0 to 6, whether the character is a vowel or a consonant, and whether the character is uppercase or lowercase. We adapt an existing BiLSTM CRF implementation suited to the segmentation task.[6] For the feature-based CRF we tuned the choice of features, epsilon (which determines the convergence condition), and the number of training iterations. The best hyperparameters were an epsilon of 1e−7 and a maximum of 160 training iterations. For the BiLSTM CRF we tuned the number of training epochs and the learning rate. The best models were trained for 20 epochs, with a learning rate of 9e−4 for isiXhosa and isiZulu, and 4e−4 for isiNedebele and siSwati.

---

[5] https://github.com/TeamHG-Memex/sklearn-crfsuite.
[6] https://github.com/jidasheng/bi-lstm-crf.

Table 4. Results for the surface segmentation task with the feature-based and bidirectional LSTM CRFs. The feature-based CRF performs best across all languages and metrics.

Language	Feature CRF			BiLSTM CRF		
	P	R	F1	P	R	F1
isiZulu	97.88	96.82	**97.35**	96.64	96.64	96.64
isiXhosa	97.16	97.13	**97.14**	94.88	95.61	95.24
isiNdebele	97.94	96.62	**97.27**	96.59	96.21	96.40
siSwati	97.17	96.40	**96.78**	90.59	91.48	91.03
Average	97.54	96.74	**97.14**	94.68	94.99	94.83

4.4 Results

Table 4 shows the results of the two CRF models on the task of surface segmentation. The feature-based CRF yielded very high performance in the surface segmentation task with an average F1 score of 97.13%. Surprisingly, the performance of the BiLSTM CRF is more than 3% lower, with an average F1 score of 93.81% across the four languages. The gap is substantially larger on SiSwati than on the other languages, with an F1 score of about 5% lower. One potential reason for the lower performance of the BiLSTM CRF is the small size of the dataset. In contrast to the sequence-to-sequence models, the performance drops on SiSwati rather than on isiNdebele, suggesting that it may be harder to tune the CRF on short sequences than the sequence-to-sequence models.

While not directly comparable, [3] reported 90.16% F1 for surface segmentation of isiZulu using a semi-Markov CRF on the Ukwabelana corpus. However, in addition to using a different corpus, they performed semi-supervised training using only 1 000 annotated training examples (together with a larger unannotated corpus). For future work, we'd like to investigate further to what extend the performance gap between canonical and surface segmentation is due to the models compared to the greater inherent difficulty of the canonical segmentation task.

5 Unsupervised Segmentation

Unsupervised segmentation is important for low-resource languages as morphological annotations are unavailable for most of them. We use Morfessor [6], a widely-used model for unsupervised segmentation, to benchmark unsupervised segmentation on these datasets, following the same preprocessing and evaluation setup as for supervised surface segmentation. In particular, we use the Morfessor-Baseline model, which uses a segmentation optimization criteria based on Minimal Description Length. We compare this to a random segmentation baseline which inserts segment boundaries at random positions in a word, as a way to check whether the unsupervised models are learning anything useful. We also implemented an entropy-based model, following previous work on unsupervised segmentation of isiXhosa [14, 15].

5.1 Entropy-Based Model

Entropy [19] measures the amount of information produced by an event or process. The conditional entropy of x_i in a sequence $x_{1:i}$ for a given probability model $p(x|x_{1:i-1})$ can be defined as

$$-\sum_{\tilde{x}\in V} p(\tilde{x}|x_{1:i-1}) \log p(\tilde{x}|x_{1:i-1}), \tag{6}$$

where V is the set of possible values of sequence element x.

The intuition behind entropy-based morphological segmentation is that inside a morpheme, each consecutive character will be less surprising (so have a lower entropy) than the previous one, while at the start of a new morpheme the entropy will increase as the character is less predictable.

Previous work used smoothed character n-gram language models to estimate the entropy [14, 15]. Here we use a character-level LSTM language model instead that encodes the entire word, learning to estimate the probabilities of successive characters. We trained language models in both forward (left-to-right) and backward directions. These models are used to obtain the left and right entropies of words, respectively. We trained 2-layer LSTMs with hidden state size of 200, dropout rate 0.2, and SGD with an initial learning rate of 20 that is decreased during training.

We experimented with a number of different objective functions that use the entropies to decide where to segment a word. We found that the best strategy was to consider the sum of left and right entropies at each character position and to insert a segment boundary if the sum exceeds experimentally determined constants. We refer to this model as *Constant Entropy*. Constants 4, 3, 12 and 2.5 were used for isiNdebele, siSwati, isiXhosa and isiZulu, respectively.

We also experimented with inserting a segment boundary based on whether the entropy increases between adjacent positions, as well as an objective that compares the sum of the left and right entropies to the mean over all the entropies in the word to perform relatively thresholding. These are similar to objective functions proposed by [15]. However, in our experiments the constant entropy objective performed substantially better than either of those approaches.

5.2 Results

The results for the unsupervised models are given in Table 5. Our entropy-based models do not outperform the Morfessor baseline. The entropy-based approach outperforms the random baseline by 7.22% on average, but was 1.96% lower than Morfessor.

The results suggest that there are substantial structural differences between the languages. In particular, both models perform substantially better on siSwati

Table 5. Precision (P), Recall (R) and F1 scores for unsupervised morphological segmentation. The best performing model on each language and metric is indicated in bold.

Language	Random			Morfessor			Constant entropy		
	P	R	F1	P	R	F1	P	R	F1
isiZulu	24.15	14.97	18.48	20.37	**23.19**	**21.69**	**28.74**	14.20	19.01
isiXhosa	23.23	14.32	17.72	**27.21**	**29.04**	**28.10**	22.79	15.41	18.38
isiNdebele	25.91	15.27	19.22	20.60	**21.36**	**20.97**	**34.19**	14.81	20.67
siSwati	26.03	14.49	18.62	**44.05**	36.67	40.02	36.22	**58.85**	**44.85**
Average	24.83	14.76	18.51	28.06	**27.57**	**27.69**	**30.49**	25.82	25.73

than on the other languages. This could partly be explained by siSwati words having less segments on average than the other languages. The entropy-based model outperforms Morfessor on siSwati, with a particularly high recall of 58.8%. Both models perform only slightly above the random baseline for isiNdebele and isiZulu. For isiXhosa, the entropy model has similarly low performance, while Morfessor does 10% better, indicating that it was able to learn more structure of the language than our model.

Previous work [14,15] also found that entropy-based models do not outperform Morfessor, although theirs were based on n-gram language models instead of LSTMs. They reported scores of up to 77% boundary identification accuracy on the same test set, but preprocessed differently. We obtained similar results when evaluating Morfessor using that metric.

6 Conclusions

We developed supervised models for surface and canonical segmentation, as well as an unsupervised segmentation model, for 4 Nguni languages. Sequence-to-sequence models outperformed a rule-based baseline for canonical segmentation by a large margin, with Transformers obtaining the highest performance. The feature-based CRF obtained very high accuracies on the surface segmentation task, with an average F1 score of 97.1%, outperforming the Bi-LSTM CRF.

The strong supervised results opens new avenues to apply models for morphological segmentation to downstream language processing tasks for Nguni languages. For future work, performance could possibly be improved further through semi-supervised training, as sequence-to-sequence models usually benefit when trained on larger datasets. Multilingual training could also be investigated, due to the similarities between the languages.

The performance of all the unsupervised models are substantially lower than the supervised models. We hypothesize that substantially different models will be required to make progress in unsupervised morphological segmentation.

Acknowledgements. This work is based on research supported in part by the National Research Foundation of South Africa (Grant Number: 129850) and the South African Centre for High Performance Computing. We thank Zola Mahlaza for valuable feedback, and Francois Meyer for running an additional baseline.

References

1. Bahdanau, D., Cho, K., Bengio, Y.: Neural machine translation by jointly learning to align and translate. In: International Conference on Learning Representations (2015)
2. Bosch, S.E., Pretorius, L.: A computational approach to Zulu verb morphology within the context of lexical semantics. Lexikos **27**, 152–182 (2017). http://www. scielo.org.za/scielo.php?script=sci_arttext&pid=S2224-00392017000100007& nrm=iso
3. Cotterell, R., Müller, T., Fraser, A., Schütze, H.: Labeled morphological segmentation with semi-Markov models. In: Proceedings of the Nineteenth Conference on Computational Natural Language Learning, pp. 164–174. Association for Computational Linguistics, Beijing (2015). https://doi.org/10.18653/v1/K15-1017. https://www.aclweb.org/anthology/K15-1017
4. Cotterell, R., Vieira, T., Schütze, H.: A joint model of orthography and morphological segmentation. In: Proceedings of the 2016 Conference of the North American Chapter of the Association for Computational Linguistics: Human Language Technologies, pp. 664–669. Association for Computational Linguistics, San Diego (2016). https://doi.org/10.18653/v1/N16-1080. https://www.aclweb. org/anthology/N16-1080
5. Creutz, M., et al.: Morph-based speech recognition and modeling of out-of-vocabulary words across languages. ACM Trans. Speech Lang. Process. (TSLP) **5**(1), 1–29 (2007)
6. Creutz, M., Lagus, K.: Unsupervised models for morpheme segmentation and morphology learning. ACM Trans. Speech Lang. Process. **4**(1), 1–34 (2007). https:// doi.org/10.1145/1187415.1187418
7. Eiselen, R., Puttkammer, M.: Developing text resources for ten South African languages. In: Proceedings of the Ninth International Conference on Language Resources and Evaluation (LREC-2014), pp. 3698–3703. European Languages Resources Association (ELRA), Reykjavik (2014). http://www.lrec-conf. org/proceedings/lrec2014/pdf/1151_Paper.pdf
8. Hochreiter, S., Schmidhuber, J.: Long short-term memory. Neural Comput. **9**(8), 1735–1780 (1997)
9. Kann, K., Cotterell, R., Schütze, H.: Neural morphological analysis: encoding-decoding canonical segments. In: Proceedings of the 2016 Conference on Empirical Methods in Natural Language Processing, pp. 961–967. Association for Computational Linguistics, Austin (2016). https://doi.org/10.18653/v1/D16-1097. https:// www.aclweb.org/anthology/D16-1097
10. Kingma, D.P., Ba, J.: Adam: a method for stochastic optimization. arXiv preprint arXiv:1412.6980 (2017)
11. Lafferty, J.D., McCallum, A., Pereira, F.C.N.: Conditional random fields: probabilistic models for segmenting and labeling sequence data. In: Proceedings of the Eighteenth International Conference on Machine Learning, ICML 2001, pp. 282–289. Morgan Kaufmann Publishers Inc., San Francisco (2001)

12. Lample, G., Ballesteros, M., Subramanian, S., Kawakami, K., Dyer, C.: Neural architectures for named entity recognition. In: Proceedings of the 2016 Conference of the North American Chapter of the Association for Computational Linguistics: Human Language Technologies, pp. 260–270. Association for Computational Linguistics, San Diego (2016). https://doi.org/10.18653/v1/N16-1030. https://www.aclweb.org/anthology/N16-1030

13. Ma, X., Hovy, E.: End-to-end sequence labeling via bi-directional LSTM-CNNs-CRF. In: Proceedings of the 54th Annual Meeting of the Association for Computational Linguistics (Volume 1: Long Papers), pp. 1064–1074. Association for Computational Linguistics, Berlin (2016). https://doi.org/10.18653/v1/P16-1101. https://www.aclweb.org/anthology/P16-1101

14. Mzamo, L., Helberg, A., Bosch, S.: Evaluation of combined bi-directional branching entropy language models for morphological segmentation of isiXhosa. In: South African Forum of Artificial Intelligence Research, pp. 77–89 (2019)

15. Mzamo, L., Helberg, A., Bosch, S.: Towards an unsupervised morphological segmenter for isiXhosa. In: SAUPEC/RobMech/PRASA, pp. 166–170 (2019)

16. Ruokolainen, T., Kohonen, O., Virpioja, S., Kurimo, M.: Supervised morphological segmentation in a low-resource learning setting using conditional random fields. In: Proceedings of the Seventeenth Conference on Computational Natural Language Learning, pp. 29–37. Association for Computational Linguistics, Sofia (2013). https://www.aclweb.org/anthology/W13-3504

17. Ruzsics, T., Samardžić, T.: Neural sequence-to-sequence learning of internal word structure. In: Proceedings of the 21st Conference on Computational Natural Language Learning (CoNLL 2017), pp. 184–194. Association for Computational Linguistics, Vancouver (2017). https://doi.org/10.18653/v1/K17-1020. https://www.aclweb.org/anthology/K17-1020

18. Schuster, M., Paliwal, K.K.: Bidirectional recurrent neural networks. IEEE Trans. Sig. Process. 45(11), 2673–2681 (1997)

19. Shannon, C.E.: A mathematical theory of communication. Bell Syst. Tech. J. 27(3), 379–423 (1948). https://doi.org/10.1002/j.1538-7305.1948.tb01338.x

20. Spiegler, S., van der Spuy, A., Flach, P.A.: Ukwabelana - an open-source morphological Zulu corpus. In: Proceedings of the 23rd International Conference on Computational Linguistics (Coling 2010), pp. 1020–1028. Coling 2010 Organizing Committee, Beijing (2010). https://www.aclweb.org/anthology/C10-1115

21. Sutskever, I., Vinyals, O., Le, Q.V.: Sequence to sequence learning with neural networks. In: Advances in Neural Information Processing Systems, pp. 3104–3112 (2014)

22. Taljard, E., Bosch, S.E.: A comparison of approaches to word class tagging: disjunctively vs. conjunctively written Bantu languages. Nord. J. Afr. Stud. 15(4), 428–442 (2006)

23. Vaswani, A., et al.: Attention is all you need. In: Advances in Neural Information Processing Systems, pp. 5998–6008 (2017)

Exploring Layerwise Decision Making in DNNs

Coenraad Mouton[1,2]([envelope]) [ORCID] and Marelie H. Davel[1] [ORCID]

[1] Faculty of Engineering, North-West University, South Africa and CAIR, Potchefstroom, South Africa
[2] South African National Space Agency (SANSA), Pretoria, South Africa
http://engineering.nwu.ac.za/must

Abstract. While deep neural networks (DNNs) have become a standard architecture for many machine learning tasks, their internal decision-making process and general interpretability is still poorly understood. Conversely, common decision trees are easily interpretable and theoretically well understood. We show that by encoding the discrete sample activation values of nodes as a binary representation, we are able to extract a decision tree explaining the classification procedure of each layer in a ReLU-activated multilayer perceptron (MLP). We then combine these decision trees with existing feature attribution techniques in order to produce an interpretation of each layer of a model. Finally, we provide an analysis of the generated interpretations, the behaviour of the binary encodings and how these relate to sample groupings created during the training process of the neural network.

Keywords: Deep neural networks · Decision trees · Interpretability · Rule extraction · Binary encodings

1 Introduction

Deep Neural Networks (DNNs) have become the standard, state-of-the-art solution to many machine learning tasks. However, the underlying decision-making process is still considered hidden (often referred to as a "black box"), and does not directly offer any human-interpretable insight. To rectify this lack of transparency, several interpretability methods have been developed. The most popular of these are feature attribution methods, which provide an indication of the relevance of certain input features to the output of the model, such as Deep Learning Important FeaTures (DeepLIFT) [9], Layer-wise Relevance Propagation (LRP) [1], and SHapley Additive exPlanations (SHAP) [7].

While certainly useful, these techniques tend to focus on understanding the way in which a machine learning model links inputs to outputs when considering the model as a whole. We use a different approach, and consider the internal structures created at each individual layer of a DNN. More specifically, we make use of the node activation values at each layer and encode this as a binary string

© Springer Nature Switzerland AG 2022
E. Jembere et al. (Eds.): SACAIR 2021, CCIS 1551, pp. 140–155, 2022.
https://doi.org/10.1007/978-3-030-95070-5_10

representing each training sample. We then use these discrete binary encodings to derive a decision tree from each layer in a ReLU-activated multilayer perceptron (MLP). As opposed to neural networks, decision trees provide interpretable structures which inherently explain their internal decision making. By combining the derived decision trees with a simple mean-sample visualization method, we are able to explore the model's internal classification procedure.

The layout of the paper is as follows: In Sect. 2 we provide background on (1) binary encodings and how they are obtained from each layer in a neural network and (2) existing decision tree induction methods applied to neural networks. Following this, in Sect. 3, we study the behaviour of the binary encodings by measuring the number of unique and duplicate encodings at several layers for different architectures and data sets. In Sect. 4 we introduce our algorithm for decision tree induction, before measuring the accuracy and size of the derived decision trees. Finally, in Sect. 5 we visualize these decision trees and shed light on the internal classification mechanisms underlying the neural network.

2   Background

In this section we first discuss binary encodings and how they are derived from a neural network, before discussing other existing methods of decision tree induction.

2.1   Nodes as Binary Classifiers

Davel et al. [3] have shown that in feedforward ReLU-activated neural networks, each node in any given layer can be viewed as a binary classifier, given that a certain node only results in an activation value greater than 0 for a subset of the training samples. This is due to the fact that for certain samples the node passes through no information, and for others the pre-activation value is passed through as is. We use the terms "ON" to refer to cases where the node output is greater than zero, and "OFF" otherwise. Through the ON and OFF state of each node, the training samples are partitioned into their respective classes, and thus each hidden layer can be viewed as the combination of several cooperating classifiers.

In the same work, the discrete dynamics of ReLU-activated MLPs was further explored, by encoding the activation values of each layer as a string of binary activation values indicating the ON or OFF state of each node for a given sample. The resulting string is referred to as a "binary encoding", or simply "encoding", the terminology we also use. They then demonstrated that in the shallower layers of the network, virtually each sample in a given training set has its own unique encoding. In deeper layers however, the encodings become highly class specific, meaning most samples of the same class share an encoding. This behaviour was shown to be reproducible over many different architectures and two separate data sets.

In Sect. 3.1 we verify these findings using our own networks and measurements, and then further explore this phenomenon in Sect. 3.2.

2.2 Decision Tree Induction

Several other methods have been developed for extracting decision trees from neural networks, with varying levels of success. Sato and Tsukimoto [8] introduced the CRED (Continuous/discrete Rule Extractor via Decision tree induction) algorithm, which extracts decision trees using the continuous activation values of nodes in a neural network. However, this algorithm is only applicable to networks consisting of a single hidden layer [4]. Zilke et al. [11] extended the CRED algorithm to networks of multiple hidden layers, but due to its computational complexity it is not suitable for tasks with a large number of input features (such as image classification).

These methods extend the decision tree extraction to the input features, and furthermore consider the neural network in its entirety. Conversely, we consider each hidden layer as a separate classifier, and opt to relate each layer's decision tree to the input features through a heatmap based method. This allows each decision tree to remain small in size, and thus easily interpretable, and furthermore allows us to explain each layer individually.

3 The Behaviour of Binary Encodings

In this section we explore the phenomenon of binary encodings, and how they relate to sample-groupings in a neural network.

3.1 Unique Encodings

To confirm the findings of Davel et al. [3], and provide an understanding of the behaviour of binary encodings at different layers of a network, we devise the following experiment: We train 10 ReLU-activated MLPs on the MNIST data set [6], with a depth of 1 to 10 hidden layers, where each layer has a width of 100. A bias node is added to the first layer only[1]. We then measure the number of unique binary encodings for all 55,000 training samples at each individual layer for all 10 networks. We repeat this experiment using a layer width of 20; and do the same for the Fashion-MNIST data set (FMNIST) [10] with layer widths of 100 and 40. The results for all four sets of networks are shown in Fig. 1. We refer to these networks by their dataset and width, namely: MNIST-100, FMNIST-100, MNIST-20, and FMNIST-40.

We use a training set size of 55,000 samples (where a 'sample' is a single image), while 5,000 separate samples are used for validation. Each data set has a separate test set of 10,000 samples. All networks are trained to 100% train accuracy. (We do not employ early stopping.) We use the Adam optimizer [5], with

---

[1] This simplifies theoretical analysis without compromising performance of a ReLU-activated MLP [3].

cross-entropy as loss function and perform learning rate decay: every *step_size* epochs the learning rate is multiplied by a decay constant *gamma*. Standard hyperparameter settings are used (batch size of 128, no regularisation), except for the initial learning rate, decay step size, and decay gamma which are optimized on the validation set to ensure interpolation, as shown in Table 1, along with the range of test set accuracy for each set of models.

Table 1. Training hyperparameters and accuracy for MNIST and FMNIST models with 1 to 10 hidden layers and varying widths

Data set	Width	Learning rate	Decay gamma	Decay step size	Train accuracy (%)	Test accuracy (%)
MNIST	100	0.001	0.990	5	100.00	97.82 to 98.19
FMNIST	100	0.001	0.990	5	100.00	87.96 to 89.10
MNIST	20	0.002	0.500	100	100.00	94.62 to 96.12
FMNIST	40	0.002	0.850	50	100.00	85.23 to 86.70

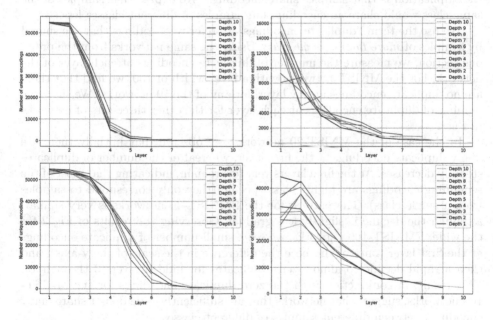

Fig. 1. Number of unique encodings per layer for MNIST and FMNIST networks with 1 to 10 hidden layers. Top left: MNIST-100. Top right: MNIST-20. Bottom left: FMNIST-100. Bottom right: FMNIST-40

Observing the MNIST and FMNIST networks with a layer width of 100 in Fig. 1, a clear pattern emerges. Initially, in the first layer, nearly every sample has its own unique encoding, as we find the number of unique encodings to be close to the total number of samples in the training set (55,000 samples) for all the networks. As the depth increases, we observe a sharp decline, indicating that encodings are shared by many samples. Finally, for the deeper networks, we observe that very few encodings remain in the last few hidden layers, implying that there are only one or two encodings shared by all the samples of a class. This is concurrent with the observations initially made by Davel et al. [3].

For the narrower networks (MNIST-20 and FMNIST-40) the general pattern appears to be similar, except that the initial number of unique encodings in the first layers is much lower (note the difference in scale of the y-axis). This seems to indicate that by decreasing the width, the network is forced to share encodings among samples, even in the first layer.

In the following section we study the behaviour of these encodings more closely.

3.2   Duplicate Encodings

Given that the number of encodings decreases as the network depth increases, the implication is that samples share encodings. We expect that samples of the same class would share an encoding, but samples of different classes less so.

We use the term "duplicate encodings" to refer to encodings that are shared by samples of *more than a single class*. Using the same networks from the previous section, we measure the number of duplicate encodings at each layer of the network. For the MNIST networks with a layer width of 100, we find that there are no duplicate encodings at any layer, for any of the 10 networks. We show the number of duplicate encodings at each layer for the other three sets of networks in Fig. 2.

In the case of the MNIST-20 networks, we observe that initially there are many duplicate encodings at the first layer, whereafter the number of duplicates steadily decreases. At the final layers very few remain, indicating that most of the remaining encodings are highly class specific (they only correspond to samples from a single class). The pattern for the FMNIST-40 networks is very similar, although the decline is slightly less gradual. Observing the results of Fig. 2 for the wide, FMNIST-100 networks, we see a small number of duplicate encodings at the first layer (once again, note the difference in the scale of the y-axis), and then a rapid decline to almost zero duplicates for hidden layers 3 through 10. This result, in conjunction with the zero duplicate encodings for the MNIST-100 networks, suggest that networks that are sufficiently wide do not share many encodings between different samples of different classes.

While we have identified that duplicate encodings do occur, we now consider how and why they occur. Through visual inspection of samples of different classes that share an encoding, we identify 3 distinct scenarios that cause duplicate encodings to occur in the narrow MNIST and FMNIST networks. We use the term "idiosyncratic" to refer to samples that are visually very dissimilar to their class-majority, and "typical" for samples that are visually similar to the majority

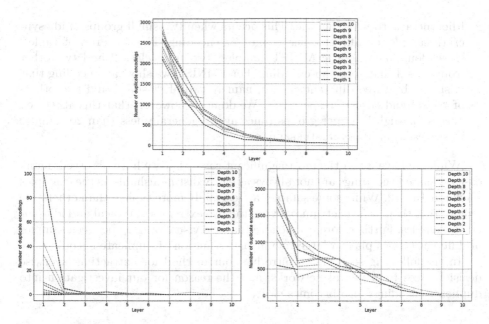

Fig. 2. Number of cross-class duplicate encodings per layer for MNIST and FMNIST networks with 1 to 10 hidden layers. Top: MNIST-20. Bottom left: FMNIST-100. Bottom right: FMNIST-40

of samples from that class. The different cases are listed below, and an example of each case for both data sets is shown in Table 2. All examples are found at the fifth hidden layer of a MNIST-20 and FMNIST-40 network with 10 hidden layers.

1. Idiosyncratic-to-typical: This occurs when a single, or very few (generally less than 20), idiosyncratic sample(s) share an encoding with many other, more typical samples from a different class. This can further be split into two sub-cases:

   (a) Idiosyncratic-to-many: In this case, the few idiosyncratic samples from one class shares an encoding with a very large number of samples from another class. We show two examples of this in the first row of Table 2. For MNIST, we find that 4 idiosyncratic samples from class 5 share an encoding with 3,221 samples from class 3. In the case of FMNIST, we show how a single idiosyncratic sample from the "shirt" class shares an encoding with 2,189 other samples from the "trouser" class.

   (b) Idiosyncratic-to-few: A duplicate encoding is shared between a few idiosyncratic samples of one class and a small subgroup of samples of another class. In the second row of Table 2 we show how a strange sample from class 7 shares an encoding with 45 samples from class 1 for MNIST. Similarly, for FMNIST we show an encoding that is shared by one sample from the "coat" class and 53 others of the "shirt" class.

2. Idiosyncratic-to-idiosyncratic: This occurs when two small groups of idiosyncratic samples of different classes share an encoding. The third row of Table 2 shows four idiosyncratic MNIST samples, two from class 2 and two other from class 3 that share an encoding. For FMNIST we show an encoding that is shared by three different classes, namely two of "t-shirt" and two others of "shirt" and "dress" respectively. We do note, however, that this also often occurs for slightly larger groups (once again, generally less than 20 samples in size each) of idiosyncratic samples.

While we have listed the most significant cases that we have observed, many cases of shared encodings are not always as easily distinguishable as the examples shown in Table 2. While some samples are certainly more typical than others, we believe that there is a spectrum between the two extremes of typical and idiosyncratic samples. Furthermore, we believe that the visual overlap between samples of different classes plays a large role in the formation of duplicate encodings.

In the following section, we introduce our method for extracting layerwise decision trees from neural networks, and the reason for our investigation into duplicate encodings also becomes clear.

Table 2. Examples of different cases of duplicate encodings, where a single encoding is shared by samples of more than one class. All examples are found at the fifth hidden layer of a depth-10 MNIST-20 and FMNIST-40 network.

Case	MNIST	FMNIST	Description
Idiosyncratic to many			**MNIST**: Idiosyncratic samples (4) from class 5 share an encoding with many (3,221) samples of class 3. **FMNIST**: A single idiosyncratic sample of class "shirt" shares an encoding with 2,189 samples of class "trouser".
Idiosyncratic to few			**MNIST**: A single idiosyncratic sample of class 7 shares an encoding with 45 samples of class 1. **FMNIST**: A single idiosyncratic sample of class "coat" shares an encoding with 53 samples of class "shirt".
Idiosyncratic to idiosyncratic			**MNIST**: Four idiosyncratic samples from classes 2 and 3 share an encoding. **FMNIST**: Four idiosyncratic samples from the classes "t-shirt" (2), "shirt" (1), and "dress" (1) share an encoding.

4   Layerwise Decision Trees

Given the knowledge of binary encodings and their behaviour expressed in the previous section, we now use these encodings to extract a decision tree at each layer of a ReLU-activated MLP, in order to better understand the internal classification procedure of the network. First, in Sect. 4.1, we explain our decision tree extraction algorithm. In the following section (Sect. 4.2) we show the accuracy of these decision trees at each layer and compare them to that of the neural network from which they are derived.

4.1   Algorithm

We follow a straightforward approach to convert a given layer into a decision tree. First we find the activation values of each node for each sample at a specific layer. Following this, we then convert these activation values to binary encodings: a w-dimensional vector of 0's and 1's for each sample, with w the width of the layer being probed. Hereafter we identify the unique and duplicate encodings. We then label each encoding according to the class it corresponds to. If there is more than one class for the encoding (a duplicate), we label it according to the class of the majority of the samples. We can then further prune this list of encodings and their corresponding labels by disregarding any that occur for less samples than a given threshold, with the threshold becoming an important hyperparameter. The remaining list of encodings are then used as the training dataset with which to construct a decision tree. The training set therefore consists of a set of unique binary encodings, each associated with a single class.

This implies that the decision tree algorithm only has access to the ON and OFF states of the nodes as features when building a tree. Nodes that are ON then provides a 'path' of node states that are required for each class, e.g. if nodes a and b are ON, the sample belongs to class 1, etc. For decision tree induction, we use the CART (Classification and Regression Tree) algorithm [2] and the Gini index [2] as splitting criterion. Due to the fact that some classes might have more unique encodings than others, we treat the data set as balanced, meaning the respective classes are equally weighted. We do not limit the depth of the decision trees or apply any pruning. Experiments are conducted using the CART implementation from *scikit-learn*[2].

To evaluate the accuracy of a decision tree, we pass each sample of the train or test set through the neural network, find its binary encoding at the specific layer that the decision tree represents, and then pass this encoding as input to the decision tree for classification.

4.2   Results

To determine the efficacy of the proposed decision tree extraction algorithm, we use the same setup as in Sect. 3, but generate 3 versions of each network, using

---

[2] https://scikit-learn.org/stable/modules/tree.html

3 different random initialization seeds. For each network and seed, we extract a decision tree from each layer, and measure its accuracy on the train and test data sets. We then take the mean accuracy of the different seeds, and also include error bars indicating the standard error. We show the average train accuracy (green) and test (red) accuracy for each decision tree at each layer in Fig. 3. We also indicate the average test accuracy of the neural network with a horizontal blue line. For these results, we use a threshold of 0 when creating the decision trees, meaning no encodings are disregarded from the training data set.

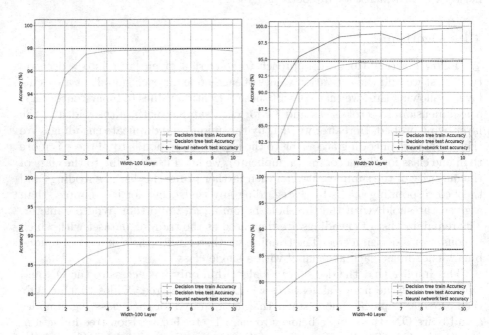

Fig. 3. Decision tree train (green) and test (red) accuracy per layer for MNIST and FMNIST networks with 10 hidden layers averaged over three initialization seeds, with a threshold of 0. The mean test accuracy of the neural network is shown by the horizontal blue line. Error bars indicate the standard error. Top left: MNIST-100. Top right: MNIST-20. Bottom left: FMNIST-100. Bottom right: FMNIST-40 (Color figure online)

Observing the results in Fig. 3 for the wide MNIST-100 and FMNIST-100 networks, we see that the decision trees achieve 100% train accuracy at virtually every layer. This is due to the small number of duplicate encodings (or 0 duplicates in the case of MNIST), meaning very few samples are unaccounted for by the binary encodings. Furthermore, the test accuracy of the decision trees in the deeper layers also match the test accuracy of the model. This implies that the test set samples produce encodings which are very similar to those produced by the train set. For the narrower MNIST-20 and FMNIST-40 networks, we observe a steady increase in train accuracy as the network depth increases. Once again, this is due to the number of duplicate encodings decreasing along with the depth of the network. We also observe that the decision trees in the deeper layers very closely approximate the test accuracy of the network.

While we find that our decision tree algorithm works well and provides good accuracy, it can only provide a clear interpretation of the layerwise decision making of the neural network if it is sufficiently concise. We measure the size of each decision tree by finding the number of "split nodes", where a split node is a feature used as a splitting criterion in the tree, in other words, each node in the tree that is not a leaf node. In Fig. 4 we show the average number of split nodes for each decision tree at each hidden layer. We once again include error bars indicating the standard error for the three initialization seeds used.

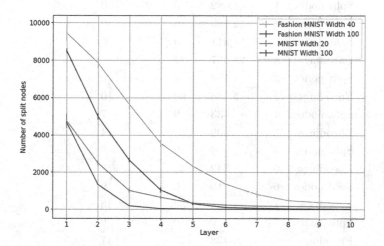

Fig. 4. The number of split nodes for each decision tree per layer for MNIST and FMNIST networks with 10 hidden layers averaged over three initialization seeds. Error bars indicate the standard error.

Figure 4 shows that the decision trees generated in the shallower layers are exceptionally large, with over 4,000 features for MNIST and over 8,000 for FMNIST in the first layer. This implies that each node in the layer is re-used many times as a splitting criterion when constructing the decision tree. However, in the deeper layers we observe that the number of split nodes used by the decision tree is less than the total number of nodes in that specific layer of the neural network.

Naturally, decision trees that are very large are not easily interpretable, however we can rectify this by applying a threshold when generating the encodings for the decision tree data set (as discussed earlier in Sect. 4.1). Making use of the MNIST-100 network, we measure the number of unique encodings, and number of split nodes, after applying a threshold of 0, 100 and 1,000. This implies that any encoding that does not occur for at least 0, 100 or 1,000 samples respectively are discarded. Results are shown in Table 3, again averaged over three seeds, and rounded to the nearest integer. We also show the mean train and test accuracy of the decision tree at each layer after applying the specified threshold in Table 4.

Table 3. Average number of encodings and number of split nodes of decision trees extracted at each layer of a MNIST-100 network with different thresholds applied. Average is obtained over three different initialization seeds.

Total	Layer	Threshold		
		0 samples	100 samples	1000 samples
Encodings	1	54,739	0	0
Split nodes	1	4,682	0	0
Encodings	2	52,265	0	0
Split nodes	2	1,341	0	0
Encodings	3	26,357	27	0
Split nodes	3	184	6	0
Encodings	4	5,236	80	10
Split nodes	4	33	9	7
Encodings	5	900	62	14
Split nodes	5	14	9	9
Encodings	6	342	39	17
Split nodes	6	10	9	9
Encodings	7	161	32	13
Split nodes	7	9	9	9
Encodings	8	138	25	17
Split nodes	8	9	9	9
Encodings	9	187	34	13
Split nodes	9	9	9	9
Encodings	10	196	32	15
Split nodes	10	9	9	9

It is clear that applying a threshold of 100 or 1,000 for the first 2 or 3 layers respectively results in zero encodings remaining in the decision tree's data set. This is to be expected, as originally observed in Fig. 1: very few samples share encodings in the shallow layers of the network. However, after applying a threshold at the fourth hidden layer the number of encodings is drastically decreased, along with only a slight decrease in accuracy. This is due to the fact that the majority of samples for each class are contained in very few encodings. In conjunction with this, we observe a similar decrease in the number of split nodes of each decision tree, implying that each decision tree (once visualized) would provide a more interpretable explanation of the classification procedure for each layer. Finally, it is quite remarkable that for the final hidden layer

Table 4. Average train and test accuracy of decision trees extracted at each layer of a MNIST-100 network with different thresholds applied. Average is obtained over three different initialization seeds.

Data set	Layer	Accuracy (%)		
		Threshold 0	Threshold 100	Threshold 1,000
Train	1	100.00	0.00	0.00
Test	1	89.60	0.00	0.00
Train	2	100.00	0.00	0.00
Test	2	95.67	0.00	0.00
Train	3	100.00	61.50	0.00
Test	3	97.47	61.05	0.00
Train	4	100.00	97.08	77.19
Test	4	97.77	94.79	75.58
Train	5	100.00	98.99	94.33
Test	5	97.85	96.41	92.08
Train	6	100.00	99.33	99.06
Test	6	97.84	96.88	96.65
Train	7	100.00	99.66	98.32
Test	7	97.85	97.29	95.67
Train	8	100.00	99.76	98.55
Test	8	97.85	97.41	96.03
Train	9	100.00	99.84	99.19
Test	9	97.78	97.48	96.87
Train	10	100.00	99.75	97.97
Test	10	97.81	97.28	95.75

(the tenth layer) the number of encodings can be reduced to only 15, and the decision tree still achieves an excellent train and test accuracy (97.97% and 95.75% respectively).

In conclusion, the results of Tables 3 and 4 show that one can disregard encodings that do not correspond to many samples and significantly decrease the size of each decision tree. Furthermore, by selecting the correct threshold, the decision tree can be kept concise and still achieve relatively high accuracy on both the train and test data sets. In the following section we demonstrate a visualization of these decision trees and how they explain the layerwise decision making in a neural network.

5 Decision Tree Visualization

We visualize the layerwise classification procedure for each class as a unique combination of node states, in the form of IF-THEN rules. Green edges indicate that a node is required to be ON, while red indicates that a node must be OFF. After each split node, we show two heatmaps, each consisting of the average of all samples for which the unique combination of node states are active: one indicating if the node is ON, and one indicating if the node is OFF. Leaf nodes are shown as pink circles indicating the class.

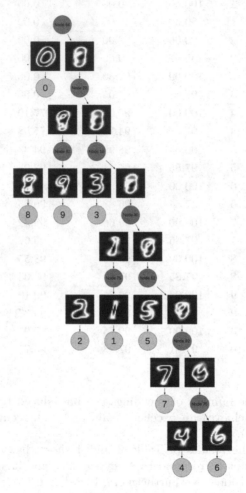

Fig. 5. Visualization of a decision tree constructed from binary encodings found at the last hidden layer of a MNIST-100 network with 10 hidden layers. (Color figure online)

For example, consider Fig. 5, where we show a visualization of a decision tree constructed from the binary encodings of the tenth (last) hidden layer of the MNIST-100 network, with no threshold applied. The root node, node 66, shows a heatmap of all the samples for which the node is ON (green edge) and another for all the samples for the node is OFF (red edge). The following split node,

node 20, then shows heatmaps consisting of all the samples for which the node is ON or OFF AND for which the root node is OFF, etc. Through showing the 'cumulative' heatmaps at each decision point we are able to visualize how the samples of the training set are partitioned by each node's state.

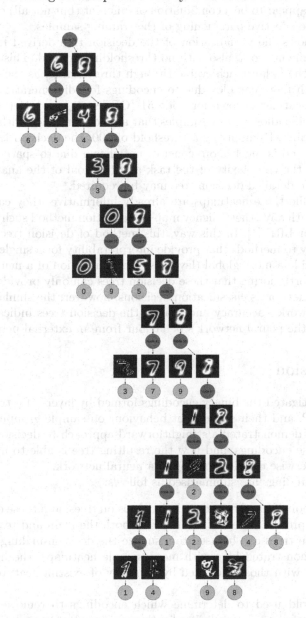

Fig. 6. Visualization of a decision tree constructed from binary encodings found at the fifth hidden layer of a MNIST-100 network with 10 hidden layers.

The visualization in Fig. 5 clearly shows how each node acts as a binary classifier, by partitioning the training set samples with its respective ON or OFF state. Certain nodes appear to only activate for samples of a single class, for example node 66 is clearly only active for samples from class 0. However, several others appear to be a combination of different (but not all) classes, which allows for more effective partitioning of the training samples.

Figure 6 shows the visualization of the decision tree derived from the fifth layer of the same network, also with no thresholding applied. This visualization clearly shows the balance achievable through thresholding, as the classification process is much more complex due to encodings for idiosyncratic samples. For example, the heatmaps shown for node 51 (OFF state) and 41 (ON state) are clearly for specific idiosyncratic samples that are not contained within their class majority encoding. By applying a threshold of 100, the decision tree resembles that of Fig. 5, and is much more concise (not shown due to space constraints). Depending on the complexity of the task and the goal of the analysis, a more concise or more detailed decision tree may be required.

Finally, while these heatmaps are already informative, they can readily be swapped out with any other saliency map visualization method such as SHAP [7], DeepLift [9], or LRP [1]. In this way, this method of decision tree induction is complementary to methods that provide interpretability for a single sample, and is able to provide a more global (layerwise) interpretation of a neural network.

It is also worth noting that these decision trees can only provide an approximation of the network's classification decisions, however, the similarity between the neural network's accuracy and that of the decision trees indicate that they closely mimic the neural network's behaviour from an external perspective.

6 Conclusion

We have investigated the binary encodings formed by layers of a trained ReLU-activated MLP, and their subsequent behaviour on sample groupings. Furthermore, we have demonstrated a straightforward approach to decision tree induction using these encodings, and how the resulting tree is able to illuminate the underlying layerwise decision making of a neural network.

Our main findings are summarised as follows:

- Binary encodings can be used to derive decision trees, and these decision trees are able to provide excellent accuracy on both the train and test data sets.
- The decision trees can be used to visualize the decision-making process of a model. Demonstrated here with mean sample heatmaps, the heatmaps can be replaced with those produced by a variety of existing feature attribution methods.
- The threshold used to determine which encodings to remove controls the complexity of the tree (and visualization produced). Depending on the goal of the analysis, a more concise or more detailed tree can be produced.

– Duplicate encodings occur when an encoding is shared by samples of more than a single class. Our analysis shows that these duplicates are caused, in part, by idiosyncratic samples which are visually very dissimilar to their class majority.

In terms of future work, we wish to first verify these results on more complex data sets before extending the process to additional attribution techniques and more complex architectures. We have already seen that activation functions that are not piecewise (such as sigmoid functions) can also be used to produce binary encodings, and that such encodings can be extracted from layers of more complex architectures. We aim to build on these observations to extend the current process to additional DNN architectures. Finally, we would like to assess this method on a real-world application, in order to better understand its usefulness in practice, and the extent to which it can be used to supplement other interpretability methods.

References

1. Bach, S., Binder, A., Montavon, G., Klauschen, F., Müller, K.R., Samek, W.: On pixel-wise explanations for non-linear classifier decisions by layer-wise relevance propagation. PloS One **10**(7), 1–46 (2015). https://doi.org/10.1371/journal.pone.0130140
2. Breiman, L., Friedman, J., Stone, C., Olshen, R.: Classification and Regression Trees. Taylor & Francis, New York (1984)
3. Davel, M., Theunissen, M., Pretorius, A., Barnard, E.: DNNs as layers of cooperating classifiers. In: Proceedings of the AAAI Conference on Artificial Intelligence, vol. 34, no. 04, pp. 3725–3732 (2020). https://doi.org/10.1609/aaai.v34i04.5782
4. Hailesilassie, T.: Rule extraction algorithm for deep neural networks: a review (2016)
5. Kingma, D., Ba, J.: Adam: a method for stochastic optimization. In: International Conference on Learning Representations (2014)
6. LeCun, Y., Cortes, C., Burges, C.: MNIST database of handwritten digits. http://yann.lecun.com/exdb/mnist/
7. Lundberg, S.M., Lee, S.I.: A unified approach to interpreting model predictions. In: Proceedings of the 31st International Conference on Neural Information Processing Systems, pp. 4768–4777 (2017)
8. Sato, M., Tsukimoto, H.: Rule extraction from neural networks via decision tree induction. In: IJCNN 2001. International Joint Conference on Neural Networks. Proceedings (Cat. No. 01CH37222), vol. 3, pp. 1870–1875 (2001). https://doi.org/10.1109/IJCNN.2001.938448
9. Shrikumar, A., Greenside, P., Kundaje, A.: Learning important features through propagating activation differences. In: Proceedings of the 34th International Conference on Machine Learning - Volume 70, pp. 3145–3153. ICML 2017 (2017). JMLR.org
10. Xiao, H., Rasul, K., Vollgraf, R.: Fashion-MNIST: a novel image dataset for benchmarking machine learning algorithms. CoRR abs/1708.07747 (2017)
11. Zilke, J.R., Loza Mencía, E., Janssen, F.: DeepRED – Rule extraction from deep neural networks. In: Calders, T., Ceci, M., Malerba, D. (eds.) DS 2016. LNCS (LNAI), vol. 9956, pp. 457–473. Springer, Cham (2016). https://doi.org/10.1007/978-3-319-46307-0_29

Automatic Baggage Threat Detection Using Deep Attention Networks

Yashay Rampershad⬤, Serestina Viriri$^{(\boxtimes)}$⬤, and Mandlenkosi Gwetu⬤

School of Mathematics, Statistics and Computer Science,
University of KwaZulu-Natal, Durban, South Africa
viriris@ukzn.ac.za

Abstract. Detecting threats in densely packed luggage is challenging for aviation security due to the partial occlusion or self-occlusion of prohibited items. Computer-aided systems have assisted security personnel to an extent. However, they require in the loop manipulation of X-ray baggage images to improve visibility of concealed prohibited items. Researchers have proposed several methods to detect threats automatically, but the occlusion problem is still prevalent. This paper proposes a novel attention mechanism that leverages spatial and channel-wise information of a given intermediate feature map. The mechanism can be seamlessly placed into existing Deep Convolutional Neural Network (DCNN) architectures. It sequentially infers the channel and spatial attention that recalibrates feature responses of the network by highlighting visual cues and dulling cues that do not contribute to the semantics of an image. In our experimentation, the proposed attention mechanism is implemented into Faster Region-based Convolutional Neural Network (Faster-RCNN) and thoroughly validated on publicly available datasets such as OPXray, SIXray and HIXray. It outperforms prior methods on the OPIXray, achieving a mean average precision (mAP) of 91.20%. For completeness, we also validate the proposed approach on ImageNet and MS-COCO datasets; it achieves an accuracy of 77.12 top-1 and 93.46 top-5 on ImageNet; and 39.7 mAP on MS-COCO.

Keywords: Baggage threat · Deep attention network · Object detection · Occlusion · Faster-RCNN

1 Introduction

In commercial travel, ensuring passenger safety has become a critical task since the terrorist attacks on September 11th, 2001. This tragic event had revolutionised aviation security internationally. To mitigate threats, computer-aided technologies were introduced, such as facial recognition, behavioural profiling and CT screening. Despite the technological advances, aviation security personnel is required to inspect several thousand baggage X-ray scans every day. They go through rigorous training to acquire the skills to detect prohibited objects effectively. However, they are subject to fatigue and stress, which impairs their

© Springer Nature Switzerland AG 2022
E. Jembere et al. (Eds.): SACAIR 2021, CCIS 1551, pp. 156–173, 2022.
https://doi.org/10.1007/978-3-030-95070-5_11

cognitive ability. Due to the densely packed nature of the baggage, inspectors face several challenges in detecting prohibited items at an image level, such as object occlusion, low saliency of objects, large intra-class variation and the low prevalence of threats [34].

Several methods have been proposed utilising computer vision methods to assist with the detection of prohibited items. These techniques are often adapted from common object detection and classification. However, they still have some limitations, as the items in the baggage are often overlapped and occluded, resulting in noisy X-ray images, which inhibits accurate detection.

This work presents a novel attention mechanism that can be easily inserted into popular object detectors. The attention mechanism leverages spatial and channel information to produce refined feature maps that highlight influential semantic information. Our experimentation shows that our novel attention mechanism that increases the discriminative ability of common object detectors. The main contributions of this work are:

- A novel attention mechanism that has been thoroughly evaluated and benchmarked on publicly available datasets such as OPIXray, HIXray and SIXRay.
- An evaluation of the transferability of the attention mechanism, as we benchmark the mechanism on MS-COCO [19] and ImageNet (ILSVRC2012) [17].

The paper is organised as follows: Sect. 2 discusses similar works, Sect. 3 describes the proposed attention mechanism and the integration into existing architectures, Sect. 4 presents the implementation details, experimental results and a comprehensive discussion of the results, Sect. 5 concludes the paper.

2   Related Work

2.1   Classical Computer Vision Methods

Early research in baggage threat detection used classical computer vision and machine learning (ML) methods to detect or classify prohibited items in X-ray scans. The prior methods [4,18,20] often followed the visual-bag-of-word (VBOW) strategy. It is usually performed in three stages: a key point descriptor such as SURF, SIFT or KAZE was used for feature extraction, each keypoint is clustered by K-means clustering and the fixed size vectors are classified by a ML algorithm (such as Random Forests, Support Vector Machines). In a review study, Mery et al. [20] benchmarked classical methodologies; their results indicated that methods that used feature descriptors are often slow due to the excessive key points produced during feature extraction and the processing of high-dimensionality feature vectors. However, despite their computational performance, classical methods performed well.

2.2   Deep Learning Methods

As deep learning (DL) started to trend, evidence indicated that DL outperformed ML methods in common object detection. Consequently, Mery et al. [20]

and Akcay et al. [2] introduced the first DL methods by utilizing the transfer learning paradigm in threat recognition; their work validated that deep convolutional neural networks (DCNNs) outperform ML methods. Furthermore, they highlighted several challenges DCNNs face: it requires large amounts of data (class-balanced) to produce accurate results, the sensitivity to affine transformations, and the misclassification of partially occluded objects. They emphasized the need for a diverse dataset or data augmentation to mitigate this issue. Given the success of DL in common object detection and these prior works, subsequent literature focused on DL methodologies in prohibited item detection [3,7,33]. Some researchers focused on the class-imbalance problem [1,9]; they often used Generative Adversarial Networks (GAN) to perform anomaly detection. Miao et al. [21] proposed a novel method called Class-balanced Hierarchical Refinement (CHR) framework that strayed away from the GAN strategy and introduced the SIXray dataset. In their experimentation CHR outperformed baseline classification architectures.

To focus on image-level classification, researchers primarily used class-balanced datasets. Xu et al. [33] introduced the use of attention mechanisms to recognize prohibited items. They employed a lateral inhibition mechanism to suppress noise in the image and perform weak localization by evaluating the activated neurons in the network (similar to class activation mapping). Hu et al. [15] proposed a novel attention-based model where they attached an attention head to a Feature Pyramid Network (FPN) to generate a spatial attention mask. They use the attention mask to attenuate noise and refine features in the classification head. Their approach has shown a noticeable improvement over other classification methods on the SIXRay dataset. The common trend that became apparent in the literature is that researchers often used a single-stage (YOLO, RetinaNet or FCOS) and seldomly used two-stage detection methodologies (Faster-RCNN). Researchers favoured single-shot detection because of their speed, as high throughput is a requirement for baggage threat detection systems. However, two-stage detectors have proven to have more accurate detection rates [3].

Addressing the occlusion problem, Wei et al. [31] introduced a professionally annotated dataset, OPIXray. Furthermore, they proposed a novel attention mechanism that can be attached to any DCNN architecture. The attention mechanism leverages edge and material information to generate an attention distribution map that spatially highlights important regions in the input image. Furthermore, they built upon their work by introducing an over-sampling training strategy that emphasizes learning complex examples. In both of their works they evaluated their approaches on single-shot detectors and showed that their methods outperform prior methods. Hassan et al. [10,12,13] introduced unconventional methodologies that perform instance segmentation on highly occluded threat objects. They proposed a novel use of structure tensors to highlight transitional contours of partially occluded objects; their work produced good results on the OPIXray and SIXRay datasets. However, they modified the SIXRay dataset by adding more annotations to the intra-classes of threat objects, which can be attributed to their success.

3   Proposed Method

Given an input feature map, $F \in \mathbb{R}^{C \times H \times W}$ we sequentially infer a 1D channel attention map $B(F) \in \mathbb{R}^{C \times 1 \times 1}$ and a 2D spatial attention map $S(F) \in \mathbb{R}^{1 \times H \times W}$. The attention enhanced feature maps are summarised as below:

$$F' = F \otimes B(F) \tag{1}$$

$$F'' = F' \otimes S(F') \tag{2}$$

The output of each attention mechanism is multiplied element-wise $\otimes$.

In our work, we use the ResNet [14] architecture for feature extraction, as this is widely used and enables us to perform comparisons with other attention mechanisms. Thus, we place the attention mechanism before the residual connection shown in Fig. 1. The following sections describe each constituent part of the UCS (U-Net Channel Spatial) attention mechanism.

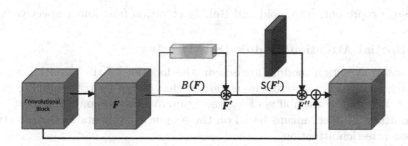

Fig. 1. An overview of the entire residual block and implementation of UCS

3.1   Channel Attention Module (CAM)

Each channel of the feature map can be conceptualised as a feature detector. Therefore, by exploiting the inter-channel dependencies, CAM highlights the most influential features of the convolutional block. The spatial dimension is aggregated using three pooling methods to produce the channel attention map. We empirically confirm that using these three pooled feature vectors increases the discriminative ability of the network. In addition, we utilise a shared network to produce the channel attention map, which is similar to [32] as this reduces the number of parameters. The module is described in detail below.

The spatial information of the feature map is aggregated using adaptive maximum, minimum and average pooling. Each feature vector produced from aggregation is passed to a shared network. The shared network contains three convolutional blocks B_1, B_2 and B_3 where each block consists of 1×1 convolutions (denoted as $f^{1 \times 1}, g^{1 \times 1}, d^{1 \times 1}, k^{1 \times 1}$ and $p^{1 \times 1}$). Blocks B_1, B_2 and B_3 output feature map sizes are $\mathbb{R}^{C/r \times 1 \times 1}$, $\mathbb{R}^{C/r \times 1 \times 1}$ and $\mathbb{R}^{C \times 1 \times 1}$, respectively. We utilise a ratio r to control the degree of dimensionality reduction, as this assists in reducing the number of parameters and this forces the network to learn important features. The output of B_1 and B_2 are added together to reinforce the feature representation, a similar idea to Inception blocks [25]. The output is passed on to, B_3 where the feature representation is then reconstructed to the input dimension, and we add a residual connection from the pooled vectors to the output of B_3. Finally, the outputs for each pooled feature vector are added together, and a sigmoid function is applied, thus generating the channel attention. The channel attention module is diagrammatically shown in Fig. 2 and is summarised below:

$$
\begin{aligned}
B_1(\mathbf{F}) &= \sigma(f^{1 \times 1}(\mathbf{F})) \\
B_2(\mathbf{F}) &= \sigma(g^{1 \times 1}(d^{1 \times 1}(\mathbf{F}))) \\
B_3(\mathbf{F}) &= \sigma(k^{1 \times 1}(p^{1 \times 1}(\mathbf{F}))) \\
H(\mathbf{F}) &= \sigma(B_3(B_1(\mathbf{F}) + B_2(\mathbf{F})) + \mathbf{F}) \\
A(\mathbf{F}) &= \tau(H(AvgPool(\mathbf{F})) + H(MaxPool(\mathbf{F})) + H(MinPool(\mathbf{F})))
\end{aligned}
\tag{3}
$$

where σ, τ represents a sigmoid and ReLU activation functions respectively.

3.2   Spatial Attention Module (SAM)

The spatial attention module focuses on the location of the essential features spatially, and it suppresses feature responses that do not contribute to the global context. Inspired by the ability of segmentation models, we conjecture that using spatial attention mechanisms based on the semantic segmentation architectures will generate rich attention.

To compute the spatial attention: the input feature maps are aggregated along the channel axis using minimum, maximum and average pooling, similar to channel attention. The pooling operation applied on the channel axis has been effective in highlighting important spatial locations. The resultant feature maps are concatenated and passed to a small U-NET network [24] to generate spatial attention $S(F) \in \mathbb{R}^{H \times W}$.

The U-NET $U(\mathbf{F})$ architecture has been modified in the following ways: we use transpose convolutions in place of bilinear interpolation up-sampling layers, the number of input channels per double convolutional block is given by 2^{n+i}; $i = 0, 1, \ldots, z - 1$ where n, z is the depth of the network and the minimum channel exponent respectively (we empirically determined $n = 4, z = 3$), the number of down-sampling and up-sampling blocks is given by $n - 1$, and the output size of the attention map is $\mathbb{R}^{H \times W \times 1 \times 1}$. The attention mechanism is diagrammatically shown in Fig. 2 and summarised below:

$$
S(\mathbf{F}) = \sigma(U([AvgPool(\mathbf{F}); MinPool(\mathbf{F}); MaxPool(\mathbf{F})]))
\tag{4}
$$

where σ represents the sigmoid activation function.

3.3 Organization of Modules

Given the evidence in [32], placing the channel and spatial attention modules sequentially yielded better results compared to the inverse or parallel arrangement. Thus, we adopt the same arrangement in our approach.

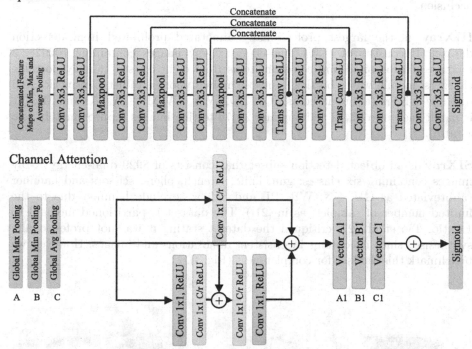

Fig. 2. Detailed architecture of each module in the UCS attention mechanism. The spatial attention module pools the features of the residual block and concatenates the resultant feature maps, passing them through the U-Net network and then applies a sigmoid function to normalize the output. The channel attention module performs global pooling of the residual block, each pooled vector is passed to the shared network; the resultant feature vectors are collected, summed and normalized.

4 Experiments

4.1 Datasets

To evaluate the effectiveness of our proposed approach, we perform several experiments on the following benchmark security inspection datasets OPIXray [31], HIXray [26] and SIXRay [21]. The characteristics of each dataset is described in the following subsections:

OPIXray is prohibited item dataset which was designed and professionally annotated by security personnel to address the occlusion problem. The dataset consists of 8885 dual-energy X-ray images containing objects of 5 classes, namely folding knives, straight knives, scissors, utility knives, and multi-tool knives (abbreviated as FO, ST, SC, UT and MU). It is partitioned into 7109 training and 1776 testing set images (approximately 4 to 1 ratio). Furthermore, the testing set is separated into three different levels of occlusion, from low to high occlusion.

HIXray is the largest professionally annotated prohibited item detection dataset. It consists of 45364 dual-energy X-ray images containing 102928, a mixture of prohibited and common items from eight classes, namely portable chargers, mobile water bottles, laptops, mobile phones, tablets, cosmetics and metallic-lighters (abbreviated as PO1, PO2, WA, LA, MP, TA, CO and ML). It is partitioned into 82452 training and 20476 testing images (approximately 4 to 1 ratio).

SIXray is an object detection subset that consists of 8929 dual-energy X-ray images containing six classes: gun, knife, wrench, pliers, scissors and hammer (abbreviated as GU, KN, WR, PL and SC; we exclude hammer due to the limited number of samples, as in [21]). The dataset is partitioned into a 4 to 1 ratio. Tao et al. [27] critiqued the dataset stating it was not professionally synthesised since it contains inconsistent annotations and images. However, we benchmark this dataset for completeness (Fig. 3).

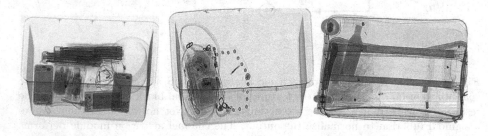

Fig. 3. Samples from each dataset. LTR: OPIXray, HIXray, and SIXRay

4.2   Experiment Detail Settings

Platform Details. The proposed framework was implemented using the MMDetection Framework [5]. All experimentations were conducted in the same hardware environment: Intel(R) Xeon(R) CPU E5-2690 v3, 128 GB DDR3 RAM and 8 Nvidia V100 GPUs. The software platform was based on Pytorch 1.7.1 with CUDA Toolkit 11.1.

Network. In our experimentation, we utilise ResNet50 [14] with FPN (Feature Pyramid Networks) as a deep backbone feature extractor. We also primarily use the Faster-RCNN [23] detection methodology for all attention-related experiments.

Parameter Settings. The proposed detector is trained using the following settings and hyper-parameters defined in Table 1. Since OPIXray and SIXray are similar in size, the parameters were replicated for each experiment. HIXray is significantly larger dataset compared to OPIXray and SIXray; therefore, we utilise a larger batch size and learning rate.

Evaluation Metric. We evaluate the results using the interpolated mean Average Precision (mAP) defined by PASCAL VOC [8] common object detection challenge.

Table 1. Settings and hyperparameters

	SIXray	OPIXray	HIXray
Epochs	20	20	20
Optimizer	SGDM	SGDM	SGDM
Learning rate	0.025	0.025	0.2
Momentumm	0.9	0.9	0.9
LR step schedule	11,15	11,15	11,15
Batch size	4	4	16
Image size	512×512	512×512	512×512

4.3   Comparison of SOTA Attention Mechanisms

First, we evaluate the effectiveness of UCS against several other deep attention mechanisms integrated into Faster-RCNN. Table 2 shows that UCS on the OPIXray dataset outperforms prior mechanisms by 1.1% and 3.4% over the baseline detector.

Similarly on HIXray dataset, UCS improves over prior methods, including the baseline detector, by 0.2%. However, the range is 1.1%, and the second-best performing method is the baseline detector, we conclude that deep attention mechanisms does not exhibit any performance advantage when used in this setting. We assume that the detectors cannot detect threats accurately due to class imbalance and the small image size.

Evaluating on the SIXRay dataset and observed that CBAM [32] outperforms other attention mechanisms by 0.4% and a 0.5% improvement over the baseline detector. The good performance can be attributed to the lightweight nature of the mechanism and exploits spatial information. UCS performed the second-worst we speculate that due to the noisy nature of the images, the three pooled feature vectors encapsulates the noise, and the detector cannot effectively suppress noisy features responses.

Despite the negligible performance gain on the HIXRay and SIXRay datasets, it should be noted that these datasets are not specifically designed for the occlusion problem, but we include their results for completeness.

Table 2. Shows the results of various attention mechanisms

		BASE	CBAM [32]	SE [16]	GC [29]	FCA [22]	ECA [28]	UCS*
OPIXray	FO	88,7	85,5	85,1	89,1	89,9	89,1	89,0
	ST	59,4	66,0	62,0	64,9	64,5	64,9	68,3
	SC	94,6	96,1	95,0	94,9	94,1	94,9	96,6
	UT	78,7	81,1	80,8	79,2	80,0	79,2	81,9
	MU	88,6	87,8	89,6	89,2	90,3	89,2	90,8
	mAP	82.0	84.3	83.3	83.8	83.8	83.8	**85.4**
HIXray	PC1	93.3	92,0	93,2	92,2	93,0	92,3	93,5
	PC2	91.0	90,2	90,3	88,0	89,5	90,8	90,4
	WA	90,8	87,0	89,8	87,5	89,8	89,9	90,8
	LA	97.9	97,9	97,7	97,8	98,1	97,6	98,2
	MP	97.2	96,1	96,4	96,0	95,4	96,9	96,6
	TA	93.5	93,7	94,4	93,8	93,8	94,1	94,0
	CO	56.8	56,1	55,8	57,0	55,9	53,8	56,5
	NL	2.6	4,6	0,3	3,9	5.7	0.8	4.5
	mAP	77.9	77.2	77.2	77.0	77.7	77.7	**78.1**
SIXray	GU	88,9	88,9	88,3	88,5	88.4	88,7	87.0
	KN	79,0	82,3	80,2	81,1	82.1	81,7	81.7
	WR	82,4	79,9	73,0	79,3	80.9	79,6	79.9
	PL	86,2	85,3	85,2	84,9	84.9	85,5	84.7
	SC	86,3	89,1	86,8	88,4	87.2	85,5	87.1
	mAP	84.6	**85.1**	82.7	84.4	84.7	84.2	84.1

4.4   Ablation Study

The Channel Attention Mechanism. We analyse the effect of the channel attention mechanism (CAM) by adding it to each residual block of ResNet to exploit inter-channel dependencies of the network by weighting the output of each residual block in the architecture. Referring to Table 3, we observe a 2.1% improvement in mAP over the baseline detector. Furthermore, we observe a significant improvement in classes that are difficult to detect; the AP of straight knife, scissors and utility knives classes increased by 6.2%, 2% and 2.6%, respectively. The straight knives are difficult to detect due to self-occlusion, and since it has a low material density it often blends in with the metallic structure of the bag. Similarly, with utility knives, however, they have high density thus it has a more contrasting appearance.

The Spatial Attention Mechanism. In this experiment, we analyse the effect of the spatial attention. Therefore, we added SAM to each residual block of ResNet.

Referring to Table 3, we observe similar results to CAM; however, the AP of straight knives has increased to 9.3% over the baseline detector and 3.1% over CAM. However, folding knives AP has decreased by 1.7% from the baseline. We speculate that there is a slight inter-class variability overlap between FO and ST such that when spatial attention is generated, the features learned are not discriminative enough to distinguish between these two classes.

The Combination of CAM and SAM. We analyse the effect of both attention mechanisms. The utilization of both mechanisms has yielded good results, as they work together and complement each other. The AP for each class is the maximum of both SAM and CAM, shown in Table 3. Overall, we observed a 2.4% improvement over the baseline and a 1.3% over each mechanism. Based on the results, we can conclude that the detector can learn more discriminative features by leveraging both channel and spatial information (Fig. 4).

Table 3. The performance of each component of UCS.

Model	FO	ST	SC	UT	MU	mAP
R50	88.7	59.4	94.6	78.7	88.6	82.0
+CAM	88.0	65.6	96.6	81.3	88.9	84.1
+SAM	87.0	68.7	94.9	81.8	88.1	84.1
+UCS	**90.1**	**68.7**	96.4	81.2	**89.9**	**85.3**

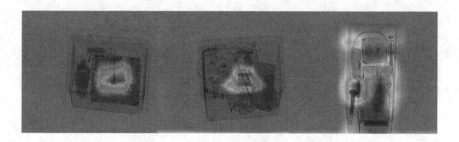

Fig. 4. Depicts the class activation map of the UCS model.

The Reduction Ratio. CAM internally reduces the size of the input vector by a hyperparameter r. In this experiment, we varied the hyperparameter to analyze the effect dimensionality reduction.

Referring to Table 4, we see that with a smaller reduction ratio, UCS performed worse. This result directly contradicts our findings in Sect. 4.6, as we see an increase in performance with a decreased ratio. A decreased ratio increases the number of parameters, which directly correlates to an increase in performance [32].

Table 4. The effect of dimensionality reduction.

Model	Param	FO	ST	SC	UT	MU	mAP
R50 + UCS	$r = 16$	90.1	68.7	96.4	81.2	89.9	85.3
R50 + UCS	$r = 32$	**89.0**	**68.3**	**96.6**	**81.9**	**90.8**	**85.4**

The Effect of Larger Image Sizes. In this experiment, we analyse the effect of increasing the image size. From Table 5, it is evident that a larger image size increases mAP, as larger images contain more contextual information; thus, the output feature maps throughout the network are up-scaled. Therefore, the network is able to learn finer details of objects (more especially smaller objects).

We observed a 3.4% increase in mAP; the most notable improvements were the straight knives class AP which increased by 7.1%, and the utility knives by 6.9% by using a large image. We speculate that the performance increase of these classes can be attributed to the accurate detection of smaller objects, as there are many viewpoint variations in densely packed baggage, which decreases the apparent size of threat objects.

Table 5. The effect of increasing the image size.

Model	Size	FO	ST	SC	UT	MU	mAP
+UCS	512	89.0	68.3	96.6	81.9	90.8	85.4
+UCS	**1024**	**91.1**	**75.4**	**96.8**	**88.8**	**92.3**	**88.9**

The Effect of Deformable Convolutions. DCNNs have difficulty learning basic geometric transformations (such as scaling, rotations, translations etc.), and they do not have an internal mechanism to aid the learning process. Thus, it relies on data augmentation to learn partial invariance to transformations. To address this, Dai et al. [6] introduced deformable convolutions that are capable of learning transformations implicitly. Thus, given the stochastic orientation and viewpoint variations of objects in densely packed baggage, we experimented with deformable convolutions in our proposed approach.

Analysing the results in Table 6, we observe a large improvement in mAP by 2.5%. The most notable improvement was the straight knife class, which increased by 7.8%. Furthermore, the AP increased throughout the classes. Based on the results, we can conclude that DCN makes the detector more robust to transformations.

Table 6. The effect of using deformable convolutions.

Model	FO	ST	SC	UT	MU	mAP
+UCS	91.1	75.4	96.8	88.8	92.3	88.9
+UCS + DCN	**92.5**	**83.2**	**96.9**	**89.6**	**93.6**	**91.2**

The Effect of Occlusion. In this experiment, we analyze the effect of detection performance when objects are subjected to varying levels of occlusion. The OPIXray dataset has three occlusion levels low, moderate and high (OL 1, OL 2, and OL 3) (Fig. 5).

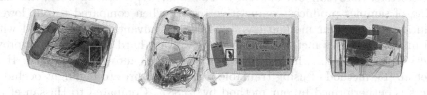

Fig. 5. Partially occluded samples.

Referring to Table 7, the mAP for OL 1 has improved by 4.6% over the baseline method. We observe a significant increase in AP of 11.7%, 5.3% and 4.6% in the straight, utility and multi-tool knives classes, respectively. We see a similar trend for OL 2 and 3, where mAP has improved by 3.9% and 3.4%. However, there are a few outliers in OL 2 the utility knife class decreased by 3.8% and in OL 3 the scissors class decreased by 4.6%. Overall, the detection accuracy of partially occluded prohibited objects does increase with the use of the UCS attention mechanism (Fig. 6).

4.5 Comparison of Prior Literature

In this section, we compare UCS with prior literature in the field. Based on the results and observations in our ablation studies, we use the best performing model, which is Faster-RCNN with ResNet50-UCS-DCN trained on high-resolution images.

Table 7. The impact on detection performance on increasing levels of occlusion.

Model	Occlusion level	FO	ST	SC	UT	MU	mAP
Baseline	O1	89,8	63,4	94,3	82	86,3	83.2
	O2	87.0	49,6	94.0	76,4	87.0	78.8
	O3	82,1	60,1	97,9	68,6	88,1	79.4
UCS	O1	88,4	75,10	97,6	87,3	90,5	87.8
	O2	90,6	61,10	96,9	72,6	92,4	82.7
	O3	87,3	65,60	93,3	76,3	91,5	82.8

Evaluations on OPIXray. The proposed model was evaluated on the OPIXray dataset. It achieved 91.2% mAP, outperforming prior methods. Compared to Wei et al. [30] our method outperforms DOAM (De-occlusion Attention Module) by 8.79% mAP. Due to DOAM being placed at the beginning of a DCNN architecture, we conjecture that this is suboptimal placing because the DOAM module changes the natural RGB representation of images. Thus, it cannot efficiently utilize transfer learning because the DCNN has to learn new representations of low-level filters. Despite this their studies indicated a performance gain over baseline detectors. Analyzing our method to Tao et al. [27] follow-up work, the hard mining of samples produces competitive results when compared to our lower-resolution models. Our method has a 7.4% mAP advantage over DOAM with hard mining. But this method evidently shows that hard mining does improve detection performance, which could be implemented into our approach. Hassan et al. [13] method of using trainable tensor structures to highlight occluded objects is outperformed by our method by 15.88%. Compared to Hassan et al. [11] later work of tensor-pooling our method shows a 7.24% improvement. Both their works utilize coherent tensor structures, in their later work they introduced a model that increases the saliency of low density objects which led to an increase in performance. Despite their success in their work, we conjecture that the use of coherent tensor structures reduces the amount of semantic information in the image which inhibits accurate detection (Table 8).

Table 8. Results of prior literature on the OPIXray dataset.

Model	FO	ST	SC	UT	MU	mAP
Hassan et al. [13]	80.24	56.13	89.34	72.89	78.02	75.32
Wei et al. [31]	86.71	68.58	90.23	78.84	87.67	82.41
Tao et al. [27]	83.80	72.73	90.03	80.77	87.80	83.80
Hassan et al. [12]	85.28	76.49	88.03	89.41	80.62	83.96
Tao et al. [26]	94.80	77.60	98.20	88.90	93.80	90.6
UCS (ours)	**92.5**	**83.2**	**96.9**	**89.6**	**93.6**	**91.2**

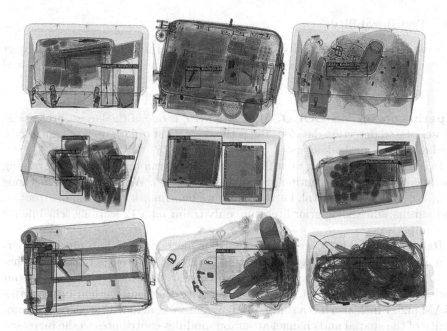

Fig. 6. Visual examples showcasing the detection of the proposed framework. Top: OPIxray Middle: HIXray Bottom: SIXray

Evaluations on HIXray. Since HIXray was recently introduced (2021) it has not been widely adopted in the field. Our method has achieved 82.60% mAP, which is 0.6% behind Tao et al. [26] method. Analyzing each category, our method is outperformed by all categories except the cosmetic (CO) class, where our method performs 3.7% better. The cosmetics class (CO) is difficult to recognize as it has a diverse range of shapes, and plastics appear orange in colour, which often blends in the background [27]. Since LIM emphasizes boundary activations it struggles with object contours that blend in with the background, as opposed to our method (Table 9).

Table 9. Results of prior literature on the HIXray dataset.

	PO1	PO2	WA	LA	MP	TA	CO	NL	mAP
Tao et al. [26]	96.1	95.1	93.9	98.2	98.3	96.4	65.8	21.3	83.2
UCS (ours)	**95.0**	**93.9**	**92.1**	**97.9**	**97.0**	**95.1**	**69.5**	**20.3**	**82.6**

4.6   Transferability

We evaluate the transferability of our approach in the field of common object detection and image classification by benchmarking on the MS-COCO [19] and ImageNet [17] datasets.

Experiments on MS-COCO. MS-COCO [19] is one of the largest professionally annotated detection datasets and is the de-facto standard used to benchmark novel detection methodologies.

In our experimentation, we utilize the following training protocol: 2x training schedule, SGD with momentum and a batch size of 16. We evaluate the methods using MS-COCO 5k-minival. Furthermore, we benchmark the common attention mechanisms, since some prior literature only trains on a 1x learning schedule for fair comparisons.

Referring to Table 10, we observe that our method exhibits competitive performance with other SOTA attention mechanisms. UCS outperforms all other mechanisms for detecting small and large objects; furthermore, this validates our results in Sects. 4.3 and 4.4. However, we notice that our method outperforms CBAM [32], which also has a similar design, and we conclude that increased complexity of the spatial and channel attention modules contributes to the increased in discriminative ability.

Table 10. Performance of SOTA attention mechanism on MS-COCO dataset

Model	mAP	mAP: 50	mAP: 75	mAP: small	mAP: medium	mAP: large
–	38.4	59.0	42.0	21.5	42.1	50.3
SE	39.1	60.1	42.3	22.5	42.8	52.0
CBAM	39.2	60.6	42.1	22.9	43.2	50.6
FCANet	39.5	61.1	42.3	23.7	42.8	49.6
UCSr32	**39.6**	**60.9**	**42.7**	**22.9**	**43.2**	**52.0**
ECA	39.7	60.9	43.3	23.3	43.3	51.5
UCSr16	**39.7**	**61.0**	**43.0**	**24.1**	**43.3**	**52.1**
EMP	39.8	61.3	43.4	23.2	43.6	51.4
GC	39.9	61.4	43.0	23.4	43.6	51.3

Experiments on ImageNet. We evaluate our approach on the ImageNet-1k image classification task. ImageNet [17] is one of the largest classification datasets, which consists of 1.2 million images from 1000 different classes. In our experimentation, we follow the standard training protocol [14,32], where we train ResNet50-UCS for 90 epochs; using SGD with Momentum with a learning rate of 0.1 and a learning rate step scheduler every 30 epochs.

From Table 11, we observe that our attention mechanism improves the baseline architecture by 1.92% in top-1 and 0.94% in top-5 accuracy. Furthermore, our approach outperforms SE-Net by 0.41% in top-1 and 0.08% in top-5 (we consider this result to be negligible). Our attention mechanism does not show any increase in accuracy over other attention mechanisms. We conjecture that our network is less successful due to the small size of the training images.

Comparing the parameters of the attention mechanisms our model has 2.6M more parameters compared to SE-Net and CBAM, this is due to using more pooled features and the residual dimensionality reduction layer of CAM.

Table 11. Attention mechanisms benchmarked on ImageNet

Model	Params	Top-1	Top-5
ResNet	24.37M	75.20	92.52
SENet	26.77M	76.71	93.38
UCS	**29.43M**	**77.12**	**93.46**
CBAM	26.77M	77.34	93.69
ECA-Net	24.37M	77.48	93.68

5 Conclusion

This paper presented an attention mechanism UCS a novel approach to improve the representation power of object detectors. By refining both channel and spatial information of DCNN's, our module is able highlight influential feature responses. Furthermore, our approach introduces a new perspective on utilizing spatial attention mechanisms based on semantic segmentation models to produce rich spatial information. In our experimentation, our approach achieved state-of-the-art results on the OPIXray dataset and achieved second best results on the HIXray dataset. Moreover, we verified the effectiveness of UCS on large benchmark datasets, and we observed competitive results.

In future work, our method can be expanded by introducing residual connections between each attention mechanism to leverage prior knowledge. Furthermore, similar to [26], our method can be implemented into the feature pyramid network to observe any improvement.

Acknowledgement. This research is funded and supported by the National Research Foundation (NRF), University of KwaZulu-Natal (UKZN) and the Center for High Performance Computing (CHPC).

References

1. Akcay, S., Atapour-Abarghouei, A., Breckon, T.P.: GANomaly: semi-supervised anomaly detection via adversarial training. In: Jawahar, C.V., Li, H., Mori, G., Schindler, K. (eds.) ACCV 2018. LNCS, vol. 11363, pp. 622–637. Springer, Cham (2019). https://doi.org/10.1007/978-3-030-20893-6_39

2. Akcay, S., Breckon, T.P.: An evaluation of region based object detection strategies within X-ray baggage security imagery. In: 2017 IEEE International Conference on Image Processing (ICIP), pp. 1337–1341. IEEE, Beijing, September 2017. https://doi.org/10.1109/ICIP.2017.8296499

3. Akcay, S., Kundegorski, M.E., Willcocks, C.G., Breckon, T.P.: Using deep convolutional neural network architectures for object classification and detection within X-ray baggage security imagery. IEEE Trans. Inform. Forensic Secur. **13**(9), 2203–2215 (2018). https://doi.org/10.1109/TIFS.2018.2812196

4. Bastan, M., Byeon, W., Breuel, T.: Object recognition in multi-view dual energy X-ray images. In: Proceedings of the British Machine Vision Conference 2013, pp. 130.1–130.11. British Machine Vision Association, Bristol (2013). https://doi.org/10.5244/C.27.130

5. Chen, K., Wang, J.: MMDetection: open MMLab detection toolbox and benchmark. arXiv:1906.07155 [cs, eess], June 2019

6. Dai, J., et al.: Deformable convolutional networks. arXiv:1703.06211 [cs], June 2017

7. Jain, D.K.: An evaluation of deep learning based object detection strategies for threat object detection in baggage security imagery. Pattern Recognit. Lett. **120**, 112–119 (2019). https://doi.org/10.1016/j.patrec.2019.01.014

8. Everingham, M., Van Gool, L., Williams, C.K.I., Winn, J., Zisserman, A.: The pascal visual object classes (VOC) challenge. Int. J. Comput. Vis. **88**(2), 303–338 (2010). https://doi.org/10.1007/s11263-009-0275-4

9. Griffin, L.D., Caldwell, M., Andrews, J.T.A., Bohler, H.: "Unexpected item in the bagging area": anomaly detection in X-ray security images. IEEE Trans. Inf. Forensics Secur. **14**(6), 1539–1553 (2019). https://doi.org/10.1109/TIFS.2018.2881700

10. Hassan, T., Akçay, S., Bennamoun, M., Khan, S., Werghi, N.: Cascaded structure tensor framework for robust identification of heavily occluded baggage items from multi-vendor X-ray scans, p. 16

11. Hassan, T., Akçay, S., Bennamoun, M., Khan, S., Werghi, N.: Tensor pooling-driven instance segmentation framework for baggage threat recognition. Neural Comput. Appl., 1–12 (2021). https://doi.org/10.1007/s00521-021-06411-x

12. Hassan, T., et al.: Meta-transfer learning driven tensor-shot detector for the autonomous localization and recognition of concealed baggage threats. Sensors **20**(22), 6450 (2020). https://doi.org/10.3390/s20226450

13. Hassan, T., Werghi, N.: Trainable structure tensors for autonomous baggage threat detection under extreme occlusion. In: Ishikawa, H., Liu, C.-L., Pajdla, T., Shi, J. (eds.) ACCV 2020. LNCS, vol. 12627, pp. 257–273. Springer, Cham (2021). https://doi.org/10.1007/978-3-030-69544-6_16

14. He, K., Zhang, X., Ren, S., Sun, J.: Deep residual learning for image recognition. In: 2016 IEEE Conference on Computer Vision and Pattern Recognition (CVPR), pp. 770–778. IEEE, Las Vegas, June 2016. https://doi.org/10.1109/CVPR.2016.90

15. Hu, B., Zhang, C., Wang, L., Zhang, Q., Liu, Y.: Multi-label X-Ray imagery classification via bottom-up attention and meta fusion. In: Ishikawa, H., Liu, C.-L., Pajdla, T., Shi, J. (eds.) ACCV 2020. LNCS, vol. 12627, pp. 173–190. Springer, Cham (2021). https://doi.org/10.1007/978-3-030-69544-6_11

16. Hu, J., Shen, L., Sun, G.: Squeeze-and-excitation networks. In: 2018 IEEE/CVF Conference on Computer Vision and Pattern Recognition, pp. 7132–7141 (2018). https://doi.org/10.1109/CVPR.2018.00745

17. Krizhevsky, A., Sutskever, I., Hinton, G.E.: ImageNet classification with deep convolutional neural networks. In: Advances in Neural Information Processing Systems, vol. 25. Curran Associates, Inc. (2012)

18. Kundegorski, M., Akcay, S., Devereux, M., Mouton, A., Breckon, T.: On using feature descriptors as visual words for object detection within X-ray baggage security screening. In: 7th International Conference on Imaging for Crime Detection and Prevention (ICDP 2016), p. 12(6.). Institution of Engineering and Technology, Madrid (2016). https://doi.org/10.1049/ic.2016.0080
19. Lin, T.Y., et al.: Microsoft COCO: common objects in context. arXiv:1405.0312 [cs], February 2015
20. Mery, D., Svec, E., Arias, M., Riffo, V., Saavedra, J.M., Banerjee, S.: Modern computer vision techniques for X-Ray testing in baggage inspection. IEEE Trans. Syst. Man Cybernet. Syst. **47**(4), 682–692 (2017). https://doi.org/10.1109/TSMC.2016.2628381
21. Miao, C., et al.: SIXray: a large-scale security inspection X-Ray benchmark for prohibited item discovery in overlapping images. In: 2019 IEEE/CVF Conference on Computer Vision and Pattern Recognition (CVPR), pp. 2114–2123. IEEE, Long Beach, June 2019. https://doi.org/10.1109/CVPR.2019.00222
22. Qin, Z., Zhang, P., Wu, F., Li, X.: FcaNet: frequency channel attention networks. In: Proceedings of the IEEE/CVF International Conference on Computer Vision (ICCV), pp. 783–792, October 2021
23. Ren, S., He, K., Girshick, R., Sun, J.: Faster R-CNN: towards real-time object detection with region proposal networks. arXiv:1506.01497 [cs], January 2016
24. Ronneberger, O., Fischer, P., Brox, T.: U-Net: convolutional networks for biomedical image segmentation. arXiv:1505.04597 [cs], May 2015
25. Szegedy, C., et al.: Going deeper with convolutions. arXiv:1409.4842 [cs], September 2014
26. Tao, R., et al.: Towards real-world X-ray security inspection: a high-quality benchmark and lateral inhibition module for prohibited items detection. arXiv:2108.09917 [cs], August 2021
27. Tao, R., et al.: Over-sampling de-occlusion attention network for prohibited items detection in noisy X-ray images. arXiv:2103.00809 [cs], March 2021
28. Wang, Q., Wu, B., Zhu, P., Li, P., Zuo, W., Hu, Q.: ECA-Net: efficient channel attention for deep convolutional neural networks. In: 2020 IEEE/CVF Conference on Computer Vision and Pattern Recognition (CVPR), pp. 11531–11539. IEEE, Seattle, June 2020. https://doi.org/10.1109/CVPR42600.2020.01155
29. Wang, X., Girshick, R., Gupta, A., He, K.: Non-local neural networks. In: 2018 IEEE/CVF Conference on Computer Vision and Pattern Recognition, pp. 7794–7803. IEEE, Salt Lake City, June 2018. https://doi.org/10.1109/CVPR.2018.00813
30. Wei, Y., Tao, R., Wu, Z., Ma, Y., Zhang, L., Liu, X.: Occluded prohibited items detection: an X-ray security inspection benchmark and de-occlusion attention module. In: Proceedings of the 28th ACM International Conference on Multimedia, pp. 138–146. ACM, Seattle, October 2020. https://doi.org/10.1145/3394171.3413828
31. Wei, Y., Liu, X.: Dangerous goods detection based on transfer learning in X-ray images. Neural Comput. Appl. **32**(12), 8711–8724 (2019). https://doi.org/10.1007/s00521-019-04360-0
32. Woo, S., Park, J., Lee, J.Y., Kweon, I.S.: CBAM: convolutional block attention module. arXiv:1807.06521 [cs], July 2018
33. Xu, C., Han, N., Li, H.: A dangerous goods detection approach based on YOLOv3. In: Proceedings of the 2018 2nd International Conference on Computer Science and Artificial Intelligence - CSAI 2018, pp. 600–603. ACM Press, Shenzhen (2018). https://doi.org/10.1145/3297156.3297199
34. Yu, C.: The role of human factors in airport baggage screening. Undergraduate Res. J. **9**, 146–155 (2018)

Knowledge Representation
and Reasoning

A Rational Entailment for Expressive Description Logics via Description Logic Programs

Giovanni Casini[1,2]([⊠]) and Umberto Straccia[1]

[1] ISTI - CNR, Pisa, Italy
{giovanni.casini,umberto.straccia}@isti.cnr.it
[2] CAIR - University of Cape Town, Cape Town, South Africa

Abstract. Lehmann and Magidor's *rational closure* is acknowledged as a land-mark in the field of non-monotonic logics and it has also been re-formulated in the context of *Description Logics* (DLs). We show here how to model a rational form of entailment for expressive DLs, such as $\mathcal{SROIQ}$, providing a novel reasoning procedure that compiles a non-monotone DL knowledge base into a *description logic program* (dl-program).

1 Introduction

One of the main non-monotonic formalism, namely Lehmann and Magidor's *rational closure* [23], is acknowledged as a landmark for non-monotonic reasoning due to its logical properties. Rational closure, that falls under the more general class of the rational entailment relations [23], has been proposed in the context of *Description Logics* (DLs) [1], starting from basic DLs, such as $\mathcal{ALC}$ [3,4,8,9,11,17,18], and re-formulated for low-complexity DLs, as $\mathcal{EL}_\perp$ [12,15], as for expressive ones, up to $\mathcal{SROIQ}$ [2].

Here we show an implementation of a rational entailment relation for an expressive DL such as $\mathcal{SROIQ}$ [19]. The main contribution of this paper is that we re-formulate the decision procedure for rational closure by compiling a non-monotone DL knowledge base into a *description logic program* (dl-program) [13]. Dl-programs have been proposed to combine DLs with *Answer Set Programming* [14], an established approach to implement non-monotonic reasoning for rule-based languages. In this way our approach can be easily implemented on top of existing reasoners supporting dl-programs, such as DLV[1].

We proceed as follows. In Sect. 2 we briefly present the logical systems we will refer to in the definition of our method, which is worked out in Sect. 3. Eventually, in Sect. 4 we briefly recall related work and then we conclude.

2 Preliminaries

For the sake of completeness and to ease the reading, we introduce here a minimum of basic notions.

---

[1] http://www.dlvsystem.com.

© Springer Nature Switzerland AG 2022
E. Jembere et al. (Eds.): SACAIR 2021, CCIS 1551, pp. 177–191, 2022.
https://doi.org/10.1007/978-3-030-95070-5_12

2.1   Description Logic Programs

Normal Logic Programs. Assume a first-order vocabulary $\Phi = \langle P, C \rangle$, with C a set of constants $\{a, b, \dots\}$ and P a set of predicates $\{p, q, \dots\}$, and let X be a set of variables $\{x, y, \dots\}$, with P, C, X mutually disjoint. A *term* t is either a variable from X or a constant from C, and an *atom* is an expression $p(t_1, \dots, t_n)$, where p is a n-ary predicate in P and each t_i is a term. A *literal* l is an atom or its negation (via connective $\neg$), while a negation-as-failure literal (*NAF-literal*) is of the form *not* l, where l is a literal. A *rule* r is an expression of the form ($m \geq k \geq 0$)

$$a \leftarrow b_1, \dots, b_k, \textit{not } b_{k+1}, \dots, \textit{not } b_m \,, \tag{1}$$

where $a, b_1, \dots, b_m$ are literals. Intuitively, a rule has to be read as "if we know that $b_1, \dots, b_k$ are true, but we are not aware that $b_{k+1}, \dots, b_m$ are true, then we can conclude a". We indicate by $H(r)$ (head of r) the literal a, by $B^+(r)$ (positive body of r) the set $\{b_1, \dots, b_k\}$ and by $B^-(r)$ (negative body of r) the set $\{b_{k+1}, \dots, b_m\}$. A *normal program* P is a finite set of rules, while a *positive program* P is a finite set of rules in which $B^-(r) = \emptyset$ for every rule r.

As usual, atoms, literals, rules and programs are considered *ground* if they do not contain any variable. The *Herbrand Universe* of a program P (HU_P) is the set of all the constants that appear in P, while the *Herbrand Base* of P (HB_P) is the set of all the literals that can be constructed from the predicates in P and the constants in HU_P. A ground instance of a rule r is obtained substituting every variable occurring in r with a constant symbol in HU_P, and, given a program P, $ground(P)$ is the set of all ground instances of rules in P.

From the semantics point of view, an interpretation I of a program P is a *consistent* subset of HB_P, i.e. $I \subseteq HB_P$ and there is no atom a such that both a and $\neg a$ are in I. The truth value of a literal l is true, false, or unknown in I iff, respectively, $l \in I$, $\neg l \in I$, or $\{l, \neg l\} \cap I = \emptyset$, where $\neg\neg a$ is a. The satisfiability of a program P is reduced to the satisfiability of its rules expressed in ground form: that is, I is a *model* of a program P iff it is a model of $ground(P)$, i.e. if $B^+(r) \subseteq I$ and $B^-(r) \cap I = \emptyset$, then $H(r) \in I$ for every rule in $ground(P)$.

In case of a positive program P, the *answer set* of P is the least model of P with respect to set inclusion: the fact that P is positive guarantees the uniqueness of its answer set [13]. If P is not positive, the notion of *answer set* is defined via the so-called *Gelfond-Lifschitz transformation* (see, *e.g.* [14]). Specifically, consider a program P and an interpretation $I \subseteq HB_P$. The *Gelfond-Lifschitz transformation* of P relative to I gives back a positive program P^I, and it is obtained from $ground(P)$ with the following procedure:

– delete from $ground(P)$ every rule r s.t. $B^-(r) \cap I \neq \emptyset$; and
– from the remaining rules delete the negative part of the body.

In this way, we end up with a positive program P^I, and I is an *answer set* for P iff I is the answer set for the positive ground program P^I. We indicate with $ans(P)$ the set of the answer sets of a program P. Eventually, we define a *cautious* (resp., *brave*) consequence relation $\models_c$ ($\models_b$) as follows: $P \models_c l$ ($P \models_b l$) iff the literal l is true in any (some) answer set of P.

Example 1. Let P be a program composed of the following rules:

$$feline(a) \leftarrow$$
$$feline(b) \leftarrow$$
$$big(b) \leftarrow$$
$$docile(x) \leftarrow feline(x), not\ big(x)\ .$$

Consider the interpretation $I = \{feline(a), feline(b), big(b), docile(a)\}$. Then P^I is defined as follows:

$$feline(a) \leftarrow$$
$$feline(b) \leftarrow$$
$$big(b) \leftarrow$$
$$docile(a) \leftarrow feline(a)\ .$$

It is straightforwardly verified that I is the least model of P^I and, thus, I is an answer set of P (actually, it is the only one).

Description Logics. We shall refer here to an expressive DLs, namely $\mathcal{SROIQ}$ (for more details about it, we refer the reader to [19]). The $\mathcal{SROIQ}$ signature is composed of a set of *concept names* $\mathcal{At} = \{A, B, \ldots\}$, a set of *role names* $\mathcal{S} = \{R, S, \ldots\}$, and a set $\mathcal{O}$ of *individuals* $\{a, b, \ldots\}$. The set of roles is $\mathcal{R} = \mathcal{S} \cup \{R^- \mid R \in \mathcal{S}\} \cup \{U\}$, where R^- is the inverse of a role R (R^{--} is R) and U is the universal role. We can also compose the roles in $\mathcal{R}$ into finite chains such as $R_1 \circ \ldots \circ R_n$. The set $\mathcal{C}$ of $\mathcal{SROIQ}$ concepts is defined inductively as:

(i) $\mathcal{At} \subseteq \mathcal{C}$;
(ii) $\top, \bot \in \mathcal{C}$;
(iii) if $\{a_1, \ldots, a_n\} \subseteq \mathcal{O}$, then $\{a_1, \ldots, a_n\} \in \mathcal{C}$;
(iv) if $C, D \in \mathcal{C}$, then $C \sqcap D, C \sqcup D, \neg C \in \mathcal{C}$;
(v) if $C \in \mathcal{C}, R \in \mathcal{R}$, then $\exists R.C, \forall R.C, \geq_n R.C, \leq_n R.C, \exists R.\texttt{Self} \in \mathcal{C}$.

Condition (iii) indicates that the enumerated sets of individuals (*nominals*) can be used also in the TBox as concepts. An interpretation is a pair $\langle \Delta^{\mathcal{I}}, \cdot^{\mathcal{I}} \rangle$, where $\Delta^{\mathcal{I}}$ is a nonempty set, called *domain*, and the *interpretation function* $\cdot^{\mathcal{I}}$ assigns to every individual a member of the domain $\Delta^{\mathcal{I}}$, to every concept name a subset of $\Delta^{\mathcal{I}}$, and to every role name a subset of $\Delta^{\mathcal{I}} \times \Delta^{\mathcal{I}}$. The function $\cdot^{\mathcal{I}}$ is extended to all the concepts and roles in the following way:

- $\{o_1, \ldots, o_n\}^{\mathcal{I}} = \{o_1^{\mathcal{I}}, \ldots, o_n^{\mathcal{I}}\}$;
- $(C \sqcap D)^{\mathcal{I}} = C^{\mathcal{I}} \cap D^{\mathcal{I}}$;
- $(C \sqcup D)^{\mathcal{I}} = C^{\mathcal{I}} \cup D^{\mathcal{I}}$;
- $(\neg C)^{\mathcal{I}} = \Delta^{\mathcal{I}} / C^{\mathcal{I}}$;
- $(\exists R.C)^{\mathcal{I}} = \{x \subset \Delta^{\mathcal{I}} \mid \exists y.(x, y) \in R^{\mathcal{I}} \wedge y \in C^{\mathcal{I}}\}$;
- $(\forall R.C)^{\mathcal{I}} = \{x \in \Delta^{\mathcal{I}} \mid \forall y.(x, y) \in R^{\mathcal{I}} \rightarrow y \in C^{\mathcal{I}}\}$;
- $(\geq_n R.C)^{\mathcal{I}} = \{x \in \Delta^{\mathcal{I}} \mid \#\{y \mid (x, y) \in R^{\mathcal{I}} \wedge y \in C^{\mathcal{I}}\} \geq n\}$;

- $(\leq_n R.C)^{\mathcal{I}} = \{x \in \Delta^{\mathcal{I}} \mid \#\{y \mid (x,y) \in R^{\mathcal{I}} \wedge y \in C^{\mathcal{I}}\} \leq n\}$;
- $(\exists R.\mathtt{Self})^{\mathcal{I}} = \{x \in \Delta^{\mathcal{I}} \mid (x,x) \in R^{\mathcal{I}}\}$;
- $(R^-)^{\mathcal{I}} = \{(a,b) \mid (b,a) \in R\}$;
- $(U)^{\mathcal{I}} = \Delta^{\mathcal{I}} \times \Delta^{\mathcal{I}}$;
- $(R_1 \circ \ldots \circ R_n)^{\mathcal{I}} = \{(a,b) \mid \exists x_1, \ldots, x_{n-1}.(a,x_1) \in R_1^{\mathcal{I}}, (x_1,x_2) \in R_2^{\mathcal{I}}, \ldots, (x_{n-1},b) \in R_n^{\mathcal{I}}\}$.

where $\#S$ is the cardinality of set $S \subseteq \Delta^{\mathcal{I}}$. A *DL knowledge base* L is a triple $\langle \mathcal{A}, \mathcal{T}, \mathcal{R} \rangle$, where $\mathcal{A}$ is an *ABox*, containing information about the individuals, $\mathcal{T}$ is a *TBox*, containing information about the relations between the concepts, and $\mathcal{R}$ is an *RBox*, containing information about the roles. The form of the allowed axioms are described in Table 1, with their respective semantics ($n \geq 1$).

Table 1. Axioms of *ABox*,*TBox* and *RBox*.

	Axiom name	Syntax	Semantics
ABox	Concept membership axiom	$C(a)$	$a^{\mathcal{I}} \in C^{\mathcal{I}}$
	Role membership axiom	$R(a,b)$	$(a^{\mathcal{I}}, b^{\mathcal{I}}) \in R^{\mathcal{I}}$
TBox	Concept inclusion axiom	$C \sqsubseteq D$	$C^{\mathcal{I}} \subseteq D^{\mathcal{I}}$
RBox	Role inclusion axiom	$R_1 \circ \ldots \circ R_n \sqsubseteq S$	$(R_1 \circ \ldots \circ R_n)^{\mathcal{I}} \subseteq S^{\mathcal{I}}$
	Transitivity	$Trans(R)$	$R^{\mathcal{I}}$ is transitive
	Functionality	$Fun(R)$	$R^{\mathcal{I}}$ is a function
	Reflexivity	$Ref(R)$	$R^{\mathcal{I}}$ is reflexive
	Irreflexivity	$Irr(R)$	$R^{\mathcal{I}}$ is irreflexive
	Symmetry	$Sym(R)$	$R^{\mathcal{I}}$ is symmetric
	Asymmetry	$Asy(R)$	$R^{\mathcal{I}}$ is asymmetric
	Disjointness	$Dis(R,S)$	$R^{\mathcal{I}}$ and $S^{\mathcal{I}}$ are disjoint

A RBox has further to comply with an additional syntactical restriction: that is, a RBox has to be *regular*, which essentially prevents a RBox from containing cyclic dependencies among roles that are known to lead to undecidability [20]. For ease of presentation we do not include the definition here and refer the reader to [19, Definition 2] instead. We use $C = D$ as a shorthand of the concept inclusion axiom $\top \sqsubseteq (\neg C \sqcup D) \sqcap (\neg D \sqcup C)$. With $\models$ we denote the classical, monotonic, consequence/entailment relation, which is defined as usual.

Note also that every ABox axiom can be reformulated as an equivalent TBox axiom. In particular, $C(a)$ can be reformulated as $\{a\} \sqsubseteq C$, while $R(a,b)$ is equivalent to $\{a\} \sqsubseteq \exists R.\{b\}$. Consequently, in what follows we will not consider ABoxes.

Description Logic Programs. A *description logic program* (*dl-program*) is composed of a pair $\mathcal{K} = \langle L, P \rangle$, where L is a DL knowledge base and P is a set of *dl-rules* [13], which we are going to specify next. The DL knowledge base L is defined over a vocabulary composed of a set of concept names $\mathcal{At}$, a set of role names $\mathcal{S}$, and a set $\mathcal{O}$

of individuals, while P is defined over a vocabulary $\Phi = \langle P, C \rangle$, with C a set of constants and P a set of predicates, and with X a set of variables. We assume that the predicative part of the two formalisms are independent, that is $\mathcal{At} \cup \mathcal{S}$ is disjoint from P, while the same domain of individuals is shared, that is $HU_P \subseteq C \subseteq \mathcal{O}$.

Dl-programs use the notions of *dl-query* and *dl-atom* to be used in rule bodies to express queries to the DL knowledge base L. That is, a *dl-query* $Q(\mathbf{t})$ can have various forms, but to what concerns us, it is sufficient to consider the following ones:

- a concept membership axiom $C(t)$ (so, $\mathbf{t} = t$);
- a role membership axiom $R(t_1, t_2)$ (so, $\mathbf{t} = \langle t_1, t_2 \rangle$).

On the other hand, a *dl-atom* is an expression of the form[2]

$$DL[S_1 \uplus p_1, \ldots, S_m \uplus p_m; Q](\mathbf{t})$$

with $m \geq 0$, where each S_i is either a concept or a role ($S_i \in \mathcal{C} \cup \mathcal{R}$), and each p_i is a predicate symbol from P, unary if S_i is a concept, binary otherwise, and $Q(\mathbf{t})$ is a dl-query. The operator $\uplus$ is functional to the updating of the DL knowledge base L with factual information obtained from the activation of the rules in the program. That is, each $S_i \uplus p_i$ indicates that the extension of S_i is increased by the extension of p_i.

Now, a *dl-rule* r is of the form (1), where any literal $b_1, \ldots, b_m \in B(r)$ may be a dl-atom and a *dl-program* is a pair $\mathcal{K} = \langle L, P \rangle$, where L is a DL knowledge base and P is a set of dl-rules.

From a semantics points of view, for an interpretations $I \subseteq HB_P$, we say that I is a *model* of a ground literal or dl-atom l under L ($I \models_L l$) iff

- if $l \in HB_P$, then $I \models_L l$ iff $l \in I$;
- if l is a ground dl-atom $DL[\lambda, Q](\mathbf{c})$, where $\lambda = S_1 \uplus p_1, \ldots, S_m \uplus p_m$, then $I \models_L l$ iff $L(I; \lambda) \models Q(\mathbf{c})$, where $L(I; \lambda) = L \cup \bigcup_{i=1}^m A_i(I)$, with, for $1 \leq i \leq m$, $A_i(I) = \{S_i(\mathbf{e}) \mid p_i(\mathbf{e}) \in I\}$,

As usual, an interpretation I is a *model* of a ground dl-rule r iff $I \models_L l$ for all $l \in B^+(r)$ and $I \not\models_L l$ for all $l \in B^-(r)$ implies $I \models_L H(r)$. I is a *model* of a dl-program $\mathcal{K} = \langle L, P \rangle$ (written $I \models \mathcal{K}$) iff $I \models_L r$ for all $r \in ground(P)$. We say that $\mathcal{K}$ is *satisfiable* if it has a model.

Let $KB = \langle L, P \rangle$ be a dl-program. The *strong dl-transform* of P w.r.t. L and I (denoted sP_L^I) is the set of all dl-rules obtained from $ground(P)$ by deleting

- every dl-rule r s.t. $I \models_L l$ for some $l \in B^-(r)$;
- from the remaining dl-rule r all literals in $B^-(r)$.

Note that (i) $\langle L, sP_L^I \rangle$ has only monotonic dl-atoms and no NAF-literals anymore; and (ii) a *positive* dl-program, if satisfiable, has a least model [13]. Now, a *strong answer set* of $\mathcal{K} = \langle L, P \rangle$ is an interpretation $I \subseteq HB_P$ s.t. I is the least model of $\langle L, sP_L^I \rangle$. We denote with $ans_s(\mathcal{K})$ the set of the strong answer sets of $\mathcal{K}$. l is a *cautious (brave)*

---

[2] The definition given here is again simpler than the original one, as we consider only the form strictly required for our proposal.

consequence of $\mathcal{K}$, indicated as $\mathcal{K} \models_{s,c} l$ ($\mathcal{K} \models_{s,b} l$) iff l is true in every (some) strong answer of $\mathcal{K}$.

Note that given a dl-program $\mathcal{K} = \langle L, P \rangle$ and an answer set I of $\mathcal{K}$, I is a minimal model of $\mathcal{K}$ [13].

Example 2. Consider a dl-program $\mathcal{K} = \langle L, P \rangle$. Let $L = \langle \mathcal{T} \rangle$, with

$$\mathcal{T} = \{\{a\} \sqsubseteq Cat, \{b\} \sqsubseteq Feline, \{b\} \sqsubseteq Big\},$$

and consider a dl-program P composed of the following rules:

$$feline(x) \leftarrow DL[Cat](x)$$
$$docile(x) \leftarrow DL[Feline \uplus feline; Feline](x), not\ DL[Big](x).$$

It can easily be shown that $\mathcal{K}$ has a unique answer set

$$I = \{feline(a), docile(a)\}.$$

In fact, I is the least model of the following set sP_L^I of dl-rules:

$$feline(b) \leftarrow DL[Cat](b)$$
$$feline(a) \leftarrow DL[Cat](a)$$
$$docile(a) \leftarrow DL[Feline \uplus feline; Feline](a).$$

2.2   Rational Closure for $\mathcal{ALC}$

For convenience, we recap here some salient notions related to *rational closure* (RC) for DLs, specifically for the DL $\mathcal{ALC}$ (see, *e.g.* [8]).

Remark 1. We remind that $\mathcal{ALC}$ concepts are inductively defined as (i) $At \subseteq \mathcal{C}$; (ii) $\top, \bot \in \mathcal{C}$; (iii) if $C, D \in \mathcal{C}$, then $C \sqcap D, C \sqcup D, \neg C \in \mathcal{C}$; (iv)] if $C \in \mathcal{C}, R \in \mathcal{R}$, then $\exists R.C, \forall R.C \in \mathcal{C}$.

Now, a *defeasible concept inclusion* axiom is of the form $C \mathrel{\vcenter{\hbox{$\scriptstyle\sqsubset$}}\mkern-3mu\sim} D$, where, without loss of generality, C and D are assumed to be atomic concepts or their negation. The expression $C \mathrel{\vcenter{\hbox{$\scriptstyle\sqsubset$}}\mkern-3mu\sim} D$ has to be read as 'if an individual falls under the concept C, typically it falls also under the concept D'. A *defeasible* DL knowledge base is a pair $L = \langle \mathcal{T}, \mathcal{D} \rangle$, where $\mathcal{T}$ (the *TBox*) is a finite set of concept inclusion axioms of the form $C \sqsubseteq D$, where C, D are $\mathcal{ALC}$ concepts, and $\mathcal{D}$ (the *DBox*) is a finite set of defeasible concept inclusion of the form $C \mathrel{\vcenter{\hbox{$\scriptstyle\sqsubset$}}\mkern-3mu\sim} D$.

We next briefly describe the decision procedure for RC for $\mathcal{ALC}$, referring in particular to the one presented in [3], that in turn has been obtained by refining the one presented in [8]. Consider $L = \langle \mathcal{T}, \mathcal{D} \rangle$. The first step of the procedure is to assign a rank to each defeasible axiom in $\mathcal{D}$. The rank of the defeasible axioms indicates, in case of conflictual information, which axiom is associated to more specific premises, and has the priority over the axioms associated to more general premises. Central to this step is the exceptionality procedure Exceptional$(\cdot)$ (see below). The procedure makes use of the notion of *materialisation*, to reduce concept exceptionality checking to entailment checking, were the *materialisation* of $\mathcal{D}$ is defined as $\overline{\mathcal{D}} := \{\neg C \sqcup D \mid C \mathrel{\vcenter{\hbox{$\scriptstyle\sqsubset$}}\mkern-3mu\sim} D \in \mathcal{D}\}$.

Procedure Exceptional(L)

> **Input**: A DL knowledge base $L = \langle \mathcal{T}, \mathcal{D} \rangle$
> **Output**: $\mathcal{E} \subseteq \mathcal{D}$

1 $\mathcal{E} := \emptyset$;
2 **foreach** $C \mathrel{\reflectbox{$\sqsubset$}} D \in \mathcal{D}$ **do**
3 $\quad$ **if** $\mathcal{T} \models \bigsqcap \overline{\mathcal{D}} \sqsubseteq \neg C$ **then**
4 $\quad\quad$ $\mathcal{E} := \mathcal{E} \cup \{C \mathrel{\reflectbox{$\sqsubset$}} D\}$
5 **return** $\mathcal{E}$

Procedure ComputeRanking(L)

> **Input**: A DL knowledge base $L = \langle \mathcal{T}, \mathcal{D} \rangle$
> **Output**: $L^* = \langle \mathcal{T}^*, \mathcal{D}^* \rangle$ and an exceptionality ranking $\mathcal{E}$

1 $\mathcal{T}^* := \mathcal{T}$;
2 $\mathcal{D}^* := \mathcal{D}$;
3 **repeat**
4 $\quad$ $i := 0$;
5 $\quad$ $\mathcal{E}_0 := \mathcal{D}^*$;
6 $\quad$ $\mathcal{E}_1 := \text{Exceptional}(\langle \mathcal{T}^*, \mathcal{E}_0 \rangle)$;
7 $\quad$ **while** $\mathcal{E}_{i+1} \neq \mathcal{E}_i$ **do**
8 $\quad\quad$ $i := i + 1$;
9 $\quad\quad$ $\mathcal{E}_{i+1} := \text{Exceptional}(\langle \mathcal{T}^*, \mathcal{E}_i \rangle)$;
10 $\quad$ $\mathcal{D}^*_\infty := \mathcal{E}_i$;
11 $\quad$ $\mathcal{T}^* := \mathcal{T}^* \cup \{C \sqsubseteq D \mid C \mathrel{\reflectbox{$\sqsubset$}} D \in \mathcal{D}^*_\infty\}$;
12 $\quad$ $\mathcal{D}^* := \mathcal{D}^* \setminus \mathcal{D}^*_\infty$;
13 **until** $\mathcal{D}^*_\infty = \emptyset$;
14 $\mathcal{E} := (\mathcal{E}_0, \ldots, \mathcal{E}_{i-1})$;
15 **return** $(L^* = \langle \mathcal{T}^*, \mathcal{D}^* \rangle, \mathcal{E})$;

The ranking of the defeasible axioms is done via the ComputeRanking($\cdot$) procedure.

In short, the ComputeRanking($\cdot$) takes as input $L = \langle \mathcal{T}, \mathcal{D} \rangle$ and gives back a new semantically equivalent knowledge base $L = \langle \mathcal{T}^*, \mathcal{D}^* \rangle$ (with $\mathcal{T} \subseteq \mathcal{T}^*$ and $\mathcal{D}^* \subseteq \mathcal{D}$), where possibly some defeasible information in $\mathcal{D}$ has been identified as strict and added to $\mathcal{T}$. Also, a sequence of $\subseteq$-ordered subsets of $\mathcal{D}$ ($\mathcal{E}_0, \ldots, \mathcal{E}_{i-1}$), with increasing level of specificity. That is, in case of potential conflicts, the axioms in a set $\mathcal{E}_j$, $j \geq 0$, have the priority over the axioms in any $\mathcal{E}_i$, $0 \leq i < j$. Now, by considering the ranking $\mathcal{E}_0, \ldots, \mathcal{E}_{i-1}$, we can define a ranking function r that associates to every defeasible concept inclusion in $\mathcal{D}$ a number, representing its level of exceptionality: that is,

$$r(C \mathrel{\reflectbox{$\sqsubset$}} D) = \begin{cases} j & \text{if } C \mathrel{\reflectbox{$\sqsubset$}} D \in \mathcal{E}_j \text{ and } C \mathrel{\reflectbox{$\sqsubset$}} D \notin \mathcal{E}_{j+1} \\ \infty & \text{if } C \mathrel{\reflectbox{$\sqsubset$}} D \in \mathcal{E}_j \text{ for every } j . \end{cases}$$

Similarly, we may associate a rank to a concept C in the following way: consider the result $(L^* = \langle \mathcal{T}^*, \mathcal{D}^* \rangle, \mathcal{E} = (\mathcal{E}_0, \ldots, \mathcal{E}_n))$ of ComputeRanking($\cdot$). Then

$$r(C) = \begin{cases} j & \text{if } T^* \models \bigcap \overline{\mathcal{E}}_j \sqsubseteq \neg C \text{ and } T^* \not\models \bigcap \overline{\mathcal{E}}_{j+1} \sqsubseteq \neg C \\ \infty & \text{if } T^* \models \bigcap \overline{\mathcal{E}}_j \sqsubseteq \neg C \text{ for every } j. \end{cases}$$

Note that $r(C \mathrel{\vert\!\sim} D) = r(C)$. Now, we will say that $C \mathrel{\vert\!\sim} D$ is *entailed* by the rational closure of a DL knowledge base L (denoted $L \vdash_{\text{rat}} C \mathrel{\vert\!\sim} D$) iff $r(C) < r(C \sqcap \neg D)$ [23, Theorem 5.17]). Finally, the procedure `RationalClosure`$(\cdot)$ determines whether $L \vdash_{\text{rat}} C \mathrel{\vert\!\sim} D$. We recall that the defined entailment relation is indeed as so-called *rational consequence relation* [23], *i.e.* satisfies the following properties:

(REF) $L \vdash_{\text{rat}} C \mathrel{\vert\!\sim} C$ Reflexivity

(LLE) $\dfrac{L \vdash_{\text{rat}} C \mathrel{\vert\!\sim} F \;\; L \models C = D}{L \vdash_{\text{rat}} D \mathrel{\vert\!\sim} F}$ Left Logical Equival

(RW) $\dfrac{L \vdash_{\text{rat}} C \mathrel{\vert\!\sim} D \;\; L \models D \sqsubseteq F}{L \vdash_{\text{rat}} C \mathrel{\vert\!\sim} F}$ Right Weakening

(CT) $\dfrac{L \vdash_{\text{rat}} C \mathrel{\vert\!\sim} D \;\; L \models C \sqcap D \mathrel{\vert\!\sim} F}{L \vdash_{\text{rat}} C \mathrel{\vert\!\sim} F}$ Cut (Cumulative Trans.)

(OR) $\dfrac{L \vdash_{\text{rat}} C \mathrel{\vert\!\sim} F \;\; L \vdash_{\text{rat}} D \mathrel{\vert\!\sim} F}{L \vdash_{\text{rat}} C \sqcup D \mathrel{\vert\!\sim} F}$ Left Disjunction

(RM) $\dfrac{L \vdash_{\text{rat}} C \mathrel{\vert\!\sim} F \;\; L \not\vdash_{\text{rat}} C \mathrel{\vert\!\sim} \neg D}{L \vdash_{\text{rat}} C \sqcap D \mathrel{\vert\!\sim} F}$ Rational Monotony

---

Procedure RationalClosure(L, α)

   Input: $L = \langle T, \mathcal{D} \rangle$ and a query $\alpha = C \mathrel{\vert\!\sim} D$.
   Output: `true` if $L \vdash_{\text{rat}} C \mathrel{\vert\!\sim} D$, `false` otherwise
1   $(L^* = \langle T^*, \mathcal{D}^* \rangle, \mathcal{E} = (\mathcal{E}_0, \ldots, \mathcal{E}_n)) :=$ ComputeRanking(L);
2   $i := 0$;
3   **while** $T^* \models \bigcap \overline{\mathcal{E}}_i \sqcap C \sqsubseteq \bot$ *and* $i \le n$ **do**
4     $\lfloor \quad i := i + 1$;
5   **if** $i \le n$ **then**
6     $\lfloor \quad$ **return** $T^* \models \bigcap \overline{\mathcal{E}}_i \sqcap C \sqsubseteq D$;
7   **else**
8     $\lfloor \quad$ **return** $T^* \models C \sqsubseteq D$;

We refer the reader to [3] for further explanations and details and limit our presentation to a concluding example.

Example 3. Assume a DL knowledge base $\langle T, \mathcal{D} \rangle$ with

$$T = \{Cat \sqsubseteq Feline, Tiger \sqsubseteq Feline, Tiger \sqsubseteq Big, BigFeline = Feline \sqcap Big \}$$
$$\mathcal{D} = \{Feline \mathrel{\vert\!\sim} Agile, Feline \mathrel{\vert\!\sim} Docile, BigFeline \mathrel{\vert\!\sim} \neg Docile \}.$$

By applying the ranking procedure, we end up with

$$r(Cat) = r(Feline) = 0$$
$$r(Feline \mathrel{\vreset} Agile) = r(Feline \mathrel{\vreset} Docile) = 0$$

$$r(Tiger) = r(Feline \sqcap Big) = 1$$
$$r(BigFeline \mathrel{\vreset} \neg Docile) = 1 \,.$$

So, for instance, we can conclude that

$$\mathcal{K} \vdash_{\mathsf{rat}} Cat \mathrel{\vreset} Docile \,, \mathcal{K} \vdash_{\mathsf{rat}} Cat \mathrel{\vreset} Agile \,, \mathcal{K} \vdash_{\mathsf{rat}} Cat \mathrel{\vreset} \neg Big$$
$$\mathcal{K} \vdash_{\mathsf{rat}} Tiger \mathrel{\vreset} \neg Docile \,, \mathcal{K} \vdash_{\mathsf{rat}} Cat \mathrel{\vreset} \neg Tiger \,.$$

3 Rational Entailment for DLs via Dl-Programs

In this section we show that, starting from a non-monotonic DL ($\mathcal{SROIQ}$) knowledge base $L = \langle \mathcal{T}, \mathcal{R}, \mathcal{D} \rangle$, we can compile L into a dl-program $\mathcal{K} = \langle \langle \mathcal{T}^*, \mathcal{R} \rangle, P \rangle$ such that the conditions for rational consequence relations are preserved. So, consider a defeasible $\mathcal{SROIQ}$ knowledge base $L = \langle \mathcal{T}, \mathcal{D} \rangle$. Our approach consists of two steps: a ranking step and a compilation step.

Ranking Step. To L we apply the procedure ComputeRanking(L) described in Sect. 2.2[3] and, thus, we end up with a new defeasible DL knowledge base $L^* = \langle \mathcal{T}^*, \mathcal{R}, \mathcal{D}^* \rangle$ that correctly separates the strict and the defeasible information contained in the original pair $L = \langle \mathcal{T}, \mathcal{R}, \mathcal{D} \rangle$, and a ranking value $r(C \mathrel{\vreset} D)$ for every defeasible axiom $C \mathrel{\vreset} D \in \mathcal{D}^*$.

Note that in order to adapt the procedures Exceptional($\cdot$) and ComputeRanking($\cdot$) to $\mathcal{SROIQ}$ it is sufficient to consider also $\mathcal{R}$ into the ranking procedure: the inputs of both the procedures is a DL knowledge base $L = \langle \mathcal{T}, \mathcal{R}, \mathcal{D} \rangle$ instead of $L = \langle \mathcal{T}, \mathcal{D} \rangle$, and line 3 in Procedure Exceptional($\cdot$) is modified from $\mathcal{T} \models \sqcap \overline{\mathcal{D}} \sqsubseteq \neg C$ to $\mathcal{T} \cup \mathcal{R} \models \sqcap \overline{\mathcal{D}} \sqsubseteq \neg C$. The set $\mathcal{R}$ comes out untouched from the ranking procedure, since $\mathcal{D}$ is the only ranked set, and the only possible new strict information is of the form $C \sqsubseteq D$, with C and D concepts, hence it can affect only the content of $\mathcal{T}$. Hence, starting from a knowledge base $\langle \mathcal{T}, \mathcal{R}, \mathcal{D} \rangle$ we end up with a ranked knowledge base $\langle \mathcal{T}^*, \mathcal{R}, \mathcal{D}^* \rangle$.

Dl-program Compilation Step. Given $L^* = \langle \mathcal{T}^*, \mathcal{R}, \mathcal{D}^* \rangle$ from the ranking step, we now compile the defeasible information in $\mathcal{D}^*$ into a a set of dl-rules P, which together with $\mathcal{T}^*, \mathcal{R}$ defines then the final dl-program $\mathcal{K} = \langle \langle \mathcal{T}^*, \mathcal{R} \rangle, P \rangle$.

To alleviate the reading, let $L = \langle \mathcal{T}, \mathcal{R}, \mathcal{D} \rangle := \langle \mathcal{T}^*, \mathcal{R}, \mathcal{D}^* \rangle$; that is, we assume that $\langle \mathcal{T}, \mathcal{R}, \mathcal{D} \rangle$ has already been ranked via the previous ranking step. Now, define a signature $\Phi = \langle \mathsf{P}, \mathsf{C} \rangle$ with $\mathsf{C} = \mathcal{O}$, while P is composed of the predicates $(c, d, e, \dots)$ representing at the level of programs the concept names in $\mathcal{T} \cup \mathcal{D}$, *i.e.* for each concept

---

[3] Of course, Exceptional($\cdot$) and, thus, ComputeRanking($\cdot$), can be applied to a DL $\mathcal{SROIQ}$ knowledge base L as the classical entailment relation for $\mathcal{SROIQ}$ is decidable.

C in $\mathcal{A}t$ we have an unary predicate c representing it in the rules. We will use the same name with or without the uppercase initial letter to indicate if it is a concept in DL (*e.g.*, *Male*) or a predicate in P (*e.g.*, *male*), respectively. Let us also recall that for each $C \mathrel{\underset{\sim}{\sqsubseteq}} D \in \mathcal{D}$, C and D are either atomic concepts or their negation. Given the ranking of the defeasible axioms in $\mathcal{D}$, let

$$\mathcal{D}_k = \{C \mathrel{\underset{\sim}{\sqsubseteq}} D \mid C \mathrel{\underset{\sim}{\sqsubseteq}} D \in \mathcal{D} \text{ and } r(C \mathrel{\underset{\sim}{\sqsubseteq}} D) = k\}$$

be the subset of $\mathcal{D}$ composed of the axioms with rank value k. Now, define the set

$$\mathfrak{A}_{\mathcal{D}_k} = \{C \mid C \mathrel{\underset{\sim}{\sqsubseteq}} D \in \mathcal{D}_k\}$$

as the set of all the antecedents of the defeasible axioms of rank k. Moreover, we consider also the set of the consequents of the defeasible axioms

$$\mathfrak{C}_{\mathcal{D}} = \{D \mid C \mathrel{\underset{\sim}{\sqsubseteq}} D \in \mathcal{D}\}.$$

Now, for every axiom $C \mathrel{\underset{\sim}{\sqsubseteq}} D \in \mathcal{D}$ of rank k, we create a pair of rules of the form[4]

$$
\begin{aligned}
d(x) &\leftarrow DL[\lambda; C](x), \\
&\quad not\ DL[\lambda; \textstyle\bigsqcup \{C' \mid C' \in \mathfrak{A}_{\mathcal{D}_m}, \text{ with } m > k\}](x), \\
&\quad not\ \neg d(x) \\
\neg d(x) &\leftarrow DL[\lambda; \neg D](x).
\end{aligned}
\tag{2}
$$

Additionally, for all $C \in \mathfrak{A}_{\mathcal{D}_m}$ with $m > 1$, we also consider a rule

$$\neg c(x) \leftarrow not\ DL[\lambda; C](x). \tag{3}$$

In all rules above, $\lambda = \{E \uplus e, \neg E \uplus \neg e \mid E \in \mathfrak{C}_{\mathcal{D}}\}$. Note that the size of the grounding of the compiled dl-program is polynomially bounded by the size of the defeasible DL knowledge base.

The intuitive meaning of the rule (2) is the following: assume we have an individual a that is an instance of concept C, which is the antecedent of the defeasible axiom $C \mathrel{\underset{\sim}{\sqsubseteq}} D$ of rank k; if a is not an instance of any other $\mathcal{D}$-antecedent that is more exceptional than C, *i.e. not* $DL[\lambda; \bigsqcup\{C' \mid C' \in \mathfrak{A}_{\mathcal{D}_m}, \text{ with } m > k\}](x)$ holds, and $d(a)$ is consistent with our knowledge base, then we can conclude $d(a)$.

On the other hand, the purpose of rule (2) is to update P, in case we derive in L that the conclusion of a defeasible axiom is negated and, thus, the defeasible axiom cannot be applied. λ is necessary to update the DL-base L with the conclusions drawn at the program level.

Finally, rules of form (3) impose that the individuals we are dealing with are as typical as possible. That is, if we are not aware that an exceptional premise applies to them (any concept in $\mathfrak{A}_{\mathcal{D}_m}$, with $m > 1$), then we assume that it doesn't apply (*e.g.*, if we note that a is a bird, but we are not aware that it is a penguin, then we presume that it is not a penguin). In the following, we illustrate our technique via an example.

---

[4] We assume to simplify double negation: that is, for a concept name F, $\neg\neg F$ is F, and similarly, for a logic program predicate f, $\neg\neg f$ is f. See also Example 4 later on.

Example 4. Assume we have a DL vocabulary with $\mathcal{A}t = \{B, P, F, I, Fi, W,$
$Preyins, Preyfish\}$, $\mathcal{S} = \{Prey\}$, and $\mathcal{O} = \{a, b\}$, were the symbols stand for;
$B \mapsto bird$, $P \mapsto penguin$, $F \mapsto flies$, $I \mapsto insect$, $Fi \mapsto fish$, $W \mapsto has\ wings$,
$Preyins \mapsto eats\ insects$, $Preyfish \mapsto eats\ fishes$, while $Prey$ is the relation *preys on*.
The DL base $L = \langle T, \mathcal{D} \rangle$ is composed of

$$T = \{\{a\} \sqsubseteq B, \{b\} \sqsubseteq P, P \sqsubseteq B, I \sqsubseteq \neg Fi,$$
$$Preyins = \forall Prey.I \sqcap \exists Prey.\top,$$
$$Preyfish = \forall Prey.Fi \sqcap \exists Prey.\top \}$$

$$\mathcal{D} = \{B \mathrel{\widetilde{\sqsubseteq}} F, P \mathrel{\widetilde{\sqsubseteq}} \neg F, B \mathrel{\widetilde{\sqsubseteq}} Preyins, P \mathrel{\widetilde{\sqsubseteq}} Preyfish, B \mathrel{\widetilde{\sqsubseteq}} W \}.$$

Now, it can be verified that the ranking step returns the following ranking of axioms $\mathcal{D}$:

$$\mathcal{D}_0 = \{B \mathrel{\widetilde{\sqsubseteq}} F, B \mathrel{\widetilde{\sqsubseteq}} Preyins, B \mathrel{\widetilde{\sqsubseteq}} W \}$$
$$\mathcal{D}_1 = \{P \mathrel{\widetilde{\sqsubseteq}} \neg F, P \mathrel{\widetilde{\sqsubseteq}} Preyfish \}.$$

Therefore, $\mathfrak{A}_{\mathcal{D}_0} = \{B\}$, $\mathfrak{A}_{\mathcal{D}_1} = \{P\}$, $\mathfrak{C}_{\mathcal{D}} = \{F, \neg F, Preyins, Preyfish, W\}$.
The compilation step proceeds now as follows. We define a vocabulary $\Phi = \langle P, C \rangle$ with
$C = \{a, b\}$, while P is composed of predicates that represent at the program level the DL
atomic concepts and roles: that is, $P = \{b, p, f, i, fi, w, preyins, preyfish, prey\}$. The
program P, resulting from the compilation step, is composed of the following rules:

$$f(x) \leftarrow DL[\lambda; B](x), not\ DL[\lambda; P](x), not\ \neg f(x)$$
$$\neg f(x) \leftarrow DL[\lambda; \neg F](x)$$

$$preyins(x) \leftarrow DL[\lambda; B](x), not\ DL[\lambda; P](x), not\ \neg preyins(x)$$
$$\neg preyins(x) \leftarrow DL[\lambda; \neg Preyins](x)$$

$$w(x) \leftarrow DL[\lambda; B](x), not\ DL[\lambda; P](x), not\ \neg w(x)$$
$$\neg w(x) \leftarrow DL[\lambda; \neg W](x)$$

$$\neg f(x) \leftarrow DL[\lambda; P](x), not\ f(x)$$
$$f(x) \leftarrow DL[\lambda; F](x)$$

$$preyfish(x) \leftarrow DL[\lambda; P](x), not\ \neg preyfish(x)$$
$$\neg preyfish(x) \leftarrow DL[\lambda; \neg Preyfish](x)$$

$$\neg p(x) \leftarrow not\ DL[\lambda; P](x),$$

with

$$\lambda = \{F \uplus f, \neg F \uplus \neg f, W \uplus w, \neg W \uplus \neg w, Preyins \uplus preyins,$$
$$\neg Preyins \uplus \neg preyins, Preyfish \uplus preyfish, \neg Preyfish \uplus \neg preyfish \}.$$

Now, note that the only answer set to the program P is the interpretation

$$I = \{f(a), preyins(a), w(a), \neg p(a), \neg f(b), preyfish(b)\} \,.$$

In fact, I is the least model of the grounded positive program P^I

$$f(a) \leftarrow DL[\lambda; B](a)$$
$$preyins(a) \leftarrow DL[\lambda; B](a)$$
$$w(a) \leftarrow DL[\lambda; B](a)$$
$$\neg f(b) \leftarrow DL[\lambda; P](b)$$
$$preyfish(b) \leftarrow DL[\lambda; P](b)$$
$$\neg p(a) \leftarrow \,.$$

So, we obtain the intuitive conclusions that, if we are aware about an individual that it is just a bird, we can conclude that, presumably, it flies, eats insects and has wings. On the other hand, if we are informed that it is a penguin, we can conclude that it doesn't fly and eats fishes.

As well known and already noted in [8], having *nominal concepts* may end up in having multiple extensions, *i.e.*, in our context, we may have multiple strong answer sets as shown with the following simple example.

Example 5. Consider a knowledge base $L = \langle T, D \rangle$, with

$$T = \{\{a\} \sqsubseteq \exists R.\{b\}, C = D \sqcap \forall R.\neg D \,\}$$
$$D = \{\top \sqsubseteq C\} \,.$$

By applying our method we obtain the following program P

$$c(x) \leftarrow DL[\lambda; \top](x), not \,\neg c(x)$$
$$\neg c(x) \leftarrow DL[\lambda; \neg C](x) \,.$$

Now, it can be verified that from the dl-program $\mathcal{K} = \langle L, P \rangle$ we obtain now two strong answer sets: namely,

$$I = \{c(a), \neg c(b) \,\}$$
$$I' = \{c(b), \neg c(a) \,\} \,.$$

Nevertheless, the main result of this paper is that each strong answer set defines a rational consequence relation. In fact, we consider the content of the DL base updated with the content of an answer set I by means of the operator $\uplus$. That is, we define a consequence relation $\models_{PI}$ where, $\mathcal{K} = \langle L, P \rangle \models_{PI} C(a)$ iff the DL base L augmented, using $\uplus$, with the content of a strong answer set I of $\mathcal{K}$, entails $C(a)$. Specifically, we can show that

Proposition 1. *Given $\mathcal{K} = \langle L, P \rangle$, were L contains a $\mathcal{SROIQ}$ TBox and a $\mathcal{SROIQ}$ RBox, P is the result of compiling L into dl-rules, and a strong answer set I of $\mathcal{K}$. Then the consequence relation $\models_{PI}$ satisfies the following properties:*[5]

---

[5] For ease of comprehension, we write concept assertions as $D(b)$ in place of the equivalent inclusion axiom $\{b\} \sqsubseteq D$ in expressions like $L \cup \{D(b)\}$.

REF_{DL} $\langle L, P \rangle \models_{PI} C(a)$ for every $C(a) \in L$

$$\text{LLE}_{DL} \quad \frac{\langle L \cup \{D(b)\}, P \rangle \models_{PI} C(a) \quad L \models D = E}{\langle L \cup \{E(b)\}, P \rangle \models_{PI} C(a)}$$

$$\text{RW}_{DL} \quad \frac{\langle L, P \rangle \models_{PI} C(a) \quad L \models C \sqsubseteq D}{\langle L, P \rangle \models_{PI} D(a)}$$

$$\text{CT}_{DL} \quad \frac{\langle L \cup \{D(b)\}, P \rangle \models_{PI} C(a) \quad \langle L, P \rangle \models_{PI} D(b)}{\langle L, P \rangle \models_{PI} C(a)}$$

$$\text{OR}_{DL} \quad \frac{\langle L \cup \{D(b)\}, P \rangle \models_{PI} C(a) \quad \langle L \cup \{E(b)\}, P \rangle \models_{PI} C(a)}{\langle L \cup \{(D \sqcup E)(b)\}, P \rangle \models_{PI} C(a)}$$

$$\text{RM}_{DL} \quad \frac{\langle L, P \rangle \models_{PI} C(a) \quad \langle L, P \rangle \not\models_{PI} \neg D(b)}{\langle L \cup \{D(b)\}, P \rangle \models_{PI} C(a)}$$

Proof. (Sketch) The proofs for REF_{DL}, LLE_{DL} are RW_{DL} are straightforward, considering the set-theoretic semantics of DLs.

In what follows, given the strong answer set I, the expression I^{DL} indicates the obvious translation of the answer set into the DL base L, so that $\langle L, P \rangle \models_{PI} C(a)$ iff $L \cup I^{DL} \models C(a)$.

For CT_{DL}, if I is an answer set for both $\langle L, P \rangle$ and $\langle L \cup \{D(b)\}, P \rangle$, then we have $L \cup \{D(b)\} \cup I^{DL} \models C(a)$ and $L \cup I^{DL} \models D(b)$, and, since every classical DL consequence relation $\models$ satisfies CT, we have $L \cup I^{DL} \models C(a)$, i.e. $\langle L, P \rangle \models_{PI} C(a)$.

For OR_{DL}, if I is an answer set for both $\langle L \cup \{D(b)\}, P \rangle$ and $\langle L \cup \{E(b)\}, P \rangle$, it must be an answer set also for $\langle L \cup \{(D \sqcup E)(b)\}, P \rangle$: since $\models$ is monotonic, it is not possible to derive from $L \cup \{(D \sqcup E)(b)\}$ some element of the set $B^-(r)$ of some r in P that could not be derived from $L \cup \{D(b)\}$ or $L \cup \{E(b)\}$; hence a rule can be eliminated from P only if also $L \cup \{D(b)\}$ or $L \cup \{E(b)\}$ would eliminate it. Given the validity of OR for $\models$, we have that $L \cup \{D(b)\} \cup I^{DL} \models C(a)$ and $L \cup \{E(b)\} \cup I^{DL} \models C(a)$ imply $L \cup \{(D \sqcup E)(b)\} \cup I^{DL} \models C(a)$, i.e. $\langle L \cup \{D(b)\}, P \rangle \models_{PI} C(a)$.

For RM_{DL}, assume $\langle L, P \rangle \models_{PI} C(a)$ and $\langle L, P \rangle \not\models_{PI} \neg D(b)$. It is sufficient to show that the answer set I must be an answer set also for $\langle L \cup \{D(b)\}, P \rangle$. Assume the opposite, *i.e.* I is not an answer set for $\langle L \cup \{D(b)\}, P \rangle$. Then, there must be in P a rule r associated to a defeasible axiom with rank equal to k s.t. *not* $\alpha \in B^-(r)$, where α is some literal s.t. $L \not\models \alpha^{DL}$ and $L \cup \{D(b)\} \models \alpha^{DL}$ (α^{DL} is the translation of α into the DL-language). In such a case, r must have been a ground rule of form

$$e(c) \leftarrow DL[\lambda; C](c), not\ DL[\lambda; \bigsqcup\{C' \mid$$
$$C' \in \mathfrak{A}_{D_m}, \text{with } m > k\}](c), not \neg e(c) .$$

α cannot be $\neg e(c)$, since from the activation of the rule we would have $\langle L, P \rangle \models_{PI} e(c)^{DL}$, and consequently $\langle L, P \rangle \models_{PI} \neg D(b)$, which contradicts the hypothesis. As a consequence, α must be the dl-atom of the form *not* $DL[\lambda; \bigsqcup\{C'\}](c)$. But then again, the activation of the rule for the individual c under $\langle L, P \rangle$ implies that the individual c is ranked at the value k (the rank of an individual a is the rank of $\{a\}$, *i.e.* $r(\{a\})$).

Having every C' a higher ranking value than k, and so also $\bigsqcup\{C'\}$, we can conclude $\langle L, P \rangle \models_{PI} \neg \bigsqcup\{C'\}(c)$, from which, again, we have $\langle L, P \rangle \models_{PI} \neg D(b)$, contrary to hypothesis. This concludes the proof.

4   Related Work

Several non-monotonic DLs exist, but somewhat related to our proposal are [2–6, 8, 9, 11, 12, 15–18, 24, 25], as they address the application of the preferential semantics [23]. As far as we know, [2, 5, 6] are the only works that consider also a DL as expressive as $\mathcal{SROIQ}$. [5, 6] propose a language, associated to a preferential semantics, that is more expressive than the one presented here, allowing the representation of many forms of defeasibily. However, at the moment such a logic is still missing a mature entailment relation. Bonatti [2] defines a semantic construction that extends rational closure to $\mathcal{SROIQ}$: the previous proposals [3, 12, 18] rely on the *disjoint model union property*, that does not hold for a DL as expressive as $\mathcal{SROIQ}$, while Bonatti proposes an alternative construction based on *stable rankings*, that is applicable for every DLs. We are not aware of any approach that relies on dl-programs, but [15, 16] propose an ASP-based decision procedure for the DL $\mathcal{SROEL}$, relying on a Datalog encoding of the DL knowledge base.

5   Conclusions

The introduction of rational monotonicity into the field of dl-programs allows the use of a non-monotonic formalism that at the same time satisfies important logical properties and gives back intuitive conclusions. From the implementation point of view, our proposal allows to compile the decision procedures into dl-programs and, thus, it can be implemented on top of existing reasoners supporting dl-programs such as DLV.

Regarding future work, we believe that two aspects are particularly urgent. Firstly, a comparison with the semantic characterisation of rational closure for $\mathcal{SROIQ}$ in [2].

Also, we would like to address the computational complexity of our approach. So far, we know that computing the rankings can be done in polynomial number of calls [8, 12] to an oracle deciding $\mathcal{SROIQ}$ entailment (the latter is complete for 2NEXP [21]). It remains to be seen whether, by reasoning similarly as done in [13], in which it has been shown that w.r.t. $\mathcal{SHOIN}$ the existence of answer sets, cautious and brave reasoning problems are complete for P^{NEXP} (recall that the entailment problem for $\mathcal{SHOIN}$ is complete for NEXP [26]), the same problems are complete for P^{2NEXP} w.r.t. our $\mathcal{SROIQ}$ setting, *i.e.* solvable in polynomial time by relying on an oracle for 2NEXP.

Eventually, from the inferential point of view rational closure has some well-known weaknesses: while there can be intuitive, desirable conclusions that cannot be derived [22], it remains an important basic construction that can be extended into richer entailment relations such as those proposed in [7, 10, 11, 17]. Future work will be partly dedicated to extending the present method to some of these entailment relations.

Acknowledgments. This research was supported by TAILOR, a project funded by EU Horizon 2020 research and innovation programme under GA No. 952215.

References

1. Baader, F., Calvanese, D., McGuinness, D., Nardi, D., Patel-Schneider, P.: The Description Logic Handbook. Cambridge University Press, Cambridge (2003)

2. Bonatti, P.A.: Rational closure for all description logics. Artif. Intell. **274**, 197–223 (2019)
3. Britz, K., Casini, G., Meyer, T., Moodley, K., Sattler, U., Varzinczak, I.: Principles of KLM-style defeasible description logics. ACM Trans. Comput. Log. **22**(1), 1:1–1:46 (2021)
4. Britz, K., Meyer, T., Varzinczak, I.J.: Concept model semantics for dl preferential reasoning. In: DL 2011 (2011)
5. Britz, K., Varzinczak, I.: Context-based defeasible subsumption for dSROIQ. In: COMMONSENSE 2017. CEUR Workshop Proceedings, vol. 2052. CEUR-WS.org (2017)
6. Britz, K., Varzinczak, I.: Towards defeasible SROIQ. In: DL-17. CEUR, vol. 1879 (2017)
7. Casini, G., Meyer, T., Moodley, K., Nortjé, R.: Relevant closure: a new form of defeasible reasoning for description logics. In: Fermé, E., Leite, J. (eds.) JELIA 2014. LNCS (LNAI), vol. 8761, pp. 92–106. Springer, Cham (2014). https://doi.org/10.1007/978-3-319-11558-0_7
8. Casini, G., Straccia, U.: Rational closure for defeasible description logics. In: JELIA-10, pp. 77–90. No. 6341 in LNAI, Springer (2010)
9. Casini, G., Straccia, U.: Defeasible inheritance-based description logics. In: IJCAI 2011, pp. 813–818 (2011)
10. Casini, G., Straccia, U.: Lexicographic closure for defeasible description logics. In: Proceedings of the Eighth Australasian Ontology Workshop - AOW 2012, pp. 28–39. No. 969 in CEUR Workshop Proceedings, CEUR (2012)
11. Casini, G., Straccia, U.: Defeasible inheritance-based description logics. J. Artif. Intell. Res. **48**, 415–473 (2013). https://doi.org/10.1613/jair.4062
12. Casini, G., Straccia, U., Meyer, T.: A polynomial time subsumption algorithm for nominal safe $\mathcal{ELO}_\perp$ under rational closure. Inf. Sci. **501**, 588–620 (2019)
13. Eiter, T., Ianni, G., Lukasiewicz, T., Schindlauer, R., Tompits, H.: Combining answer set programming with description logics for the semantic web. Artif. Intell. **172**(12–13), 1495–1539 (2008)
14. Gelfond, M., Lifschitz, V.: Classical negation in logic programs and disjunctive databases. New Gen. Comput. **9**, 365–385 (1991)
15. Giordano, L., Dupré, D.T.: ASP for minimal entailment in a rational extension of SROEL. Theory Pract. Log. Program. **16**(5–6), 738–754 (2016)
16. Giordano, L., Dupré, D.T.: Reasoning in a rational extension of SROEL. In: DL 2016. CEUR Workshop Proceedings, vol. 1577. CEUR-WS.org (2016)
17. Giordano, L., Gliozzi, V.: A reconstruction of multipreference closure. Artif. Intell. **290** (2021)
18. Giordano, L., Gliozzi, V., Olivetti, N., Pozzato, G.: Semantic characterization of rational closure: From propositional logic to description logics. Artif. Intell. **226**, 1–33 (2015)
19. Horrocks, I., Kutz, O., Sattler, U.: The even more irresistible SROIQ. In: KR-06, pp. 57–67. AAAI Press, Palo Alto (2006)
20. Horrocks, I., Sattler, U.: Decidability of $\mathcal{SHIQ}$ with complex role inclusion axioms. Art. Intell. **160**, 79–104 (2004)
21. Kazakov, Y.: $\mathcal{RIQ}$ and $\mathcal{SROIQ}$ are harder than $\mathcal{SHOIQ}$. In: KR-08, pp. 274–284 (2008)
22. Lehmann, D.: Another perspective on default reasoning. Ann. Math. Art. Int. **15**, 61–82 (1995)
23. Lehmann, D., Magidor, M.: What does a conditional knowledge base entail? Artif. Intell. **55**(1), 1–60 (1992). https://doi.org/10.1016/0004-3702(92)90041-U
24. Pensel, M., Turhan, A.: Reasoning in the defeasible description logic $\mathcal{EL}_\perp$. Int. J. Appr. Reas. **103**, 28–70 (2018)
25. Straccia, U.: Default inheritance reasoning in hybrid kl-one-style logics. IJCAI-93, pp. 676–681 (1993)
26. Tobies, S.: Complexity results and practical algorithms for logics in knowledge representation. Ph.D. thesis, RWTH-Aachen (2001)

Explanation for KLM-Style Defeasible Reasoning

Lloyd Everett[1], Emily Morris[1]([✉]), and Thomas Meyer[1,2]

[1] University of Cape Town, Cape Town, South Africa
[2] Centre for Artificial Intelligence Research, Cape Town, South Africa

Abstract. Explanation services are a crucial aspect of symbolic reasoning systems but they have not been explored in detail for defeasible formalisms such as KLM. We evaluate prior work on the topic with a focus on KLM propositional logic and find that a form of defeasible explanation initially described for Rational Closure which we term *weak justification* can be adapted to Relevant and Lexicographic Closure as well as described in terms of intuitive properties derived from the KLM postulates. We also consider how a more general definition of defeasible explanation known as strong explanation applies to KLM and propose an algorithm that enumerates these justifications for Rational Closure.

Keywords: Knowledge representation and reasoning · Defeasible reasoning · KLM approach · Rational closure · Relevant closure · Lexicographic closure · Explanations

1 Introduction

Explanation services indicate to users of symbolic reasoning systems which parts of their knowledge base lead to particular conclusions. This is helpful particularly when the reasoner is giving unexpected results since it allows the user to identify the culprit knowledge base statements and thus debug their knowledge base [10]. Explanation services have also been found to improve knowledge base comprehension, particularly if the user is not familiar with the knowledge base [1], and to improve users' confidence in the reasoning system [2]. There is also some evidence that formalisms of explanation can be theoretical tools in their own right; for example, Casini et al. [4] base their work on Relevant Closure fundamentally on classical justification, a form of classical explanation.

Although well-understood in the classical case, explanation has not yet been explored in detail for defeasible reasoning apart from some foundational work [3,8]. Our work aims to improve our understanding of explanation for defeasible propositional logic and where relevant to provide algorithms for the practical implementation of explanation services.

There are many approaches to defeasible reasoning but a particularly compelling approach that has been studied at length in the literature [5–7,13,14] is

© Springer Nature Switzerland AG 2022
E. Jembere et al. (Eds.): SACAIR 2021, CCIS 1551, pp. 192–207, 2022.
https://doi.org/10.1007/978-3-030-95070-5_13

the KLM approach suggested by Kraus, Lehmann and Magidor [11]. One of the major appeals of KLM is that it can be viewed from two different angles, each with its own advantages: either using a series of postulates asserting behaviours we intuitively expect of the defeasible reasoning formalism, or using a model-theoretic semantics perhaps not as obviously intuitive but more amenable to computation by means of reasoning algorithms. These two perspectives are linked by results in the literature [6,9,13]. Formalisms of defeasible entailment explored in the literatue for KLM include *Rational Closure* [13], *Relevant Closure* [4] and *Lexicographic Closure* [12].

Chama [8] proposes an algorithm for the evaluation of defeasible justifications for Rational Closure. We term this notion of defeasible justification *weak justification* and adapt this result to the cases of Relevant Closure and Lexicographic Closure. We then consider how this notion relates to *strong explanation*, a more general notion of defeasible explanation given by Brewka and Ulbricht [3] which has not yet been explored for KLM, and propose an algorithm for enumerating strong justifications for the case of Rational Closure using a revised definition of strong justification. Our final result characterises weak justification using properties with intuitive interpretations based on the KLM postulates.

2 Background

2.1 Classical Propositional Logic

We begin with a finite set $\mathcal{P} = \{p, q, \cdots\}$ of *propositional atoms*. The binary connectives $\wedge, \vee, \rightarrow, \leftrightarrow$ and the negation operator $\neg$ are defined recursively to form propositional *formulas*. The set of all such formulas over $\mathcal{P}$ is the *propositional language* $\mathcal{L}$. A *valuation* is a function $\mathcal{P} \rightarrow \{T, F\}$ that assigns a truth value to each atom in $\mathcal{P}$. We say that a formula $\alpha \in \mathcal{L}$ is *satisfied* by a valuation $\mathcal{I}$ if α evaluates to true according to the usual truth-functional semantics given $\mathcal{I}$. The valuations that satisfy a formula α are referred to as *models* of α, and the set of models of α is denoted $\text{Mod}(\alpha)$. By assertion, $\top$ is a propositional formula satisfied by every valuation and $\perp$ is a formula not satisfied by any valuation.

A *classical knowledge base* $\mathcal{K}$ is a finite set of propositional formulas. A valuation is a model of $\mathcal{K}$ if it is a model of every formula in $\mathcal{K}$. A knowledge base $\mathcal{K}$ *entails* a formula α, denoted $\mathcal{K} \models \alpha$, if $\text{Mod}(\mathcal{K}) \subseteq \text{Mod}(\alpha)$ and a formula α entails a formula β, denoted $\alpha \models \beta$, if $\text{Mod}(\alpha) \subseteq \text{Mod}(\beta)$. A knowledge base $\mathcal{J}$ is a *justification* for an entailment $\mathcal{K} \models \alpha$ if $\mathcal{J}$ is a subset $\mathcal{J} \subseteq \mathcal{K}$ such that $\mathcal{J} \models \alpha$ and there is no proper subset $\mathcal{J}' \subset \mathcal{J}$ such that $\mathcal{J}' \models \alpha$. Algorithms for enumerating classical justifications have been explored in detail by Horridge [10].

2.2 KLM Defeasible Entailment

Although there are many approaches to defeasible reasoning, one approach that has been studied extensively in the literature is that proposed by Kraus,

Lehmann and Magidor (KLM) [11]. This approach extends propositional logic by introducing defeasible implication $\vdash$ which can be viewed as the defeasible analogue of classical implication $\rightarrow$. Defeasible implications (DI) are expressions of the form $\alpha \vdash \beta$ where $\alpha \in \mathcal{L}, \beta \in \mathcal{L}$ and are read as 'α *typically implies* β'.

A defeasible knowledge base is then a finite set of defeasible implications and defeasible entailment $\approx$ is defined as a binary relation over defeasible knowledge baes and defeasible implications so that $\mathcal{K} \approx \alpha \vdash \beta$ reads as '$\mathcal{K}$ *defeasibly entails that α typically implies β*'. Note that while we assume that defeasible knowledge bases only contain defeasible implications, we can express any classical formula α using the defeasible representation $\neg \alpha \vdash \bot$. From here on we will assume that knowledge bases are defeasible unless stated otherwise.

Lehmann and Magidor [13] propose a series of postulates that define *rational* defeasible entailment, where each postulate can be thought of as asserting an intuitive characteristic we expect of a sensible defeasible entailment relation (hence the name *rational*). In addition to this axiomatic definition, rational entailment relations have a model-theoretic semantics which we do not discuss here but which is (in some cases) described exactly by reasoning algorithms of reasonable computational complexity. These reasoning algorithms are a central focus in this paper and we introduce Rational Closure [13], the most well-known form of defeasible entailment for KLM, in these terms.

2.3   Rational Closure

Rational Closure is a rational definition for defeasible entailment proposed by Lehmann and Magidor [13]. Casini et al. [6] present an algorithm for Rational Closure with two distinct sub-phases, shown in Algorithms 1 and 2. Essentially, the algorithm works by imposing a ranking of typicality on the knowledge base. Then, if there is an inconsistency when computing entailment, the most typical information in this ranking is removed from the knowledge base. The ranking of statements is produced by BaseRank, shown in Algorithm 2. The lower the rank of a statement, the more typical it is.

Algorithm 1: RationalClosure

Input: A knowledge base $\mathcal{K}$ and a DI $\alpha \vdash \beta$
Output: true, if $\mathcal{K} \approx_{RC} \alpha \vdash \beta$, otherwise **false**
1 $(R_0, R_1, ..., R_\infty, \text{n}) := \text{BaseRank}(K)$;
2 i := 0;
3 $R := \bigcup_{i=0}^{j<n} R_j$;
4 **while** $R_\infty \cup R \models \neg\alpha$ *and* $R \neq \emptyset$ **do**
5 | $R := R \setminus R_i$;
6 | i := i+1;
7 **end**
8 **return** $R_\infty \cup R \models \alpha \rightarrow \beta$;

Algorithm 2: BaseRank

Input: A knowledge base $\mathcal{K}$
Output: An ordered tuple $(R_0, ..., R_{n-1}, R_\infty, n)$
1 $i := 0$;
2 $E_0 := \overline{\mathcal{K}}$;
3 **repeat**
4     $E_{i+1} := \{\alpha \to \beta \in E_i \mid E_i \models \neg\alpha\}$;
5     $R_i := E_i \setminus E_{i+1}$;
6     $i := i+1$;
7 **until** $E_{i-1} = E_i$;
8 $R_\infty := E_{i-1}$;
9 $n := i\text{-}1$;
10 **return** $(R_0, ..., R_{n-1}, R_\infty, n)$;

As an illustration of the Rational Closure algorithm, consider the following example.

Example 1. Suppose one has the defeasible knowledge base $\mathcal{K}$ containing the following information.

1. Birds typically fly ($b \mathrel{|\!\sim} f$)
2. Birds typically have eyes ($b \mathrel{|\!\sim} e$)
3. Birds typically sing ($b \mathrel{|\!\sim} s$)
4. Penguins typically do not fly ($p \mathrel{|\!\sim} \neg f$)
5. Penguins are birds ($p \to b$)
6. Max is a penguin ($m \to p$)

Consider the entailment of the statement 'Max typically does not fly' ($m \mathrel{|\!\sim} \neg f$). Using `RationalClosure`, `BaseRank` is first used to compute the ranking in Fig. 1. Then we start by considering all the ranks and check whether $R_0 \cup R_1 \cup R_\infty \models \neg m$. Since this holds, R_0 is removed. We then check whether $R_1 \cup R_\infty \models \neg m$. Since this entailment does not hold, we stop removing ranks and check whether $R_1 \cup R_\infty \models m \to \neg f$. Since this entailment holds, `RationalClosure` will return **true**.

0	$b \mathrel{|\!\sim} f, b \mathrel{|\!\sim} e, b \mathrel{|\!\sim} s$
1	$p \mathrel{|\!\sim} \neg f$
∞	$p \to b, m \to p$

Fig. 1. Base ranking of statements for Example 1

It is helpful to introduce some notation closely related to these algorithms [13]:

Definition 1. *The materialisation* $\overline{\mathcal{K}}$ *of a knowledge base* $\mathcal{K}$ *is the classical knowledge base* $\{\alpha \to \beta \mid \alpha \mathrel{\vrule height 1.2ex width 0pt \sim} \beta \in \mathcal{K}\}$.

Definition 2. *The exceptionality sequence* $\mathcal{E}_0^{\mathcal{K}}, \ldots, \mathcal{E}_n^{\mathcal{K}}$ *for a knowledge base* $\mathcal{K}$ *is given by letting* $\mathcal{E}_0^{\mathcal{K}} = \mathcal{K}$, *and* $\mathcal{E}_{i+1}^{\mathcal{K}} = \{\alpha \mathrel{\vrule height 1.2ex width 0pt \sim} \beta \in \mathcal{E}_i^{\mathcal{K}} \mid \overline{\mathcal{E}_i^{\mathcal{K}}} \models \neg\alpha\}$ *for* $0 \le i < n$ *where* n *is the smallest index such that* $\mathcal{E}_n^{\mathcal{K}} = \mathcal{E}_{n+1}^{\mathcal{K}}$ *according to these equations. The final element* $\mathcal{E}_n^{\mathcal{K}}$ *is usually denoted as* $\mathcal{E}_\infty^{\mathcal{K}}$ *as it is unique in that its statements are never retracted when evaluating entailment queries.*

Definition 3. *The base rank* $\mathrm{br}_{\mathcal{K}}(\alpha)$ *of a formula* $\alpha \in \mathcal{L}$ *is the smallest index* i *such that* $\overline{\mathcal{E}_i^{\mathcal{K}}} \models \neg\alpha$. *If there is no such* i, *then let* $\mathrm{br}_{\mathcal{K}}(\alpha) = \infty$. *This is distinguished from the case of* $\mathrm{br}_{\mathcal{K}}(\alpha) = n$ *where* $\mathcal{E}_\infty^{\mathcal{K}}$ *is the first* $\mathcal{E}_i^{\mathcal{K}}$ *having* $\overline{\mathcal{E}_i^{\mathcal{K}}} \models \neg\alpha$.

We also introduce the following shorthand:

Definition 4. *For a knowledge base* $\mathcal{K}$ *and formula* α, *let* $\mathcal{E}_\alpha^{\mathcal{K}} = \mathcal{E}_r^{\mathcal{K}}$ *where* $r = \mathrm{br}_{\mathcal{K}}(\alpha)$. *The cases of* $r = \infty$ *and* $r = n$ *both correspond to* $\mathcal{E}_\alpha^{\mathcal{K}} = \mathcal{E}_\infty^{\mathcal{K}}$.

We note then that Rational Closure entailment $\mathrel{\approx}_{\mathrm{RC}}$ can alternatively be expressed as follows:

Proposition 1. *For a knowledge base* $\mathcal{K}$ *and an entailment query* $\alpha \mathrel{\vrule height 1.2ex width 0pt \sim} \beta$,

$$\mathcal{K} \mathrel{\approx}_{\mathrm{RC}} \alpha \mathrel{\vrule height 1.2ex width 0pt \sim} \beta \ \textit{iff}\ \mathrm{br}_{\mathcal{K}}(\alpha) = \infty \ \textit{or}\ \overline{\mathcal{E}_\alpha^{\mathcal{K}}} \models \alpha \to \beta.$$

3 Weak Justification

One of the main works of interest here is that of Chama [8] which proposes a notion of defeasible justification for Rational Closure according to an algorithm closely connected to the Rational Closure reasoning algorithm. The insight here is that we should follow the same process to eliminate more general statements, and once we have done so, to use classical tools to reason about the knowledge base—only in this case we obtain classical justifications instead of testing for classical entailment. We refer to these justifications as *weak justifications* to distinguish from classical justifications and the strong justifications we discuss later. We express this result for KLM propositional logic in the following definition (see Appendix A for the corresponding algorithm):

Definition 5. *A knowledge base* $\mathcal{J}$ *is a weak justification for a Rational Closure entailment* $\mathcal{K} \mathrel{\approx}_{\mathrm{RC}} \alpha \mathrel{\vrule height 1.2ex width 0pt \sim} \beta$ *if* $\overline{\mathcal{J}}$ *is a classical justification for* $\overline{\mathcal{E}_\alpha^{\mathcal{K}}} \models \alpha \to \beta$. *The set of weak justifications for* $\mathcal{K} \mathrel{\approx}_{\mathrm{RC}} \alpha \mathrel{\vrule height 1.2ex width 0pt \sim} \beta$ *is denoted* $\mathcal{J}_W(\mathcal{K}, \alpha \mathrel{\vrule height 1.2ex width 0pt \sim} \beta)$.

3.1 Relevant Closure

Casini et al. [4] propose Relevant Closure which adapts the reasoning algorithm for Rational Closure so that we only retract the statements in a less specific rank that actually disagree with more specific statements in higher ranks with respect to the antecedent of the query. Relevant Closure is not rational; it does not obey all of the axioms of rational defeasible entailment.

For the sake of brevity, we do describe the reasoning algorithm procedurally. However, the essence of the Relevant Closure reasoning algorithm can be expressed simply using the following three definitions:

Definition 6. *A knowledge base $\mathcal{J}$ is an ε-justification for $(\mathcal{K}, \alpha)$ if $\overline{\mathcal{J}}$ is a classical justification for $\overline{\mathcal{K}} \models \neg\alpha$.*

Definition 7. *A statement $\alpha \mathrel{\v+} \beta \in \mathcal{K}$ is* relevant *for $(\mathcal{K}, \gamma)$ if $a \mathrel{\v+} \beta$ is an element of some ε-justification for $(\mathcal{K}, \gamma)$. Let $R(\mathcal{K}, \gamma)$ be the set of statements in $\mathcal{K}$ that are relevant for $(\mathcal{K}, \gamma)$ and $R^-(\mathcal{K}, \gamma)$ the set of statements in $\mathcal{K}$ not relevant to $(\mathcal{K}, \gamma)$.*

Definition 8. *We have $\mathcal{K} \mathrel{\approx_{\mathrm{RelC}}} \alpha \mathrel{\vert\!\sim} \beta$ if $\overline{\mathcal{E}_\alpha^{\mathcal{K}} \cup R^-(\mathcal{K}, \alpha)} \models \alpha \rightarrow \beta$.*

What we have described here is Basic Relevant Closure, but Minimal Relevant Closure—the other definition of Relevant Closure entailment [4]—is based on a slightly altered version of relevance and the difference is not important for our purposes (i.e. minimal and basic relevance can be 'swapped out' by having $R(\cdot, \cdot)$ and $R^-(\cdot, \cdot)$ correspond to the form of relevance at hand).

Weak Justifications for Relevant Closure. We identify the following analogue of weak justification for the case of Relevant Closure entailment:

Definition 9. *A knowledge base $\mathcal{J}$ is a* weak justification *for an entailment $\mathcal{K} \mathrel{\approx_{\mathrm{RelC}}} \alpha \mathrel{\vert\!\sim} \beta$ if $\overline{\mathcal{J}}$ is a classical justification for $\overline{\mathcal{E}_\alpha^{\mathcal{K}} \cup R^-(\mathcal{K}, \alpha)}$.*

In other words, we ensure that the statements in the knowledge base considered not relevant to the query remain under our consideration when materialising just as they are when evaluating Relevant Closure entailment queries. We give a corresponding algorithm in Appendix A by adapting `WeakJustifyRC`.

3.2 Lexicographic Closure

Lexicographic Closure is another rational definition for defeasible entailment proposed by Lehmann [12] which is more permissive than Rational Closure. Like Rational Closure, Lexicographic Closure can be defined both semantically and algorithmically; we once again present the algorithmic definition. Lexicographic Closure can be seen as a refinement of Rational Closure, where we remove single statements instead of entire levels when inconsistencies arise during the reasoning process. We utilize the algorithm presented by Morris et al. [15] for propositional logic as the algorithm for Lexicographic Closure. However, while Morris et al.

Algorithm 3: LexicographicClosure

Input: A knowledge base $\mathcal{K}$ and DI $\alpha \mathrel{\vert\!\sim} \beta$
Output: true, if $\mathcal{K} \approx_{LC} \alpha \mathrel{\vert\!\sim} \beta$, otherwise **false**
1 $(R_0, ..., R_{n-1}, R_\infty, \text{n}) := \text{BaseRank}(\mathcal{K})$;
2 $i := 0$;
3 $R := \bigcup_{j=0}^{j \leq n} R_j$;
4 **while** $R_\infty \cup R \models \neg\alpha$ **and** $R \neq \emptyset$ **do**
5 $\quad$ $R := R \setminus R_i$;
6 $\quad$ $m := |R_i| - 1$;
7 $\quad$ $R_{i,m} := \bigvee_{X \in \text{Subsets}(R_i, m)} \bigwedge_{x \in X} x$;
8 $\quad$ **while** $R_\infty \cup R \cup \{R_{i,m}\} \models \neg\alpha$ **and** $m > 0$ **do**
9 $\quad\quad$ $m := \text{m-1}$;
10 $\quad\quad$ $R_{i,m} := \bigvee_{X \in \text{Subsets}(R_i, m)} \bigwedge_{x \in X} x$;
11 $\quad$ **end**
12 $\quad$ $R := R \cup \{R_{i,m}\}$;
13 $\quad$ $i := \text{i+1}$;
14 **end**
15 **return** $R_\infty \cup R \models \alpha \to \beta$;

---

refine the ranking of statements, we instead refine the removal of statements as shown in `LexicographicClosure` in Algorithm 3.

Essentially, instead of removing an entire level R_i, this refinement weakens R_i by simultaneously considering all the ways of removing j statements from the level.

Weak Justifications for Lexicographic Closure. The refined method presented in `LexicographicClosure` is equivalent to considering a series of sub-knowledge bases which are derived by replacing R_i with all the possible subsets R_i of size $m-j$, where m is the number of statements in R_i. Using this approach, the final entailment holds if the classical entailment holds in all the final sub-knowledge bases. Thus to provide a weak justification for the entailment, we can compute the classical justifications in the sub-knowledge bases and present these as the final justification. However, we wish to maintain a structure that refers to which justifications are responsible for the entailment of the statement in each sub-knowledge base. We therefore present a tuple as our final weak justification, where the i'th element of the tuple is a justification for the entailment of the statement in the i'th sub-knowledge base. This allows us to refer to individual statements in our knowledge base instead of a single combined formula.

To compute these weak justifications, we first modify `Lexicographic Closure` to create `LexicographicClosureForJustifications`. This modification is performed by returning the variable m, which represents the subset size used in the final entailment computation, and the variable i, which represents the lowest complete level used in the final entailment computation, as an ordered pair (i, m) along with the final entailment result. We can define an algorithm `WeakJustificationsLC` that then uses this information to reconstruct the appropriate sub-knowledge bases and compute the justifications for each sub-knowledge base using classical methods as was done for Rational Closure. Taking the cross product of these justifications then yields the final set of tuples, which are the weak justifications. Full details of both algorithms are given in Appendix A. We demonstrate how weak justifications are computed for Lexicographic Closure in the following example.

Example 2. Suppose one has the knowledge base in Example 1 and consider once again the entailment of the statement 'penguins typically have eyes' $(p \mathrel{\vdash\hspace{-0.5em}\sim} e)$. `LexicographicClosureForJustifications` returns **true**, along with $(1, 2)$. Thus we reconstruct the sub-knowledge bases $\mathcal{K}_1 = \{b \mathrel{\vdash\hspace{-0.5em}\sim} f, b \mathrel{\vdash\hspace{-0.5em}\sim} e\} \cup R_1 \cup R_\infty$, $\mathcal{K}_2 = \{b \mathrel{\vdash\hspace{-0.5em}\sim} f, b \mathrel{\vdash\hspace{-0.5em}\sim} s\} \cup R_1 \cup R_\infty$ and $\mathcal{K}_3 = \{b \mathrel{\vdash\hspace{-0.5em}\sim} e, b \mathrel{\vdash\hspace{-0.5em}\sim} s\} \cup R_1 \cup R_\infty$. The set of all justifications for $\mathcal{K}_1$, $\mathcal{K}_2$ and $\mathcal{K}_3$ are $\mathcal{J}_1 = \{j_1, j_2\}$, $\mathcal{J}_2 = \{j_1\}$ and $\mathcal{J}_3 = \{j_2\}$ respectively, where: $j_1 = \{b \mathrel{\vdash\hspace{-0.5em}\sim} f, p \mathrel{\vdash\hspace{-0.5em}\sim} \neg f, p \rightarrow b\}$, $j_2 = \{b \mathrel{\vdash\hspace{-0.5em}\sim} e, p \rightarrow b\}$. Thus our weak justifications will be the elements of the cross products of these sets. For example, (j_1, j_1, j_2) will be a weak justification for the entailment.

4 Strong Justification for Rational Closure

While weak justifications present an intuitive and simple approach to defining defeasible explanation, their level of description is arguably limited: we are only presenting information as to why the final classical entailment holds and are thus disregarding the rest of the reasoning process such as the determination of the base rank. In this section, we apply an intuitively more comprehensive definition for defeasible explanation, referred to as strong explanation, proposed by Brewka and Ulbricht [3] to KLM style reasoning to produce what we refer to as *strong justifications*. In particular, we look at defining what constitutes a strong justification for Rational Closure and explore an algorithm for computing these strong justifications. Note that the proofs of propositions and full details for all algorithms not presented in this section are given in Appendix B.

4.1 Overview of the Approach

A strong justification is a set $\mathcal{S}$ such that for any $\mathcal{S}'$ with $\mathcal{S} \subseteq \mathcal{S}' \subseteq \mathcal{K}$, $\mathcal{S}' \approx \alpha \mathrel{\vdash\hspace{-0.5em}\sim} \beta$ and the previous statement does not hold for any $\mathcal{S}'' \subset \mathcal{S}$. This is essentially an extension of the definition for classical justification. The intuition here is that the strong justification contains 'just enough' of the statements such that the defeasible entailment always holds even if arbitrary statements from the knowledge base are added to the justification. Note that while weak justifications for Rational Closure are a subset of the knowledge base $\mathcal{K}$ that entails the final statement—and hence always obey at least one aspect of this criterion—they are not necessarily strong justifications. As an illustration of this, consider the following example:

Example 3. Suppose one has a knowledge base $\mathcal{K}$ containing the following information:

1. If something walks, it typically does not fly $(w \mathrel{|\!\sim} \neg f)$
2. If something walks, it typically has legs $(w \mathrel{|\!\sim} l)$
3. Pigeons typically fly $(p \mathrel{|\!\sim} f)$
4. Pigeons typically walk $(p \mathrel{|\!\sim} w)$

This knowledge base has the ranking shown in Fig. 2a. Consider the entailment of the statement 'if something is a pigeon and it walks then it typically flies' $(p \wedge w \mathrel{|\!\sim} f)$. The weak justification for this statement is $\mathcal{W} = \{p \mathrel{|\!\sim} f\}$.

Now consider what happens when the statement $w \mathrel{|\!\sim} \neg f$ is added to $\mathcal{W}$. Ranking $\mathcal{W} \cup \{w \mathrel{|\!\sim} \neg f\}$ yields the ranking shown in Fig. 2b. However, now when computing the entailment of $p \wedge w \mathrel{|\!\sim} f$, $R_0 \models \neg(p \wedge w)$ and so R_0 is removed. But then $\emptyset \models (p \wedge w) \rightarrow f$ is computed as the final entailment result, which does not hold. Thus $\mathcal{W}$ is not a strong justification since $\mathcal{W} \cup \{w \mathrel{|\!\sim} \neg f\}$ does not entail our statement.

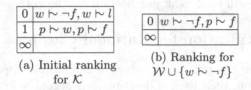

(a) Initial ranking for $\mathcal{K}$

(b) Ranking for $\mathcal{W} \cup \{w \mathrel{|\!\sim} \neg f\}$

Fig. 2. Base ranking of statements for Example 3

The issue that arises in Example 3 is that we can add statements to our set that allow us to entail the negation the antecedent α off our entailed statement but not the negation of all the antecedents of our statements in our weak justification. This leads to some of the statements in our weak justification getting 'mixed into' lower ranks in which we can still 'disprove' α, which are then removed during the algorithm. However, we can extend $\mathcal{W}$ to create the strong justification $\mathcal{S} = \{p \mathrel{|\!\sim} w, p \mathrel{|\!\sim} f\}$. Here we ensure that the weak justification is always pushed above the ranks in which we can 'disprove' p, which are the ranks that contain justifications for $\neg p$.

4.2   Algorithm

We wish to define a procedure for extending weak justifications to form strong justifications as we did for Example 3. First we define the ranking of a set $\mathcal{K}' \subseteq \mathcal{K}$ in $\mathcal{K}$ to be the rank of the statement in $\mathcal{K}'$ with the lowest ranking in $\mathcal{K}$. For example, in Fig. 2a, the set $\mathcal{K}' = \{w \mathrel{|\!\sim} \neg f, p \mathrel{|\!\sim} w\}$ has rank 0 in $\mathcal{K}$. We wish to ensure our weak justification is always ranked above the justifications for $\neg \alpha$, which we denote $\mathcal{J}_{\neg \alpha}$. We restrict ourselves to considering strong justifications for entailments where all justifications $\mathcal{J}_{\neg \alpha}$ and weak justifications have finite rank.

We start by considering every possible way of ranking the justifications $\mathcal{J}_{\neg\alpha}$ and then consider all possible ways of ranking weak justifications $\mathcal{W}$ such that they are one rank higher than the highest ranked $\mathcal{J}_{\neg\alpha}$ in $\mathcal{K}$. To do this we build up a sequences of subsets $(K_0, K_1, \ldots, K_x)$ where:

1. $br_{K_i}(\gamma) = i$
2. For all $K' \subset K_i$, $br_{K'}(\gamma) < br_{K_i}(\gamma)$

If a statement γ has rank n, that the justification for $\neg\gamma$ has rank $n - 1$. Thus we use the statement $\gamma = \alpha$ for all justifications $\mathcal{J}_{\neg\alpha}$ and $\gamma = \alpha \wedge \neg\beta$ for all weak justifications $\mathcal{W}$. We use this approach instead of defining a fixed initial set to ensure the subsets in the sequence constructed are minimal. `ComputeSubsetSequences` shown in Algorithm 4, with the sub-process `Sequences` shown in Algorithm 5, computes the appropriate sequences for weak justifications. Proposition 2 states that `ComputeSubsetSequences` will always compute at least one sequence for some weak justification.

Proposition 2. *Let $\mathcal{K}$ be a knowledge base and γ a formula. Provided $br_{\mathcal{K}}(\gamma) \neq \infty$, `ComputeSubsetSequences` returns at least one sequence of sets.*

Algorithm 4: ComputeSubsetSequences

Input: A knowledge base $\mathcal{K}$, a formula α, the rank $n \leq br_{\mathcal{K}}(\alpha)$ required for α in the final subset of a sequence

Output: Set of all sequences $(K_1, K_2, ..., K_n)$, where α has $br_{K_i}(\alpha) = i$, and each K_i is minimal

1   $i := 0$;
2   $E_0 := \overline{\mathcal{K}}$;
3   **repeat**
4      $E_{i+1} := \{\alpha \rightarrow \beta \in E_i \mid E_i \models \neg\alpha\}$;
5      $i := i+1$;
6   **until** $E_{i-1} = E_i$;
7   $E_\infty := E_{i-1}$;
8   sequences $:= Sequences((E_0, \ldots, E_\infty), \alpha, (\emptyset), n, 1)$;
9   **return** *sequences*;

Note in `Sequences`, $MinimalExtension(\alpha, A, B)$ computes the set of all sets M where M is attained by adding the minimum number of statements from A to B so that B entails α and $Minimize(A, \alpha)$ returns true if we can remove statements from A and maintain the ranking of α in A.

As a demonstration of how `ComputeSubsetSequences` creates a sequence, consider the following example.

Example 4. Consider the knowledge base and query in Example 3. `ComputeSubsetSequences` computes a single sequence (K_0, K_1, K_2) for the weak justifications, with $K_0 = \emptyset, K_1 = \mathcal{W} = \{p \mathrel{|\!\sim} w\}, K_2 = K_1 \cup \{p \mathrel{|\!\sim} w, w \mathrel{|\!\sim} \neg f\}$.

Algorithm 5: Sequences

Input: A knowledge base $\mathcal{K} = (E_0, E_1, \ldots E_\infty)$, a formula α, the current
        sequence of subsets $(K_0, \ldots, K_{i-1})$, the rank n of α in the final subset of
        the sequence, the index i of the current subset

Output: A set of sequences of length n

1 **if** $i > n$ **then**
2 | **return** $\{(K_0, \ldots, K_{i-1})\}$;
3 $\mathcal{A} := \neg\alpha \wedge (\bigwedge_{\beta \in Antecedents(K_{i-1})} \neg\beta)$;
4 $S := MinimalExtension(\mathcal{A}, E_{n-i}, K_{i-1})$;
5 $\mathcal{F} := \emptyset$;
6 **if** $S \neq \emptyset$ **then**
7 | **for** K_i in S **do**
8 | | **if** $br_{K_i}(\alpha) = i$ and $Minimize(K_i, \alpha)$ is **False** **then**
9 | | | $\mathcal{F} := \mathcal{F} \cup Sequences(\mathcal{K}, \alpha, (K_0, \ldots, K_{i-1}, K_i), n, i + 1)$;
10 | **end**
11 | **end**
12 **return** $\mathcal{F}$;

We define similar algorithms `ComputeGeneralSubsetSequences` and `GeneralSequences` for computing the sequences for all justifications $\mathcal{J}_{\neg\alpha}$. However, since we do not require these justifications to reach a certain rank, we do not need to work from E subsets. Instead statements are added from $\overline{\mathcal{K}}$. We also return a sequence when the final set can no longer be minimally extended, instead of requiring the algorithm to iterate a fixed number of times. Proposition 3 states the soundness and completeness of `ComputeSubsetSequences` for computing the minimal ways of ranking a statement.

Proposition 3. *Let $\mathcal{K}$ be a knowledge base and γ a formula. Provided $br_\mathcal{K}(\gamma) \neq \infty$, `ComputeGeneralSubsetSequences` computes exactly $M \subseteq \mathcal{K}$ such that for all $M' \subset M, br_{M'}(\gamma) < br_M(\gamma)$ i.e. M is minimal in terms of the ranking of γ.*

Given the ability to compute these sequences, we now define the formal extension of a weak justification to create a strong justification. If we choose a sequence $S_\mathcal{W}$ for some weak justification, we can consider all sequences for justifications $\mathcal{J}_{\neg\alpha}$ and use $S_\mathcal{W}$ to add the minimum number of statements to $\mathcal{W}$ to ensure it is ranked above $\mathcal{J}_{\neg\alpha}$ in each subset in each sequence. We consider each sequence $\mathcal{J}$ produced by `ComputeGeneralSubsetSequences` individually and compute all such minimal sets S for the sequence. To do this we define the algorithm `StrongSequences`. We start with S containing our weak justification and then iterate through each subset $K_i^\mathcal{J}$ in $\mathcal{J}$, checking whether $K_i^\mathcal{J} \cup S \models \neg m$ for all $m \vdash n \in S$. If this does not hold, we use $K_{i+1}^\mathcal{W}$ from our weak justification sequence and consider all the ways of adding the minimum number of required statements to S so that $K_i^\mathcal{J} \cup S \models \neg m$ for all $m \vdash n \in S'$, where S' is the previous iteration of S in a similar manner to Algorithm 5. We repeat this process until we have considered all sets in the sequence. Essentially, what we have done is create all the minimal sets S that ensure that whenever $\mathcal{J}_{\neg\alpha}$ has rank j in our sequence, our weak justifications has at least rank $j+1$.

We then consider all ways of taking a minimal set for each sequence and taking the union of these sets. The smallest set created in this manner is then taken as our strong justification. This full process is defined by the algorithm StrongJustification. Proposition 4 states the correctness of this algorithm.

Proposition 4. *Let $\mathcal{K}$ be a knowledge base and $\alpha \vdash \beta$ a defeasible implication. Provided $br_{\mathcal{K}}(\alpha) \neq \infty$, StrongJustification returns a strong justification for the entailment $\mathcal{K} \approx_{RC} \alpha \vdash \beta$.*

We provide a simple demonstration of StrongJustification using our example from the introduction.

Example 5. Consider the knowledge base and query in Example 3. Compute SubsetSequences produces the sequence in Example 4. ComputeGeneral SubsetSequences produces the single sequence $\mathcal{J} = (K_0, K_1)$ with $K_0^{\mathcal{J}} = \emptyset, K_1^{\mathcal{J}} = \{p \vdash \neg f, b \vdash f\}$. We start with $S = W = \{p \vdash f\}$ for this sequence. We then consider whether $K_1^{\mathcal{J}} \cup S \models \neg p$. Since this does not hold, we add the statement $p \vdash w \in K_2$ to S. Since there are no more subsets in $\mathcal{J}$, we return $S = \{p \vdash \neg f, p \vdash w\}$ as the single minimal set and, since there are no other sequences, S is returned as our final strong justification.

4.3 Limitations for the Approach

While we have defined strong justification as an extension of weak justifications, not every weak justification can be extended to create a strong justification. As an illustration of this, consider the following example.

Example 6. Suppose one has the knowledge base $\mathcal{K}$ shown in Fig. 3 and consider the entailment of the statement $sp \wedge p \vdash m \vee w$. This entailment has two weak justifications:

1. $\mathcal{W}_1 = \{sp \vdash f, f \vdash m\}$
2. $\mathcal{W}_2 = \{sp \vdash f, f \vdash w\}$

$\mathcal{W}_1$ cannot be extended to create a strong justification. If initially $S = \mathcal{W}_1$, then to ensure $S \cup \{p \vdash \neg f\} \approx_{RC} sp \wedge p \vdash m \vee w$, the statements $\{l \vdash \neg x, f \vdash w, w \vdash x, w \to l\}$ need to be added to S. Then $S = \{l \vdash \neg x, f \vdash w, w \vdash x, w \to l, sp \vdash f, f \vdash m\}$. But now if $f \vdash m$ is removed from S, we still have $S' \approx sp \wedge p \vdash m \vee w$ for all $S' \subseteq S \subseteq \mathcal{K}$. Thus due to the minimality property of strong justifications, $\mathcal{W}_1$ cannot be extended to create a strong justification.

It is also not the case that all strong justifications can be defined as an extension of a weak justification. As a demonstration of this fact, consider the following example.

0	$p \mathrel{\vdash\mkern-7mu\sim} \neg f, l \mathrel{\vdash\mkern-7mu\sim} \neg x$
1	$sp \mathrel{\vdash\mkern-7mu\sim} f, f \mathrel{\vdash\mkern-7mu\sim} m, f \mathrel{\vdash\mkern-7mu\sim} w, w \mathrel{\vdash\mkern-7mu\sim} x$
∞	$w \to l$

Fig. 3. Base ranking for statements in Example 6

Example 7. Suppose one has a knowledge base $\mathcal{K}$ shown in Fig. 4 and consider the entailment of the statement $p \mathrel{\vdash\mkern-7mu\sim} s$. This has the weak justification $\mathcal{W} = \{p \mathrel{\vdash\mkern-7mu\sim} \neg f, \neg f \mathrel{\vdash\mkern-7mu\sim} s\}$. However, consider rather $\mathcal{B} = \{b \mathrel{\vdash\mkern-7mu\sim} s, p \to b\}$ as the base set for extension. $\mathcal{B}$ is not a weak justification since it contains information removed during the Rational Closure algorithm. However, $\mathcal{B}$ can be extended to form the strong justification

$$\mathcal{S} = \{b \mathrel{\vdash\mkern-7mu\sim} s, \neg f \mathrel{\vdash\mkern-7mu\sim} s, r \mathrel{\vdash\mkern-7mu\sim} w, \neg f \mathrel{\vdash\mkern-7mu\sim} \neg w, \neg f \mathrel{\vdash\mkern-7mu\sim} r, p \to b\}.$$

First notice $\mathcal{S} \approx_{RC} p \mathrel{\vdash\mkern-7mu\sim} s$. Now consider what happens if any statements are added to $\mathcal{S}$. If we add any statements that cause $\mathcal{B}$ to be thrown away, namely $p \mathrel{\vdash\mkern-7mu\sim} \neg f$, the set then contains $\mathcal{W}$ and so the entailment still holds.

0	$b \mathrel{\vdash\mkern-7mu\sim} f, b \mathrel{\vdash\mkern-7mu\sim} s, r \mathrel{\vdash\mkern-7mu\sim} w$
1	$p \mathrel{\vdash\mkern-7mu\sim} \neg f, \neg f \mathrel{\vdash\mkern-7mu\sim} \neg w, \neg f \mathrel{\vdash\mkern-7mu\sim} r, \neg f \mathrel{\vdash\mkern-7mu\sim} s$
∞	$p \to b$

Fig. 4. Base ranking of statements for Example 7

5   Properties of Weak Justification

Weak justification has currently only been explored in terms of reasoning algorithms (such constructions as the exceptionality sequence $\mathcal{E}$ and base ranks) and therefore an interesting question is whether it can be characterised in a more intuitive manner. In this section, we show that for every postulate of rationality there is a corresponding property obeyed by weak justification. For the sake of simplicity, our presentation here will be limited to the case of Rational Closure and therefore we assume for this section that $\approx$ refers to $\approx_{RC}$. We begin by considering a strengthening of the postulates for rationality given by Lehmann and Magidor [13]:

1. Left logical equivalence *(LLE)*. If $\mathcal{K} \approx \alpha \leftrightarrow \beta$ and $\mathcal{K} \approx \alpha \mathrel{\vdash\mkern-7mu\sim} \gamma$ then $\mathcal{K} \approx \beta \mathrel{\vdash\mkern-7mu\sim} \gamma$.
2. Right weakening *(RW)*. If $\mathcal{K} \approx \alpha \to \beta$ and $\mathcal{K} \approx \gamma \mathrel{\vdash\mkern-7mu\sim} \alpha$ then $\mathcal{K} \approx \gamma \mathrel{\vdash\mkern-7mu\sim} \beta$.
3. *And.* If $\mathcal{K} \approx \alpha \mathrel{\vdash\mkern-7mu\sim} \beta$ and $\mathcal{K} \approx \alpha \mathrel{\vdash\mkern-7mu\sim} \gamma$ then $\mathcal{K} \approx \alpha \mathrel{\vdash\mkern-7mu\sim} \beta \wedge \gamma$.

4. *Or.* If $\mathcal{K} \approx \alpha \mathrel{|\!\sim} \gamma$ and $\mathcal{K} \approx \beta \mathrel{|\!\sim} \gamma$ then $\mathcal{K} \approx \alpha \vee \beta \mathrel{|\!\sim} \gamma$.
5. Reflexivity *(Ref)*. $\mathcal{K} \approx \alpha \mathrel{|\!\sim} \alpha$.
6. Cautious Monotonicity *(CM)*. If $\mathcal{K} \approx \alpha \mathrel{|\!\sim} \gamma$ and $\mathcal{K} \approx \alpha \mathrel{|\!\sim} \beta$ then $\mathcal{K} \approx \alpha \wedge \beta \mathrel{|\!\sim} \gamma$.
7. Rational Monotonicity *(RM)*. If $\mathcal{K} \approx \alpha \mathrel{|\!\sim} \gamma$ and $\mathcal{K} \not\approx \alpha \mathrel{|\!\sim} \neg\beta$ then $\mathcal{K} \approx \alpha \wedge \beta \mathrel{|\!\sim} \gamma$.

This is a strengthening of the KLM postulates because *LLE* has the condition $\mathcal{K} \approx \alpha \leftrightarrow \beta$ in favour of $\alpha \equiv \beta$ and *RW* has $\mathcal{K} \approx \alpha \to \beta$ in favour of $\alpha \models \beta$. (Note here that $\mathcal{K} \approx \alpha \leftrightarrow \beta$ is for example is a shorthand for $\mathcal{K} \approx \neg (\alpha \leftrightarrow \beta) \mathrel{|\!\sim} \bot$ as discussed in the background section.) This provides a more useful perspective for our purposes.

Our approach is to consider how defeasible justification applies to each of these axioms. Take for instance the example of *And*. The insight here is that if α typically implies β, and α typically implies γ, then not only should we be able to conclude that α typically implies β and γ, we should be able to conclude it *by the same token*. In this section we formalise this idea, and a similar idea for each postulate above, in relation to weak justification. The following concept helps us state these results:

Definition 10. *A knowledge base $\mathcal{D} \subseteq \mathcal{K}$ is deciding for an entailment $\mathcal{K} \approx \alpha \mathrel{|\!\sim} \beta$ if $\mathcal{D} \subseteq \mathcal{E}_\alpha^\mathcal{K}$ and $\overline{\mathcal{D}} \models \alpha \to \beta$.*

For a given entailment, any deciding knowledge base is always a superset of a weak justification and all weak justifications are deciding (refer to Definition 5). We also have the following results for deciding knowledge bases:

Proposition 5. *If $\mathcal{D}$ is a deciding knowledge base for an entailment $\mathcal{K} \approx \alpha \mathrel{|\!\sim} \beta$ and $\mathrm{br}_\mathcal{K}(\alpha) \neq \infty$, then $\mathcal{D} \approx \alpha \mathrel{|\!\sim} \beta$.*

Proposition 6. *If $\mathcal{D}$ is a deciding knowledge base for an entailment $\mathcal{K} \approx \alpha \mathrel{|\!\sim} \beta$ and we have $\mathcal{D} \approx \alpha \mathrel{|\!\sim} \beta$, then $\mathcal{J}_W(\mathcal{D}, \alpha \mathrel{|\!\sim} \beta) \subseteq \mathcal{J}_W(\mathcal{K}, \alpha \mathrel{|\!\sim} \beta)$.*

Proofs for these results, as well as all results in this section, are given in Appendix C. We can now state a result corresponding to each axiom of rational defeasible entailment:

Theorem 1. *For any knowledge bases $\mathcal{K}, \mathcal{J}_1, \mathcal{J}_2$,*

(LLE) if $\mathcal{J}_1 \in \mathcal{J}_W(\mathcal{K}, \alpha \leftrightarrow \beta)$ and $\mathcal{J}_2 \in \mathcal{J}_W(\mathcal{K}, \alpha \mathrel{|\!\sim} \gamma)$, $\mathcal{J}_1 \cup \mathcal{J}_2$ is deciding for $\mathcal{K} \approx \beta \mathrel{|\!\sim} \gamma$;

(RW)   if $\mathcal{J}_1 \in \mathcal{J}_W(\mathcal{K}, \alpha \to \beta)$ and $\mathcal{J}_2 \in \mathcal{J}_W(\mathcal{K}, \gamma \mathrel{|\!\sim} \alpha)$, $\mathcal{J}_1 \cup \mathcal{J}_2$ is deciding for $\mathcal{K} \approx \gamma \mathrel{|\!\sim} \beta$;

(And) if $\mathcal{J}_1 \in \mathcal{J}_W(\mathcal{K}, \alpha \mathrel{|\!\sim} \beta)$ and $\mathcal{J}_2 \in \mathcal{J}_W(\mathcal{K}, \alpha \mathrel{|\!\sim} \gamma)$, $\mathcal{J}_1 \cup \mathcal{J}_2$ is deciding for $\mathcal{K} \approx \alpha \mathrel{|\!\sim} \beta \wedge \gamma$;

(Or)   if $\mathcal{J}_1 \in \mathcal{J}_W(\mathcal{K}, \alpha \mathrel{|\!\sim} \gamma)$ and $\mathcal{J}_2 \in \mathcal{J}_W(\mathcal{K}, \beta \mathrel{|\!\sim} \gamma)$, $\mathcal{J}_1 \cup \mathcal{J}_2$ is deciding for $\mathcal{K} \approx \alpha \vee \beta \mathrel{|\!\sim} \gamma$.

(Ref) $\mathcal{J}_W(\mathcal{K}, \alpha \mathrel{|\!\sim} \alpha) = \{\emptyset\}$.

(CM)   if $\mathcal{K} \approx \alpha \mathrel{|\!\sim} \gamma$ and $\mathcal{K} \approx \alpha \mathrel{|\!\sim} \beta$, every $\mathcal{J} \in \mathcal{J}_W (\mathcal{K}, \alpha \mathrel{|\!\sim} \gamma)$ is deciding
         for $\mathcal{K} \approx \alpha \wedge \beta \mathrel{|\!\sim} \gamma$;

(RM)   if $\mathcal{K} \approx \alpha \mathrel{|\!\sim} \gamma$ and $\mathcal{K} \not\approx \alpha \mathrel{|\!\sim} \neg\beta$, every $\mathcal{J} \in \mathcal{J}_W (\mathcal{K}, \alpha \mathrel{|\!\sim} \gamma)$ is deciding
         for $\mathcal{K} \approx \alpha \wedge \beta \mathrel{|\!\sim} \gamma$.

6   Conclusions and Future Work

We have extended the principle of weak justification, previously only explored
for Rational Closure, to the case of Relevant and Lexicographic Closure and
proposed algorithms for enumerating these justifications. We then evaluated a
revised definition of strong justification in light of certain issues and proposed an
algorithm that enumerates these justifications for Rational Closure. This is, to
our knowledge, the first application of strong explanation to KLM and may offer
an alternative to weak justification that is perhaps more comprehensive as far as
the resulting justifications are concerned. Our final result is a characterisation
of weak justification in relation to the KLM postulates for rationality. This
provides evidence that weak justification is a sound and generalisable notion
of justification for KLM-style defeasible entailment and illustrates similarities
between weak justification for the defeasible case and classical justification for
the classical case.

Since the algorithm we propose for enumerating strong justifications and
the declarative characterisation of weak justification were limited to the case of
Rational Closure, further work might seek to apply this result to other notions
of defeasible entailment for KLM or perhaps generally to rational defeasible
entailment. Another possibility is to consider how these ideas apply to KLM
description logic [5, 7, 14].

A   Supplementary Material

The full paper with the appendix containing proofs for all propositions and
additional details for algorithms is available at: https://www.cair.org.za/sites/
default/files/2021-11/Explanation_For_KLM.pdf

References

1. Bail. S.P.: The justificatory structure of OWL ontologies. PhD thesis, University
   of Manchester (2013)
2. Biran, O., Cotton, C.: Explanation and justification in machine learning: a survey.
   In: IJCAI-17 Workshop on Explainable AI (XAI), vol. 8, pp. 8–13 (2017)
3. Brewka, G., Ulbricht, M.: Strong explanations for nonmonotonic reasoning. In:
   Description Logic, Theory Combination, and All That, pages 135–146. Springer,
   Cham (2019). https://doi.org/10.1007/978-3-030-22102-7
4. Casini, G., Meyer, T., Moodley, K., Nortjé, R.: Relevant closure: a new form of
   defeasible reasoning for description logics. In: Fermé, E., Leite, J. (eds.), Logics in
   Artificial Intelligence, pp. 92–106. Springer, Cham (2021)

5. Casini, G., Meyer, T., Moodley, K., Varzinczak, I.: Towards practical defeasible reasoning for description logics (2013)
6. Casini, G., Meyer, T., Varzinczak, I.: Taking defeasible entailment beyond rational closure. In: Calimeri, F., Leone, N., Manna, M. (eds.) JELIA 2019. LNCS (LNAI), vol. 11468, pp. 182–197. Springer, Cham (2019). https://doi.org/10.1007/978-3-030-19570-0_12
7. Casini, G., Straccia, U.: Defeasible inheritance-based description logics. J. Artif. Intell. Res. **48**, 415–473 (2013)
8. Chama, V.: Explanation for defeasible entailment. Master's thesis, Faculty of Science (2020)
9. From propositional logic to description logics: Laura Giordano, Valentina Gliozzi, Nicola Olivetti, and Gian Luca Pozzato. semantic characterization of rational closure. Artif. Intell. **226**, 1–33 (2015)
10. Horridge, M.: Justification based explanation in ontologies. The University of Manchester (United Kingdom) (2011)
11. Kraus, S., Lehmann, D., Magidor, M.: Nonmonotonic reasoning, preferential models and cumulative logics. Artif. Intell. **44**(1), 167–207 (1990)
12. Lehmann, D.: Another perspective on default reasoning. Ann. Math. Artif. Intell. **15**(1), 61–82 (1995)
13. Lehmann, D., Magidor, M.: What does a conditional knowledge base entail? Artif. Intell. **55**(1), 1–60 (1992)
14. Moodley, K.: Practical reasoning for defeasable description logics. PhD thesis, University of KwaZulu-Natal (2016)
15. Morris, M., Ross, T., Meyer, T.: Algorithmic definitions for KLM-style defeasible disjunctive datalog. South Afr. Comput. J. **32**(2), 141–160 (2020)

Machine Learning

Revisiting the Use of Noise in Evolutionary Robotics

Mathys C. du Plessis[(✉)] [iD], Antin P. Phillips, and Christiaan J. Pretorius [iD]

Nelson Mandela University, Gqeberha, South Africa
mc.duplessis@mandela.ac.za

Abstract. The injection of noise into simulator predictions during controller evolution in Evolutionary Robotics (ER) has long been used as a method of counteracting the *reality gap* problem. This study endeavoured to design and conduct experiments to quantify the impact of different levels of such noise on two different factors that are believed to contribute to the reality gap: inconsistencies in real-world robotic behaviour and inaccuracies in the simulator used in ER. These experiments were conducted on a robot performing a maze-navigation task. The results obtained in this study showed that, as was anticipated, noise injection during controller evolution does have an appreciable positive impact on the transferability of evolved controllers to the real robot. Various additional trends were observed, however, such as the limited capability of noise to aid in transferability under certain conditions. Additionally, the results of this study illustrated that different contributors to the reality gap may be optimally counteracted using different levels of noise. The results thus emphasized the importance of noise injection and of selecting optimal noise levels during the ER process.

Keywords: Evolution · Robotics · Noise · Reality gap

1 Introduction

Evolutionary Robotics (ER) harnesses the power of evolution to automatically design controllers and morphologies for robots. This research is focused on the evolution of controllers. One of the major challenges in the field is known as the *reality gap* which refers to the poor transferability of controllers evolved in simulation when executed in the real-world. One of the most common and effective means of addressing the reality gap problem is through the injection of noise into simulator predictions during the evolution process.

Two main causes of the reality gap are inconsistencies in robot behaviour in the real-world and inaccurate simulators being used during controller evolution. This research aims to systematically investigate the relationship and effect of these two causes with respect to the magnitude of noise used in ER. Experiments were designed to examine this relationship on a mobile robot traversing a maze.

The remainder of this paper is presented as follows: The ER process itself and previous investigations in ER which are applicable to the current study are

© Springer Nature Switzerland AG 2022
E. Jembere et al. (Eds.): SACAIR 2021, CCIS 1551, pp. 211–226, 2022.
https://doi.org/10.1007/978-3-030-95070-5_14

presented in Sect. 2. The study to be attempted in this work is then motivated (Sect. 3) and the experimental procedure to be used is discussed (Sect. 4). Results are presented in Sect. 5 and finally conclusions are drawn (Sect. 7).

2   Related Work

This section will briefly outline previous research relevant to the current study, by introducing the ER process, as well as the use of simulation and the role played by noise injection during this process.

2.1   Evolutionary Robotics

The ER process is a technique for developing control programs (or simply controllers) for experimental robots, which can allow these robots to perform certain tasks in their environment [1]. This is achieved by making use of an Evolutionary Algorithm (EA) [2] to iteratively evolve a population of robotic controllers. Controllers can be implemented in various ways, with Neural Networks (NNs) being a popular method [3]. By making use of ER, the development process of controllers can be achieved with minimal need for human involvement, since the ER process operates semi-autonomously. As a result of the automation in robotic development offered by ER, this field has attracted considerable interest from the robotics community.

Since the ER process is based on an EA, an important facet of ER is the assignment of a fitness value to each candidate controller in the population which is evolved during this process [4]. The fitness value assigned to a given controller gives a quantitative indication of the performance of that controller in performing the required task, relative to the other controllers in the population. The ultimate goal of ER is to maximize this fitness. Due to its iterative nature, a typical ER process will involve fitness evaluations of a large number of potential controllers. This means that evaluating the performance of each controller by uploading it to the real-world robot is often impractical, because of time constraints [5] and potential damage to robot hardware due to excessive use.

2.2   Simulation in ER

As an alternative to real-world controller evaluations in ER, robotic simulators are often used [6–12]. Such simulators are constructed to model the functioning of motors and/or sensors onboard the robot, so that the operation of candidate controllers in the ER population can be evaluated purely in software. The usage of robotic simulators can accelerate the ER process and alleviate other issues involved in performing ER in the real-world. As such, simulators have become ubiquitous in ER experiments.

The usage of simulators, however, does introduce some potential challenges in ER which need to be taken into account. Any discrepancies between robotic behaviour predicted by a simulator and the corresponding real-world behaviour of the robot, can negatively affect the performance of controllers produced by ER, when these controllers are deployed on the real-world robot. An adequate controller produced by a simulation-based ER process is thus not guaranteed to transfer successfully to reality. This divide between controller performance in simulation as opposed to the real-world is termed the *reality gap* problem [10,11]. The reality gap has been investigated extensively by ER researchers, who have suggested various techniques to reduce the impact of this problem. For the sake of brevity, an extensive discussion on these techniques will, however, not be presented here.

2.3   Noise in ER

One technique that has been suggested to deal with the reality gap problem in ER, is noise injection during evolution. Noise has been used in ER for 25 years [10], and has become standard whenever controllers are evolved in simulation. Such noise generally is used to minimize the differences between robotic behaviour in simulation and in the real-world, by introducing the noisy and unpredictable nature of the real-world into the simulator. This is done in an attempt to reduce the likelihood of the ER process exploiting inaccuracies or oversimplifications in the simulator [13]. The use of noise is not only a technique to overcome the reality gap problem, but noise is also useful when evolving NN-based controllers. The addition of noise in the inputs during training improves the training time and resultant generalisation abilities of NNs [2].

In one of the first studies in ER investigating the usage of noise, Jakobi, Husbands and Harvey [10] investigated the ER-based evolution of controllers to achieve obstacle avoidance and light seeking behaviours in a differentially steered mobile robot. Controller evolution was conducted in a simulator, with varying levels of noise injected into predictions made by the simulator during evolution. It was shown that the level of noise injected during evolution does affect the real-world transferability of evolved controllers, with the best transferability achieved when realistic levels of noise are used. Similar studies done at roughly the same time confirmed that adequate usage of noise can aid in the simulation-based ER process [14] and can also accelerate the evolution process [15].

In a more recent study, Holland, Gallagher, Griffith and O'Riordan [16] explored how the reality gap in ER can be investigated purely in simulation. This was achieved by making use of abstract and more realistic robotic models in the evolution of robotic swarm behaviour. The impact of noise during the controller evolution process was investigated by evolving controllers with noise injection and then running these controllers in a noiseless environment, and evolving controllers without noise injection and running these controllers in a noisy environment. This study illustrated that studies on noise injection in ER can be performed purely in simulation.

3   Motivation

This work assumes that the reality gap is caused by two problems. The first is that simulators are never perfectly accurate. Any physical robot will have unique characteristics that will not be modeled by a general simulator, for example, traction on one wheel may be worn, some of the servomotors may slip at high torque, or sensors may not perform as expected due to manufacturing defects. Consequently, it is inevitable that the simulator used to evaluate controllers during evolution will not be a 100% accurate model of the robot.

The second problem is the consistency (repeatability) of the real-world. Even if a simulator could be created that models a robot perfectly for a specific sequence of movements, the robot will never perform the same movements in exactly the same way when performing the same commands. Robots are sensitive to changes in temperature, air pressure, power fluctuations, friction, etc. which make robotic movements inherently inconsistent despite the best efforts of robotic engineers. Controllers evolved even in a perfect simulator will inevitably be brittle solutions if no variation is present in the simulator.

Previous studies have looked at the amount of noise which should be included in the simulator, but the aim of this paper is to explicitly investigate the relationship between the amount of noise during evolution and **a)** the consistency of the real-world and **b)** the accuracy of the simulator. The goal is to determine if noise is equally effective at addressing both these causes of the reality gap problem and to determine how much noise is appropriate for each.

4   Experimental Procedure

This section describes the experimental procedure followed in this investigation. Firstly, the task that will be used to evaluate controllers is discussed. Secondly, the simulator that will be used is briefly described. This is followed by a description of how an inconsistent real-world and an inaccurate simulator will be modelled. Finally, the evolution process and the evaluation procedure will be outlined.

4.1   Task

The robot used in this research is the differentially steered Khepera III robot which has been used in many ER papers [17, 18]. The robot is steered by varying the relative motor speeds of its two wheels and is equipped with nine infrared distance sensors around the perimeter of its body. The task that the robot had to perform involved steering to a specified goal in a Double-T Maze (TT-M), shown in Fig. 1. The TT-M has frequently been used in ER research [19, 20] because it represents a problem of reasonable complexity.

The robot always starts at a specific position on one of the arms of the maze. An input is given to the robot indicating which of the four goal positions in the maze must be visited. The robot must then move to that position using only

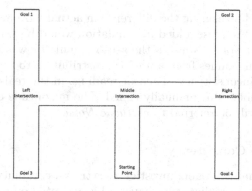

Fig. 1. The double-T maze

information from its distance sensors. Note that a single generalised controller for the robot must be devised that will enable it to travel to any of the four goals upon command. A limit is placed on the number of time-steps that the controller is executed to prevent trivial solutions which always visit all four goals. Such a solution would defeat the purpose of the exercise.

The controllers selected for this task take the form of Recurrent Long Short-Term Memory Networks (LSTM) [21,22]. This configuration has been successfully used in previous research as controllers for the TT-M task [23]. The neurons (or cells) in LSTM networks differ from normal NN neurons in that they contain a memory value which influences the firing of the neuron and which is updated every time the network fires. Each controller consists of an LSTM network with a single hidden layer of 12 neurons. Two outputs are produced by the controller: the left and the right motor speeds. The produced motor speeds are also recurrently fed back to the network as inputs, along with the nine sensor readings and four inputs which flags the goal position to visit. During execution each controller is fired every 400 ms after which the robot is moved using the produced motor speeds and new sensor readings are obtained from the robot so that the network can be fired again.

4.2   Simulator

This research considers the relationship between the amount of noise used in simulation during the ER process and the repeatability of the real-world and the accuracy of the simulator. The simulator used for experimentation has been extensively used in ER research on the Khepera III robot [17,18,24]. The two components that make up the simulator are a NN-based location simulator and a hand-crafted infrared sensor simulator.

Random noise is usually added to the location using a normal distribution during the evolution process. The standard deviation of the added noise was experimentally determined by repeatedly executing a set of commands on the real-world robot and measuring the difference in actual movements. The motivation for this is that the noise added in simulation would be similar to variations expected in the real-world. Noise in the sensor simulator was found to be most effective when adding values from a uniform distribution to the sensor readings, thus modeling the inconsistency of sensor readings in the real-world. The range of the random numbers was manually tuned. The magnitude of noise described in this paragraph will be referred to as *Basic Noise*.

4.3 Real-World Consistency

The first scenario that this paper investigates is the repeatability of robot actions. The performance of controllers thus have to be evaluated on robots that exhibit various levels of consistency when repeating the same actions. Creating such robots in the real-world would be very difficult and expensive, so a substitute real-world was created in simulation using the simulator previously discussed. The substitute real-world for this scenario involved the addition of noise to the simulator in exactly the same way as during the evolution process (i.e. the addition of random values to the simulator's predictions). Four noise levels were selected. Level 0 consists of no noise, Level 1 consists of noise levels half of *Basic Noise*, Level 2 consists of noise equal to *Basic Noise* and Level 3 consists of noise equal to double of *Basic Noise*.

Jakobi [25] stressed the need to add noise to all the bases of simulation (i.e. to the location and the sensor simulation). To explicitly investigate this notion experiments were performed for cases where only sensor noise is present, only location noise is present and both are present. The latter case involved the staggered increase of noise from both sources. Seven levels of noise were created for the case when both forms of noise is present: Level 0 - No noise from either location or sensor; Level 1 - No noise for location and half of *Basic Noise* for sensor; Level 2 - half of *Basic Noise* for location and half of *Basic Noise* for sensor; Level 3 - half of *Basic Noise* for location and *Basic Noise* for sensor; Level 4 - *Basic Noise* for location and *Basic Noise* for sensor; Level 5 - *Basic Noise* for location and double *Basic Noise* for sensor; Level 6 - double *Basic Noise* for location and double *Basic Noise* for sensor.

4.4 Inaccurate Simulator

The second scenario considered in this paper is the situation of a simulator misrepresenting the real-world. Controllers are thus evolved in an inaccurate simulated world that does not correspond to the real-world. This scenario was modelled by altering the substitute real-world simulator to differ from the simulator used during the evolution process. The alteration consisted of scaling the values produced by the substitute real-world simulator by constant values: 0.5, 0.7, 0.9, 1.0, 1.1, 1.3, 1.5. This has the effect of producing scenarios in which the simulator used during evolution overestimates the substitute real-world by factors 2.0, 1.43 and 1.11 for scale factors 0.5, 0.7 and 0.9 respectively, and underestimating the substitute real-world by factors 0.91, 0.77 and 0.67 for scale factors 1.1, 1.3 and 1.5. In other words, if a scale factor of 0.5 is used on the values produced by the substitute real-world simulator, it represents a scenario where controllers were evolved which expect the robot to move double the distance for any command and double the sensor input from any given reading. No other noise was added to the substitute real-world.

4.5 Evolution

The weights on the Recurrent LSTM network controllers were optimized using an EA and controllers were evaluated in simulation. Sets of controllers were evolved with different amounts of noise used in the simulator. As with the noise that was eventually added to substitute real-world evaluations, noise levels corresponding to sensor noise only (Levels 0 to 3), location noise only (Levels 0 to 3) and both noisy (Levels 0 to 6) were investigated.

Each controller was produced by letting a population of 100 candidate controllers evolve for 500 generations. Elitism was employed (2 individuals) and new individuals were created using Gaussian mutations and uniform crossovers. Each individual was evaluated in simulation by commanding it to visit each of the four goals 30 times (i.e. a total of 120 executions). The fitness function rewarded the controllers for remaining within the bounds of the maze, moving closer to the goal position, using few motor commands and minimising infrared sensor readings (i.e. staying far away from the maze walls). Full details of the fitness function used can be found in [20].

4.6 Experiment and Evaluation

The goal of this paper is to determine how the use of various noise levels during evolution in simulation performs in various real-world scenarios (i.e. real-worlds that has various levels of consistency and scenarios where simulators model the real-world to varying degrees of accuracy). Controllers were evolved in simulation using no noise, and then progressively higher levels of noise. Thirty controllers were evolved for each noise level. The evolved controllers were then evaluated in substitute real-worlds that modelled each of the scenarios investigated. Each of the thirty controllers evaluated in each scenario were directed to visit each of the goals in the maze thirty times. This means that each controller was evaluated in the substitute real-world 120 times. Each substitute real-world scenario thus consisted of a total of $120 \times 30 = 3600$ evaluations.

Two metrics were collected during experimentation. The first is the *Success Count*. This represents the number of the thirty evolved controllers that are deemed to be effective at performing the required task. A controller is deemed to be effective if it managed to successfully reach each of the four goals in the maze more than 50% of the time. The *Success Count* metric ensures that controllers must be able to reach any of the goals and disqualifies controllers that only managed to learn to reach three or less of the four goals.

The second metric that was collected is the *Goal Rate*. This is a percentage of the number of successful goals reached out of the 3600 substitute real-world evaluations. This metric is considered to be of secondary importance as it does not measure the ability of controllers to reach all four goals. For example, controllers that only learn to visit three of the goals will have a *Goal Rate* of 75% while the *Success Count* will be 0. Such controllers are seen as inferior to controllers that reach each of the goals 50% of the time (thus being a *Success Count* of 30) even though the *Goal Rate* of the more general controllers is only 50%. The *Goal Rate* will thus only be used to compare scenarios when controllers have identical values for *Success Count*.

5   Results

The results that were obtained clearly demonstrate the benefit of adding noise to the simulator during the evolution process. Figure 2 shows the performance of a controller that was evolved without noise and is executed in a substitute real-world without noise. The controller was tasked with visiting each of the four goal areas 25 times, but since the substitute real-world does not contain any noise there is no variation in its behaviour. The solution that was evolved is clearly extremely brittle, with many turns and redundant movements (even relying on moving through a wall to reach the goal on the top right). This controller does not perform well in a substitute real-world that contains noise, as shown in Fig. 3. When noise is present, the robot hardly ever reaches the goal regions and frequently moves outside the bounds of the maze. Compare this to the behaviour of the controller shown in Fig. 4, which was evolved with noise present in the simulation. The second controller exhibits much more successful, effective and consistent behaviour.

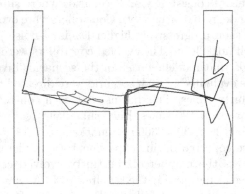

Fig. 2. Controller evolved without noise in a real-world without noise

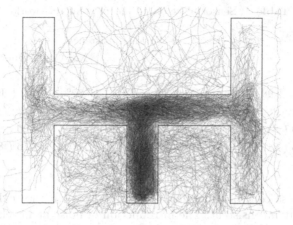

Fig. 3. Controller evolved without noise in a real-world with noise

Fig. 4. Controller evolved with noise in a real-world with noise

The results of the experimental work are summarised in Tables 1 through 6. Rows in the tables represent controllers that were evolved with successively higher levels of noise in simulation, while columns represent the evaluations of the controllers in various substitute real-world scenarios. All cells in the tables give the *Success Count* (out of 30) followed by *Goal Rate* in brackets. A *Success Count* of 28 with *Goal Rate* of 98.33% was found for the case where no noise was present in either during evolution or in the substitute real-world. Results pertaining to real-world consistency (refer to Sect. 4.3) will be discussed first.

Table 1 gives the results for the investigation into the presence of only sensor noise in simulation and in the substitute real-world. The first row of the table shows that although a high *Success Count* was achieved when using no noise in evolution when there is no noise in the real-world (i.e. a perfectly consistent

Table 1. Sensor noise only - inconsistent real-world

Noise Level	Real-World Consistency			
	← Very Consistent		Not Consistent →	
	0	1	2	3
0	*28* (98.33%)	4 (53.25%)	3 (50.22%)	2 (49.33%)
1	21 (88.33%)	*23* (90.00%)	*22* (88.22%)	*24* (84.94%)
2	19 (85.00%)	20 (87.53%)	20 (87.14%)	20 (84.78%)
3	15 (81.67%)	17 (82.03%)	18 (81.97%)	16 (81.89%)

real-world), these controllers perform very poorly when the real-world sensors are even slightly inconsistent. The introduction of noise at Levels 1 to 3 during evolution does result in controllers that are less effective in a very consistent real-world, but are considerably more effective in more realistic, inconsistent real-world environments. The grey cells indicate the best performing evolution noise level for each of the real-world scenarios. The lowest non-zero noise level tested resulted in the best performing controllers in all the inconsistent real-world tests. This would indicate that even when the real-world infrared sensors have high levels of inconsistency, the best controllers are evolved by only adding a small amount of noise in simulation.

Table 2. Location noise only - inconsistent real-world

Noise Level	Real-World Consistency			
	← Very Consistent		Not Consistent →	
	0	1	2	3
0	*28* (98.33%)	1 (43.00%)	0 (35.22%)	0 (24.19%)
1	19 (85.83%)	22 (81.92%)	19 (73.44%)	0 (48.03%)
2	21 (89.17%)	*26* (90.86%)	*26* (87.00%)	7 (63.89%)
3	21 (87.50%)	26 (90.72%)	25 (88.00%)	*16* (72.25%)

Table 2 gives the results for the investigation into only noise in location being present. Here controllers evolved without noise are even less successful when the real-world is inconsistent in terms of the location reached by the robot. This would indicate that these controllers relied heavily on a memorised sequence of movements to reach the goals and did not utilise infrared sensor inputs as required. The addition of noise during evolution resulted in controllers that are considerably more effective in inconsistent real-world scenarios. Unlike the results for the sensor only noise experiments, where best results were obtained with a small amount of noise in simulation, the location noise controllers performed the best when similar amounts of noise were used during evolution as what were present in the real-world.

Table 3. Sensor and location noise - inconsistent real-world (**NL** = Noise Level)

NL	Real-World Consistency						
	← Very Consistent			Not Consistent →			
	0	1	2	3	4	5	6
0	28 (98.33%)	5 (55.42%)	1 (42.81%)	1 (42.75%)	1 (36.83%)	0 (37.75%)	0 (23.56%)
1	21 (88.33%)	24 (89.81%)	7 (62.03%)	11 (61.25%)	3 (50.11%)	4 (52.39%)	0 (32.61%)
2	15 (81.67%)	20 (85.33%)	22 (84.39%)	21 (83.53%)	19 (76.08%)	17 (75.83%)	1 (48.28%)
3	17 (85.00%)	18 (84.19%)	21 (83.78%)	19 (83.56%)	16 (77.14%)	13 (76.94%)	0 (51.36%)
4	21 (91.67%)	26 (91.78%)	25 (90.75%)	26 (90.61%)	23 (86.78%)	24 (86.72%)	7 (63.28%)
5	21 (90.00%)	24 (90.44%)	26 (91.14%)	26 (91.67%)	25 (87.67%)	26 (87.89%)	3 (62.75%)
6	22 (89.17%)	25 (86.64%)	28 (93.03%)	29 (93.00%)	27 (90.39%)	26 (90.17%)	11 (72.94%)

The experiments where both sensor and location noise were investigated are summarised in Table 3. Once again the benefits of adding noise during evolution are evident, with the *Success Count* of one of the sets of controllers being even higher than the no noise scenario. Note that in most cases the most successful controllers are evolved with considerably more noise in simulation than what is present in the real-world (the maximum noise level investigated performed the best in all inconsistent real-world scenarios except the case when very little noise was present). This is in contrast to the results obtained when only noise from either the infrared sensors or the location was present. A possible reason for this could be that when multiple sources of inconsistency are present in the real-world, their effects are compounded to be very challenging to the controllers, thus requiring large amounts of noise during evolution.

Table 4. Sensor noise only - inaccurate simulator (**NL** = Noise Level)

NL	Simulator Accuracy						
	← Simulator Overestimates			Perfect	Simulator Underestimates →		
	2.00	1.43	1.11	1.00	0.91	0.77	0.67
0	1 (27.50%)	2 (41.67%)	2 (43.33%)	28 (98.33%)	2 (49.17%)	1 (38.33%)	0 (34.17%)
1	1 (39.17%)	5 (54.17%)	11 (68.33%)	21 (88.33%)	10 (65.83%)	10 (60.00%)	1 (52.50%)
2	1 (42.50%)	4 (56.67%)	12 (70.00%)	19 (85.00%)	13 (75.83%)	8 (62.50%)	6 (55.83%)
3	0 (43.33%)	1 (53.33%)	11 (64.17%)	15 (81.67%)	13 (72.50%)	8 (58.33%)	6 (54.17%)

Table 4 gives the first results pertaining to simulator accuracy (refer to Sect. 4.4). Once again infrared sensor noise and sensor accuracy was first considered in isolation. Each row in the table represents controllers evolved with different noise levels as in the previous experiments. The columns represent different scenarios in which the simulator overestimated or underestimated values produced in the substitute real-world. The column labelled "Perfect" corresponds to the situation where the simulator used during evolution is identical to the one used as substitute real-world (i.e. no values were scaled). The first row in the table indicates that using an inaccurate simulator is extremely detrimental, as can be seen by the extremely low values of *Success Count*. The situation is improved when using noise as can be seen in the second and third row of data where the *Success Count* is higher. However, noise only seems to be of significant benefit when the overestimation or underestimation of the simulator is small or moderate. None of the highest values for *Success Count* appears at noise Level 3 which indicates that noise is only helpful up to a point for this problem.

Table 5. Location noise only - inaccurate simulator (**NL** = Noise Level)

NL	Simulator Accuracy						
	← Simulator Overestimates			Perfect	Simulator Underestimates →		
	2.00	1.43	1.11	1.00	0.91	0.77	0.67
0	1 (27.50%)	2 (41.67%)	2 (43.33%)	*28* (98.33%)	2 (49.17%)	1 (38.33%)	0 (34.17%)
1	*1* (42.50%)	2 (60.83%)	17 (81.67%)	19 (85.83%)	15 (80.00%)	10 (70.00%)	7 (66.67%)
2	0 (42.50%)	*6* (69.17%)	*23* (90.83%)	21 (89.17%)	*23* (92.50%)	18 (85.83%)	14 (82.50%)
3	0 (33.33%)	5 (66.67%)	18 (80.83%)	21 (87.50%)	*23* (92.50%)	*20* (89.17%)	*21* (86.67%)

Table 5 summarises results for location only noise when faced with an inaccurate location simulator. Once again the inaccurate simulator can be seen to be extremely detrimental to the transferability of evolved controllers (first row). Considerably better results are achieved when using noise during evolution. However, the results indicate that noise is mostly beneficial when the simulator underestimates or only slightly overestimates the values in the real-world. Little benefit is achieved when the simulator overestimates by a large magnitude.

Table 6. Sensor and location noise - inaccurate simulator (**NL** = Noise Level)

NL	Simulator Accuracy						
	← Simulator Overestimates			Perfect	Simulator Underestimates →		
	2.00	1.43	1.11	1.00	0.91	0.77	0.67
0	1 (27.50%)	2 (41.67%)	2 (43.33%)	*28* (98.33%)	2 (49.17%)	1 (38.33%)	0 (34.17%)
1	*1* (39.17%)	5 (54.17%)	11 (68.33%)	21 (88.33%)	10 (65.83%)	10 (60.00%)	1 (52.50%)
2	0 (39.17%)	1 (57.50%)	17 (84.17%)	15 (81.67%)	16 (82.50%)	11 (73.33%)	7 (62.50%)
3	0 (43.33%)	*6* (67.50%)	16 (78.33%)	17 (85.00%)	16 (85.83%)	15 (81.67%)	12 (74.17%)
4	0 (40.00%)	2 (63.33%)	17 (87.50%)	21 (91.67%)	*23* (91.67%)	16 (85.83%)	*17* (87.50%)
5	0 (43.33%)	4 (69.17%)	20 (89.17%)	21 (90.00%)	20 (89.17%)	16 (84.17%)	16 (84.17%)
6	0 (31.67%)	4 (60.83%)	*21* (89.17%)	22 (89.17%)	22 (90.00%)	*17* (85.83%)	14 (81.67%)

Table 6 gives the results for experiments where both the sensor and location components of the simulator are inaccurate. The addition of noise is able to effectively mask the small simulator inaccuracies but is less effective for large inaccuracies, especially for cases where the simulator overestimates the real-world sensor reading and robot movements. This phenomenon is potentially task dependent. The robot learns during training in simulation to expect and respond to high sensor inputs and to cover larger distances when moving. This will result in poor performance in the real-world where sensor values never actually reach the expected threshold or where the robot does not move far enough towards its goal.

Comparing the results in Tables 3 and 6, it is clear that large amounts of noise during evolution consistently produced good results for the situation where the reality gap is caused by inconsistency in the real-world. This is not the case for experiments which investigated inaccurate simulators, where more moderate amounts of noise produced better results more often.

6   Alternate Form of Noise

The previous section reported results which used noise generated in the traditional manner. However, there are other means of adding variation during evolution. As an interesting and simple alternative, the experiments of the previous section were repeated without noise, but the starting position of the robot was randomly varied by a few centimetres at each evaluation in simulation. Although randomness is only introduced at the first step of the robot's execution, the entire resultant path that the robot travels will be unique for each evaluation. Controllers were evolved with increasing levels of start point variation and were then evaluated in the substitute real-world scenarios investigated in the previous section.

Table 7. Perturbed start position - inconsistent real-world (**OV** = Origin Variation)

OV	Real-World Consistency						
	← Very Consistent			Not Consistent →			
	0	1	2	3	4	5	6
0	28 (98.33%)	5 (55.42%)	1 (42.81%)	1 (42.75%)	1 (36.83%)	0 (37.75%)	0 (23.56%)
1	19 (85.00%)	20 (84.61%)	18 (73.47%)	19 (74.28%)	11 (61.03%)	11 (62.28%)	0 (36.75%)
2	19 (84.17%)	19 (81.97%)	18 (70.11%)	18 (70.67%)	15 (60.44%)	12 (60.08%)	1 (37.78%)
4	14 (78.33%)	19 (82.36%)	18 (75.31%)	19 (74.36%)	16 (66.00%)	17 (66.03%)	1 (40.69%)
8	14 (74.17%)	13 (72.56%)	12 (63.58%)	12 (63.78%)	11 (55.78%)	11 (55.69%)	1 (36.33%)

Table 7 gives the results for inconsistent real-world experiments. The varying origin technique resulted in considerable improvements of transferability of the evolved controllers (compare the first row to the subsequent rows), although too much variation in the start position degraded performance (refer to the last row). Note that the best *Success Count* values obtained are still lower than those found in Table 3 which suggests that, although varying the start position does assist with transferability, the more traditional method of noise addition is more effective.

Table 8. Perturbed start position - inaccurate simulator (**OV** = Origin Variation)

OV	Simulator Accuracy						
	← Simulator Overestimates			Perfect	Simulator Underestimates →		
	2.00	1.43	1.11	1.00	0.91	0.77	0.67
0	*1* (27.50%)	2 (41.67%)	2 (43.33%)	*28* (98.33%)	2 (49.17%)	1 (38.33%)	0 (34.17%)
1	0 (35.83%)	*3* (61.67%)	*16* (77.50%)	19 (85.00%)	*17* (80.83%)	12 (70.00%)	6 (56.67%)
2	0 (38.33%)	3 (54.17%)	15 (70.83%)	19 (84.17%)	15 (71.67%)	13 (66.67%)	*9* (60.00%)
4	0 (40.00%)	1 (58.33%)	15 (76.67%)	14 (78.33%)	12 (75.83%)	*13* (68.33%)	9 (56.67%)
8	0 (32.50%)	2 (44.17%)	11 (66.67%)	14 (74.17%)	11 (67.50%)	12 (65.00%)	9 (55.83%)

The results for inaccurate simulator scenarios (Table 8) also demonstrated the benefit of varying the robot's start position, however, as was the case with the results in Table 6, the benefits are limited to small simulator inaccuracies and cases where the simulator underestimates the real-world values. Once again the traditional noise injection method is more effective.

7   Conclusions

The results in this paper confirms that the inclusion of noise in simulation dramatically improves the transferability of controllers evolved using the ER process. By comparing scenarios where noise is only present in the sensors, only present in location, and present in both it was shown that the source of inconsistencies in the real world does have an effect in the amount of noise that is most appropriate in simulation. Multiple sources of inconsistencies appear to be best remedied with large amounts of noise. Despite the success of noise inclusion to address the reality gap, the results of this work showed that there is a limit to what can be achieved in very inconsistent environments.

Noise inclusion was less successful in the presence of inaccurate simulators. Inaccurate simulators can only be partially remedied and modest amounts of noise appear to give the best results. The results show that the type of inaccuracy determines whether noise will be helpful. Noise was more effective at masking simulator inaccuracies when the simulator underestimates values.

Varying the start position showed that other methods of producing noise can also be beneficial, but the method tested was not as effective as the traditional noise introduction method.

Future work could include reproducing the results of this paper with various real robots in the real-world. The type and complexity of tasks is also expected to influence the effectiveness of noise. Investigating other tasks could be an extension of the current work.

References

1. Pratihar, D.K.: Evolutionary Robotics - A Review. Sadhana 28(6), 999–1009 (2003)
2. Engelbrecht, A.P.: Computational Intelligence: An Introduction, 2nd edn. Wiley, West Sussex (2007)

3. Doncieux, S., Bredeche, N., Mouret, J., Eiben, A.E.G.: Evolutionary robotics: what, why, and where to. Front. Robot. AI **2**, 4 (2015)
4. Nelson, A.L., Barlow, G.J., Doitsidis, L.: Fitness functions in evolutionary robotics: a survey and analysis. Robot. Autonom. Syst. **57**(4), 345–370 (2009)
5. Koos, S., Mouret, J., Doncieux, S.: The transferability approach: crossing the reality gap in evolutionary robotics. IEEE Trans. Evol. Comput. **17**(1), 122–145 (2012)
6. Farooq, S.S., Kim, K.J.: Evolution of neural controllers for simulated and real quadruped robots. In: IEEE International Conference on Robot, Vision and Signal Processing, pp. 295–298 (2013)
7. Belter, D., Skrzypczyński, P.: A biologically inspired approach to feasible gait learning for a hexapod robot. Int. J. Appl. Math. Comput. Sci. **20**(1), 69–84 (2010)
8. Glette, K., Klaus, G., Zagal, J.C., Torresen, J.: Evolution of locomotion in a simulated quadruped robot and transferral to reality. In: International Symposium on Artificial Life and Robotics (2012)
9. Jakobi, N.: Running across the reality gap: octopod locomotion evolved in a minimal simulation. In: Evolutionary Robotics, pp. 39–58 (1998)
10. Jakobi, N., Husbands, P., Harvey, I.: Noise and the reality gap: the use of simulation in evolutionary robotics. In: Morán, F., Moreno, A., Merelo, J.J., Chacón, P. (eds.) ECAL 1995. LNCS, vol. 929, pp. 704–720. Springer, Heidelberg (1995). https://doi.org/10.1007/3-540-59496-5_337
11. Mouret, J., Chatzilygeroudis, K.: 20 years of reality gap: a few thoughts about simulators in evolutionary robotics. In: Genetic and Evolutionary Computation Conference Companion, pp. 1121–1124 (2017)
12. Zagal, J.C., Ruiz-del Solar, J.: Combining simulation and reality in Evolutionary Robotics. J. Intell. Robot. Syst. **50**, 19–39 (2007)
13. Bongard, J.C.: Evolutionary robotics. Commun. ACM **56**(8), 74–83 (2013). https://doi.org/10.1145/2493883
14. Miglino, O., Lund, H.H., Nolfi, S.: Evolving mobile robots in simulated and real environments. Artifi. Life **2**(4), 417–434 (1995)
15. Seth, A.K.: Noise and the pursuit of complexity: a study in evolutionary robotics. In: Husbands, P., Meyer, J.-A. (eds.) EvoRobots 1998. LNCS, vol. 1468, pp. 123–136. Springer, Heidelberg (1998). https://doi.org/10.1007/3-540-64957-3_68
16. Holland, J., Gallagher, C., Griffith, J., O'Riordan, C.: Identifying the reality gap between abstract and realistic models using evolved agents and simulated kilobots. In: 2018 IEEE International Conference on Robotics and Biomimetics (ROBIO), pp. 224–230. IEEE (2018)
17. Pretorius, C.J., du Plessis, M.C., Gonsalves, J.W.: A comparison of neural networks and physics models as motion simulators for simple robotic evolution. In: Evolutionary Computation (CEC), 2014 IEEE Congress on, pp. 2793–2800. IEEE (2014)
18. Woodford, G.W., Pretorius, C.J., du Plessis, M.C.: Concurrent controller and simulator neural network development for a differentially-steered robot in evolutionary robotics. Robot. Autonom. Syst. **76**, 80–92 (2016)
19. Jakobi, N.: Half-baked, ad-hoc and noisy: minimal simulations for evolutionary robotics. In: Fourth European Conference on Artificial Life, vol. 4, p. 348. MIT press (1997)
20. Phillips, A.P., du Plessis, M.C.: Towards the incorporation of proprioception in evolutionary robotics controllers. In: International Conference on Robotic Computing, IEEE (2019)
21. Hochreiter, S., Schmidhuber, J.: Long short-term memory. Neural comput. **9**(8), 1735–1780 (1997)

22. Gers, F.A., Schmidhuber, J.: Recurrent nets that time and count. In: Proceedings of the IEEE-INNS-ENNS International Joint Conference on Neural Networks. IJCNN 2000. Neural Computing: New Challenges and Perspectives for the New Millennium, vol. 3, pp. 189–194. IEEE (2000)
23. Phillips, A.P., du Plessis, M.C.: Evolutionary robotics controllers with proprioception facilitated by neural network based simulators. In: Unpublished (2020)
24. Leonard, B.A., du Plessis, M.C., Woodford, G.W.: Bootstrapped neuro-simulation as a method of concurrent neuro-evolution and damage recovery. Robot. Autonom. Syst. **124**, 103398 (2020). https://doi.org/10.1016/j.robot.2019.103398
25. Jakobi, N.: Evolutionary robotics and the radical envelope-of-noise hypothesis. Adapt. Behav. **6**(2), 325–368 (1997)

Avoiding Unexpected Obstacles During Robotic Navigation Using Rapidly-Exploring Random Trees and a Neural Network Simulator

Bouwer Botha$^{(\boxtimes)}$ and Mathys C. du Plessis

Nelson Mandela University, Gqeberha, South Africa
{s218063113,mc.duplessis}@mandela.ac.za

Abstract. Well-known environments allow for the creation of open-loop robotic controllers (controllers that do not rely on sensor feedback). Unexpected obstacles in the robot path would render an open-loop controller useless and would require a sophisticated and complex closed-loop controller. This problem is addressed by the developed approach that uses command sampling and neural network based localization to temporarily take control and safely navigate around unexpected obstacles, when detected. Control is then relinquished back to the base controller to perform the original task. Experiments performed on a real robot highlight the viability of the approach for short-term navigation, but adjustments are required for longer paths.

Keywords: Simulator neural networks · Rapidly-Exploring Random Trees · Motion planning · Simultaneous localization and mapping · Robotics

1 Introduction

Motion planning is a fundamental research area in robotics that has been extended from basic robot planning to more complex and diverse applications. Examples of current issues being investigated are planning under uncertainty or in dynamic environments [1]. Implementations are not limited to robotics and have seen applications in games [2] and virtual surgery [3].

A substantial amount of effort has been invested in developing robotic controllers. These controllers issue commands to a robot to manipulate the robot and perform a task. For certain applications, the controllers are developed before execution and may neglect certain considerations, such as unplanned obstacles. Collisions with these obstacles could not only cause damage to the robot but also impede its ability to complete its original task. Simultaneous Localization and Mapping (SLAM) has proven very useful [4] in assisting with collision-free movement, by allowing a robot to map its environment (by using sensor/image

© Springer Nature Switzerland AG 2022
E. Jembere et al. (Eds.): SACAIR 2021, CCIS 1551, pp. 227–241, 2022.
https://doi.org/10.1007/978-3-030-95070-5_15

data) and locate itself in the environment. Motion planning in these environments is often dependent on inverse kinematics. Due to most systems not being uniquely invertible, the inverse kinematics of a robot is often more difficult to determine than the forward kinematics [5].

This research is focused on a scenario where an open-loop controller is created before robot execution to enable the robot to perform a task. Unexpected obstacles may appear in the environment that were unknown during the development phase. An approach, called Neuro-Simulation Assisted Control Intervention, is suggested where control is temporarily released by the controller when an obstacle is encountered. A Rapidly-Exploring Random Trees based algorithm then determines a new collision-free path for the robot (by making use of a Neural Network Simulator) which returns the robot to a later point on the original path of the controller. This approach aims to avoid potential SLAM requirements such as inverse kinematics and high-quality sensors. The feasibility and shortcomings of this approach are highlighted by performing experiments on a real robot.

Section 2 of this paper discusses existing literature. The suggested approach is discussed in Sect. 3 and 4. The details surrounding experiments carried out are discussed in Sect. 5. The results of the experiments are given in Sect. 6 and the conclusions drawn are presented in Sect. 7.

2 Related Work

2.1 Background

Robotic controllers differ depending on the robot and can take many different forms. Examples of controllers could be a sequence of motor commands [6], a Neural Network [7] or a series of periodic motor control functions [8]. Open-loop controllers do not provide feedback (like sensor data) from the machine to the controller and rely solely on predetermined inputs. Closed-loop controllers tend to be more complex and make use of feedback to be able to self-correct during execution.

2.2 Rapidly-Exploring Random Trees

A Rapidly-Exploring Random Tree (RRT) is a sampling-based algorithm [9] (and an associated data structure) that has been widely used in motion planning due to its application not being limited to problems with low degrees of freedom [10]. This algorithm was introduced [11] as an efficient data structure and sampling scheme that can quickly search constrained (by obstacles or other dynamic constraints) high dimensional spaces. The base RRT has been shown [10] to come arbitrarily close (converge in probability) to any point in a convex or non-convex space.

The basic algorithm (Algorithm 1) starts by initializing the tree with the root node corresponding to the starting point. A new state in the configuration space (x_{rand}) is then randomly selected and the tree is extended in that direction. This

Algorithm 1. RRT(*destination*)

initializeTree(*root*)
for $k = 1$ to K do
  $x_{rand} \leftarrow$ randomState()
  $x_{near} \leftarrow$ nearestNeighbor(x_{rand})
  if notInTree($x, x_{near}, x_{new}, u_{new}$)and safe($x_{new}, u_{new}$) then
    addToTree(x_{new}, u_{new})
    if distance($x_{new}, destination$) $< D$ then
      return x_{new}
    end if
  end if
end for

---

extension is accomplished by searching the tree to find the node that is "closest" (x_{near}) to the new randomly selected point. A new node (x_{new}) is then created that is a fixed distance (from x_{near}) in the direction of the randomly selected node (x_{rand}). This newly created node is then added to the tree by connecting it to x_{near} through the use of a newly created edge. The process of selecting a random new state and expanding the tree in that direction is repeated K times. For the purpose of single-query motion planning (i.e. a single starting and goal state), the algorithm can be terminated preemptively if the newly added node is deemed close enough to the destination (in which case there exists a set of nodes and edges in the tree that correspond to path from the start point to the destination). The algorithm caters for obstacles by only adding new nodes if the path between x_{near} and x_{new} is unobstructed.

2.3 Simultaneous Localization and Mapping

Given that a mobile robot is placed at an unknown location and environment, Simultaneous Localization and Mapping (SLAM) attempts to allow the robot to build a consistent map (in an incremental manner) of the environment while simultaneously determining its location within the created map. In SLAM both the path of the robot as well as the location of all landmarks are estimated without having any prior knowledge of where they are [12].

The two main components in a SLAM algorithm are the motion model (which describes the effect of the input/command on the robot's state) and the observation model (which describes the effect of the observation on the mapped environment). Physics/Odometry based models are generally used to localize motion, whereas the maps are generally created in a topological or grid format. SLAM algorithms typically make use of statistical techniques to find the most likely state and map of the environment given the observations and commands executed by the robot [13].

2.4   Simulator Neural Networks

Real world evaluation and training of robotic controllers can often be a long and tedious process with mechanical and energy considerations (such as damage to the robot). Simulators can be used to shorten the process, but have their own shortcomings stemming from inaccuracies of the simulation leading to controllers trained in simulation not performing as expected (referred to as the reality gap). Furthermore, creating sufficiently accurate physics-based simulators can be a complex and lengthy task that requires extensive knowledge of the robot's dynamics.

Research [7,14,15] has been conducted to address the complex task of creating simulators, used for the training of evolutionary robotics (ER) controllers, with sufficient accuracy to lessen the gap between the simulated and real environment. Simulators that make use of Artificial Neural Networks (ANNs) instead of mathematical models have been proven [15] to be suitable alternatives. ANNs are used to predict specific aspects of the robot's behavior in reality. Random commands are performed on the robot and measured state changes are used to train the neural networks. After successful training, the ANN can act as a Simulator Neural Network (SNN) which maps robot commands to resulting robot movements. These models can then be used to interpolate outputs for different input data. The promising ability of these NNs to generalize and be tolerant to noise has also been investigated [14]. The use of simple architectures for these SNNs allow for real-time calculation of results.

3   Neuro-Simulation Assisted Control Intervention

This paper suggests an approach, called Neuro-Simulation Assisted Control Intervention (NSACI), which is aimed at temporarily assuming robot control when unexpected obstacles occur on the navigational path of an existing open-loop controller. NSACI employs facets of SLAM, but does not require high quality sensors, odometry or tracking-based localization, or the inverse kinematics of the robot. The benefit of NSACI is that a simple open-loop base controller can easily be hand crafted or created using techniques like evolutionary robotics (ER) or reinforcement learning to make a robot traverse an environment, while the complexities of unexpected obstacles are handled by closed-loop NSACI during robot execution.

NSACI assumes control from the base controller when an obstacle is detected using distance sensors. An adaptation of the RRT algorithm is then used to plot a temporary path around the obstacle towards a safe (i.e. not blocked by an obstacle) goal state of the base controller. This is achieved by generating an approximation map of the environment in an incremental manner. If, at any stage, the generated temporary path is found to have an unsafe movement (i.e. the potential for collision), then a new temporary path (based on the updated map) is generated. Once the robot arrives at a state close to its original simulated path, its orientation is adjusted (by rotating the robot in place) so that control can be relinquished to the base controller and movement can continue along the original path.

A novel aspect of NSACI is that it makes use of a SNN to determine goal states, validate branches of the RRT (refer to Sect. 4) and to generate an approximation of a map of the environment in an incremental manner. SNNs have previously only been used in ER for controller evolution, so NSACI demonstrates a new use of SNNs during the actual execution and control phase of the robotics process. The light-weight nature of the SNN and adapted RRT (described in Sect. 4), means that NSACI is computationally inexpensive and not memory intensive. NSACI can therefore be executed on low cost on-board robot processors.

4   Adaptations to RRT

Normal RRT's are expanded by randomizing states in the configuration space and then expanding the nearest node in the tree in the direction of the sampled state (if possible). This approach requires parsing the tree to find the nearest node for each extension, which could prove difficult when dealing with robots that cannot easily be moved in any direction. It would also require finding the command that can perform the extension (i.e. the command u_{new} that can move the robot from x_{near} to x_{new} in Algorithm 1). Finding this command requires calculation of the inverse kinematics of the robot.

Algorithm 2. AdaptedRRT(destination)

---

  initializeTree($root$)
  for $k = 1$ to K **do**
    x_{near} ←selectFromTree($tree$)
    for $j = 1$ to J **do**
      u_{new} ← randomCommand()
      x_{new} ← SNN.getState(x_{near}, u_{new})
      if notInTree($x_{near}, x_{new}, u_{new}$) **and** safe($x_{new}, u_{new}$) **then**
        addToTree(x_{new}, u_{new})
        if distance($x_{new}, destination$)$< D$ **then**
          return x_{new}
        end if
      end if
    end for
  end for
  return $null$

As illustrated in the pseudo code given in Algorithm 2, the proposed adaptation is to first select the state and then randomize commands from the chosen state to expand the tree. The SNN is used to map the randomized commands to state configurations, which are added to the tree with the edges connecting the nodes being the randomized commands. The commands used to move from one state to another are therefore guaranteed to be possible and do not have to be calculated using inverse kinematics.

5   Methodology

5.1   Experimental Setup

Experiments were carried out on a Khepera III robot [16]. The robot has two wheels and is differentially steered by sending commands via a serial Bluetooth connection. It is controlled by sending the robot pairs of left and right wheel velocities at different points in time. Around the base of the robot, there are 9 infrared proximity sensors that can be used for the detection of nearby obstacles. The readings for these sensors are obtainable from the robot and are updated sequentially every 33 ms. The readings are sensitive to ambient light and very noisy, with sequences of readings differing for the same environment and robot configuration during multiple executions.

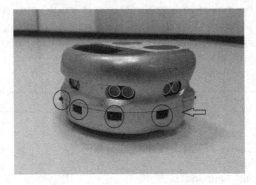

Fig. 1. The Khepera III robot used for the experiment. Four of the infrared sensors can be seen around the base.

The testing area is a flat 270 × 180 cm slip-resistant board. Mounted on the ceiling above the testing area is a camera that can be used (in conjunction with colored tracking markers on the robot) to track and estimate the location (x and y coordinates) and orientation (θ) of the robot on the testing area. This tracker was used to ensure relatively similar (subject to tracking error) starting positions and orientations of the robot during experimentation. No tracking data was ever communicated to the robot or used for any processing purposes during experimentation. Obstacles were simulated using cylinders ($\approx$6 cm diameter) that were covered with reflective tape. Experiments featured up to 7 obstacles and the exact configurations that were tested are described in the corresponding experiment.

Open-loop controllers were generated which contained a sequence of commands to be executed to move the robot from start to destination. All controller commands were executed for 400 ms. This timing was subject to variable latency when communicating new commands to the robot via the serial connection.

5.2   Implementation Details

Command Processing. Command processing was done in real-time and was initialized with the list of base commands (parsed from the open-loop controller). This list corresponded to all commands needed to move the robot from the starting point to the original destination. The SNN used this list to generate an estimation of the original path that would be followed if no obstacles had been present. This list was then used in conjunction with a second list of commands (initially empty) which was used to store any RRT-generated paths (used for obstacle avoidance). Commands were processed sequentially with the secondary list of commands being given priority (i.e. processed first if there were any). Processed commands were removed from the appropriate list (base or secondary) and the robot's destination after executing the command was estimated using the SNN. Each command was processed in one of two ways:

- If the movement generated by this command was deemed collision-free, then the command was communicated to the robot for execution. After 350 ms, the sensor readings were requested from the robot and the map updated.
- If the movement generated by the command was unsafe, the robot was stopped (sent a (0;0) wheel velocity command). The next safe state in the simulated original path was then determined. A RRT was built from the stopped position of the robot to the next safe state. The secondary list was then assigned the commands corresponding to the calculated path. The list of base commands was shortened to exclude unsafe commands.

The sequential processing of these commands was performed until all safe base controller commands were processed.

Simulator Neural Network. The motion simulator (developed by [15]) consisted of three ANNs responsible for simulating the robot's change in x position (Δx), y position (Δy) and angle ($\Delta \theta$) respectively. This configuration was found to produce more accurate results than a single NN. All three ANNs had the following 5 inputs: the previous left wheel velocity, the previous right wheel velocity, the current left wheel velocity, the current right wheel velocity and the time that the current command would be executed for.

RRT. When a node was selected to be processed, 50 commands were randomized and the corresponding states were predicted using the SNN. The collision-free candidates were then evaluated and 5 of the sampled velocities were added to the tree as children of the current node (based on their heuristic value).

Branches that were too long (*length* > *L*) were removed from the solution. If a tree node was generated that was suitably close to the next safe state (within 1 cm), then the node was returned and the list of commands retrieved. A single command to adjust the angle (by rotating the robot in place) was calculated and appended to the end of the list. A piece-wise heuristic was chosen to evaluate nodes for selection. Initially, commands that moved the robot towards the goal state were more favorable (i.e. the Euclidean distance was used). At a later stage, the robot's orientation was also taken into account with commands that resulted in the robot moving towards and facing the goal state after execution being more favourable.

Due to there being 1 225 000 000 possible commands that could be sent to the robot ($-17500 \leq v_{left}, v_{right} \leq 17500$ where $v_{left}, v_{right} \in Z$), some restrictions were imposed on the sampling strategy. Wheel velocities were limited to positive values and only a single wheel velocity was randomized (following a uniform distribution). The other wheel velocity was then set to $17500 - v$ (where v was the sampled value). Due to very small integer differences in sampled velocities producing negligible differences, a step size of 100 was introduced meaning that there was a total of 176 ([0,175]) different velocities that could be sampled. The heuristic described previously was used to evaluate each sampled velocity, with the 3 best (heuristic-wise) candidates being added to the tree along with a middle of the pack candidate and the worst candidate.

Control commands (turning 90° to the left or right, turning around and reversing) were added to the root of the tree to allow the robot to orientate itself correctly initially, if necessary.

Mapping Method. A 2-D array matching the dimensions of the testing surface (270 × 180) was used as an occupancy grid. This meant that each 1 cm × 1 cm square had a cell in the grid with a value between 0 and 1, which was indicative of the collision chance. All cells were initialized with a value of 0.5. The robot's form was simplified to a circle with a 7 cm radius. Testing for potential collisions would therefore be done by calculating whether any cells within a 7 cm radius of the x and y coordinates have high values (≥ 0.51).

The 9 sensors were assumed to have a visibility angle of 40° and a render distance of 12 cm. All sensors were assumed to be on the circumference of the 7 cm radius circle representing the robot. When a reading was received (a value between 0 and 4000), the value was fit to a distance bucket k (an integer value between 1 and 12). Cells ($c_{i,j}$) within the sensor's visibility were updated as follows:

$$c_{i,j} = \begin{cases} 0.2 & d_{i,j} < k \\ \frac{100 - d_{i,j}}{100} & \text{otherwise} \end{cases}$$

where $d_{i,j}$ is the distance between the sensor and the cell $c_{i,j}$. A cell value was the average of all observations relating to that cell. Cells that the robot moved through during execution were assumed to be empty and got assigned a fixed value of 0.

5.3   Analysis

Experiments were performed on two different open-loop controllers. The first controller (controller A) moved the robot in a straight line (corresponding to 55 commands where the robot had identical wheel velocities). The second controller (controller B) moved the robot in a curved path around the testing area and back to a position close to the starting point (140 commands). The path of the robot was recorded when these controllers were executed without any obstacles being present. The resultant path followed by the robot using these controllers are given in Fig. 2.

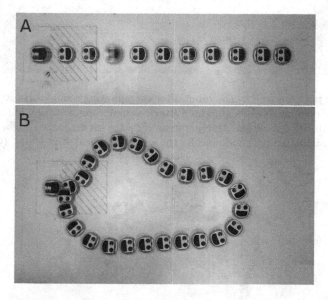

Fig. 2. Composite images of the paths followed by the robot using the base controllers in the absence of obstacles.

The viability of the solution was tested by incrementally placing obstacles in the original path of the robot and rerunning the proposed solution (starting from the same position). A maximum of 7 obstacles were placed on the experimental surface. The final destination of the robot (once all the commands were executed) was observed and compared to the original destination. Results reported are the first execution of the approach for a specific obstacle configuration.

6   Results

6.1   Experiment 1

This preliminary experiment was used to test whether Neuro-Simulated Assisted Control Intervention could allow the robot to safely navigate around a single

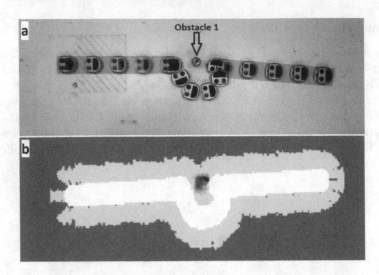

Fig. 3. a. The path followed by the robot after encountering a single obstacle. Executed base controller commands are highlighted. **b.** Heat map representation of the map built by the robot during execution. Darker areas indicate an estimated higher chance of collision. The simulated path followed by the robot is indicated in white. (Color figure online)

Fig. 4. Visualization of the navigational path (estimated using RRT and SNN) generated for the avoidance of the detected obstacle. A path was built based on the current map (at that point in time). Unexplored areas (i.e. no sensor updates to specific cells) are indicated with white. Darker shading is used to visualize higher grid values. (Color figure online)

obstacle directly in the path of the base controller. The straight line path followed by the robot in the absence of any obstacles is illustrated in Fig. 2 (labeled A). The path followed by the robot in the presence of the single obstacle is illustrated in Fig. 3a. As seen in Fig. 3a, the robot avoided the single obstacle and navigated to a position suitably close to a later state in the path. Some overcompensation with realignment was present, however, with the robot's adjustment angle being overestimated (by approximately 5°) resulting in the robot's turn being too severe (in the real world) and the robot diverging from the correct (straight line) path. This overcompensation can be attributed to the simulated path of the solution (around the obstacle) needing a larger angle correction than actually necessary as well as inaccuracies in the turning command sent to adjust the angle. This ultimately resulted in the robot finishing a distance of 9.43 cm away from the original destination for the single obstacle case.

The heat map representation of the map built is illustrated in Fig. 3b. By comparing the mapped path (before and after the obstacle avoidance) with the real path in Fig. 3a, it can be seen that the angular drift is only present in the real world and not in the simulated path. All RRT sampled commands (both safe and unsafe) at the point of collision detection are illustrated in Fig. 4. These commands were overlaid onto the map (that was built at that point in time). By observing the branch density close to the starting point, it can be seen that multiple different paths are generated initially that could not be branched any further due to the mapped obstacle. Upon finally generating a path that could orientate the robot to move around the obstacle, there were minimal unnecessary pathways that were explored.

6.2   Experiment 2

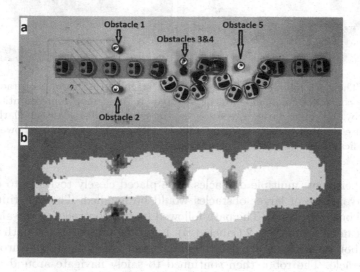

Fig. 5. a. The path followed by the robot after encountering various obstacles. Executed base controller commands are highlighted. **b.** Heat map representation of the map built by the robot during execution for the multiple obstacle case. Darker areas indicate an estimated higher chance of collision. The simulated path followed by the robot is indicated in white. (Color figure online)

The sensitivity of the implemented approach was tested on the straight line controller (original path illustrated in Fig. 2) by monitoring whether the robot could safely move between obstacles without falsely detecting collisions. The path followed in the presence of the placed obstacles is illustrated in Fig. 5a. The robot not only avoided all obstacles, but also preserved as much of the original path as possible by safely navigating between the sets of obstacles placed in its path. The altered path is very similar (when possible) to the actual path. The only inaccuracy seems to be the simulator's estimation of the length of the path, resulting in the robot moving further than the original destination by approximately 15 cm. The heat map representation of the map built for this environment is illustrated in Fig. 5b. The inaccuracies of the sensors can be seen by comparing the size of map representations of the obstacles (darker shaded regions) with the actual obstacles in Fig. 5a. Mapped obstacles are substantially larger than the actual obstacles.

6.3   Experiment 3

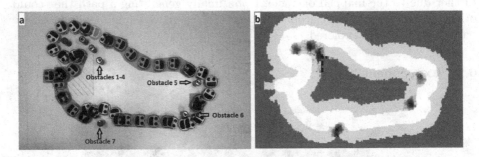

Fig. 6. a. The path followed by the robot after encountering various obstacles. Executed base controller commands are highlighted. **b.** Heat map representation of the map built by the robot during execution for the multiple obstacle case. Darker areas indicate an estimated higher chance of collision. The simulated path followed by the robot is indicated in white. (Color figure online)

In this experiment, multiple obstacles were placed closely together to evaluate how the avoidance of larger obstacles would be handled. The experiment was performed on controller B. The path followed by this controller in the absence of obstacles can be seen in Fig. 2 (labeled B). Figure 6a illustrates the path followed by the robot during this experiment. The robot safely navigated around the larger obstacle. The robot then continued to safely navigate around all other obstacles and finished within 10 cm of the original destination. By comparing the positions of the obstacles in Fig. 6a with the map generated (Fig. 6b), it can be seen that the mapped layout of these obstacles is very similar to the actual layout.

It should be noted that more often than not, multiple paths are generated at different points while moving around the same obstacle(s) (as seen in Fig. 7 and 8). This is due to the robot exploring new areas not yet covered by short range sensor data and refining the map. By comparing the maps in Fig. 7 and 8,

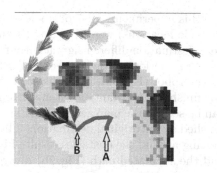

Fig. 7. Visualization of the navigational path (estimated using RRT and SNN) generated for the avoidance of the detected obstacles. Point A indicates where the original collision detection took place.

Fig. 8. The path generated shortly after Fig. 7 when it was determined that the previously generated path was unsafe as well. Point B indicates the position where it was detected that the temporary path generated previously (Fig. 7) was unsafe.

it can be seen that the left obstacle was not yet sensed, resulting in a path being generated that navigated the robot towards the obstacle. Upon reaching a point close to the aforementioned obstacle, the map was updated and an impending collision was detected. This resulted in a new path being generated which successfully avoided the first set of obstacles and navigated the robot to a later point in its base command list. The segment connecting point A and B in Fig. 8 is used to illustrate the path followed by the robot to move from point A to point B (i.e. the segment of the first generated path that was executed on the robot).

6.4 Experiment 4

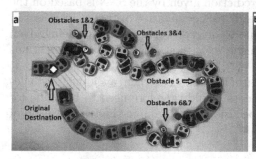

Fig. 9. a. The path followed by the robot after encountering multiple obstacles. Executed base controller commands are highlighted. b. Heat map representation of the map built by the robot during execution for the multiple obstacle case.

For this experiment, all 7 obstacles were used and different configurations (i.e. obstacle locations) were tested until an inadequate result was found (where the final destination differed significantly from the original destination). This experiment was performed on base controller B (Fig. 2). By looking at the path followed by the robot (Fig. 9a), it can be seen that the robot safely avoided all obstacles, but finished a substantial distance from the base controller. A closed loop (path) can be seen in the map generated (Fig. 9b). According to the simulator, the robot finished at the original destination. The accumulation of localization errors when moving around the obstacles resulted in incorrect angle adjustments being made and the simulated path (Fig. 9b) diverging from the actual path.

7 Conclusions

Through the use of Neuro-Simulation Assisted Control Intervention, the two existing controllers used for experimentation could not only safely avoid unexpected obstacles, but also determine adequate paths around these obstacles. This allowed for these controllers to be applied to multiple different environment configurations and still safely navigate a similar path. Successful navigation was achieved even when several obstacles were placed on the path, which required multiple interventions using NSACI. This showed that control could successfully be switched from the base controller to NSACI and back more than once. The results were achieved in the absence of positional tracking, perfect sensors and inverse kinematics. Through the use of a simple Neural Network architecture, state estimations and safe path calculations were computationally inexpensive and done in real-time.

The implemented approach appears to always find a safe path around obstacles, but not necessarily the best/shortest path. The main threat to the effectiveness of the approach is angular drift where the SNN's predicted orientation ($\hat{\theta}$) differs significantly from the actual orientation (θ). This inaccuracy leads to incorrect angle adjustments being made after successfully moving around obstacles. Seeing as the future state prediction given by the SNN is based on the current state as well, this inaccuracy leads to a cumulative drift that increases in size as more commands get parsed. Due to no real-world state data being given to the robot at any point in time during execution, the necessary corrections can't be made.

Data association issues are a cause for concern when avoiding obstacles while navigating long paths. Adjustments would therefore need to be made for longer/more complex paths (such as occasionally obtaining the true location of the robot).

References

1. Elbanhawi, M., Simic, M.: Sampling-based robot motion planning: a review. IEEE Access **2**, 56–77 (2014)

2. Bayazit, O., Song, G., Amato, N.: Enhancing randomized motion planners: exploring with haptic hints. In: Proceedings 2000 ICRA. Millennium Conference. IEEE International Conference on Robotics and Automation. Symposia Proceedings (Cat. No. 00CH37065), vol. 1, pp. 529–536 (2000)
3. Chang, H., Li, T.Y.: Assembly maintainability study with motion planning. In: Proceedings of 1995 IEEE International Conference on Robotics and Automation, vol. 1, pp. 1012–1019 (1995)
4. Chen, Y., Huang, S., Fitch, R.: Active slam for mobile robots with area coverage and obstacle avoidance. IEEE/ASME Trans. Mech. **25**(3), 1182–1192 (2020)
5. Dinh, B.H., Dunnigan, M.W., Reay, D.S.: A practical approach for position control of a robotic manipulator using a radial basis function network and a simple vision system. WSEAS Trans. Syst. Ctrl. **3**(4), 289–298 (2008)
6. Woodford, G.W., Pretorius, C.J., du Plessis, M.C.: Concurrent controller and simulator neural network development for a differentially-steered robot in evolutionary robotics. Robot. Auton. Syst. **76**(C), 80–92 (2016)
7. Pretorius, C.J., du Plessis, M.C., Cilliers, C.B.: A neural network-based kinematic and light-perception simulator for simple robotic evolution. In: IEEE Congress on Evolutionary Computation, pp. 1–8 (2010)
8. Cully, A., Clune, J., Tarapore, D., Mouret, J.B.: Robots that can adapt like animals. Nature **521**(7553), 503–507 (2015)
9. Rodriguez, Tang, X., Lien, J.M., Amato, N.: An obstacle-based rapidly-exploring random tree. In: Proceedings 2006 IEEE International Conference on Robotics and Automation. ICRA 2006, pp. 895–900 (2006)
10. LaValle, S., Kuffner, J.: Rapidly-exploring random trees: progress and prospects. In: Proceedings of International Workshop on Algorithmic Foundations of Robotics (WAFR) (2000)
11. LaValle, S.: Rapidly-exploring random trees : a new tool for path planning. Technical Report (1998)
12. Durrant-Whyte, H., Bailey, T.: Simultaneous localization and mapping: part I. IEEE Rob. Autom. Mag. **13**(2), 99–110 (2006)
13. Taheri, H., Xia, Z.: SLAM; definition and evolution. Eng. Appl. Artif. Intell. **97**, 104032 (2021)
14. Woodford, G.W., Plessis, M.C.D., Pretorius, C.J.: Evolving snake robot controllers using artificial neural networks as an alternative to a physics-based simulator. In: 2015 IEEE Symposium Series on Computational Intelligence, pp. 267–274 (2015)
15. Pretorius, C.J., du Plessis, M.C., Gonsalves, J.W.: A comparison of neural networks and physics models as motion simulators for simple robotic evolution. In: 2014 IEEE Congress on Evolutionary Computation (CEC), pp. 2793–2800 (2014)
16. K Team Khepera III. https://www.k-team.com/mobile-robotics-products/old-products/khepera-iii. Accessed 05 Apr 2021

Low Rank Matrix Approximation
for Imputing Missing Categorical Data

Joseph Muthui Wacira[1,2], Dinna Ranirina[1,3(✉)], and Bubacarr Bah[1,3] (iD)

[1] African Institute for Mathematical Sciences (AIMS), Cape Town, South Africa
{joemuthui,dinna,bubacarr}@aims.ac.za
[2] Department of Mathematics and Applied Mathematics,
University of Western Cape, Bellville, South Africa
[3] Department of Mathematical Sciences, Stellenbosch University,
Stellenbosch, South Africa

Abstract. The use of matrix completion to recover low-rank matrices with missing entries has been widely studied. This has many applications especially in recommendation systems. However, these studies have mainly focused on numerical data, and less has been done towards the completion of a matrix with categorical data.

In this work, we apply a special matrix completion algorithm that works for more general categorical data, and can be applied to a higher number of categories than two. The algorithm is a low-rank matrix completion algorithm (LRMC) based on the minimization of the nuclear norm and uses multiple linear transformations to impute missing categorical entries. This LRMC algorithm is compared with the state-of-the-art iterative imputer and k-nearest neighbors (KNN) algorithms, which serve as benchmarks. Simulations on real datasets show that the LRMC algorithm performs better when the matrix is low-rank; otherwise, their performances are similar.

Keywords: Matrix completion · Categorical data · Low-rank matrix · KNN · Iterative-Imputer · Nuclear norm · Recommender system

1 Introduction

The science of learning the information behind some given data has been the target of many researchers over the past decades in many different research areas including Mathematics, Statistics and Machine Learning (ML). It is common knowledge in ML that the performance of an ML model depends a lot on the quality of the data used to build the model. One key factor affecting the quality of the data is missing or corrupted entries and many methods/techniques have been developed over the years to replace these missing or corrupted entries [1–3]. Besides the desire to fill in missing entries as a pre-processing step to perform other ML tasks like regression or classification, there are many other applications of filling in missing entries of a dataset. Most popular among these applications is recommendation systems and a good example is the Netflix problem [4,5].

© Springer Nature Switzerland AG 2022
E. Jembere et al. (Eds.): SACAIR 2021, CCIS 1551, pp. 242–256, 2022.
https://doi.org/10.1007/978-3-030-95070-5_16

In practice for computational purposes, data is in the form of a matrix and filling the missing entries is a matrix completion problem. The matrix completion problem has been approached in various ways and one highly studied approach has been the low-rank matrix approximation [5–7]. However, much focus has been devoted to matrices with missing numeric and real value entries, even if the entries take only finite discrete values (solutions are usually round-off to the nearest integer in this case). Many interesting applications (recommendation systems, biostatistics, predictive medicine, or any data-driven study) deal with missing categorical values. Essentially, imputing missing entries of a one-hot encoding of categorical data is 1-bit matrix completion [8]. The theory of 1-bit matrix is well established but to the best of our knowledge no significant practical use and comparison of this method to popular ML imputation approaches has been done. Moreover, in a situation where the categorical matrix being completed is not low rank, approaches like matrix completion with multiple linear transformations (MCMT) could be used to exploit low-rankness in the submatrices to fill in the missing entries [9]. This approach of combining 1-bit matrix completion and MCMT has not been used before.

Related Works. Various methods have been suggested to impute missing data. In statistics for instance, there are many well-established imputation algorithms implemented in the R data science ecosystem like *Amelia, mi, mice,* and *miss-Forest,* see [10] for the *R MICE* package and references therein for the others. Similarly in ML and two popularly used algorithms especially in scikit-learn [11] are the Iterative-Imputer and the k-nearest neighbor imputer (henceforth referred to as the KNN-Imputer), perhaps popularized by [12]. The underlying principle in many of the above-mentioned algorithms is some form of averaging. Unfortunately, although the calculations are usually quick, the algorithms can be affected by outliers and become unstable. Hence the motivation behind the choice of methods based on matrix completion which is based on the concept of having a set of much less numerous vector bases generating all the observations. In other words, the large data matrix is assumed to be low rank.

The solution of the matrix completion problem through low rank matrix approximation has also been well studied. Theoretical limits and guarantees are established [6, 13, 14]. Optimization algorithms with optimal convergence rates and guarantees have been proposed [7, 16–18]. These results were generally derived with real-value missing data in mind. It is fair to say also that methods based on matrix completion have been developed, such as 1-bit matrix completion transforming the categorical data matrix into incomplete binary matrices with only two categories (0 for missing values and 1 or −1 otherwise) [8,19]. Other techniques have also been developed for much faster convergence and efficient recovery, such as the MCMT algorithm which instead uses the low rank of the sub-matrices, which is beneficial when the entire matrix is not low rank [9].

Contributions. The contributions of this work can be summarized as follows. Firstly, the proposition of a low rank matrix approximation algorithm for imputing missing values of categorical data, when the categories are one-hot encoded, leading to the LRMC-Imputer. In addition, we propose using MCMT for the case where the matrix is not low-rank, leading to the MCMT-Imputer. For an efficient application of the approach, we further propose a fast optimization algorithm to solve the resulting minimization problem and a special pre-processing step, which involves computational strategies that induce low-rankness in the data matrix. Finally, we demonstrate the superior performance of our proposed low-rank matrix approximation based algorithm (LRMC-Imputer and MCMT-Imputer) to selected state-of-the-art imputers: KNN-Imputer and Iterative-Imputer [12].

Organization of Paper. The rest of the paper is organized as follows. Section 2 introduces the concept of matrix completion and computational strategies that improve the performance of the low rank matrix completion methods. In Sect. 3 a brief description of the optimization algorithm is given. In Sect. 4, simulations are presented where the proposed algorithm is compared with two well known algorithms in ML (Iterative-Imputer and KNN-Imputer). Finally, Sect. 5 summarizes the results and discusses the limitations of this approach as well as the possible extensions.

2   Matrix Completion

In this section, we briefly outline what is low-rank matrix completion and also introduce the low-rank matrix completion with multiple linear transformations method. We conclude the section with a description of a very helpful pre-processing step to our approach.

2.1   Low-Rank Matrix Completion

The rank of a matrix, say $\mathbf{A}$, is defined as the dimension of the vector space generated by its columns. This corresponds to the maximal number of linearly independent columns of $\mathbf{A}$. Low-rank matrix completion (LRMC) is a matrix completion technique that is based on the assumption that most matrices are of low rank and hence few columns explain the entire matrix. For example, in the movie rating matrix from the famous Netflix problem [4]. The user rating is dependent on a few factors about the movie, which might include the director, genre, and/or the release year of the movie. This implies that the matrix to be recovered is approximately low rank.

LRMC exploits the low rank properties to complete or predict the missing values of a matrix, say $\mathbf{X} \in \mathbb{R}^{m \times n}$ which is a partial observation of a matrix $\mathbf{M} \in \mathbb{R}^{m \times n}$. In order to recover matrix $\mathbf{M}$ from matrix $\mathbf{X}$, we solve a constrained rank minimization problem as follows

$$\min_{\mathbf{X}} \quad \text{rank}(\mathbf{X}), \qquad \text{subject to} \quad x_{ij} = m_{ij}, \ (i,j) \in \Omega, \tag{1}$$

where Ω is the set of indices for the observed (non-missing) entries. Problem 1 can be redefined by employing the sampling operator $\mathcal{P}_\Omega$, which for a matrix $\mathbf{X}$ is

$$\mathcal{P}_\Omega(\mathbf{X}) = \begin{cases} x_{ij}, & \text{if } (i,j) \in \Omega \\ 0, & \text{otherwise.} \end{cases}$$

Therefore, (1) becomes

$$\min_{\mathbf{X}} \ \text{rank}(\mathbf{X}) \quad \text{subject to} \quad \mathcal{P}_\Omega(\mathbf{X}) = \mathcal{P}_\Omega(\mathbf{M}). \tag{2}$$

The rank minimization problem is generally NP-hard and therefore computationally intractable since all algorithms for exactly solving (2) are doubly exponential in dimension $\max(m,n)$ in both theory and practice [7]. This explains why most of the algorithms solve an approximate problem. It has been proven that the tightest convex relaxation of the rank is the nuclear norm $||.||_*$, which is the convex envelope of the rank [5]. The nuclear norm is the sum of all singular values of a matrix, i.e.

$$||\mathbf{X}||_* = \text{tr}(\mathbf{X}^T\mathbf{X}) = \sum_{i=1}^{\min(m,n)} \sigma_i(\mathbf{X}) = ||\sigma(\mathbf{X})||_1, \tag{3}$$

where σ is a vector of singular values, σ_i, $i = 1, 2, \ldots, \min(m,n)$. The rank minimization (2) is typically solved via its convex surrogate [7].

$$\min_{\mathbf{X}} \ ||\mathbf{X}||_* \quad \text{subject to} \quad \mathcal{P}_\Omega(\mathbf{X}) = \mathcal{P}_\Omega(\mathbf{M}). \tag{4}$$

Details about conditions for optimal recovery of the true matrix like *coherence* and *sparsity of observed entries* are skipped, the interested reader is referred to [6,13,14] and references therein. Similarly, for efficient algorithms (except for the singular-value thresholding algorithm to be discussed in the next section) with optimal convergence rates and guarantees, the interested reader is referred to [7,16–18] and references therein.

2.2 Matrix Completion Under Multiple Linear Transformation

In this section we present an LRMC algorithm that we will apply to recover the categorical data matrix. Many algorithms discussed in the previous section rely heavily on the low-rank nature of the matrix to be recovered as a whole. This assumption often does not hold, especially in cases where the matrix has discrete values (as is the case with the categorical data matrix). It is for this reason, [9] presents an efficient problem reformulation dubbed Matrix Completion under Multiple linear Transformation (MCMT). It utilizes the low-rankness of sub-matrices instead of the entire matrix. This approach favors our problem of categorical data matrix completion as many real-world categorical data matrices are full rank.

The MCMT approach proposes that a matrix can be broken down into K submatrices, which are presumed to be approximately low-rank. This approach redefines the nuclear norm of a matrix as a sum of K nuclear norms of submatrices; and therefore instead of minimizing the nuclear norm, we minimize the sum of K nuclear norms, i.e.

$$\min_{\mathbf{X} \in \mathbb{R}^{m_1 \times m_2}} \sum_{i \in [K]} ||\beta_i(\mathbf{X})||_* \quad \text{subject to} \quad \mathcal{P}_\Omega(\mathbf{X}) = \mathcal{P}_\Omega(\mathbf{M}), \quad (5)$$

where $[K]$ is a set of submatrices, $m_1 \times m_2$ is the dimension of these submatrices and β_i is a linear transformation.

Multiple analyses and formulations of the linear transformation have been well studied in [9]. An unconstrained reformulation of (5) is given by

$$\min_{\mathbf{X} \in \mathbb{R}^{m_1 \times m_2}} \frac{1}{2} ||\mathcal{P}_\Omega(\mathbf{X}) - \mathcal{P}_\Omega(\mathbf{M})||_F^2 + \lambda \sum_{i \in [K]} ||\beta_i(\mathbf{X})||_*, \quad (6)$$

where $|| \cdot ||_F$ is the Frobenious norm and λ is a regularization parameter, see [9].

2.3 Creating Low-Rankness in Categorical Data Matrices

One of the key ingredients for the success of our method is a computational strategy, which is a pre-processing step that creates low-rank categorical data matrices. The strategy has two components: (i) shuffling data points and (ii) reshaping the resulting categorical data matrix from the one-hot encoding. For instance, in the univariate case a dataset of d categories and N samples, we have a $d \times N$ data matrix after the one-hot encoding. For computational purposes we convert the zeros in the one-hot encoding to -1, which means columns corresponding to observed data will have $d-1$ values of -1 and 1 entry of 1. Columns corresponding to missing data are represented by d zeros.

We observe that this $d \times N$ matrix is full-rank and in addition having many columns with all zeros makes accurate recovery impossible. Therefore, we propose reshaping the matrix to an $m \times n$ matrix for $m > d$ with the expectation that the resulting matrix will be low-rank, i.e. with a rank $r < m$ (note that we can have $r \geq d$). How to optimally do the reshaping of the matrix is not clear and different reshaping will result into different ranks. However, what is most important is getting a low-rank matrix, the approach works as long as the matrix is low-rank. Intuitively, shuffling the data based on the user's knowledge of the data can increase the chances of forming a low-rank matrix and avoiding columns with all zeros. Hence with this strategy we create low-rank matrices on which we can apply LRMC. If this fails work, MCMT could still work on the submatrices. Therefore, the reshaping from $d \times N$ to $m \times n$ even if it does not result into a low-rank matrices, will be helpful for performance of MCMT and avoiding columns of all zeros.

3   Optimization Algorithm

Here we present the efficient optimization algorithm we used to solve both the original LRMC in (4) and MCMT in (6). This is an application of the Fast Iterative-Shrinkage Thresholding Algorithm (FISTA) [15] to the Singular Value Thresholding (SVT) [16] method for solving (4).

3.1   Singular Value Thresholding

Even though the minimization problem (4) can be solved by just minimizing the nuclear norm via convex and semi-definite programming, the process is computationally expensive when matrices become larger. SVT was proposed by [16] to curb this problem.

The main idea of this technique is to add the regularization term into the nuclear norm minimization (4). The general formulation of SVT is

$$\min_{\mathbf{X}} \ \tau||\mathbf{X}||_* + \frac{1}{2}||\mathbf{X}||_{\mathrm{F}}, \qquad \text{subject to} \quad \mathcal{P}_\Omega(\mathbf{X}) = \mathcal{P}_\Omega(\mathbf{M}), \qquad (7)$$

where $\tau \geq 0$ is the regularization parameter. This approach is considered as a proximal objective of nuclear norm minimization. The parameter τ acts as a trade-off between the nuclear norm and the Frobenious norm. As τ becomes larger, (7) is dominated by the nuclear norm.

Problem 7 can be solved by solving its Lagrangian. Posing Problem 7 as a Lagrangian has the advantage that the SVT can be extended to other problems which involve nuclear norm minimization with constraints. Now let us define

$$f_\tau(\mathbf{X}) := \tau||\mathbf{X}||_* + \frac{1}{2}||\mathbf{X}||_{\mathrm{F}},$$

and let $\mathbf{Y}$ be the dual variable, then the Lagrangian is given by

$$\mathcal{L}(\mathbf{X}, \mathbf{Y}) = f_\tau(\mathbf{X}) + \langle \mathbf{Y}, \mathcal{P}_\Omega(\mathbf{M}) - \mathcal{P}_\Omega(\mathbf{X}) \rangle. \qquad (8)$$

By principle of duality in mathematical optimization, we let $\hat{\mathbf{X}}$ and $\hat{\mathbf{Y}}$ be the primal and dual optimal solutions respectively. Then by strong duality, which states that the primal and dual optimal objectives are equal, we have

$$\max_{\mathbf{Y}} \min_{\mathbf{X}} \ \mathcal{L}(\mathbf{X}, \mathbf{Y}) = \mathcal{L}(\hat{\mathbf{X}}, \hat{\mathbf{Y}}) = \min_{\mathbf{X}} \max_{\mathbf{Y}} \ \mathcal{L}(\mathbf{X}, \mathbf{Y}). \qquad (9)$$

The SVT algorithm finds the solutions, $\hat{\mathbf{X}}$ and $\hat{\mathbf{Y}}$ iteratively by starting with $\mathbf{Y}_0 = \mathbf{0}_{m \times n}$ then updates $\mathbf{X}_k$ and $\mathbf{Y}_k$ such that

$$\mathbf{X}_k = \operatorname*{argmin}_{\mathbf{X}} \mathcal{L}(\mathbf{X}, \mathbf{Y}_{k-1}), \qquad \mathbf{Y}_k = \mathbf{X}_{k-1} + \delta_k \frac{\partial \mathcal{L}(\mathbf{X}_k, \mathbf{Y})}{\partial \mathbf{Y}}, \qquad (10)$$

where δ_k is a positive step-size for all $k \geq 1$.

Recall that $\mathbf{X}_k$ can be expressed as

$$\mathbf{X}_k = \operatorname*{argmin}_{\mathbf{X}} f_\tau(\mathbf{X}) - \langle \mathbf{Y}_{k-1}, P_\Omega(\mathbf{X}) \rangle = \operatorname*{argmin}_{\mathbf{X}} \tau||\mathbf{X}||_* + \frac{1}{2}||\mathbf{X} - \mathbf{Y}_{k-1}||_{\mathrm{F}}^2.$$

It has been shown in [16] that, if $\mathbf{Z}$ is a matrix whose singular value decomposition is given by

$$\mathbf{Z} = \mathbf{U}\Sigma\mathbf{V}^T, \tag{11}$$

and we define $t_+ := \max(t, 0)$ for $t \in \mathbb{R}$, then

$$D_\tau(\mathbf{Z}) = \operatorname*{argmin}_{\mathbf{X}} \tau||\mathbf{X}||_* + \frac{1}{2}||\mathbf{X} - \mathbf{Y}_{k-1}||_F^2, \tag{12}$$

where $D_\tau(\mathbf{Z})$ is a singular value thresholding operator defined as

$$D_\tau(\mathbf{Z}) = \mathbf{U}\mathrm{diag}(\{(\sigma_i(\mathbf{Z}) - \tau)_+\})\mathbf{V}^T. \tag{13}$$

SVT has a computational complexity $\mathcal{O}(rmn)$ where r is the rank of an $m \times n$ matrix and requires $\mathcal{O}\left(\epsilon^{-1/2}\right)$ iterations to obtain a solution with ϵ error [16].

3.2   FISTA for Matrix Completion

FISTA proposed by [15] is an improvement of the Iterative Shrinkage Thresholding Algorithm (ISTA), see Chap. 12 of [20] for a general introduction to these methods. The convergence rate of ISTA is $\mathcal{O}\left(k^{-1}\right)$; while that of FISTA is $\mathcal{O}\left(k^{-2}\right)$, where k is the number of iterations [15, 21]. Therefore, using FISTA for SVT greatly speeds up the computations.

Both FISTA and ISTA solve problems of the form

$$\min \; \{F(x) \equiv f(x) + g(x)\}, \tag{14}$$

and in matrix completion we require to solve the unconstrained problem (6). We therefore set,

$$f(x) = \frac{1}{2}||\mathcal{P}_\Omega(\mathbf{X}) - \mathcal{P}_\Omega(\mathbf{M})||_{\mathrm{F}}^2, \quad \text{and} \quad g(x) = \lambda \sum_i ||\beta_i(\mathbf{X})||_*. \tag{15}$$

It is straight forward to show that these functions satisfy the FISTA conditions, details skipped. There are issues about step-size choices, we took a constant step-size. We thus wrap up this part by summarizing the implementation details and presenting the FISTA matrix completion technique below, used to solve (6).

Algorithm 1: FISTA for Matrix Completion (NN-min)

Result: Y_{k+1}

$\mathbf{Z}_0 = \mathbf{X}_0 = \mathbf{Y}$;

$t_1 = 1$;

for $k \geq 0$ **do**

$\quad [\hat{\mathbf{Z}}_k]_{i,j} = \begin{cases} [\mathbf{Z}_k]_{i,j} & \text{if}(i,j) \in \Omega \\ [0] & \text{if } (i,j) \notin \Omega \end{cases}$ (Put back in known entries);

$\quad \mathbf{X}_{k+1} = \mathbf{SVST}(\hat{\mathbf{Z}}_k, \lambda)$;

$\quad t_{k+1} = \frac{1+\sqrt{1+4t_k^2}}{2}$ ([21]);

$\quad Y_{k+1} = x_k + \frac{t_{k-1}}{t_{k+1}}(x_k - x_{k-1})$ (Momentum) ;

end

The **SVST** step in Algorithm 1 applies the shrinkage operator (13).

4   Numerical Experiments

We perform simulations to compare our proposed LRMC approach for the categorical data matrix with the KNN-Imputer and the Iterative-Imputer. We chose these two imputers to compare due to their popularity as state-of-the-art in the Machine Learning community [11]. We tested the algorithms on two real-world datasets. In addition we wanted to investigate the effect of low-rankness to the three approaches. The datasets we carefully chosen so that reshaping one of the datasets always resulted in full matrices; while reshaping the other yielded low-rank matrices. For the full rank case, we used the hair color dataset, which has four categories i.e. black, blond, brown and red. It contained 800 observations/samples. For the low rank simulations, we used an eye color dataset which has four categories i.e. blue, hazel, brown and green. It also contained 800 observations/samples. Based on the earlier notation, $d = 4$ and $N = 800$ in both datasets. Both datasets can be accessed from [22].

For each of the datasets (hair color and eye color or full rank and low-rank respectively) different levels of observed data are investigated, i.e. 20% to 90% (in intervals of 10) of observed (non-missing) data. At each level of observed (missing) data, ten masks are generated uniformly at random and the missing values are imputed ten times. In the following subsections, we outline the process, the outcomes for each method using the confusion matrices and accuracy plots. The results are presented for when the reshaped matrix is low-rank or full rank.

4.1   KNN-Imputer

The KNN-Imputer adopted from the scikit-learn package [11], applies the k-nearest neighbors' method to complete the missing entries. It applies the Euclidean distance as a metric to impute the missing values. The KNN-Imputer does not allow text data and therefore the need to do one-hot encoding of our data. In addition to the pre-processing step mentioned above, if a complete row was missing, all entries in that row were assigned NaN to differentiate between the zeros in the binary tuple and the zeros in the missing rows. The KNN-Imputer was applied to the preprocessed data for different k values and the best k was chosen based on the percentage accuracy and used in the comparisons below.

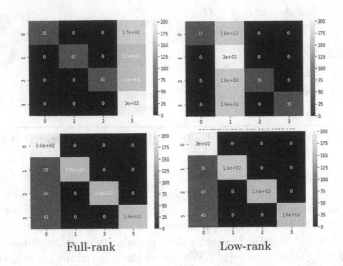

Full-rank   Low-rank

Fig. 1. Confusion matrix indicating the misclassified classes using the KNN-Imputer, where 0, 1, 2, 3 correspond to classes 1, 2, 3, 4 respectively, for full rank and low rank matrices and levels of observed data. *Top row:* 20% and *Bottom row:* 80%.

Figure 1 shows examples of confusion matrices for levels 20% and 80% of observed entries for both low- and full rank matrices. From the two sets of classification matrices, it can be observed that the performance of the KNN-Imputer is independent of the rank of the reshaped matrix. Hence their performance are similar for the same levels of observed data. The plots in Fig. 1 also confirm that with more observed data the KNN-Imputer does perform better.

4.2   Iterative-Imputer

The Iterative-Imputer is also adopted from scikit-learn [11], where each feature is modeled as a function of the other features. It is an approach for imputing missing values by modeling each feature with missing values as a function of other features in a round-robin fashion. We repeated the simulations using the same masks on the preprocessed dataset and chose the best n-neighbors based on accuracy using the most frequent strategy.

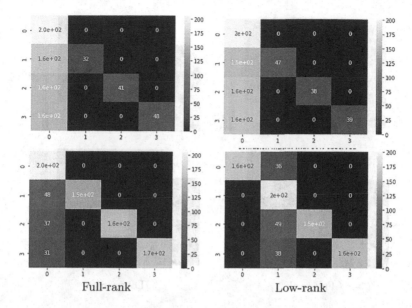

Fig. 2. Confusion matrix indicating the misclassified classes using the Iterative-Imputer, where 0, 1, 2, 3 correspond to classes 1, 2, 3, 4 respectively, for full rank and low-rank matrices and levels of observed data. *Top row:* 20% and *Bottom row:* 80%.

Figure 2 also shows examples of confusion matrices for levels 20% and 80% of observed entries for both low- and full rank matrices. From the two sets of classification matrices, it can be observed that the performance of the Iterative-Imputer, like the KNN-Imputer, is also independent of the rank of the reshaped matrix. Hence their performance is relatively the same for the same levels of observed data. Again the plots in Fig. 2 also confirm that with more observed data the KNN-Imputer does better.

4.3   LRMC-Imputer

The LRMC-Imputer applies the LRMC method to the missing categorical data. The data used in this approach is further preprocessed. Firstly, the one-hot encoded binary matrix for the observed categories is changed to −1 and 1 matrix, where −1 replaces 0. The missing categories are encoded into a vector of zeros. The columns of the 4×800 data matrix are reshuffled and the resulting matrix is reshaped into a matrix with dimensions that make it either approximately low-rank or full rank, but also ensuring that sparsity property is satisfied and that no complete row or column is missing. In particular, the original 4×800 categorical data matrix was reshuffled and reshaped into a matrix of 50×64. We then apply the LRMC algorithm to the data to impute the missing values.

Figure 3 also shows examples of confusion matrices for levels 20% and 80% of observed entries for both low- and full rank matrices. From the two sets of clas-

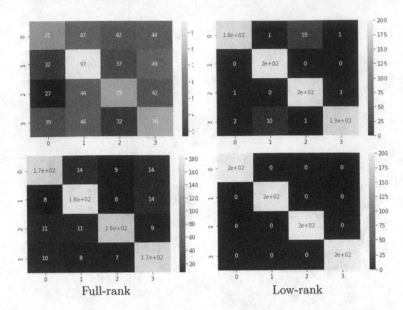

Full-rank   Low-rank

Fig. 3. Confusion matrix indicating the misclassified classes using the LRMC-Imputer, where 0, 1, 2, 3 correspond to classes 1, 2, 3, 4 respectively, for full rank and low rank matrices and levels of observed data. *Top row:* 20% and *Bottom row:* 80%.

sification matrices, it can be observed that the LRMC-Imputer performs better when the matrix is approximately low-rank as compared to an approximately full rank matrix. We have observed that the confusion matrices may have an extra row and column, whose predicted value is zero. In the example plots in Fig. 3 our algorithm recovered the whole matrix albeit some entries wrongly. This why the confusion matrix did not show an extra column and row of zeros. This is caused by the classes that the algorithm was unable to assign a specific class. Unassigned classes are caused by missing a complete column or row. This could be resolved by doing a post-processing step that uses, for instance KNN-Imputer or Iterative-Imputer. However, we kept the results as they are to highlight this issue. Note that even if the unassigned classes are counted as errors (as we do here) the performance of the LRMC-Imputer is at par or better than the KNN-Imputer or the Iterative-Imputer. This is what we do in our accuracy results in the next section.

4.4   Performance Comparisons

Here we perform a comparative analysis of the three methods discussed above and two more imputers, i.e. the MCMT-Imputer, which is the MCMT implementation of the LRMC-Imputer and the Simple-Imputer another popular imputer from scikit-learn [11]. Recall the MCMT-Imputer applies low-rank matrix completion on submatrices of the original matrix. The hope is that if the submatrices are low-rank whilst the original matrix is not, the MCMT-Imputer will

perform better than the LRMC-Imputer. The Simple-Imputer is a less sophisticated imputer than the Iterative-Imputer, see [11].

The accuracy of the methods will be computed using the following formula,

$$\text{accuracy} = \frac{\text{Number of accurate classification}}{\text{Total number of observations}} \times 100\% \ .$$

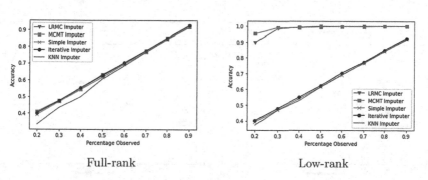

Full-rank   Low-rank

Fig. 4. The plot of accuracy against percentage observed data ranging from 0.2 to 0.9,
for an approximately full rank matrix and approximately low-rank matrix respectively.

Figure 4 shows plots of the accuracies of the five methods for different percentages of observed (missing) entries and for the approximately full rank and
approximately low-rank matrices respectively. The plots are the means over ten
realizations of simulations. In all realizations the optimal settings of the KNN-
Imputer and the Iterative-Imputer were used. In the left plot of Fig. 4 we see
that performance of the matrix completion approaches (LRMC-Imputer and
MCMT-Imputer) are similar to the other imputers, even though the matrix is
not low-rank and our MCMT-Imputer was not recovering low-rank submatrices either. In the right plot of Fig. 4 we observe that the MCMT-Imputer and
LRMC-Imputer perform much better than the others, also LRMC and MCMT
achieve perfect recovery with 50% missing observations for low-rank matrices.

We see similar results to the above, which is based on mean performance,
when we look at the accuracies of the imputer for all the realizations (different
problem instances). In this regard, we also generated the box plots for three of the
approaches, i.e. KNN-Imputer, Iterative-Imputer and LRMC-Imputer as shown
in Fig. 5. The box plots showed that the average accuracies were not affected
by outliers in most cases. All approaches produced few outliers, meaning they
always return solutions very close to the optimal solution possible. The plots
also confirm the remarkable perfect recovery of LRMC-Imputer for ≥50% of the
observed data.

5   Discussion

This work proposed a matrix completion approach for missing categorical data,
where the matrix comes from the one-hot encoding of the categorical data.

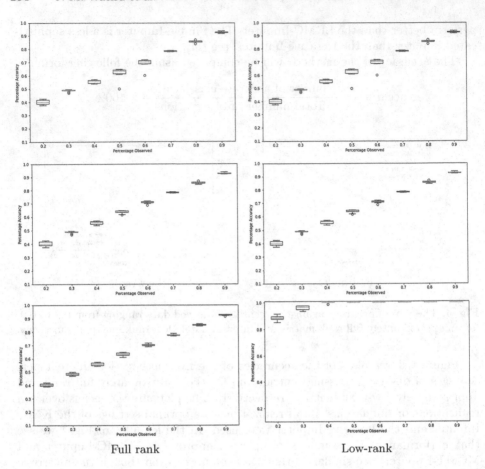

Full rank   Low-rank

Fig. 5. The box plots of accuracy against percentage observed data ranging from 0.2 to 0.9 for different ranks: full rank in first column and low-rank in second column; also for the three of the imputers: *Top row:* KNN-Imputer, *Middle row:* Iterative-imputer and *Bottom row:* LRMC-Imputer.

We use low-rank matrix approximation to perform the matrix completion assuming the data matrix is low-rank. In the case that the matrix is full rank we suggested using an MCMT approach, which performs low-rank matrix completion on the submatrices of the original matrix. In addition, we propose a preprocessing strategy of reshuffling the data and reshaping the matrix to create low-rank matrices. The work also proposed an optimal optimization procedure combining FISTA with SVT, which led to fast computations of the low-rank matrix approximation optimization formulation. Finally, the proposed imputers (LRMC and MCMT) were compared to the state-of-the-art in ML (scikit-learn) packages.

Results of the experiments demonstrate superior performance of the matrix completion based approaches over the selected scikit-learn algorithms. To be precise, in the case where the encoding of the categorical data leads to approximately full rank matrices all the methods perform relatively the same. However, if the matrices are approximately low-rank, the matrix completion based approaches perform exceedingly better than the benchmark ML algorithms. A Python software package is being prepared from this work.

The matrix completion approach shows promising results, even though its theory is well known in the signal processing community, it is not clear if this is the case for ML community. This work demonstrates this for the ML audience and it is just a scratch of the surface, many more can be done to further improve the method. The method has many challenges and possible avenues for improvement. Firstly, despite the efficient implementation we explored here, the method is still more computationally expensive than the ML methods. However, even though it may be possible to reduce the computational cost gap, this might not be a big issue since imputing missing data is usually a pre-processing step that is done offline. Secondly, the success of our method depends on creating low-rankness in the matrices we try to complete by reshuffling and reshaping the matrices. It is an open question how to optimally create low-rankness. Thirdly, the MCMT approach is a natural solution to the preceding point but looping through all submatrices makes the approach more computationally expensive and it is also not clear what is the best way to choose the submatrices. Nonetheless, it is interesting to note that in the results presented here the MCMT was not optimized, yet it performed at par with the other approaches.

References

1. Rubin, D.B.: Inference and missing data. Biometrika **63**(3), 581–592 (1976). https://doi.org/10.2307/2335739
2. Little, R.J.A., Rubin, D.B.: Statistical Analysis with Missing Data. John Wiley & Sons Inc., New York (1986). https://doi.org/10.2307/1165119
3. Roy, B.: All About Missing Data Handling, Missing Data Imputation Techniques. Towards Data Science, 3 September 2019. https://towardsdatascience.com/all-about-missing-data-handling-b94b8b5d2184
4. Bennett, J., Lanning, S.: The Netflix prize. In: Proceedings of KDD Cup and Workshop, vol. 2007, p. 35, August 2007. https://doi.org/10.1145/1345448.1345459
5. Fazel, M.: Matrix rank minimization with applications. Ph.D. thesis, Stanford University (2002). https://faculty.washington.edu/mfazel/thesis-final.pdf
6. Recht, B., Fazel, M., Parrilo, P.A.: Guaranteed minimum-rank solutions of linear matrix equations via nuclear norm minimization. SIAM Rev. **52**(3), 471–501 (2010). https://doi.org/10.1137/070697835
7. Candès, E., Recht, B.: Exact matrix completion via convex optimization. Commun. ACM **55**(6), 111–119 (2012). https://doi.org/10.1145/2184319.2184343
8. Davenport, M.A., Plan, Y., van den Berg, E., Wootters, M.: 1-bit matrix completion. Inf. Infer. J. IMA **3**(3), 189–223 (2014). https://doi.org/10.1093/imaiai/iau006
9. Li, C., He, W., Yuan, L., Sun, Z., Zhao, Q.: Guaranteed matrix completion under multiple linear transformations. In: Proceedings of the IEEE/CVF Conference on Computer Vision and Pattern Recognition (CVPR), pp. 11136–11145 (2019). https://doi.org/10.1109/CVPR.2019.01139

10. van Buuren, S., Groothuis-Oudshoorn, K.: MICE: multivariate imputation by chained equations in R. J. Stat. Softw. **45**, 1–67 (2011). https://doi.org/10.18637/jss.v045.i03
11. Pedregosa, F., et al.: Scikit-learn: machine learning in Python. J. Mach. Learn. Res. **12**, 2825–2830 (2011). http://www.jmlr.org/papers/volume12/pedregosa11a/pedregosa11a.pdf
12. Troyanskaya, O., et al.: Missing value estimation methods for DNA microarrays. Bioinformatics **17**(6), 520–525 (2001). https://doi.org/10.1093/BIOINFORMATICS/17.6.520
13. Emmanuel, J.: Candès and Terence Tao: the power of convex relaxation: near-optimal matrix completion. IEEE Trans. Inf. Theor. **56**(5), 2053–2080 (2010). https://doi.org/10.1109/TIT.2010.2044061
14. Candès, E.J., Plan, Y.: Matrix completion with noise. Proc. IEEE **98**(6), 925–936 (2010). https://doi.org/10.1109/JPROC.2009.2035722
15. Beck, A., Teboulle, A.: A fast iterative shrinkage-thresholding algorithm for linear inverse problems. SIAM J. Imag. Sci. **2**(1), 183–202 (2009). https://doi.org/10.1137/080716542
16. Cai, J.F., Candès, E.J., Shen, Z.: A singular value thresholding algorithm for matrix completion. SIAM J. Optim. **20**(4), 1956–1982 (2010). https://doi.org/10.1137/080738970
17. Fornasier, M., Rauhut, H., Ward, R.: Low-rank matrix recovery via iteratively reweighted least squares minimization. SIAM J. Optim. **21**(4), 1614–1640 (2011). https://doi.org/10.1137/100811404
18. Mohan, K., Fazel, M.: Iterative reweighted algorithms for matrix rank minimization. J. Mach. Learn. Res. **13**(1), 3441–3473 (2012). https://doi.org/10.5555/2503308.2503351
19. Cao, Y., Xie, Y.: Categorical matrix completion. In 2015 IEEE 6th International Workshop on Computational Advances in Multi-Sensor Adaptive Processing (CAMSAP), pp. 369–372, December 2015. https://doi.org/10.1109/CAMSAP.2015.7383813
20. Facchinei, F., Pang, J.-S.: Finite-Dimensional Variational Inequalities and Complementarity Problems. ORFE, vol. 2. Springer, New York (2003). https://doi.org/10.1007/b97543
21. Nesterov, Y.: Smooth minimization of non-smooth functions. Math. Program. **103**, 127–152 (2005). https://doi.org/10.1007/s10107-004-0552-5
22. csv/datasets/HairEyeColor.csv: Datasets distributed with R Git Source Tree - rdataset is a collection of 597 datasets that were originally distributed alongside the statistical software environment "R" and some of its add-on packages. Datasets distributed with R. From Scilab. https://forge.scilab.org/index.php/p/rdataset/source/tree/master/csv/datasets/HairEyeColor.csv

Implementing Quantum-Kernel-Based Classifiers in the NISQ Era

Shivani Mahashakti Pillay[1,2,3]($\boxtimes$), Ilya Sinayskiy[2,4], Edgar Jembere[1,3], and Francesco Petruccione[2,4]

[1] School of Mathematics, Statistics, and Computer Science,
University of KwaZulu-Natal, Durban, South Africa
`217039130@stu.ukzn.ac.za`
[2] Quantum Research Group, School of Chemistry and Physics,
University of KwaZulu-Natal, Durban, South Africa
[3] Centre for Artificial Intelligence Research (CAIR), Cape Town, South Africa
[4] National Institute for Theoretical and Computational Sciences (NITheCS),
Johannesburg, South Africa
`https://cair.org.za`

Abstract. There is an intrinsic link between operations that can be performed on a quantum computer and kernel methods. This has inspired the development of quantum-kernel-based classifiers that exploit the ability of quantum computers to efficiently perform operations in large Hilbert spaces. This work performs a proof of principle demonstration of a quantum-kernel-based classifier applied to the binary classification of various non-linearly separable datasets. For each classification task, a quantum device provided by the IBM Quantum (IBMQ) platform is used to estimate a kernel matrix. A number of novel strategies comprised of combinations of existing post-processing methods are then applied to the matrix to mitigate the effects of noise from the quantum device, readout error and account for the effects of finite sampling. The application of certain strategies is shown to improve the quality of the kernel matrices estimated by the quantum device. The raw and post-processed kernel matrices are fed into a classical support vector machines (SVM) that learns a model to perform the classification. For each classification task, the classifiers exhibits high accuracies that are comparable to the classifiers that use ideal, simulated kernel matrices. The classifiers that use certain post-processed kernel matrices exhibit higher accuracies than the classifiers that use the raw kernel matrices. This demonstrates the effectiveness of quantum-kernel-based classifiers in the Noisy Intermediate Scale Quantum (NISQ) computing era as well as the power of certain of post-processing strategies.

Keywords: Kernel methods · Quantum-kernel-based classifier · Support vector machine · Binary classification · Post-processing strategies

1 Introduction

One of the goals of Quantum Machine Learning (QML) is to leverage the non-classical properties of quantum devices to solve problems in machine learning.

© Springer Nature Switzerland AG 2022
E. Jembere et al. (Eds.): SACAIR 2021, CCIS 1551, pp. 257–273, 2022.
https://doi.org/10.1007/978-3-030-95070-5_17

Classification problems, in particular, have received considerable attention and a number of quantum classifiers have been developed [1]. These classifiers include the quantum neural network [2–9], the quantum decision tree [10], the quantum nearest neighbour algorithm [11,12], the quantum support vector machine [13] and other quantum kernel methods [14–18].

Recently, quantum kernel methods have gained considerable traction. There are two main approaches to quantum kernel methods: quantum variational classifiers and quantum-kernel-based classifiers [16,17]. While quantum variational classifiers use a variational short-depth circuit to train the parameters of some decision boundary, quantum-kernel-based classifiers execute short-depth circuits to perform the kernel estimation on a quantum computer and train the classification model of some kernel method like the SVM on a classical computer.

Quantum-kernel-based classifiers have recently been proven to provide powerful advantages in fault-tolerant settings [19,20]. Liu et al. have constructed a learning problem based on the discrete logarithm problem and have proven that a quantum-kernel-based classifier can achieve a rigorous and robust speed-up over all classical learners [19]. To solve the same learning problem, Huang et al. have introduced a projected quantum kernel method that also provides a rigorous speed-up over all classical learners [20]. It is also worth mentioning that quantum-kernel-based classifiers may be preferable to quantum variational classifiers in fault-tolerant settings since training variational quantum algorithms has recently been shown to be NP-hard [21].

There is also interest in the effectiveness of these classifiers in the NISQ era [22–24]. For instance, Peters et al. have demonstrated that a quantum-kernel-based classifier can be used to successfully classify high dimensional data without performing any dimensionality reduction [24]. Demonstrating the effectiveness of quantum-kernel-based classifiers in the NISQ era would reveal a practical use case for machine learning with quantum computers, a long sought after goal in the field of QML.

When using near-term quantum computers, there are three sources of error: device noise, readout error and finite sampling. Numerous post-processing methods to suppress the effects of device noise and finite sampling on estimated quantum kernel matrices have been implemented [25,26]. While the effect of some of these methods on the classification accuracies of quantum-kernel-based classifiers has not yet been investigated, these methods have been shown to improve the quality of the estimated kernel matrices by increasing their alignment to the ideal, simulated kernel matrices. To combat the effects of readout error, a simple readout error correction method [27] has been applied to estimated quantum kernels [17,24]. The effectiveness of the readout error correction method and the methods to suppress the effects of device noise and finite sampling has inspired the investigation of the effectiveness of post-processing strategies consisting of combinations of these methods.

In this work, a quantum-kernel-based classifier is used to perform binary classification on various non-linearly separable datasets. The quantum kernel estimation is performed using a real quantum computer that executes circuits proposed in [17, 28]. The resulting kernel matrix is used to train and test a SVM. Even with the current noise levels, the quantum-kernel-based classifiers that use the real quantum computer for the kernel estimation achieve high classification accuracies, comparable to the accuracies obtained by the quantum-kernel-based classifiers that use an ideal simulator for the kernel estimation. It is demonstrated that the quality of the kernel matrices estimated by the real device can be improved by applying certain novel post-processing strategies designed to combat the effects of device noise, finite sampling and readout error. The improvement is quantified using the Relative Improvement in Alignment [25] to the ideal kernel matrices. The post-processing strategies that achieve the highest Relative Improvement in Alignment are presented. It is also demonstrated that, in some cases, the classifiers that use the post-processed kernel matrices achieve higher accuracies than the classifiers that use the raw kernel matrices.

The rest of this paper is structured as follows: Sect. 2 presents the quantum kernel estimation technique used in this study, the methods used in the post-processing strategies and how they are combined as well as a short description of the SVM. Section 3 presents the data that constitutes each classification task and the experimental setup. Section 4 presents the effects of the post-processing strategies on the quality of the estimated kernel matrices, the accuracies obtained by the quantum-kernel-based classifiers on the various classification tasks and a discussion on these results. Lastly, Sect. 5 presents some concluding remarks.

2   Methods

For the quantum-kernel-based quantum classifier implemented in this work, a quantum computer is used to estimate the kernel for each pair of data vectors in a given 2-dimensional dataset. The kernel values are all stored in a kernel (or Gram) matrix. The kernel matrix is then used to train and test a SVM on a classical computer.

2.1   Quantum Kernel Estimation

At the core of all quantum kernel estimation techniques[1] is the idea that quantum computers can be used to estimate kernels through two operations: the encoding of classical data vectors into quantum states and a quantum measurement of those states [16]. In this section, a short summary of the quantum kernel estimation technique [17, 28] used in this work is presented.

A 2-dimensional classical data vector $\mathbf{x} \in \mathbb{R}^2$, $\mathbf{x} = (x_1, x_2)$ is encoded into a set of real-valued encoding functions $\Phi(\mathbf{x}) = \{\phi_1(\mathbf{x}), \phi_2(\mathbf{x}), \phi_{1,2}(\mathbf{x})\}$. These encoding functions are then used to define a unitary operator $\mathcal{U}_{\Phi(\mathbf{x})}$ which is applied to the initial state $|00\rangle$. The resulting quantum state can be written as $|\Phi(\mathbf{x})\rangle = \mathcal{U}_{\Phi(\mathbf{x})} |00\rangle$. This effectively maps the data vector into a feature Hilbert space $\mathbb{C}^{2^2}$.

---

[1] A brief introduction to quantum computing and kernels can be found in Sections A and B, respectively, of the Supplementary Material [29].

The unitary operator $\mathcal{U}_{\Phi(\mathbf{x})}$ is defined as:

$$\mathcal{U}_{\Phi(\mathbf{x})} = U_{\Phi(\mathbf{x})} H^{\otimes 2} U_{\Phi(\mathbf{x})} H^{\otimes 2} , \tag{1}$$

where

$$U_{\Phi(\mathbf{x})} = \exp\left(i\phi_1(\mathbf{x}) Z \otimes I + i\phi_2(\mathbf{x}) I \otimes Z + i\phi_{1,2}(\mathbf{x}) Z \otimes Z \right) , \tag{2}$$

and H is a unitary operator known as the Hadamard gate, I is the 2×2 identity matrix, Z is the Pauli-Z matrix and $\otimes$ denotes the tensor product for matrices.

The kernel can then be defined as the squared state overlap between two states in this feature Hilbert space

$$k(\mathbf{x}, \mathbf{z}) = |\langle \Phi(\mathbf{x}) | |\Phi(\mathbf{z}) \rangle|^2 . \tag{3}$$

This can be estimated as:

$$k(\mathbf{x}, \mathbf{z}) = |\langle 00 | \mathcal{U}_{\Phi(\mathbf{x})}^\dagger \mathcal{U}_{\Phi(\mathbf{z})} | 00 \rangle|^2 , \tag{4}$$

where $\mathcal{U}_{\Phi(\mathbf{x})}^\dagger$ is the complex conjugate transpose of $\mathcal{U}_{\Phi(\mathbf{x})}$.

Practically, $\mathcal{U}_{\Phi(\mathbf{x})}$ is applied to a 2-qubit system through a quantum circuit shown in Fig. 1. The circuit that implements $U_{\Phi(\mathbf{x})}$ is shown in Fig. 2.

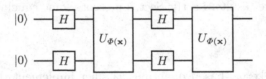

Fig. 1. Circuit representation for $\mathcal{U}_{\Phi(\mathbf{x})} |00\rangle$ which encodes the input $\mathbf{x}$ to the quantum state $|\Phi(\mathbf{x})\rangle = \mathcal{U}_{\Phi(\mathbf{x})} |00\rangle$. This effectively maps $\mathbf{x}$ into a feature Hilbert space.

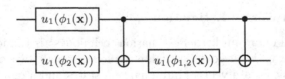

Fig. 2. Circuit representation for $U_{\Phi(\mathbf{x})}$ composed of three $u_1(\phi)$ gates and two Controlled-NOT (C-NOT) operations. $U_{\Phi(\mathbf{x})}$ is used to compose $\mathcal{U}_{\Phi(\mathbf{x})}$ as in Fig. 1.

Matrix representations for the Hadamard gate, C-NOT operation and $u_1(\phi)$ can be found in [30].

The quantity that defines the kernel in (4) represents the probability of measuring the qubits in the state $|00\rangle$ after preparing the state $\mathcal{U}_{\Phi(\mathbf{x})}^\dagger \mathcal{U}_{\Phi(\mathbf{z})} |00\rangle$. This probability can be obtained through a Z-basis measurement of the circuit shown in Fig. 3.

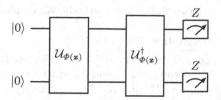

Fig. 3. Circuit representation for the Z-basis measurement of $\mathcal{U}_{\Phi(\mathbf{x})}^{\dagger}\mathcal{U}_{\Phi(\mathbf{z})}|00\rangle$. This is the circuit that will evaluate the kernel $k(\mathbf{x}, \mathbf{z})$.

2.2 Post-processing Strategies

Some degree of error is unavoidable in experiments using NISQ devices. This work will employ combinations of a number of methods to combat readout error and the effects of device noise and finite sampling. Throughout this section $K^{(\text{ideal})}$ will be used to denote the kernel matrix estimated by the ideal simulator, $K^{(\text{raw})}$ will be used to denote the raw kernel matrix estimated by the real device and $K^{(\text{post})}$ will be used to denote the raw kernel matrix after post-processing.

Device Noise Mitigation. Device noise can result from the inevitable interaction of the quantum system with its environment as well as imperfect gate implementation. The methods to combat device noise introduced in [25] use depolarizing noise to model the device noise. The knowledge that each diagonal entry of the ideal kernel matrix should be equal to 1 is used to infer the decay rate of the depolarizing channel, denoted by λ_i. This is done according to:

$$\lambda_i = \sqrt{\frac{K_{ii}^{(\text{raw})} - 2^{-N}}{1 - 2^{-N}}}, \tag{5}$$

where $K^{(\text{raw})}$ denotes i^{th} diagonal element of the the raw kernel matrix and N is the number of qubits, in our case $N = 2$.

These decay rates are then used to estimate the ideal kernel entry according to

$$K_{ij}^{(\text{post})} = \frac{K_{ij}^{(\text{raw})} - 2^{-N}(1 - \lambda_i\lambda_j)}{\lambda_i\lambda_j}, \tag{6}$$

where $K^{(\text{post})}$ denotes the post-processed kernel matrix which, in this case, contain estimates of the ideal kernel entries. Equations (5) and (6) are derived in detail by Hubregtsen et al. [25].

Three methods that make use of these relations have been developed [25] and descriptions of these methods are presented in Table 1.

Readout Error Correction. Readout error is the error due to the measurement of an unexpected state. This can sometimes result from dissipation and

Table 1. The device noise mitigation methods [25] employed in this work.

Method	Description
M-SPLIT	Each kernel entry $K_{ij}^{(\text{post})}$ is calculated using the decay rates λ_i and λ_j which are estimated using $K_{ii}^{(\text{raw})}$ and $K_{jj}^{(\text{raw})}$ respectively
M-MEAN	Each kernel entry $K_{ij}^{(\text{post})}$ is calculated using an average decay rate λ_{mean}. All or some diagonal entries $K_{ii}^{(\text{raw})}$ can be used to estimate λ_{mean}
M-SINGLE	Each kernel entry $K_{ij}^{(\text{post})}$ is calculated using a single decay rate λ_{single}. In this work and in [25], λ_{single} is calculated using the first kernel entry of the noisy matrix, $K_{00}^{(\text{raw})}$

decoherence in the physical quantum computer, a consequence of the qubits interacting with their environment. The method used in this work to combat readout error [27] has previously been applied to quantum kernel estimation [17,24] and will be denoted M-READ.

This method involves preparing $2^2 = 4$ calibration circuits where each circuit prepares a different basis input state. Each calibration circuit is executed on the noisy quantum device and the results are used to construct a calibration matrix C,

$$C_{ij} = P(|i\rangle \,|\, |j\rangle) \,,$$

where $P(|i\rangle \,|\, |j\rangle)$ is the conditional probability of measuring the basis state $|j\rangle$ when executing the calibration circuit preparing $|i\rangle$.

For each kernel estimation circuit that has been executed on the quantum computer, a noisy probability distribution $\mathbf{P}^{(\text{raw})}$ will be obtained,

$$\mathbf{P}_i^{(\text{raw})} = P(|i\rangle \,|i\rangle) \,, \tag{7}$$

where $P(|i\rangle \,|i\rangle)$ is the probability of measuring the basis state $|i\rangle$ when executing the kernel estimation circuit. An approximation for the noiseless probability distribution can then be obtained using

$$\mathbf{P}^{(\text{post})} = C^{-1}\mathbf{P}^{(\text{raw})} \,. \tag{8}$$

Kernel Regularization. The kernel matrices estimated on the real device may not be positive semi-definite and, therefore, may not be valid kernel matrices. However, a positive-semi-definite matrix is a requirement for the convergence of the optimization problem solved in the training of the SVM. A number of methods have been used in [25,26] to make the noisy kernel matrix positive semi-definite. This helps mitigate the effects of device noise, readout error and finite sampling by bringing the obtained matrix closer to the ideal, noiseless kernel matrix. The regularization methods used in this work include four methods that make use of spectral transformations and a method introduced in [25] that uses a semi-definite program.

The regularization methods that use spectral transformations first require a spectral decomposition of $K^{(\text{raw})}$,

$$K^{(\text{raw})} = \sum_{i=1}^{n} \lambda_i \mathbf{u}_i \mathbf{u}_i^T , \tag{9}$$

where λ_i refers to the eigenvalues and $\mathbf{u}_i$ the corresponding eigenvectors of $K^{(\text{raw})}$.

The spectrum of $K^{(\text{raw})}$ is then transformed according to one of the transformations[2] presented in Table 2.

Table 2. The spectral transformations used in the kernel regularization methods employed in this work.

Transformation	Abbreviation	Description
Tikhonov Regularization/ Shifting [31]	R-TIK	The smallest negative eigenvalue of $K^{(\text{raw})}$ is subtracted from all the eigenvalues of $K_{(\text{raw})}$
Thresholding/Clipping [32]	R-THR	The negative eigenvalues of $K^{(\text{raw})}$ are set to zero
Flipping [33]	R-FLP	The signs of the negative eigenvalues of $K^{(\text{raw})}$ are flipped

Lastly, a new matrix, $K^{(\text{post})}$, is composed using the transformed spectrum and the original eigenvectors of $K^{(\text{raw})}$.

The last regularization method is a semi-definite program described by:

$$\text{R-SDP}(A) = \text{argmin}\{||A' - A||_F : A' \geq 0, A'_{ii} = 1\} , \tag{10}$$

where $||X||_F = \sqrt{\langle X, X \rangle_F}$ denotes the Frobenius norm and $\langle X, Y \rangle_F = \text{Tr}(X^\dagger Y)$ is the Frobenius inner product for any matrix X and Y.

This method involves searching for the closest positive semi-definite matrix, according to the Frobenius norm, to the original $K^{(\text{raw})}$ while incorporating the knowledge that all the diagonal entries of the noiseless matrix should be 1.

---

[2] R-TIK and R-THR were originally applied to quantum kernel estimation in [25]. R-TIK, R-THR and R-FLP were originally applied quantum kernel estimation in [26].

Construction of the Post-processing Strategies. This work combines methods for device noise mitigation, readout error correction and kernel regularization to form different post-processing strategies which will follow a similar form to the strategies used in [25].

Here, the strategies consist of 4 steps, presented in Table 3:

Table 3. The four steps included in each post-processing strategy employed in this work and the options for each step.

Step		Options
1	Read-out Correction	M-READ, Id
2	Regularization	R-TIK, R-THR, R-FLP, R-SDP, Id
3	Device Noise Mitigation	M-SPLIT, M-MEAN, M-SINGLE, Id
4	Regularization	R-TIK, R-THR, R-FLP, R-SDP, Id

Picking a method at each step presented in the Table 3 would result in $(2 \times 5 \times 4 \times 5 = 200)$ combination strategies, including the option Id to apply nothing to the matrix at each step. However, some combinations are 'reducible' [25]. For example, all strategies of the form M-READ/Id, R-SDP followed by some device noise mitigation and regularization are reducible to [M-READ/Id, R-SDP, Id, Id]. This is because the device mitigation and regularization methods following R-SDP receive a positive semi-definite matrix with all diagonal entries being equal to 1. Furthermore, for any strategy that includes R-TIK, R-THR or R-FLP in the first regularization step followed by Id in the device noise mitigation step and R-TIK, R-THR or R-FLP in the second regularization step, the application of R-TIK, R-THR or R-FLP is redundant since this step would already receive a positive semi-definite matrix. When excluding these two cases and repetitions, there are 136 distinct post-processing strategies.

2.3   SVM Training and Testing

A SVM is trained and tested on the kernel matrix estimated by the real quantum device as well as all the 136 post-processed kernel matrices.

For each kernel matrix, the kernel matrix is split into a training kernel matrix and a testing kernel matrix. The training kernel matrix is used, by the classical SVM, to solve a quadratic optimization problem and construct the following decision rule:

$$\tilde{y} = \sum_{i=1}^{N} \alpha_i y_i K(\mathbf{x}_i, \tilde{\mathbf{x}}) + b \,, \tag{11}$$

where $\tilde{y}$ is the predicted class, α_i and b are the optimized parameters, $\tilde{\mathbf{x}}$ is the new, unclassified input, x_i are the training vectors and y_i are the corresponding target outputs.

The decision boundary, corresponding to this decision rule, maximizes the distance from the nearest data vectors of each class, called the support vectors. In this way, the SVM is an optimal binary classifier.

The testing kernel matrix is then used to test the decision rule. The classification accuracy of the kernel-based quantum classifier is then obtained from the results.

3   Data and Experimental Set-up

The quantum-kernel-based classifier described in this work was applied to the following 2-dimensional, non-linearly separable datasets are used: Circles, Moons, Exp and XOR. These datasets can be seen in Fig. 4. The Circles and Moons datasets were provided by the Scikit-learn datasets module (*sklearn.datasets*) and the Exp and XOR datasets were generated. All datasets have 100 data points and are balanced. For all points $\mathbf{x} = (x_1, x_2)$ in the dataset, $x_1, x_2 \in [-1, 1]$.

Five different kernels are used, each defined by one of the following sets of encoding functions [28]. The sets of encoding functions are:

$$\Phi_1 = \left\{ \phi_1(\mathbf{x}) = x_1, \phi_2(\mathbf{x}) = x_2, \phi_{1,2}(\mathbf{x}) = \pi \times x_1 \times x_2 \right\}, \tag{12}$$

$$\Phi_2 = \left\{ \phi_1(\mathbf{x}) = x_1, \phi_2(\mathbf{x}) = x_2, \phi_{1,2}(\mathbf{x}) = \frac{\pi}{2}(1 - x_1)(1 - x_2) \right\}, \tag{13}$$

$$\Phi_3 = \left\{ \phi_1(\mathbf{x}) = x_1, \phi_2(\mathbf{x}) = x_2, \phi_{1,2}(\mathbf{x}) = \exp\left(\frac{|x_1 - x_2|^2}{8/\ln(\pi)} \right) \right\}, \tag{14}$$

$$\Phi_4 = \left\{ \phi_1(\mathbf{x}) = x_1, \phi_2(\mathbf{x}) = x_2, \phi_{1,2}(\mathbf{x}) = \frac{\pi}{3\cos(x_1)\cos(x_2)} \right\}, \tag{15}$$

$$\Phi_5 = \left\{ \phi_1(\mathbf{x}) = x_1, \phi_2(\mathbf{x}) = x_2, \phi_{1,2}(\mathbf{x}) = \pi\cos(x_1)\cos(x_2) \right\}, \tag{16}$$

where the functions $\phi_{1,2}(\mathbf{x})$ are non-linear functions in the range of 2π (Max($\phi_{1,2}$)-Min($\phi_{1,2}$) $\leq 2\pi$) for $x_1, x_2 \in [-1, 1]$.

Qiskit [34], an open source software development framework was used to construct and run the quantum circuits for the quantum kernel estimation. Qiskit grants access to various simulators and real computers through the IBMQ cloud platform. For each kernel applied to each dataset, the kernel estimation is performed using the Statevector simulator (an ideal simulator) and ibmq_athens (a real quantum device), both provided by Qiskit.

Thereafter, the post-processing strategies described in Sect. 2.2 are applied to the kernel matrices estimated by the real device, resulting in 136 post-processed kernel matrices for each kernel applied to each dataset. These post-processing strategies are constructed using methods provided by PennyLane [35], an open source library for QML, using the *qml.kernels* subpackage.

One of the aims of this study was to investigate the effect of the various post-processing strategies on the kernel matrices estimated by the real device. To determine the effect of the post-processing strategies on a given raw kernel matrix, all post-processing strategies are applied to the kernel matrix. Thereafter, the quality of each post-processing strategy is determined by the Relative Improvement in Alignment [25] of the kernel matrix it yields. The Relative

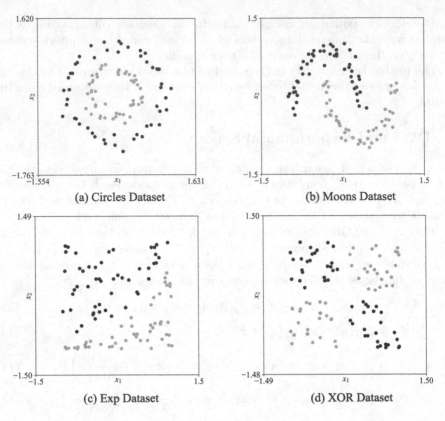

(a) Circles Dataset

(b) Moons Dataset

(c) Exp Dataset

(d) XOR Dataset

Fig. 4. Graphical representation of the four non-linearly separable 2-dimensional datasets that the quantum-kernel-based classifier was applied to.

Improvement in Alignment of a post-processed kernel matrix is given by:

$$\mathrm{RIA}(K^{(\mathrm{post})}) = \frac{A(K^{(\mathrm{post})}, K^{(\mathrm{ideal})}) - A(K^{(\mathrm{raw})}, K^{(\mathrm{ideal})})}{1 - A(K^{(\mathrm{raw})}, K^{(\mathrm{ideal})})} , \qquad (17)$$

where $A(X, X') = \frac{\langle X, X' \rangle_F}{\sqrt{\langle X, X \rangle_F \langle X, X' \rangle_F}}$ is the alignment between the two kernel matrices and gives a measure of how similar the two kernel matrices are. The Relative Improvement in Alignment as a measure allows us to express the improvement achieved by the post-processing strategy as a percentage. For example, a Relative Improvement in Alignment of 10% for $K^{(\mathrm{post})}$ means that $K^{(\mathrm{post})}$ improved the alignment of the raw kernel matrix by 10% of what is needed for the raw kernel matrix and the ideal kernel matrix to have perfect alignment.

Another aim of this study was to investigate the performance of the quantum-kernel-based classifiers using the raw kernel matrices and whether this performance could be improved by applying the post-processing strategies to these matrices. Scikit-learn [36] was used to train and test a classical SVM using each kernel matrix. This results in a total of 138 classifiers (1 ideal kernel matrix,

1 raw kernel matrix and 138 post-processed kernel matrices) for each kernel applied to each dataset.

For each dataset, an "ideal" regularization parameter was found for each set of classifiers using the same kernel. This regularization parameter, denoted by "C" in Scikit-learn, was estimated using the kernel matrix obtained from the Statevector simulator in a Bayesian Optimization method provided by Scikit-learn. In this method, a set of candidate hyperparameters are chosen, cross-validation is performed with each parameter and the parameter that obtained the highest classification accuracy is returned. The regularization parameters that were used are given in Section C of the Supplementary Material [29].

The performance of each classifier is measured using the classification accuracy obtained by that classifier. Since all the datasets are balanced, classification accuracy is a valid metric. In this work, the classification accuracy of each classifier was determined using 5-fold cross validation. Each dataset is divided into 5 groups and, for each unique group, the classifier is evaluated with this group as the testing set and the other 4 groups as the training set.

4   Results and Discussion

The post-processing strategies that achieved the highest Relative Improvement in Alignment on each kernel matrix are shown in Tables 4, 5, 6, and 7. Some post-processing strategies were able to improve the raw kernel matrix by 48%. For each kernel matrix, at least one post-processing strategy was able to improve the raw kernel matrix. However, perhaps counter-intuitively, it was also found that some post-processing strategies decreased the alignment of the raw kernel matrix to the ideal kernel matrix. In these cases, the post-processing strategies added to the error in the raw kernel matrices. This corresponds to a negative Relative Improvement in Alignment and the worst examples of this can be found in Section D of the Supplementary Material [29].

Many of the strategies that lead to the highest Relative Improvement in Alignment in each case included the readout-error mitigation technique. This shows that readout-error mitigation is a necessary post-processing technique. The best strategies also show that combining this technique with other post-processing strategies that exploit the properties of kernel matrices like the noise mitigation and regularization techniques is of great use.

M-SPLIT is the device noise mitigation technique that most often contributed to the best post-processing strategy in each case. However, unlike M-MEAN and M-SINGLE, this technique require all the diagonal elements to be estimated. R-THR and R-SDP are the regularization techniques that most often contributed to the best post-processing strategy in each case. This could be because both these approaches correspond to finding the closest positive semi-definite kernel matrix to the ideal kernel matrix [25]. It is also noteworthy, that in most cases, the best strategies did not include the first regularization step.

The post-processing strategy that achieved the highest relative improvement in most cases was [M-READ, Id, M-SPLIT, R-THR/R-SDP]. This post-processing strategy is a good candidate for improving the quality of other quantum kernels.

Table 4. The best post-processing strategies for the Circles dataset and the relative improvements in alignment that were achieved. Methods separated by/indicate that both methods in those strategies achieved the same alignments.

	Encoding functions				
	Φ_1	Φ_2	Φ_3	Φ_4	Φ_5
Best post-processing strategies	M-READ, Id, M-MEAN, R-THR/R-SDP	Id, Id, M-SPLIT, R-THR/R-SDP	M-READ, Id, M-SPLIT, R-THR/R-SDP	M-READ, Id, M-SPLIT, R-THR/R-SDP	M-READ, Id, M-SPLIT, R-THR/R-SDP
Relative Improvement in Alignment	0.278161	0.236903	0.312989	0.323963	0.321567

The classification accuracies obtained by each classifier, for each dataset, are shown in Fig. 5. Tables of these results can be found in Section D of the Supplementary Material [29]. $K^{(\text{ideal})}$ denotes the classifier that used the Statevector simulator for the kernel estimation, $K^{(\text{raw})}$ denotes the classifier that used the real quantum computer for the kernel estimation and $K^{(\text{post})}$ denotes the classifier that used the post-processed kernel matrix. The post-processed kernel matrix chosen was the one that achieved the highest Relative Improvement in Alignment as shown in Tables 4, 5, 6, and 7.

The classifiers using the real device perform well, even with current levels of noise and error. In most cases, accuracies comparable to the classifiers that used the ideal kernel matrices were attained. The strategies that lead to the highest relative improvements in alignment also lead to an increase in the accuracy with one exception: the strategies that lead to the highest relative improvement for the Exp dataset and Φ_1 lead to a decrease in the accuracy by 1%. Interestingly, the strategies that lead to the highest relative improvements in alignment did

Table 5. The best post-processing strategies for the Moons dataset and the relative improvements in alignment that were achieved. Methods separated by/indicate that both methods in those strategies achieved the same alignments.

	Encoding functions				
	Φ_1	Φ_2	Φ_3	Φ_4	Φ_5
Best post-processing strategies	Id, Id, M-MEAN, R-THR/R-SDP	Id, Id, M-SINGLE, R-THR/R-SDP	M-READ, Id, M-MEAN, R-THR/R-SDP	M-READ, Id, M-SINGLE, R-THR/R-SDP	M-READ, Id, M-MEAN, R-THR/R-SDP
Relative Improvement in Alignment	0.292376	0.333813	0.286295	0.296915	0.312724

Table 6. The best post-processing strategies for the Exp dataset and the relative improvements in alignment that were achieved. Methods separated by/indicate that both methods in those strategies achieved the same alignments.

	Encoding functions				
	Φ_1	Φ_2	Φ_3	Φ_4	Φ_5
Best post-processing strategies	M-READ, Id, Id, R-THR/R-SDP	Id Id M-SPLIT R-THR/R-SDP	M-READ Id M-SPLIT R-THR/R-SDP	M-READ Id M-SPLIT R-THR/R-SDP	M-READ Id M-SPLIT R-THR/R-SDP
	M-READ, R-THR, M-SPLIT, Id/R-THR/R-TIK/ R-SDP/R-FLP				
	M-READ, R-THR, Id, R-SDP				
Relative Improvement in Alignment	0.280404	0.274039	0.426255	0.425453	0.411823

Table 7. The best post-processing strategies for the XOR dataset and the relative improvements in alignment that were achieved. Methods separated by/indicate that both methods in those strategies achieved the same alignments.

	Encoding functions				
	Φ_1	Φ_2	Φ_3	Φ_4	Φ_5
Best post-processing strategies	M-READ, Id, M-SPLIT, R-THR/R-SDP	M-READ, Id, M-SPLIT, R-THR/R-SDP	Id, Id, M-SINGLE, R-THR/R-SDP	M-READ, Id, M-SPLIT, R-THR/R-SDP	M-READ, Id, M-SPLIT, R-THR/R-SDP
Relative Improvement in Alignment	0.477828	0.383002	0.238320	0.264283	0.249567

not necessarily lead to the highest increase in the classification accuracy. For example, for the Exp dataset and Φ_1, some strategies increased the accuracy to 87% and for the XOR dataset and Φ_3 some strategies increased the accuracy to 100%. In some other cases, the other post-processing strategies increased the accuracy by 1 or 2% more than the strategies that lead highest relative improvements in alignment. It was also found that, in some cases, the post-processing strategies that lead to an increase in alignment lead to a decrease in the classification accuracy. Examples of this can be found in Section D of the Supplementary Material [29]. This could be because the regularization parameters were chosen to maximise the classification accuracy obtained by a classifier that uses the ideal kernel matrix estimated by the Statevector simulator. Even though the post-processed kernel matrix may be closer to the ideal kernel matrix, the accuracy of classifier will not necessarily improve due to the non-linear relationship between the regularization parameter and the kernel matrix.

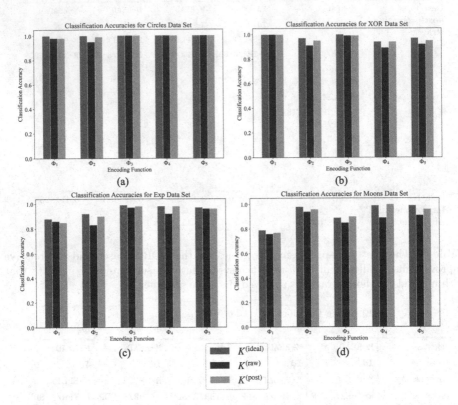

Fig. 5. (a) The classification accuracies obtained by the various quantum-kernel-based classifiers on the Circles dataset, (b) The classification accuracies obtained by the various quantum-kernel-based classifiers on the XOR dataset, (c) The classification accuracies obtained by the various quantum-kernel-based classifiers on the Exp dataset, (d) The classification accuracies obtained by the various quantum-kernel-based classifiers on the Moons dataset.

5   Conclusion

It has been shown that quantum-kernel-based classifiers can successfully be applied to binary classification problems, for non-linearly separable datasets, even with the current levels of noise. Several novel post-processing strategies that include readout error correction, noise mitigation methods and regularization methods that improve the quality of the raw kernel matrices have been identified. This improvement has also, in some cases, lead to an improvement in the classification accuracy. Readout error correction proved to be a vital post-processing step. The most promising post-processing strategy found was [M-READ, Id, M-SPLIT, R-THR/R-SDP]. The success of these finding justifies the study of quantum-kernel-based classifiers as well as the post-processing strategies that could boost their performance.

Future work could explore other post-processing strategies or develop post-processing strategies with performance guarantees. One could also look at applying quantum-kernel-based classifiers to real-world classification problems, unbalanced problems or multi-class classification problems. Finding quantum kernels that can achieve some advantage over classical kernels in the NISQ era also remains an unsolved problem.

Acknowlegdements. This work is based upon research supported by the South African Research Chair Initiative, Grant No. 64812 of the Department of Science and Innovation and the National Research Foundation of the Republic of South Africa. Support from the CSIR DSI-Interbursary Support (IBS) Programme is gratefully acknowledged. Support from the Center of Artificial Intelligence Research is appreciated. We would like to thank Mr I. J. David for his assistance in proof reading the manuscript. We acknowledge the use of IBM Quantum services for this work. The views expressed are those of the authors and do not reflect the official policy or position of IBM or the IBM Quantum team.

References

1. Li, W., Deng, D.-L.: Recent advances for quantum classifiers. arXiv preprint arXiv:2108.13421 (2021)
2. Schuld, M., Petruccione, F.: Supervised Learning with Quantum Computers, vol. 17. Springer (2018)
3. Zoufal, C., Lucchi, A., Woerner, S.: Quantum generative adversarial networks for learning and loading random distributions. NPJ Quant. Inf. **5**(1), 1–9 (2019)
4. Romero, J., Olson, J.P., Aspuru-Guzik, A.: Quantum autoencoders for efficient compression of quantum data. Quant. Sci. Technol. **2**(4), 045001 (2017)
5. Dunjko, V., Briegel, H.J.: Machine learning & artificial intelligence in the quantum domain: a review of recent progress. Rep. Prog. Phys. **81**(7), 074001 (2018)
6. Ciliberto, C.: Quantum machine learning: a classical perspective. Proc. R. Soci. Math. Phys. Eng. Sci. **474**(2209), 20170551 (2018)
7. Killoran, N., Bromley, T.R., Miguel Arrazola, J., Schuld, M., Quesada, N., Lloyd, S.: Continuous-variable quantum neural networks. Phys. Rev. Res. **1**(3), 033063 (2019)
8. Schuld, M., Sinayskiy, I., Petruccione, F.: The quest for a quantum neural network. Quant. Inf. Process. **13**(11), 2567–2586 (2014)
9. Farhi, E., Neven, H.: Classification with quantum neural networks on near term processors. arXiv preprint arXiv:1802.06002 (2018)
10. Lu, S., Braunstein, S.L.: Quantum decision tree classifier. Quant. Inf. Process. **13**(3), 757–770 (2013). https://doi.org/10.1007/s11128-013-0687-5
11. Lloyd, S., Mohseni, M., Rebentrost, P.: Quantum algorithms for supervised and unsupervised machine learning. arXiv preprint arXiv:1307.0411 (2013)

12. Wiebe, N., Kapoor, A., Svore, K.: Quantum algorithms for nearest-neighbor methods for supervised and unsupervised learning. arXiv preprint arXiv:1401.2142 (2014)
13. Rebentrost, P., Mohseni, M., Lloyd, S.: Quantum support vector machine for big data classification. Phys. Rev. Lett. **113**(13), 130503 (2014)
14. Chatterjee, R., Yu, T.: Generalized coherent states, reproducing kernels, and quantum support vector machines. arXiv preprint arXiv:1612.03713 (2016)
15. Schuld, M., Fingerhuth, M., Petruccione, F.: Implementing a distance-based classifier with a quantum interference circuit. EPL (Europhys. Lett.) **119**(6), 60002 (2017)
16. Schuld, M., Killoran, N.: Quantum machine learning in feature Hilbert spaces. Phys. Rev. Lett.**122**(4), 040504 (2019)
17. Havlíček, V., et al.: Supervised learning with quantum-enhanced feature spaces. Nature **567**(7747), 209–212 (2019)
18. Blank, C., Park, D.K., Kevin Rhee, J.-K., Petruccione, F.: Quantum classifier with tailored quantum kernel. NPJ Quant. Inf. **6**(1), 1–7 (2020)
19. Liu, Y., Arunachalam, S., Temme, K.: A rigorous and robust quantum speed-up in supervised machine learning. Nat. Phys. 1–5 (2021)
20. Huang, H.-Y., et al.: Power of data in quantum machine learning. Nat. Commun. **12**(1), 1–9 (2021)
21. Bittel, L., Kliesch, M.: Training variational quantum algorithms is np-hard. Phy. Rev. Lett.**127**(12), 120502 (2021)
22. Bartkiewicz, K., Gneiting, C., Černoch, A., Jiráková, K., Lemr, K., Nori, F.: Experimental kernel-based quantum machine learning in finite feature space. Sci. Rep. **10**(1), 1–9 (2020)
23. Kusumoto, T., Mitarai, K., Fujii, K., Kitagawa, M., Negoro, M.: Experimental quantum kernel machine learning with nuclear spins in a solid. arXiv preprint arXiv:1911.12021 (2019)
24. Peters, E.: Machine learning of high dimensional data on a noisy quantum processor. arXiv preprint arXiv:2101.09581 (2021)
25. Hubregtsen, T.: Training quantum embedding kernels on near-term quantum computers. arXiv preprint arXiv:2105.02276 (2021)
26. Wang, X., Du, Y., Luo, Y., Tao, D.: Towards understanding the power of quantum kernels in the NISQ era. arXiv preprint arXiv:2103.16774 (2021)
27. Asfaw, A., et al.: Learn quantum computation using Qiskit (2020)
28. Suzuki, Y., et al.: Analysis and synthesis of feature map for kernel-based quantum classifier. Quant. Mach. Intell. **2**(1), 1–9 (2020). https://doi.org/10.1007/s42484-020-00020-y
29. Mahashakti Pillay, S., Sinayskiy, I., Jembere, E., Petruccione,F.: Implementing-quantum-kernel-based-classifiers-in-the-NISQ-Era-Supp-Material. **11**   (2021). https://git.io/JX8cp
30. Nielsen, M., Chuang, I.: Quantum Computation and Quantum Information, 10th Anniversary edition. Cambridge University Press, Cambridge (2010)
31. Roth, V., Laub, J., Kawanabe, M., Buhmann, J.M.: Optimal cluster preserving embedding of nonmetric proximity data. IEEE Trans. Patt. Anal. Mach. Intell. **25**(12), 1540–1551 (2003)
32. Wu, G., Chang, E.Y., Zhang, Z.: An analysis of transformation on non-positive semidefinite similarity matrix for kernel machines. In: Proceedings of the 22nd International Conference on Machine Learning, vol. 8. Citeseer (2005)
33. Graepel, T., Herbrich, R., Bollmann-Sdorra, P., Obermayer, K.: Classification on pairwise proximity data. Adv. Neural Inf. Process. Syst. **11**, 438–444 (1999)

34. Abraham, H., et al.: Qiskit: an open-source framework for quantum computing (2019)
35. Bergholm, V., et al.: Automatic differentiation of hybrid quantum-classical computations (2020)
36. Pedregosa, F., et al.: Scikit-learn: machine learning in python. J. Mach. Learn. Res. **12**, 2825–2830 (2011)

A Temporal Approach to Facial Emotion Expression Recognition

Christine Asaju[✉][iD] and Hima Vadapalli[iD]

School of Computer Science and Applied Mathematics,
University of the Witwatersrand, Johannesburg, South Africa
1990591@students.wits.ac.za, hima.vadapalli@wits.ac.za

Abstract. Systems embedded with facial emotion expression recognition models enable the application of emotion-related knowledge to improve human and computer interaction and in doing so, users have a satisfying experience. Facial expressions exhibited by individuals are mostly used as non-verbal cues of communication. It is envisaged that accurate and real-time estimation of expressions and/or emotional changes will improve existing online platforms. However, further mapping of estimated expressions to emotions is highly useful in many applications such as sentiment analysis, market analysis, student comprehension among others. Feedback based on estimated emotions plays a crucial role in improving the usability of such models. However, there have been no or limited feedback mechanisms incorporated into these models. The proposed work, therefore, investigates the use of deep learning to identify and estimate emotional changes in human faces and further analysis of estimated emotions to provide feedback. The methodology involves a temporal approach including a VGG-19 pre-trained network for feature extraction, a BiLSTM architecture for facial emotion expression recognition, and mapping criteria to map estimated expressions and the resultant emotion (positive, negative, neutral). The CNN-BiLSTM model achieved an accuracy of 91% on a test set consisting of seven basic emotions of anger, disgust, fear, happy, surprise, sadness and neutral from the Denver Intensity of Spontaneous Facial Action (DISFA) data. The data set for affective States in E-Environment(DAiSEE) labeled with boredom, frustration, confusion, and engagement was used to further test the proposed model to estimate the seven basic expressions and re-evaluate the mapping model used for mapping expressions to emotions.

Keywords: Facial emotion expression recognition · Deep learning · Emotion estimation · Expression to emotion mapping

1 Introduction

Virtual interactions are becoming more widespread, especially in the aftermath of the COVID outbreak, when most firms were forced to use online setups. As a result, computer vision and machine learning research have exploded. Systems

E. Jembere et al. (Eds.): SACAIR 2021, CCIS 1551, pp. 274–286, 2022.
https://doi.org/10.1007/978-3-030-95070-5_18

are now being designed to perceive, understand, and evaluate a wide spectrum of emotions as a result of this rapid development. A range of modalities, including facial expressions, speech, posture, gesture, and physiological signals, can be used to identify human emotions. Facial emotion expression recognition is an important area of research in computer vision and machine learning.

Facial emotional expressions are spontaneous movements that occur when one or more of the facial muscles are engaged. Each or a combination of these facial muscles are typically coded as Action Units (AU) as per Facial Action Coding System [39]. Action units are the smallest, visibly significant switch in facial actions, which can be presented individually, or in combinations to depict facial expressions. Facial expressions are an important tool through which humans communicate with each other. During interactions, social information is conveyed via different types of facial expressions. It was stressed by Zhou et al. [6] that, in day-to-day communication, language, voice, and facial expression are used to transmit information and that facial emotion expressions account for 55% of the overall information communicated among these three.

Facial expressions have been proved to be universal; that is, the facial expressions exhibited by individuals from one geographical location are the same all over the world. Strong evidence of universality was discovered by Dr. Paul Ekman [1], using people of different cultures from different geographical areas. Ekman et al. [1–3] also opined that there are seven basic emotions, namely, sadness, happiness, fear, disgust, anger, contempt, and surprises. However, Jack et al. [35] on the other hand, was of the opinion that emotionally inclined facial expressions are culturally distinctive, debunking the idea that human emotions are universally expressed by the same set of six distinct facial expression signals.

Recognition of spontaneous expressions from human faces has a wide range of applications which includes human-computer interaction, automated tutoring, smart environment, driver warning systems, among others. Several machine learning approaches have been adopted to recognize an individual's emotions from their facial expressions, one of such is explored in this paper.

The remaining paper is organized in the following way: Sect. 2 discusses related research on facial expression emotion analysis. The methodology of the proposed work is presented in Sect. 3, while the results are presented in Sect. 4. Section 5 contains the discussions, while Sect. 6 provides a conclusion and sheds some light on future work.

2   Related Work

Owing to the vast range of applications based on facial expression and emotion identification, this topic in recent decades, has received widespread attention. In the work of Zadeh et al. [4], a framework for emotion recognition based on deep learning was presented. Gabor filters were employed to extract features from the samples collected from the JAFFE (Japanese Female Facial Emotion) data set. A Convolutional Neural Network (CNN) was utilized to classify the data into seven basic emotions of anger, disgust, fear, sad, happy, surprise and neutral. This cascade of Gabor filters and CNNs achieved an accuracy of 87% when compared to standard CNN which reported accuracy of 51%.

Wu et al. [5] proposed a cascade of decision and Gabor filter-based technique for unconstrained FER, with the belief that less difficult expressions are recognized first. They trained five models in a cascade to recognize a specific facial emotion. Happy emotion was classified by the first binary classifier, achieving the highest accuracy, second binary classifier classified surprise, with the second highest accuracy, the third binary classifier classified neutral emotion and the fourth model classified sad, while the last model was a three-class classifier for angry, disgust, and fear. Average accuracy of 77.6% was achieved on the FER2013 dataset using the final set of classifiers.

A deep CNN that recognizes 5 different human emotions, namely anger, neutral, sad, happy and surprise was presented by Pranav et al. [7]. Their model achieved an accuracy of 78.04% on test dataset, using 2D CNN for recognition. Guetari et al. [8] presented an automatic approach for distinguishing basic facial emotions such as joy, anger, sadness, contempt, surprise, fear, and neutral in video streams. JAFFE and the extended Cohn Kanade (CK+) data sets were used in the experiments. The study reached a best accuracy of 56.54% and 89.73% on JAFFE and CK+ data sets using bi-linear VGG-19 architecture.

John et al. [9] proposed a real-time facial emotion recognition system by implementing a hybrid method of feature extraction, pre-processing methods like facial landmark and HOG were integrated into a CNN. Both JAFEE and FER2013 datasets were used for experiments. Their method achieved an accuracy of 74.4% and 90.69% on FER2013 and JAFFE datasets respectively. Vulpe-Griborasi et al. in [10], hyper-parameters of a CNN were optimized to increase the ability of the architecture for the recognition of facial emotion. This was achieved by generating and training models based on Random Search algorithms. The optimal model was trained and evaluated using the FER2013 dataset and accuracy of 72.16% was reported.

Srivastava et al. [11] proposed the use of deep learning to identify seven main human emotions such as anger, disgust, fear, happiness, sadness, surprise and neutral. Their work further maps the classified emotion expressions to the corresponding emojis. This was achieved by training a CNN model both for feature extraction and classification using samples from the FER2013 dataset. Their work achieved an accuracy of 90.4%, 87.4%, 90.8%, 89.4%, 84.2%, 89.8% and 85.2% in classifying anger, disgust, fear, happy, neutral, sad, and surprise emotions respectively.

Qiu et al. [12] proposed a facial expression recognition framework that relies only on facial landmarks. In their framework, the facial landmark feature was first extracted and fed into a shallow network called a Multi-Layered Perceptron (MLP) for classification. Their framework produced an accuracy of 87.7% on CK+ dataset.

Despite the various methods that have been developed in recent years, developing an effective system for facial emotion identification remains a technological issue that has not been entirely overcome. In essence, a number of issues have yet to be effectively addressed. As a result, the authors seek to contribute to previous work in the proposed research by employing a temporal approach to facial emotion recognition, mapping of the estimated emotions into positive, negative and neutral emotion types. The estimated emotions were further mapped with affective states of boredom, engagement, confusion and frustration for further analysis. Such recognition and estimation of emotional states have the potential to improve existing e-learning platforms and help generate appropriate feedback to end-users.

The proposed study used transfer learning for extracting discriminate features using a CNN architecture and a bidirectional LSTM for capturing and encoding both spatial and temporal features from facial emotion data to estimate the presence of basic emotions such as anger, disgust, happy, fear, surprise, sadness and neutral. The use of LSTM has been notable for its ability to learn order dependency [38] in sequential data. Estimated emotions are further mapped into high-level emotion labels such as positive, negative and neutral which provides a general idea about the type of emotion experienced by users during a session. To achieve this, a Visual Geometry Group (VGG-19) pre-trained CNN network is fine-tuned for the extraction of facial features from image samples obtained from DISFA database. VGG-19 pre-trained network for feature extraction is motivated due to its remarkable performance compared to other pre-trained CNNs [Murali et al., Wen et al., Apostolopoulos et al., and Bouaafia et al.] [31–34]. Further experiments to consolidate the emotions to affective states mapping is carried out using samples from DAiSEE dataset.

3 Methodology

The proposed research comprises of the following stages: Stage 1: feature extraction using pre-trained VGG-19 and Bi-LSTM classifier for training and validation for emotion recognition, Stage 2: model testing using samples from DISFA and DAiSEE datasets Stage 3: mapping of the basic emotions into positive, negative, and neutral emotions. Figure 1 gives the framework of the proposed model.

3.1 Experimental Data

DISFA dataset was used for the baseline experiments. This dataset consists of samples from 27 adult subjects, that include 12 females and 15 males from different regions of the globe. Each participant was asked to watch a 4-min video clip that lasted 242 s and the response was recorded. The video that was observed by the participant is supposed to depict spontaneous action units in response to the video clips' reactions. The video that was observed by the participants are made up of 9 portions, the majority of which were sourced from YouTube [13]. The participants' facial emotional behavior was filmed at a high resolution of 1024×768 pixels under equal illumination for each participant.

The current work used a total of 26,603 video sequences from the sample video. A total of 24,329 video sequences were used for training and validation, while 2,274 video sequences were used to test the model.

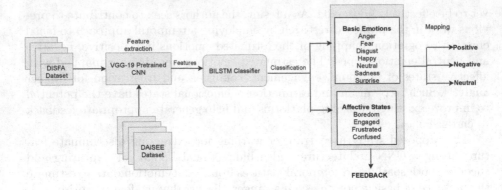

Fig. 1. The CNN-BiLSTM framework

DAiSEE was used in the second experiment to verify the mapping of emotions from the first experiment. DAiSEE is a publicly available data set that consists of 9,068 video sequences captured from 112 Asian subjects. The dataset was categorized into four emotional states namely, boredom, engagement, confusion, and frustration using crowd annotations, Gupta et al. [16]. The current work used 2,727 sample video sequences for further testing the proposed model.

3.2   Feature Extraction

The feature from the frame sequences that were used for training, validation and initial testing were extracted using the VGG-19 pre-trained network. VGG-19 is a variant of VGG models that is composed of 19 layers which include; 16 convolutions layers, 3 fully connected layers, 5 max pool layers, and 1 softmax layer as presented by Simonya et al. [17]. VGG-19 was trained on the ImageNet database and can classify 100- categories of objects according to George et al. [18]. The pre-trained VGG-19 accepts the input video sequences which have been split into different frames of images. The frames were reshaped to 224×224×3 each, which is the input size required by the VGG-19 network, and passed through the VGG-19 network for the extraction of discriminate features of the input images. The images forward propagate through the network and the propagation stops at the last max-pool layer, where the value of the output shape was 512 which was used as the feature vector. The network therefore produced a 2D vector of size 24,329 × 512.

3.3   Classification

A bi-directional LSTM was used for categorizing the discriminating features extracted by the VGG-19 pre-trained CNN into various estimated emotion expressions. The bi-directional LSTM is an expanded version of the LSTM model that is made up of two LSTMs: the first LSTM is applied to the input sequence data in the forward direction, while the second LSTM takes in the reverse structure of the input sequence. This type of LSTM structure aids in the learning of long-term dependencies and has the potential to increase a model's accuracy according to Rahman et al., and Graves et al. [19,20]. Baldi et al. and Xia et al. [22,23] also stressed that application of LSTM in a bidirectional setup will lead to an improvement in learning long-term dependencies and invariably, will improve the accuracy of the model.

In a bidirectional LSTM, the forward hidden layer h_t^f processes the input in ascending order, that is t= 1,2,3....T, while the backward hidden layer h_t^b processes the input sequence in descending order that is, t= T,.....3,2,1. Lastly, both layers are combined to generate output Y_t [21]. Thus, a biLSTM is implemented using the following equations:

$$h_t^f = \tanh(W_{xh}^f xt + W_{hh}^f h_{t-1}^f + b_h^f) \tag{1}$$

$$h_t^b = \tanh(W_{xh}^b xt + W_h^b hh_{t+1}^b + b_h^b) \tag{2}$$

$$Y_t = W_{hy}^f h_t^f + W_{hy}^b h_t^b + by \tag{3}$$

Where tanh is an activation function of the hidden layer, W is a weight matrix and W_{xh} is a weight connecting input (x) to the hidden layer (h), and b is a bias vector for both the forward and backward hidden layers h_t^f and h_t^b as given in Eqs. (1) and (2).

3.4 Evaluation Metrics

The proposed model was evaluated using the following metrics: accuracy, precision, recall, and F-1 score. The precision (P), recall (R), and F1 score computations are listed below.

$$Precision(P) = \frac{TP}{TP + FP} \tag{4}$$

$$Recall(R) = \frac{TP}{TP + FN} \tag{5}$$

$$F1\ Score = \frac{2 * P * R}{P + R} \tag{6}$$

where TP denotes True Positive, TN denotes True Negative, FP denotes False Positive, and FN denotes False Negative.

3.5 Experiment Details

The proposed framework was implemented on a computer with an Intel Core i7 8th generation processor, 16GB of RAM, and the Linux operating system. The codes were run in a tensor-flow environment, with a tensor-board used to display the training/validation epochs, accuracy, and loss. The work stages include:

Training and Validation. The input to the biLSTM is a sequence of frames, where we have 24329 × 512 number of features from each frame and were split into a training dataset and validation datasets, then input to the bi-LSTM classifier for classification. The bi-LSTM network performs the learning task on both the training and validation input features, considering both the temporal and spatial features of the samples then gives a classification accuracy over the validation data set With a batch size of 128 and a maximum of 100 epochs. The trained temporal model was tested with the remaining DISFA dataset which had not been part of the model training previously. An average accuracy of 91% was achieved on seven basic emotions of anger, disgust, fear, happiness, sadness, surprise, and neutral.

Mapping of Recognised Emotions. Following the classification, the researchers looked through a variety of sources to map the identified emotion expressions of anger, disgust, fear, happiness, sadness, surprise, and neutral into positive, negative, and neutral categories. The sources include the mapping provided by Sathik et al., Kapoor et al., Pan et al., and Zakka et al. [24–27]. Upon experimentation, the baseline mappings were adapted based on the experimental results that were put together to consolidate the emotion mappings.

Table 1 provides a summary of the mapping results of various emotions based on literature for the study.

Table 1. Initial mapping of the basic emotions to positive, negative and neutral categories

Emotions	Authors				
	Sathik et al.	Kapoor et al.	Pan et al.	Zakka et al.	Current study
Anger	Negative	Negative	Positive	Negative	**Negative**
Disgust	-	Negative	Negative	Negative	**Negative**
Fear	Positive	Positive	-	Positive	**Positive**
Happy	-	Positive	Positive	Positive	**Positive**
Sadness	Negative	Negative	-	Negative	**Negative**
Surprise	Positive	Positive	Positive	Positive	**Positive**
Neutral	-	-	Positive	Positive	**Neutral**

4 Experiments Results

The results of the test experiments conducted on the test sample set from DISFA and DAiSEE are discussed in the following sections.

4.1   Test Result on DISFA Dataset

The model was tested with 2,274 unseen sequence samples from DISFA dataset which resulted in an accuracy of 91% in classifying the seven basic emotions. Figure 2 illustrates the confusion matrix of the test experiment from the CNN-biLSTM framework. Table 2 presents the evaluation metrics from the test experiments. This study also compared the result of the experiment with related studies and is presented in Table 3.

Table 2. Evaluation metrics for the DISFA test experiment

Emotion	Precision	Recall	F1-Score	Samples
Anger	0.99	0.95	0.97	434
Disgust	0.99	0.95	0.97	267
Fear	0.71	0.62	0.66	204
Happy	0.92	0.95	0.93	470
Neutral	1.00	0.99	1.00	330
Sadness	0.80	0.81	0.81	253
Surprise	0.81	0.92	0.86	316
			0.91	2,274

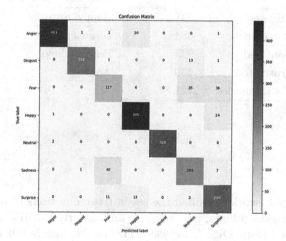

Fig. 2. The confusion matrix depicting the results obtained on DISFA test datset

Table 3. Comparison of results with related studies

Authors	Dataset	Model	Accuracy
Akay et al. [28]	DISFA	Stacked CNN	55%
Hernandez et al. [29]	DISFA	DeepFN	69.7%
Hinduja et al. [30]	DISFA+	CNN	79%
Amal et al. [36]	FER2013	CNN	73.12%
Boughida et al. [37]	DAiSEE	ResNet + TCN	63.9%
Current Study	DISFA	CNN-BILSTM	91%

4.2   Testing the Framework on DAiSEE Dataset

The work explored the mapping further through a second testing. The goal was to estimate the labels for samples from DAiSEE dataset which had been labelled for affective states, and see if the estimated emotion expressions do map onto their relevant affective states. The proposed framework was tested on 2,727 unlabelled sample video sequences from DAiSEE dataset. The results from the experiments are shown in Table 4.

Table 4. Testing with DAiSEE

DAiSEE Labels	Number tested	Estimated emotion from CNN-biLSTM
Engaged	691	Happy, Surprise
Boredom	683	Disgust
Confused	923	Fear, Sadness
Frustrated	430	Anger
Total samples	2727	

5   Discussion

The suggested framework classified the seven basic emotions of anger, fear, disgust, happy, neutral, sadness, and surprise and reported a 91% accuracy when tested on samples from DISFA dataset. The model misclassified 3% of anger emotion samples, 3% of disgust emotion samples, 34% of fear emotion samples, 7% of happy emotion samples, 19% of sadness emotion samples, and 14% of surprise emotion samples. In general, the model has produced results that are comparable to those of other recent studies as shown in Table 3.

Based on a review of relevant literature, the classified emotions were further mapped into positive, negative, and neutral categories. To determine the first mappings, the researchers used another dataset, the DAiSEE dataset, which included labels for the emotional states of boredom, engagement, frustration, and confusion. From the second experimental results it was noted that "engaged" affective state was estimated as happy and surprise emotions. "Engaged" affective state is considered as a positive state and so are the happy and surprise expressions [24–27]. This consolidates our initial mapping of both happy and surprise emotion expressions as positive. Similarly, "confused" affective states was estimated as fear and sadness emotions by the trained CNN-biLSTM framework. "Confused" affective state is considered as a negative affective state and so is sadness emotions [24–27], but fear was considered as positive affective state, but the model maps it to confused affective states, which is negative affect. This also consolidates our initial mapping of sadness emotion expression as negative and fear is been verified to be a negative emotion as against the literature survey. "Boredom" affective state was estimated by the trained CNN-biLSTM framework as disgust emotion expression. "Boredom" affective states is considered a negative emotion, so also is disgust emotion [25–27]. This also consolidates our initial mapping of disgust emotion expression as negative. "Frustrated" affective state was estimated as anger emotion expression, and "frustrated" affective state is considered a negative state, so is anger emotion [24–27]. This also consolidates our initial mapping of anger emotion expression as negative.

The work therefore verifies the initial mapping in Table 1. As a result, the research concludes that the seven basic emotions expression can likewise be mapped to these affective states. This can be used to gain a better grasp and estimation of a user's emotions during an online session.

6   Conclusion and Future Works

Automatic emotion recognition based on facial expression is an interesting study area in computer vision and machine learning that has been presented and utilized in several fields including security, health, and human-machine interactions. Researchers in this domain are interested in developing strategies to understand, code, and extract facial expressions to improve prediction. With deep learning's astonishing success, several architectures were proposed in the literature to improve the performance of facial emotion expression recognition systems. Despite the extensive success of conventional facial recognition systems based on the extraction of handcrafted features, researchers have turned to deep learning in the last decade owing to their such numerous applications.

In the online scenario, estimating the user's affective states through their facial emotion recognition and further mapping them into affective states is useful for providing feedback to users. The real-time estimation of affective states is useful in areas such as education, to understand the learner's comprehension during an online learning session; in online advertising and market analysis to know which product is fascinating to the audience; in health sectors where doctors can interact virtually with patients, and understand the patients through their facial emotion expression; in sentiment analysis to understand emotions through written texts and so on.

The proposed study combines the use of machine learning models, a CNN-biLSTM model, existing datasets and mappings between emotion expression and affective states which has the potential to enhance the user behavior understanding.

Experimental results on the test dataset were a classification accuracy of 91% for the discriminate classification of anger, disgust, fear, happy, sadness, surprise, and neutral emotions. The proposed CNN-biLSTM architecture outperformed the models proposed by Akay et al., Hernandez et al., Hinduja et al., Amal et al., and Boughida et al. [28–30, 36, 37]. The estimated emotions were then mapped onto positive, negative or neutral states based on the initial mapping. To further consolidate the mapping, experiments were carried where affective states (engaged, frustrated, confused and boredom) were mapped onto positive, negative and neutral states. The work deduced from the experiments, that, it is possible to estimate the user's affective states using the facial emotion expression recognition, mapping the estimated emotions to positive, negative and neutral emotions, and analyzing the result from the mapping. Similarly, the estimated emotion can be mapped into the affective states of boredom, engaged, confused and frustrated. It was noted that positive emotions and positive affective states correlate, and so do the negative emotions and negative affective states.

It is envisaged that estimating emotion and or affective states will help improve the existing online platforms and can be used for useful feedback generation.

The proposed framework can be further enhanced by incorporating new modalities such as physiological signals, voice, text and body language. It is also worth exploring combining modalities such as facial data and text to better estimate ones' emotional state.

References

1. Ekman, P., Keltner, D.: Universal facial expressions of emotion. In: Segerstrale, U.P., Molnar, P. (eds.) Nonverbal Communication: Where Nature Meets Culture, vol. 27, p. 46 (1997)
2. Ekman, P., Cordaro, D.: What is meant by calling emotions basic. Emot. Rev. 3(4), 364–70 (2011)
3. Ekman, P.: Basic emotions. Handbook Cogn. Emot. 98(45–60), 16 (1999)
4. Zadeh, M.M., Imani, M., Majidi, B.: Fast facial emotion recognition using convolutional neural networks and Gabor filters. In: 2019 5th Conference on Knowledge Based Engineering and Innovation (KBEI) 2019, pp. 577–581. IEEE (2019)
5. Wu, Y., Zhang, L., Chen, G., Michelini, P.N.: Unconstrained facial expression recogniton based on cascade decision and Gabor filters. In: 2020 25th International Conference on Pattern Recognition (ICPR), 10 January 2021, pp. 3336–3341. IEEE (2021)
6. Zhou, J., Zhang, S., Mei, H., et al.: A method of facial expression recognition based on Gabor and NMF. Pattern Recogn. Image Anal. 26(1), 119–124 (2016)
7. Pranav, E., Kamal, S., Chandran, C.S., Supriya, M.H.: Facial emotion recognition using deep convolutional neural network. In: 2020 6th International Conference on Advanced Computing and Communication Systems (ICACCS), 6 March 2020, pp. 317–320. IEEE (2020)

8. Guetari R, Chetouani A, Tabia H, Khlifa N. Real time emotion recognition in video stream, using B-CNN and F-CNN. In: 2020 5th International Conference on Advanced Technologies for Signal and Image Processing (ATSIP), 2 September 2020, pp. 1–6. IEEE (2020)

9. John, A., Abhishek, M.C., Ajayan, A.S., Sanoop, S., Kumar, V.R.: Real-time facial emotion recognition system with improved preprocessing and feature extraction. In: 2020 Third International Conference on Smart Systems and Inventive Technology (ICSSIT), 20 August 2020, pp. 1328–1333. IEEE (2020)

10. Vulpe-Grigoraşi, A., Grigore, O.: Convolutional neural network hyperparameters optimization for facial emotion recognition. In: 2021 12th International Symposium on Advanced Topics in Electrical Engineering (ATEE), 25 March 2021, pp. 1–5. IEEE (2021)

11. Srivastava, S., Gupta, P., Kumar, P.: Emotion recognition based emoji retrieval using deep learning. In: 2021 5th International Conference on Trends in Electronics and Informatics (ICOEI), 3 June 2021, pp. 1182–1186. IEEE (2021)

12. Qiu, Y., Wan, Y.: Facial expression recognition based on landmarks. In: 2019 IEEE 4th Advanced Information Technology, Electronic and Automation Control Conference (IAEAC), 20 December 2019, vol. 1, pp. 1356–1360. IEEE (2019)

13. Mavadati, S.M., Mahoor, M.H., Bartlett, K., Trinh, P., Cohn, J.F.: DISFA: a spontaneous facial action intensity database. IEEE Trans. Affect. Comput. 4(2), 151–60 (2013)

14. Benitez-Quiroz, C.F., Wang, Y., Martinez, A.M.: Recognition of action units in the wild with deep nets and a new global-local loss. In: ICCV 2017, pp. 3990–3999 (2017)

15. Kollias, D., Zafeiriou, S.: A multi-task learning and generation framework: valence-arousal, action units and primary expressions. arXiv preprint arXiv:1811.07771 (2018)

16. Gupta, A., D'Cunha, A., Awasthi, K., Balasubramanian, V.: DAiSEE: towards user engagement recognition in the wild. arXiv preprint arXiv:1609.01885 (2018)

17. Simonyan, K., Zisserman, A.: Very deep convolutional networks for large-scale image recognition. arXiv preprint (2014)

18. George, D., Shen, H., Huerta, E.A.: Deep transfer learning: a new deep learning glitch classification method for advanced LIGO. arXiv preprint arXiv:1706.07446 (2017)

19. Rahman, M., Watanobe, Y., Nakamura, K.: A bidirectional LSTM language model for code evaluation and repair. Symmetry 13(2), 247 (2021)

20. Graves, A., Jaitly, N., Mohamed, A.R.: Hybrid speech recognition with deep bidirectional LSTM. In: 2013 IEEE Workshop on Automatic Speech Recognition and Understanding, pp. 273–278. IEEE (2013)

21. Siami-Namini, S., Tavakoli, N., Namin, A.S.: The performance of LSTM and BiLSTM in forecasting time series. In: 2019 IEEE International Conference on Big Data (Big Data), pp. 3285–3292. IEEE (2019)

22. Baldi, P., Brunak, S., Frasconi, P., Soda, G., Pollastri, G.: Exploiting the past and the future in protein secondary structure prediction. Bioinformatics 15(11), 937–46 (1999)

23. Xia, T., Song, Y., Zheng, Y., Pan, E., Xi, L.: An ensemble framework based on convolutional bi-directional LSTM with multiple time windows for remaining useful life estimation. Comput. Ind. 115 103182 (2020)

24. Sathik, M., Jonathan, S.G.: Effect of facial expressions on student's comprehension recognition in virtual educational environments. SpringerPlus 2(1), 1–9 (2013)

25. Kapoor, A., Mota, S., Picard, R.W.: Towards a learning companion that recognizes affect. In: AAAI Fall Symposium 2001, vol. 543, pp. 2–4 (2001)
26. Pan, M., Wang, J., Luo, Z.: Modelling study on learning affects for classroom teaching/learning auto-evaluation. Science 6(3), 81–6 (2018)
27. Zakka, B.E., Vadapalli, H.: Estimating student learning affect using facial emotions. In: 2020 2nd International Multidisciplinary Information Technology and Engineering Conference (IMITEC), pp. 1–6. IEEE (2020)
28. Akay, S., Arica, N.: Stacking multiple cues for facial action unit detection. Vis. Comput. 1–16 (2021). https://doi.org/10.1007/s00371-021-02291-3
29. Hernandez, J., McDuff, D., Fung, A., Czerwinski, M.: DeepFN: towards generalizable facial action unit recognition with deep face normalization. arXiv preprint arXiv:2103.02484 (2021)
30. Hinduja, S., Canavan, S.: Real-time action unit intensity detection. In: 2020 15th IEEE International Conference on Automatic Face and Gesture Recognition (FG 2020), p. 916 (2020). https://doi.org/10.1109/FG47880.2020.00026
31. Murali, S., Deepu. R., Shivamurthy, R.C.: ResNet-50 vs VGG-19 vs training from scratch: a comparative analysis of the segmentation and classification of Pneumonia from chest x-ray images. In: Global Transitions Proceedings (2021)
32. Wen, L., Li, X., Li, X., Gao, L.: A new transfer learning based on VGG-19 network for fault diagnosis. In: 2019 IEEE 23rd International Conference on Computer Supported Cooperative Work in Design (CSCWD), 6 May 2019, pp. 205–209. IEEE (2019)
33. Apostolopoulos, I.D., Mpesiana, T.A.: Covid-19: automatic detection from x-ray images utilizing transfer learning with convolutional neural networks. Phys. Eng. Sci. Med. 43(2), 635–40 (2020)
34. Bouaafia, S., Messaoud, S., Maraoui, A., Ammari, A.C., Khriji, L., Machhout, M.: Deep pre-trained models for computer vision applications: traffic sign recognition. In: 2021 18th International Multi-Conference on Systems, Signals and Devices (SSD), 22 March 2021, pp. 23–28. IEEE (2021)
35. Jack, R.E., Garrod, O.G., Yu, H., Caldara, R., Schyns, P.G.: Facial expressions of emotion are not culturally universal. Proc. Nat. Acad. Sci. 109(19), 7241–4 (2012)
36. Amal, V.S., Suresh, S., Deepa, G.: Real-time emotion recognition from facial expressions using convolutional neural network with Fer2013 dataset. In: Karuppusamy, P., Perikos, I., García Márquez, F.P. (eds.) Ubiquitous Intelligent Systems. SIST, vol. 243, pp. 541–551. Springer, Singapore (2022). https://doi.org/10.1007/978-981-16-3675-2_41
37. Boughida, A., Kouahla, M.N., Lafifi, Y.: A novel approach for facial expression recognition based on Gabor filters and genetic algorithm. Evol. Syst. 1–15 (2021). https://doi.org/10.1007/s12530-021-09393-2
38. Brownlee, J.: A Gentle Introduction to Long Short-Term Memory Networks by the Experts. Mach. Learn. Mastery 1, 19 (2017)
39. Clark, E.A., et al.: The facial action coding system for characterization of human affective response to consumer product-based stimuli: a systematic review. Front. Psychol. 11, 920 (2020)

Full Rotation Hyper-ellipsoid Multivariate Adaptive Bandwidth Kernel Density Estimator

Terence L. van Zyl[✉][iD]

Institute for Intelligent Systems, University of Johannesburg,
Johannesburg, South Africa

Abstract. Adaptive bandwidth kernel density estimators (AB-KDEs) have received attention from the academic community due to an analytical promise of increased performance over classical estimators. However, the field is fragmented, and there exists no comprehensive comparison of the existing state-of-the-art AB-KDEs. We provide a comparison of some state-of-the-art and classical AB-KDE methods as well as a computational framework. We also present a novel implementation of a full principal axes rotation hyper-ellipsoid variant of the k-Nearest Neighbours algorithm and a Gaussian extension to K-NN. The extensive experimental results show the fixed bandwidth rule-of-thumb methods achieve satisfactory results. Further, the balloon estimators are shown to be superior in the higher dimensional spaces, with higher modes or data on non-linear manifolds. The sample point estimators show utility when data are scarce in low dimensions. The empirical results show that our full rotation hyper-ellipsoid estimator and our Gaussian K-NN are state-of-the-art and will have a significant positive impact on data analysis algorithms. Especially algorithms which depend upon underlying density estimates on "complex" higher-dimensional data.

Keywords: Kernel density estimator · Adaptive bandwidth · Multivariate

1 Introduction

The increased move towards using adaptive bandwidth kernel density estimators (AB-KDEs) in non-linear, high—volume,—mode, and—dimensional spaces necessitates empirical evidence around which of the plethora of methods one should be utilising. The utility of AB-KDEs in these spaces is especially prevalent in applications such as pilot function estimation, machine learning, background modelling, and anomaly detection [20, 26, 30, 34, 36].

Specific applications extend to activities like geospatial regions' analysis, epidemiology, pattern classification and region of interest tracking in computer vision [3, 4, 8, 10, 19, 27, 38]. Other uses include the summarization of Bayesian

© Springer Nature Switzerland AG 2022
E. Jembere et al. (Eds.): SACAIR 2021, CCIS 1551, pp. 287–303, 2022.
https://doi.org/10.1007/978-3-030-95070-5_19

posteriors, in classification, for discriminant analysis and in Monte Carlo methods [5].

A substantial body of work has been dedicated to the theoretical analysis of AB-KDE methods [25]. Additionally, studies have been done that empirically compare these methods in lower-dimensional spaces [12,23]. However, an empirical comparison of the various AB-KDE methods and classical methods under different non-linear manifold embeddings, modes, sample sizes and dimensionality is lacking. It is important to acknowledge no work could cover the breadth or depth of this field. Instead, we have selected the methods most commonly found in R, Python and the literature.

In this paper, an empirical comparison, using simulated synthetic data, of a subset of AB-KDE methods is presented. Further, we present two novel extensions to the balloon estimators that outperform the present methods in the high dimensional multi-modal spaces. The two new novel methods are a full rotation hyper-ellipsoid "Terrel K-NN" balloon estimator and "Gaussian K-NN" balloon estimator.

The remainder of the paper follows as background in Sect. 2, our proposed methods in Sect. 3, methodology in Sect. 4 and the results and discussion in Sect. 5. The below experiments, as well as the implementations of the AB-KDEs considered in this paper, are available online at https://github.com/tvanzyl/adaptive_bandwidth_kde.

2   Multivariate Adaptive Bandwidth Kernel Density Estimators

AB-KDEs are divided into two major groups: balloon estimators and sample point estimators. Balloon estimators try to optimise the bandwidth $\mathbf{H}(\mathbf{y})$ of the KDE

$$\hat{f}(\mathbf{y}) = \frac{1}{n\,|\mathbf{H}(\mathbf{y})|} \sum_{i=1}^{n} K\left(\mathbf{H}(\mathbf{y}), (\mathbf{x}_i - \mathbf{y})\right) \tag{1}$$

given the point $\mathbf{y}$ at which sampling of the probability estimate is taking place and a set of samples $\mathbf{x}_i \in X$. Sample point estimators optimise the bandwidth $\mathbf{H}(\mathbf{x}_i)$ to be used for each of the sample points $\mathbf{x}_i \in X$ such that the KDE is given by

$$\hat{f}(\mathbf{y}) = \frac{1}{n} \sum_{i=1}^{n} \frac{1}{|\mathbf{H}(\mathbf{x}_i)|} K\left(\mathbf{H}(\mathbf{x}_i), (\mathbf{x}_i - \mathbf{y})\right). \tag{2}$$

In considering the above Eqs. 1 and 2 it is assumed that K is the multivariate Gaussian kernel unless stated otherwise. Further, the bandwidth $\mathbf{H}$ may be regularised as follows [22]: $\mathbf{H} \in \mathcal{H}_1$: scalar bandwidths $\{h^2; h > 0\}$, $\mathbf{H} \in \mathcal{H}_2$: diagonal bandwidths $\{\mathrm{diag}(h_1^2, \ldots, h_d^2); h_i > 0\}$ vector, and $\mathbf{H} \in \mathcal{H}_3$: full covariance bandwidth matrices $\{\mathbf{\Sigma}\}$.

2.1   Balloon Estimators

Balloon estimators exploit properties in the region of $\mathbf{y}$ to select the bandwidth. The most straightforward approach is through the use of the ratio of the nearest neighbours to the volume that encapsulates that set of points. These approaches are called K-Nearest Neighbour (K-NN) balloon estimators. Other mechanisms used to determine the local properties of $\mathbf{y}$ include Bayesian statistics.

Concerning the K-NN approaches, selection of k, the number of nearest neighbours, is crucial. Three rules are explored, these are Kung *et al.* [16], Hansen *et al.* 2009 [15] and the square root law. Given a d-dimensional space and n samples, for Hansen *et al.* [15] k is given by: $k = n^{4/(4+d)}$. Kung *et al.* [16] proposes that a better choice of k is given by: $k = (d-1)n^{1/d}$. Another popular choice for k is the simple square root law found in some software packages such as R. Here k is given by: $k = n^{1/2}$ and is equivalent to Kung when $d = 2$. The value of k drives the size of the bandwidth such that in Eq. 1 $\mathbf{H} \rightarrow \mathbf{H}(\mathbf{y}, k)$ is a function of $\mathbf{y}$ and k.

The second choice is that of a kernel K to be used. Loftsgaarden *et al.* 1965 [18] proposed the use of the volume of a d dimensional unit ball V_d as the kernel:

$$K \rightarrow V_d^{-1} \mathbb{1}_{[(\mathbf{x}_i - \mathbf{y}) \in \mathbf{H}(\mathbf{y}, k)]}, \tag{3}$$

where the bandwidth/radius $\mathbf{H}(\mathbf{y}, k)$ is the distance to the kth nearest point to $\mathbf{y}$, and $\mathbb{1}_{[]}$ is the indicator function. We take the normalization term $|\mathbf{H}(\mathbf{y}, k)| = R^d$ with $R = \max(\mathbf{H}(\mathbf{y}, k))$ as the distance to the kth nearest neighbour of $\mathbf{y}$.

Substituting K into Eq. 1 results in the "Loftsgaarden K-NN" balloon estimator of the form:

$$\hat{f}(\mathbf{y}) = \frac{k}{nR^d V_d} \tag{4}$$

Further to the above set of balloon estimators, we also consider the following Bayesian balloon estimators [17]. The first case uses the L_1 loss function and results in the "Lima Entropy" balloon estimator with a bandwidth given by:

$$\mathbf{H}(\mathbf{y}) = \frac{\left[\sum_{i=1}^{n} \omega_i \Delta_i^{-1}\right]^{-1}}{e+1}. \tag{5}$$

The second case uses the L_2 loss function resulting in the "Lima Quadratic" balloon estimator where the bandwidth is given by:

$$\mathbf{H}(\mathbf{y}) = \frac{\sum_{i=1}^{n} \omega_i \Delta_i}{e+1}. \tag{6}$$

In both of the "Lima ..." balloon estimators,

$$\omega_i = \frac{|\Delta_i|^{-(e+1)/2}}{\sum_{j=1}^{n} |\Delta_j|^{-(e+1)/2}} \quad \text{and} \quad \Delta_i = (\mathbf{y} - \mathbf{x}_i)(\mathbf{y} - \mathbf{x}_i)' + \Sigma_0 \tag{7}$$

where Σ_0 is the covariance matrix over the samples, and $e = n^{2/(d+4)} + p$.

2.2 Sample Point Estimators

The sample point estimators are somewhat more varied. We consider approaches that try to partition the data in some way and use either clustering, a pilot function, an entropy/likelihood measure or the K-NNs as a proxy to local density. In these methods, first, some approximate of the local density is arrived at. Second, we optimise a global parameter to scale the bandwidth appropriately. Two approaches to the optimisation of these global parameters are considered here. The first approach is back substitution. The assumption is the equation will converge to the actual estimate. We use a rule-of-thumb pilot density estimator for the initial value. The second is the Cross-validation Least Squares (CVLS) algorithm in d-dimensions. The reader is referred to Hall *et al.* 1983 [13] for a review of Cross-validation.

The first set of sample point estimators suggest that the local bandwidth $\mathbf{H}(\mathbf{x}_i)$ at a given sample point $\mathbf{x}_i$ can be adapted by optimising:

$$\mathbf{H}(\mathbf{x}_i) = (\Lambda_i)^{-\alpha}\,\mathbf{H}_0 \tag{8}$$

where α is the sensitivity parameter, $\mathbf{H}_0$ is a global bandwidth scaling factor and Λ_i are the local bandwidth scaling factors.

Silverman *et al.* [28] suggested that the local bandwidth factors Λ_i be the ratio of the density at $\mathbf{x}_i$ using a pilot function $\hat{f}(\mathbf{x}_i|\mathbf{H}_0)$ and the geometric mean g of the local densities, and that $\alpha = 1/2$ as per Abramson *et al.* [1]. This configuration gives rise to the "Silverman Pilot" sample point estimator, with a local bandwidth given by:

$$\mathbf{H}(\mathbf{x}_i) = \left(\frac{\hat{f}(\mathbf{x}_i|\mathbf{H}_0)}{g}\right)^{-\frac{1}{2}}\mathbf{H}_0 \tag{9}$$

where the pilot function $\hat{f}(\dots)$ is a KDE that uses a non-adaptive bandwidth and $\mathbf{H}_0$ is a pilot estimate of $\mathbf{H}$.

A good initial choice for $\mathbf{H}_0$ is obtained with a rule-of-thumb estimator. By back substitution of Eq. 9 through $\mathbf{H}_0 \leftarrow \mathbf{H}(\mathbf{x}_i)$ it is possible to optimise the adaptive bandwidth. It is also possible, as suggested by Silverman *et al.* 1986 [28] to optimise $\mathbf{H}_0$ directly using CVLS.

The next sample point estimator we consider is the "Breiman Pilot" sample point estimator. Breiman *et al.* 1977 [6] suggested that we could adapt the bandwidth $\mathbf{H}(\mathbf{x}_i)$ at a given sample point $\mathbf{x}_i$ through the use of the K-NNs, leading to a local bandwidth, to be used in Eq. 2, of the form:

$$\mathbf{H}(\mathbf{x}_i) = (R)^{-\frac{1}{d}}\,\mathbf{H}_0 \tag{10}$$

where R is the distance from $\mathbf{x}_i$ to the furthest of its K-NNs. Like in Eq. 2 for the K-NN balloon estimators we again define $|\mathbf{H}(\mathbf{x})| = |\mathbf{H}_0 R I_d| = (\mathbf{H}_0 R)^d$ and optimise through CVLS.

In the "Wu Cluster" sample point estimator, Wu *et al.* 2007 [32] suggested that $\Lambda_i = b(\mathbf{x}_i)$ be a function of the average local clustering of $\mathbf{x}_i$ within the dendrogram formed through average distance hierarchical clustering. For comparability, and unlike in the original paper, CVLS is used once again to optimise $\mathbf{H}_0$ in

$$\mathbf{H}(\mathbf{x}_i) = b(\mathbf{x}_i)\mathbf{H}_0. \tag{11}$$

Another class of sample point estimators adapt the bandwidth locally by maximising the likelihood of the AB-KDE given $\mathbf{H}(\mathbf{x}_i)$. For a review of this class of classifiers, the reader is referred to [30]. All of these bandwidths are adapted through an iterative scheme, and a lower bound is set as per van de Walt *et al.* 2017 [30] to regularise these methods. Two maximum likelihood (ML) adaptive kernel density estimators are considered.

The "Barnard ML" sample point estimator is given by an adaptive bandwidth [2]:

$$\mathbf{H}(\mathbf{x}_i) \leftarrow \frac{\sum_{j \neq i} (\mathbf{x}_i - \mathbf{x}_j)(\mathbf{x}_i - \mathbf{x}_j)^T K\left(\mathbf{H}(\mathbf{x}_i), (\mathbf{x}_i - \mathbf{y})\right)}{\sum_{j \neq i} K\left(\mathbf{H}(\mathbf{x}_i), (\mathbf{x}_i - \mathbf{y})\right)} \tag{12}$$

where $\mathbf{H} \in \mathcal{H}_2$.

The "VdWalt ML" sample point estimator is given by an adaptive bandwidth [30]:

$$\mathbf{H}(\mathbf{x}_i) \leftarrow \frac{\sum_{i=1}^{n} \frac{\sum_{j \neq i}(\mathbf{x}_i - \mathbf{x}_j)(\mathbf{x}_i - \mathbf{x}_j)^T K(\mathbf{H}(\mathbf{x}_i),(\mathbf{x}_i - \mathbf{y}))}{\hat{f}_{-1}(\mathbf{x}_i)}}{\sum_{i=1}^{n} \frac{\sum_{j \neq i} K(\mathbf{H}(\mathbf{x}_i),(\mathbf{x}_i - \mathbf{y}))}{\hat{f}_{-1}(\mathbf{x}_i)}} \tag{13}$$

where

$$\hat{f}_{-1}(\mathbf{y}) = \frac{1}{n-1} \sum_{i=1}^{n} \frac{1}{|\mathbf{H}(\mathbf{x}_i)|} K\left(\mathbf{H}(\mathbf{x}_i), (\mathbf{x}_i - \mathbf{y})\right) \tag{14}$$

is the leave-one-out AB-KDE and $\mathbf{H} \in \mathcal{H}_1$ and $\mathbf{H} \in \mathcal{H}_2$.

Finally, the "Sain Partition" sample point estimator, a classical method in low dimensional settings, is not considered. It is unclear how it should be extended to higher-dimensional spaces without the partitions becoming overly sparse [22].

2.3   Goodness of Fit Measures

To compare the above AB-KDEs we considered the following goodness-of-fit measures [7]: Integrated Mean Absolute Error (IMAE); Integrated Mean Squared Error (IMSE), Jensen-Shannon Divergence (JS); Kullback-Leibler Divergence (KD), and Differential Entropy (DE). It should be noted that only JS was the only one shown to converge sufficiently and consistently given a reasonable sample size [7]. This conclusion was upheld by our own experiments using an unseen sample of 2000 points and evaluating the previous set of goodness-of-fit measures on the experiments outlined below. As a result, JS with base two was chosen as a reasonable metric.

3   Proposed Balloon Methods

Terrel *et al.* 1992 [29] and Hall *et al.* 1994 [14] suggested the use of the radii of the smallest ellipsoid centred at $\mathbf{y}$ that encompasses the k nearest neighbours as the set $\mathbf{H}(\mathbf{y}, k)$ in Eq. 3 and the normalization term $|\mathbf{H}(\mathbf{y}, k)| = \prod \mathbf{H}(\mathbf{y}, k)$. However, these implementations were only attempted with axis aligned ellipsoids. We expand upon this work by considering a novel full rotation hyper-ellipsoid "Terrel K-NN" balloon estimator expressed as:

$$\hat{f}(\mathbf{y}) = \frac{k}{n \prod r_j V_d} \tag{15}$$

where r_j are the radii of said ellipsoid. In our implementation the rotation of the ellipsoid has been allowed to vary freely together with the volume by utilising the Minimum Volume Enclosing Ellipsoid algorithm of Moshtagh *et al.* 2005 [21].

The above K-NN balloon estimators lead one to consider what would occur if the kernel K was for instance replaced by Gaussian kernel with $\mathbf{H}(\mathbf{y}, k)$ as a covariance matrix. We further introduce the novel "Gaussian K-NN" balloon estimator where:

$$\mathbf{H}(\mathbf{y}, k) = \frac{R^d I_d}{\chi^2(0.6826, d)} \tag{16}$$

with χ^2 as the Chi-Squared distribution with dimensions as degrees of freedom and I_d the identity matrix. The resultant covariance matrix assumes that the radius R is effectively the 68.26[th] Percentile confidence ellipsoid. The Chi-Squared distribution does add additional hyper-parameters.

4   Empirical Experiments

The ten selected simulations are predominately from the literature and have been extended in some cases into higher dimensions. These are selected as they are the most commonly used simulations evidenced by the number of references next to each. The first five synthetic datasets are classical bivariate simulations from the literature and have the short names $e1 - 5$. Let $N(\bar{\mu}; \Sigma)$ denote a multivariate normal density with mean $\bar{\mu} = [\mu_1, \ldots, \mu_d]$ and covariance matrix Σ, then the functional forms of these synthetic dataset are given by:

$e1$: "Bimodal J" [31,35],

$$\frac{1}{2}N\left([2,2]; \begin{bmatrix} 1 & -\frac{9}{10} \\ -\frac{9}{10} & 1 \end{bmatrix}\right) + \frac{1}{2}N\left([-\frac{3}{2}, -\frac{3}{2}]; \begin{bmatrix} 1 & \frac{3}{10} \\ \frac{3}{10} & 1 \end{bmatrix}\right)$$

$e2$: "Skewed" [22,31,32],

$$\frac{1}{5}N\left([0,0]; \begin{bmatrix} 1 & 0 \\ 0 & 1 \end{bmatrix}\right) + \frac{1}{5}N\left([\frac{1}{2}, \frac{1}{2}]; \begin{bmatrix} \frac{4}{9} & 0 \\ 0 & \frac{4}{9} \end{bmatrix}\right) + \frac{3}{5}N\left([\frac{13}{12}, \frac{13}{12}]; \begin{bmatrix} \frac{25}{81} & 0 \\ 0 & \frac{25}{81} \end{bmatrix}\right)$$

e3: "Trimodal Gavel" [17,31,32,37],

$$\frac{9}{20}N\left([-\frac{6}{5},\frac{6}{5}];\begin{bmatrix}\frac{9}{25} & \frac{27}{250}\\ \frac{27}{250} & \frac{9}{25}\end{bmatrix}\right) + \frac{9}{20}N\left([\frac{6}{5},-\frac{6}{5}];\begin{bmatrix}\frac{9}{25} & -\frac{27}{125}\\ -\frac{27}{125} & \frac{9}{25}\end{bmatrix}\right) + \frac{2}{20}N\left([0,0];\begin{bmatrix}\frac{1}{16} & \frac{1}{80}\\ \frac{1}{80} & \frac{1}{16}\end{bmatrix}\right)$$

e4: "Trimodal λ" [22,31,37], and

$$\frac{3}{7}N\left([-1,0];\begin{bmatrix}\frac{9}{25} & \frac{63}{250}\\ \frac{63}{250} & \frac{49}{100}\end{bmatrix}\right) + \frac{3}{7}N\left([1,\frac{2}{\sqrt{3}}];\begin{bmatrix}\frac{9}{25} & 0\\ 0 & \frac{49}{100}\end{bmatrix}\right) +$$

$$\frac{1}{7}N\left([1,-\frac{2}{\sqrt{3}}];\begin{bmatrix}\frac{9}{25} & 0\\ 0 & \frac{49}{100}\end{bmatrix}\right) \quad (17)$$

e5: "Bimodal T" [17,37]:

$$\frac{1}{2}N\left([1,1];\begin{bmatrix}1 & 1\\ 1 & \frac{1}{2}\end{bmatrix}\right) + \frac{1}{2}N\left([-1,-1];\begin{bmatrix}1 & 1\\ 1 & -\frac{1}{2}\end{bmatrix}\right).$$

The synthetic datasets e6–8 are also taken from the literature but have been extended to d-dimensional space in some cases. The functional forms of these densities are given by:

e6: "Unimodal d-dimensions" with [11,37]:

$$\Sigma = \begin{bmatrix} 1 & \frac{9}{10} & \cdots & \frac{9}{10} \\ \frac{9}{10} & \ddots & & \vdots \\ \vdots & & \ddots & \frac{9}{10} \\ \frac{9}{10} & \cdots & \frac{9}{10} & 1 \end{bmatrix}$$

such that $N\left([0,\ldots,0];\Sigma\right)$.

e7: "Bimodal d-dimensions" with [11,37]:

$$\Sigma(\rho) = \frac{1}{1-\rho^{d-1}}\begin{bmatrix} 1 & \rho^1 & \cdots & \rho^{d-1} \\ \rho^1 & \ddots & & \vdots \\ \vdots & & \ddots & \rho^1 \\ \rho^{d-1} & \cdots & \rho^1 & 1 \end{bmatrix}$$

such that $\frac{1}{2}N\left([4,\ldots,4];\Sigma(\frac{9}{10})\right) + \frac{1}{2}\left([1,\ldots,1];\Sigma(\frac{7}{10})\right)$.

e8: "Bimodal 4-dimensions" with [17,37]:

$$\Sigma_1 = \begin{bmatrix} 1 & \frac{6}{10} & \frac{6}{10} & \frac{6}{10} \\ \frac{6}{10} & 1 & \frac{6}{10} & \frac{6}{10} \\ \frac{6}{10} & \frac{6}{10} & 1 & \frac{6}{10} \\ \frac{6}{10} & \frac{6}{10} & \frac{6}{10} & 1 \end{bmatrix} \quad \text{and} \quad \Sigma_2 = \begin{bmatrix} 1 & \frac{5}{10} & \frac{7}{10} & \frac{5}{10} \\ \frac{5}{10} & 1 & \frac{5}{10} & \frac{7}{10} \\ \frac{7}{10} & \frac{5}{10} & 1 & \frac{5}{10} \\ \frac{5}{10} & \frac{7}{10} & \frac{5}{10} & 1 \end{bmatrix}$$

such that $\frac{1}{2}N\left([1,\ldots,1];\Sigma_1\right) + \frac{1}{2}\left([-1,\ldots,-1];\Sigma_2\right)$.

The synthetic datasets e9–10 are not from the literature and have been constructed to test higher numbers of modes in d—dimensional space and the density estimation of a non-linear manifold. The forms of these synthetic datasets are given by:

e9: "m-modes d-dimensions" with a mixture of m randomly parametrised Gaussian distributions in d dimensional space. μ for each of the Gaussians is a d vector of uniformly distributed values in $[-0.5, 0.5]$. We use the make_sp_matrix of sklearn to generate a random Σ for each of the Gaussians.

e10: "∞-modes d-dimensions" is a hyper-ellipsoid in $d > 1$ dimensional space with the observations sampled uniformly from the surface of the ellipsoid:

$$1 = \sum_{i=1}^{d} \frac{y_i^2}{r_i^2}.$$

For each observation $\mathbf{x}$, some random noise $N([0, \dots, 0]; vI_d)$ is added where $v = 0.05\|\mathbf{x}\|$ is the scaled L_2 norm and makes the variance proportional to the distance from the centre of the ellipsoid.

4.1 Experimental Permutations

To evaluate the previous methods with respect to sample size, dimensionality and number of modes, the following parameters where considered: For dimensionality, $d \in 2, 3, 4, 5, 6$ and 7 are evaluated. Practically at dimensions 5 and higher, we will already start to feel the curse of dimensionality without incurring the increased computational cost for dimensions 8 and above [29]. The sample size $n \in 110, 175, 350, 800, 2100$ and 5700 correspond to the minimum recommended sample sizes at these dimensionalities [9,24].

We explore the effect of both modes and sample size in the region around $d \in 4, 6$. Terrell et al. 1992 [29] consider this to be a transition point for the efficiency of balloon estimators over sample point estimators. To evaluate the effect of changing sample size with fixed dimensions, we consider sample sizes of $\pm 10\%, \pm 30\%$ and $\pm 50\%$ of the minimum recommended sizes above. For number of modes $m \in 2, 3, 4, 5, 6$ and ∞ are evaluated. Here, ∞ refers to data lying on a non-linear manifold.

4.2 Experimental Evaluation and Ranking

For each synthetic dataset simulation and each method, the experiment is run 30 times. The JS values of the runs are pairwise ranked for all methods using a one-sided Kolmogorov-Smirnov (KS) statistic with $p = 0.05$ as per Zeng et al. 2017 [33]. If the results of the KS statistic are not significant, both methods receive a zero, otherwise, the worse performing method of the two receives the score. The final ranking for a method is the mean of its scores. The JS with base 2 ranges from 0–1 with 0 being no difference between the AB-KDE method and the actual distribution. As a result, the KS statistic has the same range with the maximum difference between two AB-KDEs being 1. The range of mean JS-KS rankings is also 0–1 with 0 being no difference and 1 the maximum difference.

The above JS-KS ranking broadly agrees with rankings obtained utilizing either the mean or median of the JS scores across all runs. However, the JS-KS ranking is less sensitive to outliers, ignores comparisons of non-significant differences and eliminates the need to consider the distribution of the results. We do however in some instances plot the actual JS scores where we wish to discuss the effects of increasing or decreasing certain experimental parameters, like dimensionality.

5   Results and Discussion

Let us consider initially the classical experiments from the literature. We have included all the AB-KDE methods and their scores using the JS-KS ranking as described in Subsect. 4.2 in Table 1. As per Farmen *et al.* 1999 [12] we see that AB-KDE methods do not substantively and consistently outperform constant bandwidth KDE methods such as Rule-of-Thumb $\mathcal{H}_2$ and $\mathcal{H}_3$ in a 2-dimensional setting.

We also note that sample point estimators generally outperform balloon estimators in 2-dimensional setting as per previous analytical arguments by Terrell *et al.* 1992 [29]. It is also interesting that $\mathcal{H}_2$ methods generally outperform their $\mathcal{H}_3$ counterparts. Given the computational cost of optimising the $\mathcal{H}_3$ parameter space, this parity in ranking is worth acknowledging.

Of particular interest is the synthetic dataset $e1$, where we see that both the sample point and balloon estimators perform well. It is worth noting the significant variance in the K-NN balloon estimators, over smoothing of Lima Entropy and the remarkable similarities between the sample point estimators. Aesthetically, Vd Walt Maximum Likelihood seems to be most representative. Synthetic dataset $e3$ is equally interesting as Wu Clustering does exceptionally well, and in $e5$ we see Lima Entropy doing remarkably well.

In the remainder of this discussion, we consider the higher-dimensional, higher-modes and non-linear manifold cases to evaluate how these AB-KDE methods perform when these factors are manipulated.

5.1   Increasing Sample Size Simulation Experiments

The research requires we first evaluate whether the sample sizes we have chosen are sufficient to provide meaningful results. In Fig. 1 we show the results of simulations $e8$ where we evaluate with increasing sample size how the various AB-KDE methods perform concerning their JS score. These results are similar to those of $e8$.

For readability, where a method has alternate variations, we have only included the best performing variation. Expressly, we have excluded Silverman Pilot CVLS $\mathcal{H}_2$; Silverman BackSub $\mathcal{H}_3$; Lima Entropy, Barnard; and K-NN alternatives with k values that performed worse.

Table 1. JS-KS rankings for classical simulations e1–5. $d(2)$ indicates 2-dimensions, $n(110)$ refers to a sample size, $m(2, 2, 3, 3, 3)$ describe the number of modes presented in increasing order for the experiments datasets. *(*This method)*

Name $d(2)$ $n(110)$ $m(2,2,3,3,3)$	e1	e5	e2	e3	e4
Rule-of-Thumb $\mathcal{H}_2$	0.556	0.010	0.021	0.540	0.129
Rule-of-Thumb $\mathcal{H}_3$	0.801	0.011	0.032	0.211	0.047
Silverman Pilot BackSub $\mathcal{H}_2$	0.425	**0.000**	**0.000**	0.399	0.035
Silverman Pilot BackSub $\mathcal{H}_3$	0.768	0.035	**0.000**	0.203	**0.000**
Silverman Pilot CVLS $\mathcal{H}_2$	**0.000**	0.010	**0.000**	**0.000**	0.076
Silverman Pilot CVLS $\mathcal{H}_3$	0.451	0.081	**0.000**	0.183	0.021
Breiman CVLS K-NN Kung	0.032	0.010	0.169	0.011	0.126
Breiman CVLS K-NN Hansen	0.032	0.021	0.185	0.010	0.118
Breiman CVLS K-NN Sqrt	0.032	0.010	0.169	0.011	0.126
Wu Cluster CVLS	0.072	0.044	0.050	**0.000**	0.118
*Terrell K-NN Kung	0.124	0.625	0.653	0.263	0.550
*Terrell K-NN Hansen	**0.000**	0.203	0.183	0.485	0.281
*Terrell K-NN Sqrt	0.124	0.625	0.653	0.263	0.550
Loftsgaarden K-NN Kung	0.065	0.461	0.507	0.099	0.367
Loftsgaarden K-NN Hansen	0.161	0.142	0.107	0.604	0.261
Loftsgaarden K-NN Sqrt	0.065	0.461	0.507	0.099	0.367
*Gaussian K-NN Kung	**0.000**	0.162	0.231	0.058	0.143
*Gaussian K-NN Hansen	0.114	0.111	0.062	0.519	0.225
*Gaussian K-NN Sqrt	**0.000**	0.162	0.231	0.058	0.143
Lima Entropy	0.667	0.047	0.047	0.088	**0.000**
Lima Quadratic	0.671	0.035	0.047	0.132	0.010
VdWalt ML BackSub	0.011	0.511	0.608	0.043	0.457
Barnard ML BackSub	0.299	0.831	0.890	0.303	0.797

The objective is to evaluate if the selected recommended sample sizes from the literature are indeed sufficient. Specifically, $e7$ evaluates for six dimensions and $e8$ for four dimensions since these two dimensionalities straddle the low and high dimensional threshold. In both $e7$ and $e8$ we note that with increasing sample sizes all methods performances do in fact increase. We additionally note the graphs are decreasing non-linearly and remain somewhat equidistant from left to right with an very slight elbow around 100%. These results lend confidence to the recommended sample sizes from the literature and do not provide any further information to us when selecting an AB-KDE method.

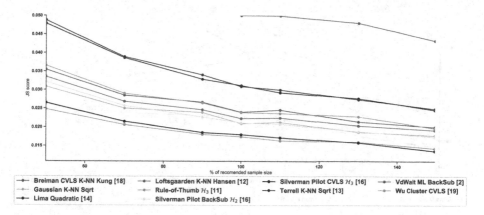

Fig. 1. JS statistic score (y-axis) of experiment e8 as a function of increasing sample sizes (x-axis)

5.2   Increasing Dimensionality Simulation Experiments

Given our increased confidence in the selected sample sizes, we focus on the impact of increasing dimensionality on the performance of the AB-KDE methods. In Fig. 2 we present the results of synthetic dataset e6, where we evaluate with increasing dimensionality how the various AB-KDE methods perform with respect to their JS score. We chose synthetic dataset e6 for this evaluation since it is unimodal and as such allows us to evaluate just the increases in dimensionality. As in Subsect. 5.1, we exclude the redundant methods. The sample point estimators do especially well in lower-dimensional spaces, but their performance decreases as the dimensions increase. Alternatively, the balloon estimators, although not necessarily outperforming, performance increases in dimensions beyond four. By seven dimensions, both Loftsgaarden-KNN and our Gaussian-KNN outperform the best sample point estimators. Since we did not optimise our choice of k, we suspect the balloon estimators may be capable of doing even better. These results are consistent with the theoretical analysis provided in the literature [29]. We note that most methods cannot outperform the static Rule-of-Thumb KDE in this unimodal experiment for dimensions less than seven.

5.3   Increasing Mode Simulation Experiments

Given the results relating to increases in dimensionality, we consider the conditions under which AB-KDE methods outperform the static Rule-of-Thumb KDE noted in the classical 2-dimensional experiments of Subsect. 5. The aforementioned experiments hint towards the higher number of modes in the data being a factor that the AB-KDE methods are able to exploit. Tables 2 and 3 show the results of e9 in which we increase the number modes in the 4 and 6 dimensional settings respectively. Redundant results have been excluded for

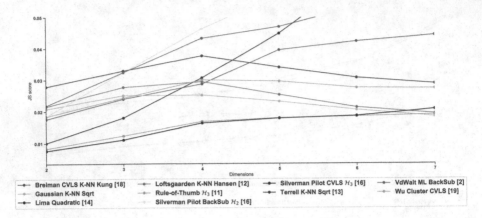

Fig. 2. JS statistic score (y-axis) of synthetic dataset $e6$ as a function of increasing dimensionality (x-axis).

readability. We note that in the lower dimensional (4-dimensions) setting, the results are largely mixed with sample point, rule-of-thumb and balloon methods all doing equally well. We point out that our "Gaussian K-NN" is consistently among the top performers in this lower-dimensional space despite being a balloon estimator. These results demonstrate that the AB-KDE methods perform on par with the static Rule-of-Thumb KDE method in the lower dimensional setting given many hyper-ellipsoids/Gaussian modes.

Table 2. KS-JS ranking score of experiment $e9$ as a function of increasing number of modes in 4-dimensions. *(*This method)*

Name $e9$ $d(4)$ $n(350)$	$m(2)$	$m(3)$	$m(4)$	$m(5)$	$m(6)$
Rule-of-Thumb $\mathcal{H}_3$	**0.000**	**0.000**	**0.000**	**0.000**	**0.000**
Silverman Pilot BackSub $\mathcal{H}_2$	0.011	0.049	0.042	0.010	0.025
Silverman Pilot CVLS $\mathcal{H}_3$	0.011	**0.000**	**0.000**	**0.000**	**0.000**
Breiman CVLS K-NN Kung	0.115	0.093	0.042	0.085	0.192
Wu Cluster CVLS	0.011	**0.000**	0.022	0.010	0.021
*Terrell K-NN Hansen	0.311	0.257	0.294	0.297	0.267
Loftsgaarden K-NN Hansen	0.026	0.019	0.065	0.010	0.011
*Gaussian K-NN Sqrt	0.025	**0.000**	**0.000**	**0.000**	**0.000**
Lima Quadratic	0.286	0.181	0.125	0.090	0.211
VdWalt ML BackSub	0.901	0.833	0.819	0.900	0.872

In the higher dimensional (6-dimensions) settings, the balloon estimators outperform the other AB-KDE methods and the static Rule-of-Thumb KDE. One sample point method that has consistently shown good results is that of

Table 3. KS-JS ranking score of experiment e9 as a function of increasing number of modes in 6-dimensions. (*This method)

Name e9 d(6) n(2100)	m(2)	m(3)	m(4)	m(5)	m(6)
Rule-of-Thumb $\mathcal{H}_3$	0.072	**0.010**	0.050	0.132	0.043
Silverman Pilot BackSub $\mathcal{H}_2$	0.099	0.158	0.047	0.199	0.124
Silverman Pilot CVLS $\mathcal{H}_3$	0.121	0.075	0.054	0.146	0.043
Breiman CVLS K-NN Kung	0.086	0.074	0.122	0.042	0.042
Wu Cluster CVLS	0.133	0.049	**0.000**	0.071	**0.000**
*Terrell K-NN Hansen	0.426	0.325	0.254	0.229	0.200
Loftsgaarden K-NN Hansen	**0.000**	**0.000**	**0.000**	**0.033**	**0.000**
*Gaussian K-NN Sqrt	**0.000**	0.039	0.064	**0.010**	**0.000**
Lima Quadratic	0.618	0.458	0.365	0.300	0.268
VdWalt ML BackSub	0.886	0.854	0.856	0.860	0.810

Table 4. KS-JS ranking score of experiment e10 as a function of increasing number of dimensions. (*This method)

Name e10 m(∞)	d(2)	d(3)	d(4)	d(5)	d(6)	d(7)
Rule-of-Thumb $\mathcal{H}_3$	**0.029**	**0.000**	**0.000**	**0.000**	0.071	0.161
Silverman Pilot BackSub $\mathcal{H}_2$	0.069	0.085	**0.062**	0.175	0.378	0.474
Silverman Pilot CVLS $\mathcal{H}_3$	0.128	0.225	0.440	0.547	0.626	0.669
Breiman CVLS K-NN Kung	0.344	0.506	0.650	0.626	0.537	0.486
Wu Cluster CVLS	0.140	0.211	0.315	0.308	0.328	0.293
*Terrell K-NN Sqrt	0.167	0.228	0.210	0.136	**0.053**	**0.013**
Loftsgaarden K-NN Hansen	0.682	0.425	0.244	0.139	0.139	0.110
*Gaussian K-NN Sqrt	0.607	0.406	0.200	**0.037**	**0.000**	**0.000**
Lima Quadratic	**0.000**	**0.000**	0.067	0.475	0.792	0.792
VdWalt ML BackSub	0.108	0.771	0.904	0.900	0.875	0.806

Wu Cluster CVLS. We note that our Gaussian K-NN is now consistently outperforming the other methods along with Loftsgaarden K-NN. The results lead us to expect that with increasing data "complexity" the AB-KDE balloon methods results will improve further.

5.4 High Dimensional Embedded Manifold Simulation Experiment

Given the lack of distinction between AB-KDE methods with increased hyperellipsoid/Gaussian modes, experiment e10 seeks to evaluate how the methods compare given a non-linear manifold in higher dimensional spaces. The experiment was also conducted under varying sample sizes, which had only a minor impact on the outcomes.

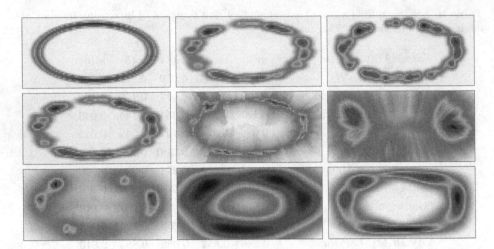

Fig. 3. 2-dimensional density estimates plots of various AB-KDE methods for experiment $e10$. From left to right top top bottom. Top: actual density, Silverman Pilot CVLS $\mathcal{H}_3$, Breiman CVLS k-NN Kung. Middle: Wu Cluster CVLS, Terrel k-NN Sqrt, Loftsgaarden k-NN Hansen. Bottom: Gaussian k-NN Sqrt, Lima Quadratic, and VdWalt ML BackSub.

In Fig. 3 we display the actual manifold in 2-dimensions alongside the estimates of the density for various AB-KDE methods. Many of the methods seem to be following the non-linear manifold well. However, in this lower-dimensional space, we see from Table 4 that the static Rule-of-Thumb and Lima Quadratic seem to be providing the best estimates. We note that the Silverman Pilot, which had outperformed the other methods in much of the previous results, is now less effective-extending the dimensionality beyond 5-dimensions results in the balloon estimators beginning to outperform the sample point estimators.

In Table 4 we see the extent to which the balloon estimators can outperform the other methods on a non-linear manifold. In the Table, we see that the weakness of the sample point estimators in the high dimensional settings on a non-linear manifold are also more apparent. By 6-dimensions, Wu Cluster is the best performing sample point estimator. Both our Terrell K-NN with full rotational hyper-ellipsoid and our Gaussian K-NN are the top-performing methods from 5-dimensions upwards. In this non-linear high dimensional manifold setting, we demonstrate the state-of-the-art results for both these methods on this task.

5.5   General Discussions

The $\mathcal{H}3$ methods outperform the $\mathcal{H}2$ methods in the high-dimensional and -mode cases. However, this comes at a high computational cost as the number of parameters to be optimised increases quadratically with dimensionality. Specifically for

Terrell K-NN, finding a hyper-ellipsoid was an order of magnitude slower than the other methods. The Gaussian K-NN performance was on par with the other methods.

6   Conclusions

A significant amount of effort has been placed on the analytical understanding of AB-KDEs. These studies focus on theoretical limits almost always not encountered in real-world data. The lack of real-world applicability of these methods is highlighted in the results by the small performance increases gained in using them over the static Rule-of-Thumb presented.

Our Gaussian K-NN is shown to obtain a state-of-the-art method as the number of modes increased in high dimensional space. Further, our Terrell K-NN method also presented state-of-the-art results alongside Gaussian K-NN when dealing with complex manifolds in a high dimensional setting. Unfortunately the Terrell K-NN come at a significant additional computational cost. The results indicate our balloon estimators provide opportunities for deeper investigation when data dimensions are high or data contain a high number of modes that lies on a non-linear manifold.

References

1. Abramson, I.S.: On bandwidth variation in kernel estimates-a square root law. Ann. Stat. **10**(4), 1217–1223 (1982)
2. Barnard, E.: Maximum leave-one-out likelihood for kernel density estimation. In: Proceedings of the Twenty-First Annual Symposium of the Pattern Recognition Association of South Africa (2010)
3. Bithell, J.F.: An application of density estimation to geographical epidemiology. Stat. Med. **9**(6), 691–701 (1990)
4. Boltz, S., Debreuve, E., Barlaud, M.: High-dimensional statistical measure for region-of-interest tracking. IEEE Trans. Image Process. **18**(6), 1266–1283 (2009)
5. Botev, Z.I., Grotowski, J.F., Kroese, D.P., et al.: Kernel density estimation via diffusion. Ann. Stat. **38**(5), 2916–2957 (2010)
6. Breiman, L., Meisel, W., Purcell, E.: Variable kernel estimates of multivariate densities. Technometrics **19**(2), 135–144 (1977)
7. Budka, M., Gabrys, B., Musial, K.: On accuracy of pdf divergence estimators and their applicability to representative data sampling. Entropy **13**(7), 1229–1266 (2011)
8. Comaniciu, D., Ramesh, V., Meer, P.: The variable bandwidth mean shift and data-driven scale selection. In: Eighth IEEE International Conference on Computer Vision. ICCV 2001. Proceedings, vol. 1, pp. 438–445. IEEE (2001)
9. DasGupta, A.: Some results on the curse of dimensionality and sample size recommendations. Calcutta Stat. Assoc. Bull. **50**(3–4), 157–178 (2000)
10. Domeniconi, C., Gunopulos, D.: Locally adaptive techniques for pattern classification. In: Encyclopedia of Data Warehousing and Mining, 2nd edn., pp. 1170–1175. IGI Global, Hershey (2009)

11. Duong, T., Hazelton, M.L.: Cross-validation bandwidth matrices for multivariate kernel density estimation. Scand. J. Stat. **32**(3), 485–506 (2005)
12. Farmen, M., Marron, J.S.: An assessment of finite sample performance of adaptive methods in density estimation. Comput. Stat. Data Anal. **30**(2), 143–168 (1999)
13. Hall, P.: Large sample optimality of least squares cross-validation in density estimation. Ann. Stat. **11**(4), 1156–1174 (1983)
14. Hall, P., Huber, C., Owen, A., Coventry, A.: Asymptotically optimal balloon density estimates. J. Multivariate Anal. **51**(2), 352–371 (1994)
15. Hansen, B.E.: Lecture notes on nonparametrics. Lect. Notes (2009). (Report) University of Wisconsin
16. Kung, Y.H., Lin, P.S., Kao, C.H.: An optimal k-nearest neighbor for density estimation. Stat. Prob. Lett. **82**(10), 1786–1791 (2012)
17. de Lima, M.S., Atuncar, G.S.: A Bayesian method to estimate the optimal bandwidth for multivariate kernel estimator. J. Nonparametric Stat. **23**(1), 137–148 (2011)
18. Loftsgaarden, D.O., Quesenberry, C.P., et al.: A nonparametric estimate of a multivariate density function. Ann. Math. Stat. **36**(3), 1049–1051 (1965)
19. Marshall, J.C., Hazelton, M.L.: Boundary kernels for adaptive density estimators on regions with irregular boundaries. J. Multivariate Anal. **101**(4), 949–963 (2010)
20. Mittal, A., Paragios, N.: Motion-based background subtraction using adaptive kernel density estimation. In: Proceedings of the 2004 IEEE Computer Society Conference on Computer Vision and Pattern Recognition. CVPR 2004, vol. 2, p. 2. IEEE (2004)
21. Moshtagh, N.: Minimum volume enclosing ellipsoid. Convex Optim. **111**, 112 (2005)
22. Sain, S.R.: Multivariate locally adaptive density estimation. Comput. Stat. Data Anal. **39**(2), 165–186 (2002)
23. Salgado-Ugarte, I.H., Perez-Hernandez, M.A., et al.: Exploring the use of variable bandwidth kernel density estimators. Stata J. **3**(2), 133–147 (2003)
24. Scott, D.W.: Feasibility of multivariate density estimates. Biometrika **78**(1), 197–205 (1991)
25. Scott, D.W., Sain, S.R.: Multidimensional density estimation. Handb. Stat. **24**, 229–261 (2005)
26. Shi, X.: Selection of bandwidth type and adjustment side in kernel density estimation over inhomogeneous backgrounds. Int. J. Geogr. Inf. Sci. **24**(5), 643–660 (2010)
27. Sibolla, B.H., Coetzee, S., Van Zyl, T.L.: A framework for visual analytics of spatiotemporal sensor observations from data streams. ISPRS Int. J. Geo Inf. **7**(12), 475 (2018)
28. Silverman, B.W.: Density Estimation for Statistics and Data Analysis, vol. 26. CRC Press, Boca Raton (1986)
29. Terrell, G.R., Scott, D.W.: Variable kernel density estimation. Ann. Stat. **20**(3), 1236–1265 (1992)
30. van der Walt, C.M., Barnard, E.: Variable kernel density estimation in high-dimensional feature spaces. Association for the Advancement of Artificial (2017)
31. Wand, M., Jones, M.: Comparison of smoothing parameterizations in bivariate kernel density estimation. J. Am. Stat. Assoc. **88**(422), 520–528 (1993)
32. Wu, T.J., Chen, C.F., Chen, H.Y.: A variable bandwidth selector in multivariate kernel density estimation. Stat. Prob. Lett. **77**(4), 462–467 (2007)

33. Zeng, G.: A comparison study of computational methods of Kolmogorov-Smirnov statistic in credit scoring. Commun. Stat. Simul. Comput. **46**(10), 7744–7760 (2017)
34. Zhang, L., Lin, J., Karim, R.: Adaptive kernel density-based anomaly detection for nonlinear systems. Knowl. Based Syst. **139**, 50–63 (2018)
35. Zhang, X., King, M., Hyndman, R.: A Bayesian approach to bandwidth selection for multivariate kernel density estimation. Comput. Stat. Data Anal. **50**(11), 3009–3031 (2006)
36. Zhong, B., Liu, S., Yao, H.: Local spatial co-occurrence for background subtraction via adaptive binned kernel estimation. In: Zha, H., Taniguchi, R., Maybank, S. (eds.) ACCV 2009. LNCS, vol. 5996, pp. 152–161. Springer, Heidelberg (2010). https://doi.org/10.1007/978-3-642-12297-2_15
37. Zougab, N., Adjabi, S., Kokonendji, C.C.: Bayesian estimation of adaptive bandwidth matrices in multivariate kernel density estimation. Comput. Stat. Data Anal. **75**, 28–38 (2014)
38. van Zyl, T.L.: Machine learning on geospatial big data. In: Big Data: Techniques and Technologies in Geoinformatics, p. 133. CRC Press, Boca Raton (2014)

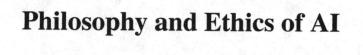

Philosophy and Ethics of AI

Is AI a Problem for Forward Looking Moral Responsibility? The Problem Followed by a Solution

Fabio Tollon[✉] [iD]

Department of Philosophy/GRK 2073 "Integrating Ethics and Epistemology of Scientific Research", Bielefeld University, Bielefeld, Germany
`fabio.tollon@uni-bielefeld.de`

Abstract. Recent work in AI ethics has come to bear on questions of responsibility. Specifically, questions of whether the nature of AI-based systems render various notions of responsibility inappropriate. While substantial attention has been given to backward-looking senses of responsibility, there has been little consideration of forward-looking senses of responsibility. This paper aims to plug this gap, and will concern itself with responsibility as moral obligation, a particular kind of forward-looking sense of responsibility. Responsibility as moral obligation is predicated on the idea that agents have at least some degree of control over the kinds of systems they create and deploy. AI systems, by virtue of their ability to learn from experience once deployed, and their often experimental nature, may therefore pose a significant challenge to forward-looking responsibility. Such systems might not be able to have their course altered, and so even if their initial programming determines their goals, the means by which they achieve these goals may be outside the control of human operators. In cases such as this, we might say that there is a gap in moral obligation. However, in this paper, I argue that there are no "gaps" in responsibility as moral obligation, as this question comes to bear on AI systems. I support this conclusion by focusing on the nature of risks when developing technology, and by showing that technological assessment is not only about the consequences that a specific technology might have. Technological assessment is more than merely consequentialist, and should also include a hermeneutic component, which looks at the societal meaning of the system. Therefore, while it may be true that the creators of AI systems might not be able to fully appreciate what the consequences of their systems might be, this does not undermine or render improper their responsibility as moral obligation.

Keywords: Responsibility gaps · Forward-looking responsibility · Technological assessment · Moral obligation

1 Responsibility and AI

Questions of responsibility have become increasingly important in the field of AI ethics. Specifically, questions of whether the nature of certain technological systems equipped with AI renders various notions of responsibility inappropriate. Substantial attention has

E. Jembere et al. (Eds.): SACAIR 2021, CCIS 1551, pp. 307–318, 2022.
https://doi.org/10.1007/978-3-030-95070-5_20

been given to backward-looking or retrospective senses of responsibility, as these come to bear on questions of moral responsibility [12, 15, 17, 20]. However, less attention has been paid to *forward-looking* senses of responsibility. This paper aims to plug this gap, and so I will concern myself with responsibility as moral obligation, a particular kind of forward-looking sense of responsibility.

Responsibility as moral obligation is a responsibility for *future* states of affairs and is concerned with the active promotion of certain societal goals, and the responsibility of agents to align what they do with these goals [17]. We must take seriously our obligation to ensure that the decisions we make today help in the pursuit of a better tomorrow. This is not to merely suggest that we take the future into account, but rather that we have an *active* obligation to steer society in a way that aligns with various important values.

For an agent to be responsible for future states of affairs, the means by which they go about getting to these future states ought to be in some sense under their control, such that if a desirable outcome is not achieved, we would be able to find them at fault. For the agent to be *responsible*, in this sense, it needs to be the case that the desired future state of affairs is somehow *up to them*. That is, it is *possible* for them to see to it that the future state comes into being. Thus, this moral obligation is predicated on the idea that agents at least have some degree of *control* over the kinds of systems they create and deploy. AI-systems, by virtue of their ability to learn from experience once deployed, and their often-experimental nature, may pose a significant challenge to responsibility as moral obligation. Such systems might not be able to have their course altered, and so even if their initial programming determines their *goals,* the means by which they achieve these goals may be outside the control of human operators. In cases such as this, we might say there is a gap in moral obligation. It is this "gap" that this paper aims to plug.

2   Task, Authority, and Obligation

Engineers and the creators of technology have a moral obligation to ensure that their products comply with certain norms and standards, and that these are in the service of socially desirable values and goals. This is not news to those working in engineering ethics and related disciplines. That engineers have a responsibility to design, for example, bridges that can bear a certain weight, buildings that can withstand certain wind speeds, and transportation systems that do not endanger passengers is nothing new or controversial. However, these obligations are closely linked with the *tasks* that engineers conduct. That is, they have a professional obligation to design and build structures that adhere to certain basic requirements. Moreover, they are also *authorities* on such matters (given their education) and are responsible for how the project is in fact carried out. This kind of responsibility is termed role responsibility and is *descriptive* in nature. It refers to whether the agent in question is in the correct kind of causal relation to an outcome, given their position in an organization or their authority. We can therefore think of this descriptive sense of responsibility as being *passive* in that it is more concerned with the legal and moral consequences that might be brought to bear on engineers should they fail to perform their task *as engineers*.

In addition to this, we have responsibility as *moral obligation*, which differs from responsibility as task and authority in that it is not so closely coupled with the *technical skills* of the engineer but is a *normative* sense of responsibility. It is also focused on responsibility for future states of affairs and is therefore not restricted to the analysis of an agent's adherence to certain professional norms. It is therefore a predominantly forward-looking sense of responsibility. We are here concerned with a *prescription* that agents have, "in terms of an obligation to do something or to see to something, or to take care of something" [16]. Here the question is not necessarily about what responsibilities they may have given their position as engineers, but rather on the responsibilities that we might expect them to rationally or reasonably assume [16]. The responsibilities we might expect them to assume are natural extensions of their roles and authority, but they are distinct in that when it comes to moral obligation there is an *active* component: they are expected to check-in, supervise, and *ensure* that some future state of affairs obtains. It is therefore important that we keep the distinction between "role responsibility", on the one hand, and moral responsibility on the other. Role responsibility has to do with certain professional norms (as noted earlier) while moral responsibility, in the forward-looking sense, has to do with responsibility for future states of affairs.

A second thing to note is that it is not controversial that these forward-looking obligations change over time: for example, added to the list of forward-looking responsibilities that current engineers have is a concern for sustainability, which may not have been a factor just 80 years ago. Nor would such a change (necessarily) lead to a "gap". What I will now investigate is whether AI systems might come to complicate our ability to make evaluations of forward-looking responsibility due to their unpredictability and their experimental nature.

3 Passive and Active Responsibility

As mentioned previously, responsibility as moral obligation is concerned with seeing to it that something is the case. For an agent to be reasonably held responsible in this sense, we expect that they could, for example, check in on the system or update it, so that the desired future state of affairs is achieved. It is their ability to intervene in this way that makes them fairly responsible. This, however, becomes difficult in the case of those developing AI-systems. AI research is an innovative and unpredictable field, due to both the vast collection of agents involved in creating these systems and the nature of AI itself. In the first case, engineers may have competing obligations towards different stakeholders (their employers, the public, etc.), and they might not be aware of what their social roles entail (whether they are scientists, businesspersons, or technicians, etc.). In the second case, the nature of AI-driven systems makes them in some sense *experimental*, in that engineers are often testing and *innovating* with potential solutions, without knowing exactly what the future consequences of their decisions may be. Additionally, once these systems are deployed, it may be impossible for engineers to actively intervene: the system would be *outside of their control.*

A gap in moral obligation may occur when we reflect on these two features. In the first case, engineers may not be aware of their obligations to other agents (due to the complicated network in which they are embedded) and therefore cannot seemingly be held responsible for a failure to meet these obligations. However, this is not unique to AI development: there are other contexts in which agents are embedded in complicated bureaucratic networks and may be unsure of their obligations due to this. For example, the scientists working on the Manhattan Project, which produced the world's first nuclear weapons during World War II, worked in massive teams of discrete groups. This was the beginning of Big Science, where scientists were not limited to working in siloed academic laboratories but were pushed into large-scale organizations with political backing (and political agendas) [18]. This kind of project was massively funded and had clearly defined objectives. The important point here is that this represented a break in the "traditional" way of doing science and created a bridge between the power of science and political power. The mingling of these two once broadly distinct spheres resulted in a complication of the scientists' understanding of their own moral obligations, as they were not "married to the science" as it were, but also to various political agendas, which they might depend on for future funding, employment, access to resources, etc. My point is not to go into the details of this affair, but rather to note that it created an organizational structure in which the role that scientists found themselves to be playing was not only restricted to science itself. As Steven Shapin put it,

> Scientists had never before possessed such authority, largesse, civic responsibility, and obligations. By free choice or not, some scientists now lived the *vita activa*, and, while there were still consequential worries about the extent to which they were indeed "normal citizens," they had never been more integrated into the civic sphere [18].

Here we can see how scientists' obligations *qua* scientists might be complicated by their new political power. This could be thought to create a gap in moral obligation, due to the often competing (or conflicting) objectives of scientific research and political objectives. If scientists are not properly trained for their new political roles, we might expect them to be unable to cope with these new obligations. It may therefore be unreasonable to expect them to fully understand their roles, especially in the early days of this mixing of political and scientific power. They might not understand their *active* responsibilities with respect to their research and how it is implemented. The point is that such complications of responsibility as moral obligation, at least in the sense of agents being answerable to different stakeholders, are not unique to AI.

Thus, the advent of AI and the teams of computer scientists behind them do not necessarily create a *unique* gap in moral obligation when we reflect on the issue of competing obligations. This does not mean the problem is solved, but rather that the question of competing stakeholders and the ways in which this challenges our ascriptions of responsibility cover much broader terrain than my present concern. Where AI might indeed pose a unique challenge, however, comes about in how it complicates the second feature of responsibility as moral obligation: the innovative and experimental nature of AI research and development may undermine the relevant *control* required for reasonable ascriptions of forward-looking responsibility. There are two aspects to this. The first concerns the *risks* that are inherent in deploying autonomous systems that are outside of human control. The second concerns our inability to predict the consequences of this technology.

4   Risks and Consequences

It seems it would be unreasonable to hold engineers responsible when they are dealing with experimental and innovative technologies. In such cases where full knowledge of the consequences is impossible to ascertain beforehand and intervention once the system is deployed is not possible, ascriptions of full responsibility do not seem to be fair. In the case of nuclear weapons and the Manhattan Project, it was relatively clear that this technology posed an existential threat to humanity should it ever be developed and deployed. While this was not a widely held belief among individual scientists at that time, there were many (such as Einstein) who were cognizant of this threat. One reason for this is the technology had a clearly defined purpose, and once developed, would be used in a very specific way. It would be deployed at targeted locations, determined by human agents. Up until the moment the bomb was dropped, there existed the possibility of human intervention, and at no point was it outside of meaningful human control. There was no sense in which the technology could set its own goals or learn from its "experiences". For the scientists (and all those involved in the project) there was therefore a sense in which they could reasonably *anticipate* the future *consequences* of what they were producing. This was true in two senses. In the first case, it was possible to anticipate the kinds of *risks* associated with the technology. Second, due to the direct nature of how the technology was to be deployed (and the nature of how the technology was tested beforehand), they could also reliably predict what the consequences of its use would be (in the sense of anticipating the level of destruction, not the effects on society overall). Obviously, these two factors are linked, but I think it is useful to consider them separately, as there may be cases where we understand the risks of a technology but do not have a clear handle on its potential consequences.

This, I think, might be what motivates the emergence of a gap in moral obligation due to AI: even if we grasp the risks, this does not necessarily entail that we can fully appreciate the potential consequences, which are often compounded by our lack of control over the system. I will argue, however, that both of these aspects can be overcome, and that there is therefore no gap in obligation. To do this I will first show that we do in fact, broadly, understand the risks of deploying AI systems (or at the very least, that we *know* about these risks), and we have frameworks in place to mitigate such risks. This will involve taking seriously that the risk of deploying a system over which we have no control might itself be a problem. Releasing fully autonomous AI out into the world is a choice we make, and we might be better off ensuring that we *always* have a sufficient level of control over such systems. Second, I will show that while an exclusive focus on consequences might allow for the emergence of a gap in responsibility, this is not the only means we have at our disposal in our assessment of technological systems.

5   Risks of AI

From the perspective of forward-looking responsibility, the question is not whether this makes blame appropriate for these systems, but rather whether such deployment creates a gap whereby developers, engineers, programmers, etc. cannot fulfil their future-orientated obligations because the AI-system has functional autonomy. That is, it can operate outside of "meaningful human control" [13]. The main concern here is the supposed fact that it would be impossible for agents to intervene with such autonomous systems, foreclosing assignments of prospective responsibility. However, this claim operates with the assumption that AI somehow has a pre-configured position in society. I will argue, however, that AI systems, while importantly different to traditional technological artefacts, are nonetheless still created and deployed by human beings, and so their position in society is always a *choice* that *we* make [5].

While it is important to note AI is different from traditional technical artefacts, the one way in which it is similar is that it is *designed by and for human agents*. When thinking about AI we should therefore not be misled by the supposed "intelligence" of such systems. Their intelligence, if they have any, is of a derivative kind, and is the product of a *human process* of research and development. For example, Joanna Bryson argues that concepts such as intentionality, consciousness, and sentience, etc. are mere sideshows to the real problems posed by AI: these being problems of *governance* [6]. Specifically, she argues that the most pressing question concerning AI is how to design our artefacts "in a way that helps us maintain enough social order so that we can sustain human dignity and flourishing" [6]. From this perspective, questions of a forward-looking gap in moral obligation do not seem to arise. While of course, the potential agential nature of AI in many contexts makes it more *difficult* and can increase the *complexity* of determining what our forward-looking obligations might be, and what the best route to achieve them might entail, this does not by itself create a *gap*. For there to be real indeterminacy, the technology would seemingly have to come out of the ether with its own set of values and goals, in which case we would have no understanding of, or contribution to, its design. However, notice that even in this extreme case, the notion of forward-looking responsibility still makes sense: even if no human agent contributed to the system, we might still *reasonably expect* those with the relevant skills and competencies to intervene, check on the system, try to stop it, etc. Although we might not *blame* them for not doing so, this does not mean that they have failed in their active responsibility.

While it is of course true that the emergence of potentially autonomous systems requires critical ethical reflection, we as human beings still have full control over *when* and *how* AI systems are developed, and thus carry the responsibility for them [5]. This is especially true if we conceive of forward-looking responsibility as being concerned not only with desirable outcomes but also with the promotion of shared values. Here we would be interested with questions regarding the *alignment* of AI research and deployment with certain values that are deemed beneficial for society [4, 7]. As more and more social processes become automated and "outsourced" to AI or algorithmic systems, we need to understand these systems as not merely technical but rather as social and political artefacts, capable of reinscribing and reifying injustice [1]. This places a forward-looking responsibility not just on programmers, engineers, and manufacturers, but also on political actors, who have a responsibility to check in on and intervene in instances of algorithmically caused harm. This is also true of those who *fund* these programs, as funders also have an obligation to, for example, ensure that their projects adhere to trustworthy practices [9].

6 Beyond Consequentialist Reasoning

The second feature that might be thought to create in moral obligation is the *experimental* and *innovative* nature of many aspects of AI research. It is often the case, especially with machine learning systems, that the correlations they generate are *novel*. Thus, in the process of training these systems, engineers and programmers cannot predict the kinds of results that will be generated. The process of creating and deploying these systems is often an iterative one, with tweaks being made here and there to avoid failure or undesirable outputs. There is therefore a sense in which those involved are *experimenting* with the available data in order to try and derive a meaningful pattern that could be put to work. This kind of work is also *innovative* in the sense that it often involves a unique commercial application of a process or product. We might take innovation to mean the "*commercialization* of *technological* inventions" [3]. Of course, innovation in a broader sense is also possible (outside of technological innovation), but for my purposes, it is enough that we come to see the novel use of AI-based systems as a species of technological innovation. With this in mind, I will aim to show that the innovative and experimental nature of AI does not create a gap in moral obligation. Although it might seem as though these features would make it impossible to predict the consequences of AI-based interventions, this does not exhaust our ability to assess technology and thus does not come to complicate our active moral obligations.

In a recent article, Armin Grunwald [10] argues that a wholly consequentialist method of Technological Assessment (TA) does not work. He insightfully suggests that we may evaluate nascent technologies not only on their potential consequences but also by looking at the *hermeneutic knowledge* that is available to us when performing such evaluations. Here we find support for the idea that technological assessment is more than merely consequentialist, and should also include a hermeneutic component, which looks at the *societal meaning* of the system [10]. This raises the possibility that concerns strictly grounded in the control condition, with respect to moral obligation and AI, might not undermine our responsibility practices. Specifically, it suggests that the experimental and innovative nature of AI research does not foreclose discussions of moral obligation for future states of affairs.

One of the key complicating factors when reflecting on the future obligations that the creators of technology might have comes from the so-called Collingridge Dilemma [8]. Basically, the dilemma is that when a given technology is still in the nascent stages of development, it is possible to influence the way it will develop significantly however, we lack knowledge of how the technology will affect society. Once the technology becomes 'embedded' in society, and we come to know its implications, however, we are then in a position where we are unable to influence its development. In essence, when change is at its easiest, the need for it cannot be foreseen, and when change is required, it is difficult to implement [10]. This dilemma, when applied to AI, is especially pernicious. This is because, with AI, we are not only dealing with new technology subject to the constraints of the Collingridge Dilemma, but also a kind of technology that is capable of *learning* from its experiences, and thus, in a way, lying beyond the scope of the Collingridge Dilemma. Such technologies, from their very beginning, might not offer us the safety and security of *ever* being able to significantly influence their trajectories once they are deployed. I will argue, however, that reflection on the potential implications of technology is more than a reflection on its potential consequences. This means that even if we cannot fully anticipate the consequences of a given technology, it does not follow that we are foreclosed from having an active moral obligation towards it.

An interesting point of departure on this journey is to reflect on the German translation of technological assessment: *Technikfolgenabschätzung*. Within this word, we find *Folgen*, which, literally, translates to "consequences" in English. Here we see how embedded the role of consequences are in TA, and rightly so. Prospective knowledge (knowledge about the future) is by its very nature uncertain, and so we need to devise a means with which we can reduce this uncertainty. This leads to attempts to develop mechanisms to *anticipate* what the future might hold, which acts as a guide to how we might structure our decision making in the present, with respect to novel technology [10].

When assessing technology, however, what exactly are we evaluating? Grunwald offers us two potential answers, and then gives reasons to reject both. He first claims that perhaps TA is an assessment of *technology*. However, this construal misses the fact there is no such thing as technology *as such*, and that technology is always embedded in a given *social environment* [10]. Second, he suggests that TA might concern itself with the *consequences of technology*. "Predicting, estimating and foresighting the possible consequences of technology belongs to TA's core business" [10]. Grunwald provides two reasons for rejecting this claim. The first is that the consequences of technology are not *just* the consequences of technology: these consequences are the result of varied and evolutionary interactions between technical, social, and institutional factors. Second, the consequences of technology do not yet exist. Therefore, strictly speaking, TA cannot be about these consequences *per se*, but only about the expectations, projections, or imaginations of *what they might be* [10]. In this way, we come to see that when evaluating technology, it is not enough to simply state that we should be concerned with the *consequences* of a specific technology, but rather we must interrogate the "*imaginations of future socio-technical configurations*" [10]. What might these "imaginations" be? Well, Grunwald argues that they need to fulfil two conditions to be proper objects of TA:

(1) Involve relations with science and technology

(2) Demonstrate that the technologies under consideration possibly have societal meaning and significance [10]

These two conditions seem natural enough. The first condition is straightforward, and once again points out that we must be conscious of the link between science and technology. The second condition introduces "societal meaning and significance", which is incredibly important to understand if we are to have a coherent means to evaluate novel technology. This criterion takes us beyond the mere consequences of the technology and prompts us to ask questions regarding the society-wide effects we may come to observe. These technologies are not simply additions to pre-given social systems, but come to influence ethical, economic, and social aspects of reality [11]. That is, we are now tasked with excavating what the technology might *mean* and are thus engaging in a distinctly *hermeneutical* project.

This draws our attention to how the projections and visions of new technologies come to shape their development. In order for scientists and researchers to secure public funds, they must convince those in charge of those funds (who are often not experts in the field) that their research will be of great importance. This often has less to do with the science or technology itself, but what these will *make possible*. In addition to this, breakthroughs in science and technology can themselves fuel the creation of new forms of meaning. For example, ultrasound scans made it possible for people to "see" the developing foetus in the womb for the first time [21]. However, the associated meaning of this technology is very different to the consequences of the technology itself. The consequences of the technology are that it makes visible what was once invisible. In addition to this, however, ultrasound also made it possible to determine the thickness of the nape of the neck of a foetus [22]. With this knowledge, parents and doctors can make an assessment of the risk that the child will be born with Down's syndrome. Thus, the technology provides a new framework for how we understand the foetus: no longer an invisible entity, but a medical subject understood in terms of disease. Significantly, such an understanding also brings to light our ability to *prevent* certain foetuses from being born, should we be able to diagnose any "abnormalities" early enough. Thus, ultrasound technologies come to mediate certain moral questions regarding abortion. This mediation role of technology is well documented and provides support to the hermeneutic approach outlined above. Instead of *only* looking at the potential consequences of the technology, we need to focus our attention on trying to give an adequate account of how we understand it. This understanding is never "stable", as it is an iterative process (often called the "hermeneutic circle"): once we take the time to understand the social meaning of a technology we do not come back to our original starting position. Rather, the process of uncovering meaning itself creates a kind of spiral, whereby new inputs are interpreted by society in a number of ways and come to influence our understanding of the technology in question.

One way to deal with unpredictability might be to focus on the decision-making procedure itself. Even if we have some unpredictability in terms of *outcomes*, we might nonetheless be able to mitigate such risks by focusing on the *process* of AI development. Such a switch in perspective has been proposed by Stilgoe *et al.* [19], where they propose their AIRR (Anticipation, Reflexivity, Inclusion, and Responsiveness) framework. The AIRR framework provides a mechanism by which engineers can be educated about their professional roles *and* the means of fulfilling their moral obligations in these roles. The focus of this framework is on the *process* of responsible research, and so the unpredictability of the system does not *necessarily* undermine the feasibility of such an approach.

What does any of this have to do with AI and moral obligation? The point of this section has been to show that when assessing a technology, unreliable knowledge about the consequences of that technology do not foreclose our ability to investigate the societal meaning that the technology may hold. Therefore, while it may be true that the creators of AI systems might not be able to fully appreciate what the consequences of their systems might be, they can still take the time to investigate their societal significance. For example, 'predictive policing' algorithms have been touted as a mechanism to assist law enforcement with determining their inspection priorities [23]. These systems are meant to increase the efficiency and efficacy of law enforcement processes by targeting 'high risk' areas and deploying more resources to those areas.

From a purely consequentialist perspective, we could say that the consequences of this technology would be greater policing in high-risk zones. However, hermeneutically, we might start to ask whether this kind of system might reinforce or create new forms of discrimination. What will the effects be of increasing police presence in high-risk areas, when those areas are historically disadvantaged? Unfortunately, with the benefit of hindsight, we can see that the results have been damaging for those communities. Hyper-surveillance partly produces increased rates of recorded crime (in the form of more arrests for petty crimes, for example), especially when the police know that they are being deployed in areas and are on the lookout for criminal behaviour, creating a guilty until proven innocent scenario [2]. This might reinforce existing racial prejudice on the part of police officers (if they are serving in historically disadvantaged communities) and may increase resentment in the community among those who feel that they are being unfairly targeted. The point of this example is that before deploying such systems, we should not merely look at the consequences of the *technology*, we also have to critically investigate how the technology will be embedded and what that might *mean* to the communities whom it will affect. Additionally, such "predictive systems" themselves operate under the assumption that attempting to predict the future will not influence the present. As the example should illustrate, and as a hermeneutical perspective illuminates, this is simply false, "as the very practice of forecasting the future partly acts directly upon the world - machine prediction plays a part in creating what exists whenever such predictions inform decision-making" [2].

Thus, those who design and implement such systems can undertake such hermeneutical analyses. There is no gap in moral obligation due to AI because here we have a mechanism that can overcome the cause of the potential gap (in the form of unpredictable consequences). In this respect, designers and developers ought to regularly check that the AI in question is performing its task in a way that is aligned with various socially desirable values (respect for human rights, equality, sustainability, etc.). This would involve understanding the specific context in which the AI is embedded, as well as how the agents interacting with it understand it, and how it affects the communities and groups within its range of influence.

However, this is not to say that this would be easy, or even that isolated engineers would be able to fulfill these obligations without education and input from researchers in the social sciences. My proposal therefore requires inter- and trans-disciplinary work so that the given societal meaning of the system can be uncovered. Such a process *demands* a diverse and pluralistic approach to technological assessment. Additionally, it might seem excessively onerous that programmers or engineers have to undertake such a hermeneutic analysis. This is especially concerning if we reflect on the gap between theory and practice that is operative in the AI ethics debate at present [14]. However, it is beyond the scope of the present paper to go into much detail with respect to how we might go about implementing such a hermeneutical perspective in applied contexts. My point here has merely been to suggest a theoretical perspective which might, when applied, yield more governable form(s) of AI systems.

7   Conclusion

In this paper, I have argued that AI systems do not create a unique gap in forward-looking responsibility. I supported this conclusion by focusing on the nature of risks when developing technology, and by showing that technological assessment is not only about the consequences that technology might have. By broadening the horizons of what constitutes technological assessment, with specific reference to societal meaning, I aimed to show that we can avoid a gap in forward looking moral responsibility. This does not mean, however, that forward-looking responsibility is not an *issue* when it comes to developing and deploying AI systems. In fact, given what I have said here, it should be clear that AI does indeed *complicate* our responsibility ascriptions. However, such complications do not lead to an insurmountable gap.

References

1. Birhane, A.: Algorithmic injustice: a relational ethics approach. Patterns **2**(1), 1–9 (2021a). https://doi.org/10.1016/j.patter.2021.100205
2. Birhane, A.: The impossibility of automating ambiguity. Artif. Life **27**, 1–18 (2021b)
3. Blok, V.: 'What Is Innovation? Laying the ground for a philosophy of innovation. Techné Res. Phil. Technol. **1**, 1–25 (2020). https://doi.org/10.5840/techne2020109129
4. Boenink, M., Kudina, O.: Values in responsible research and innovation: from entities to practices. J. Responsible Innov. **7**(3), 450–470 (2020). https://doi.org/10.1080/23299460.2020.1806451
5. Bryson, J.J.: Patiency is not a virtue: the design of intelligent systems and systems of ethics. Ethics Inf. Technol. **20**(1), 15–26 (2018). https://doi.org/10.1007/s10676-018-9448-6
6. Bryson, J.J.: The artificial intelligence of the ethics of artificial intelligence: an introductory overview for law and regulation. In: Dubber, M., Pasquale, F., Das, S. (eds.) The Oxford Handbook of Ethics of AI. Oxford University Press, New York (2020)
7. Carrier, M.: How to conceive of science for the benefit of society: prospects of responsible research and innovation. Synthese **198**(19), 4749–4768 (2019). https://doi.org/10.1007/s11229-019-02254-1
8. Collingridge, D.: The Social Control of Technology. Frances Pinter Limited, London (1980). https://doi.org/10.2307/1960465
9. Gardner, A., Smith, A.L., Steventon, A., Coughlan, E., Oldfield, M.: Ethical funding for trustworthy AI: proposals to address the responsibilities of funders to ensure that projects adhere to trustworthy AI practice. AI Ethics **15**, 1–15 (2021). https://doi.org/10.1007/s43681-021-00069-w
10. Grunwald, A.: The objects of technology assessment. Hermeneutic extension of consequentialist reasoning. J. Responsible Innov. **7**(1), 96–112 (2020). https://doi.org/10.1080/23299460.2019.1647086
11. Henry, N., Powell, A.: Sexual Violence in the Digital Age, Social and Legal Studies. Palgrave Macmillan, London (2017). https://doi.org/10.1177/09646663915624273
12. Matthias, A.: The responsibility gap: ascribing responsibility for the actions of learning automata. Ethics Inf. Technol. **6**(3), 175–183 (2004). https://doi.org/10.1007/s10676-004-3422-1
13. Mecacci, G., Santoni de Sio, F.: Meaningful human control as reason-responsiveness: the case of dual-mode vehicles. Ethics Inf. Technol. **22**(2), 103–115 (2019). https://doi.org/10.1007/s10676-019-09519-w
14. Morley, J., et al.: Ethics as a service: a pragmatic operationalisation of AI ethics. Minds Mach. **31**, 239–256 (2021). https://doi.org/10.2139/ssrn.3784238
15. Nyholm, S.: Attributing agency to automated systems: reflections on human–robot collaborations and responsibility-loci. Sci. Eng. Ethics **24**(4), 1201–1219 (2017). https://doi.org/10.1007/s11948-017-9943-x

16. van de Poel, I., Sand, M.: Varieties of responsibility: two problems of responsible innovation. Synthese **198**(19), 4769–4787 (2018). https://doi.org/10.1007/s11229-018-01951-7
17. Santoni de Sio, F., Mecacci, G.: Four responsibility gaps with artificial intelligence: why they matter and how to address them. Philos. Technol. **34**, 1057–1084 (2021). https://doi.org/10.1007/s13347-021-00450-x
18. Shapin, S.: The Scientific Life: A Moral History of a Late Modern Vocation. The University of Chicago Press, Chicago (2008). https://doi.org/10.1002/sce.20372
19. Stilgoe, J., Owen, R., Macnaghten, P.: Developing a framework for responsible innovation. Res. Policy **42**, 1568–1580 (2013). https://doi.org/10.1002/9781118551424.ch2
20. Tigard, D.W.: There is no techno-responsibility gap. Philos. Technol. **34**(3), 589–607 (2020). https://doi.org/10.1007/s13347-020-00414-7
21. Verbeek, P.P.: What Things Do. The Pennsylvania State University Press, University Park (2005). https://doi.org/10.1017/CBO9781107415324.004
22. Verbeek, P.P.: Materializing morality: design ethics and technological mediation. Sci. Technol. Human Values **31**(3), 361–380 (2006). https://doi.org/10.1097/EDE.0b013e3181
23. Yeung, K.: "Hypernudge": big data as a mode of regulation by design. Inf. Commun. Soc. **20**(1), 118–136 (2017). https://doi.org/10.1080/1369118X.2016.1186713

Re-imagining Current AI Ethics Policy Debates: A View from the Ethics of Technology

Emma Ruttkamp-Bloem[1,2]([✉]) [iD]

[1] Department of Philosophy, University of Pretoria, Pretoria, South Africa
emma.ruttkamp-bloem@up.ac.za
[2] Centre for Artificial Intelligence (CAIR), Hatfield, South Africa

Abstract. A lot has been written recently on the ineffectiveness of the current plethora of AI ethics regulations available in the public and private sectors. I approach this concern from a novel angle by critically reflecting from within the ethics of technology on current AI ethics discourse, which is mostly still deeply Cartesian, especially when it comes to policy-making. I start with an analysis of current AI ethics vocabulary and point to its value-laden and Cartesian nature. In a first step towards moving away from Cartesianism I then briefly take the reader on a journey through pertinent aspects of trans-human discourse as illustrated by Clark's proposal of human minds as 'extended'. I then consider Verbeek and Kudina's work in post-phenomenological mediation theory to enrich Clark's suggestions by acknowledging a more active role for technology in co-shaping humans and their socio-cultural worlds. As a result, via a novel notion of 'extended moral agency', I define a notion of 'moral affordance' to inform a new non-Cartesian tradition for AI ethics discourse and policy-making. Finally, I briefly comment on implications of my argument for the future of AI ethics regulation.

Keywords: Actionable AI ethics · Trans-humanism · Mediation · Moral agency · Moral appropriation · Moral affordance

1 Introduction

Given the plethora of artificial intelligence (AI) ethics regulations that recently saw the light and the subsequent discussion of its overall ineffectiveness (see, e.g., [24,29,38]) I want to suggest here, as an aide to these reflections, that we reconsider the philosophical context within which policy researchers reflect on the reasons for and content of regulation. What is the impact of the traditional Cartesian framework on AI ethics policy research? There have been many voices in the philosophy of technology through the past 100 years or so, and most recently in the late 20th century from domains such as actor network theory and post-phenomenology, pleading for reflection on limiting the impact of Cartesianism on how humans and their world and their interaction with the tools of their

E. Jembere et al. (Eds.): SACAIR 2021, CCIS 1551, pp. 319–334, 2022.
https://doi.org/10.1007/978-3-030-95070-5_21

world are portrayed. These voices suggest an active role for technology in shaping humans and their "lifeworlds" [27] (see also, e.g., [50]) within a context of accepting that the human world and human experiences have "never been modern" [33], and thus that a Cartesian framework for the philosophy (and ethics) of technology has always been inadequate, and even inappropriate.

Given the vastness of this literature and the scope of my paper, I will focus here only on a recent voice in the domain of trans-humanism, which is a domain that intersects in core places with reflection on discussions in these other two domains. At issue is the centuries old question of what it means to be human. Andy Clark [11] in his discussion of humans as "natural-born" cyborgs suggests that humans are made up of extended minds, minds extending beyond the "biological skinbag" [11] of their physical skulls, and also of extended bodies that allow for multiple embodiments in various ways. Building on insights from this discussion, I then turn to recent suggestions in post-phenomenological mediation theory that technology does not only mediate between humans and the world á la Idhe [27], but in fact co-shapes humans and their world in a never-ending hermeneutic lemniscate [31]. Taking from both these discussions and Kudina and Verbeek's work on moral appropriation (e.g., [32,40,51]), I reflect on the context within which moral norms originate and are impacted on by technology. I subsequently suggest a notion of 'moral affordance' based on Gibson's [23] notion of affordance in ecological psychology that shapes a notion of human moral agents as in fact 'extended moral agents' and then finally, I consider the possibility of a new non-Cartesian tradition in AI ethics discourse and policy-making.

In the next section I commence the discussion by considering the status of current Cartesian AI ethics narratives and the attitude of 'practical denialism' [10] these narratives often result in. I then discuss Clarks' notion of humans as 'natural-born' cyborgs. In the penultimate section, building on Kudina and Verbeek's work, I turn to re-imagining the narrative of AI ethics if it is taken to center around humans as extended moral agents who co-create qualities of moral affordance in their technologies via moral appropriation resulting from co-shaping inter-activity with technology and the socio-cultural world. In conclusion, I summarise a new non-Cartesian context for the AI ethics policy-making domain, which may be more effective against practical denialist impacts on actionable AI ethics policies than is currently the case.

2   Current AI Ethics Regulation Discourse

Consider the strange behaviour of persons fully aware of the dangers of climate change and who are genuinely shocked about the status of the health of the environment and ecosystems. A high percentage of such persons nevertheless do not in fact go into action to actively work towards mitigating the situation. So, they are not 'cognitive denialists', in the sense that they do in fact update their beliefs based on new evidence, but they are denialist on a practical level, which is perhaps an even more frustrating epistemic vice than cognitive denialism. Quassim Cassam [10] calls this the epistemic vice of 'behavioural' or 'practical denialism'. I suggest here that this kind of practical denialism also plays a significant role in the overall ineffectiveness of AI ethics regulation. While there may certainly be other reasons such as economic power and financial gain that drive this form of practical denialism in the AI ethics context, here I consider the role that the typical vocabulary of broad AI ethics policy discourses play in this state of affairs by perhaps creating false (Cartesian) perceptions of what it means to be human in a technologically mediated socio-cultural world.

To illustrate the validity of my concern, I start by briefly comparing the impact of human discourse about nature on the trajectory of the environmental sciences and its philosophy and ethics to the impact of human discourse about technology on the trajectory of AI research and its philosophy and ethics. In Jon Krakauer's book 'Into the Wild', "... the wilderness represents both the untouched and pure, which are worth aiming for, and the untamed and violent, which threaten and destroy human lives" [46, p. 79]. I suggest that to a significant extent this echoes stories about AI technology as the solution to all our problems on the one hand, and as the 'evil demon' threatening our very existence as the beings we most truly are, on the other. Uggla [46] explores how "humans' deeply ambivalent relationship with nature, which oscillates between romantic devotion to nature and attempts to conquer it" has not only influenced the nature-culture divide according to which nature is the 'other', as opposed to culture, but also environmental policy. I suggest considering whether this is true of depictions of AI technology and imagined counter-positions for humans and their world of technology in AI ethics policy too.

Firstly, in the discourses of AI ethics regulation there is a spectre of hubris illustrated for instance by current machine ethics narratives on the possibility, potential and overall desirability of 'creating' artificial moral agency. On the one hand, there are discussions around the computational tractability of building artificial moral agents (AMA's) (e.g., [1,6,7,41,53]). Writers such as Brundage [8], and Bostrom and Yudkowski [7] are openly skeptical of the possibility of functioning AMA's; Bostrom [6] and others are concerned about the implication of 'super-human' AMA's; while the more moderate writers such as Moor [39], Asaro [1], Wallach and Allen [53], Floridi and Sanders [21] who are willing to consider the concept of AMA's in principle, in general suggest some form of hierarchy of moral status to be introduced. The idea is that an equivalent level of moral agency accompanies each level of moral status.

These discussions share a concern for retaining human autonomy and, many advocate for human-centered AI i.e., they focus on AI technologies that are designed with sensitivity to their human impact, and that are intended to augment, rather than replace, human capabilities and intelligence. Of course, such approaches are welcomed. I want to highlight, however, that behind much of this debate is a fundamental belief in the preference for retaining human moral decision-making. This is also of course commendable, but, if such a belief implodes into arguments for the obvious superiority of human moral abilities, a flag should go up, as such a belief is obviously not borne out by actual events (see e.g., [3], p. 110). Raising this flag of course does not imply that all humans are untrustworthy moral agents, nor does it oppose views advocating for human moral agency on grounds of human dignity, but it does point to the need for acknowledging that there is no necessary causal relation between being human or protecting what is human, on the one hand; and being a good moral agent or ensuring a just human world, on the other. Not acknowledging this may very well lead to the kind of complacency and even practical denialism that contribute to the current paralysis of AI ethics policies – and this at a time that humanity can ill afford it.

Uggla warns that "[e]xplicitly or implicitly, regulation creates demarcations that make objects appear hazardous or harmless, important or unimportant, or natural or non-natural" ([46], p. 79). (see also [35,44].) Concepts employed in regulation are deeply value-laden [46] and political [44]. I suggest these considerations should certainly be taken into account in terms of AI ethics policy-making too. Analysing how understanding of technology and concerns for trustworthy (ethical, lawful and robust according to the EU Commission Guidelines [19]) AI are constructed in "applicable regulatory frameworks" [19] is core to understanding the underlying factors that may (accidently or deliberately) result in practical denialism, because it will tell us how human agency and human-technology relationships are defined. Just as "the 'natural' is often used as a socially and politically neutral concept, [and] the search for it remains a deeply value-laden activity that entails drawing boundaries and assigning priorities" [46] in the environmental science domain, so is the concept of technology often portrayed as neutral, while nevertheless threatening to humanity, in AI ethics policy discourses, effectively ignoring views of the mediating role of technology between humans and their world.

Feenberg ([20], p. 5) notes that to a certain extent, in many traditional philosophy of technology discourses – perhaps specifically where Cartesian discourses rule – technology is portrayed as playing the same authoritative role in contemporary human societies that religion played in pre-modern Western societies. This kind of thinking that opposes technology's function of 'control' to science's function of 'explaining', also may contribute to loading the dice against technology and in favour of hubris thus potentially ignoring both the work needed to ensure human responsibility for sound moral decisions as well as the mediating role of technology in shaping human 'lifeworlds' [27], and potentially setting the stage for complacent practical denialism rather than reflecting on actionable AI ethics policies. From within the domain of Human-Computer Interaction (HCI), McCarthy and Wright ([36], p. 2) raise a related concern when they remind that while "[w]e don't just use or admire technology ... [but] ... live with it", it is still the case that "much academic framing of technology plays down this side of the relationship between people and technology in favor of something more objective, on the basis that objective analysis is required to advance theory and change practice", which reminds strongly of the Greek concept of technē as an objective discipline.

Let us now reconsider what it means to be human – and what it is to be technology - with the aim to rethink AI ethics discourse (and resulting policy

making traditions) and to upend the "ancient western [and modern Cartesian] ...
tendency to think of the mind as so deeply special as to be distinct from the rest
of the natural order" ([11], p. 26). This serves two purposes: 1) there is a move
away from portraying technology as 'neutral' and totally separate from humans,
and 2) there is a move away from portraying humans in control and humans as
focus point as guarantees for a just world without anything else needed. In the
penultimate section this discussion will inform a post-phenomenological twist to
current AI ethics policy-making.

3 Human as Natural-Born Cyborgs

How exactly should we think of humans, technology and their world being
related? Almost four decades ago Turkle [45] already asked us to consider what
humans are becoming as technology advances. Are humans deliberately turning themselves into slaves, for instance? Let us consider such questions here by
reflecting on whether humans are not perhaps evolving in tandem with technology in ways that we have to start taking into account in broad AI ethics conversations and their related policy-making formulation. This would also throw
some light on questions such as 'what does it mean that humans build technology that they know they may not be able to control' that Haselager and
Mecacci [25] raise. Perhaps the notion of 'control' in play here is misguided?
Let us here consider these issues and whether or not we should "accept that,
just like other non-human actants, AI plays a role in the continuous construction of the collective" [30] by considering Clark's [11] notion of the human mind
as 'extended'; as merging with technology in ways that have enhanced human
cognitive architecture over centuries in ways that seem to implode any divide
between *physis* and *poēsis*.

  A central aspect of Clark's project is to convince us that the history of humanity is in fact entangled with the history of technology (rather than opposed to it
as the ancient and Cartesian stories go) given that the "tendency" of humans for
"cognitive hybridisation" is an ancient tenet of what it means to be human ([11],
p. 15). He speaks of a "cognitive fossil trail" commencing with speech and counting, through writing and numerals and the printing revolution, to the digitalisa-
tion of sound, texts and images, and suggests the various industrial revolutions
simply as markers of this trail. This historic cognitive trail represents a "cascade
of cognitive upgrades", which are "cognitive upheavals in which the effective
architecture of the human mind is altered and transformed" [11]. In this sense,
Clark ([11], p. 14) argues that humans are "... cyborgs not in the merely super-
ficial sense of combining flesh and wires but in the more profound sense of being
human-technology symbionts: thinking and reasoning systems whose minds and
selves are spread across biological brain and nonbiological circuitry" in a way
that is true to human's "own biological nature" ([11], p. 5).

  On the modernist Cartesian view, humans are depicted as somehow separate
from and superior to the world of objects because of a firm belief (the fault of the
ancient Greeks, made worse by the Renaissance's exultation in what is human,

and intensified by the Enlightenment's Cartesian drive) that what determines who they are, somehow is fundamentally internal to their minds ruled by the ever-powerful Cartesian subject. Clark takes a different path, perhaps closer to Freud, Marx and Darwin's emphasis on humans as part of nature, when he writes "[t]he human mind, if it is to be the physical organ of human reason, simply cannot be seen as bound and restricted by the biological skinbag. ... The mind is just less and less in the head" ([11], p. 14).

What does he mean? He is not suggesting that humans are machines, but he is suggesting that they are special in an extended sense. This is no post-human story he is telling, but rather a trans-human one. The special nature of the human mind is such that the tools it interacts with to enhance its cognitive architecture become invisible as separate entities to the extent that the mind extends or stretches to include these tools. It is this kind of "technological scaffolding" of the mind, that allows humans to evolve cognitively. The mind-body problem, in fact, becomes the mind-body-scaffolding problem ([11], p. 11) in this sense.

In terms of the body, Clark argues that our notion of a physical body is a mental construct that can continuously be expanded, renewed, or reconfigured. He notes that it "just doesn't matter whether the data are stored somewhere inside the biological organism or stored in the external world. What matters is how information is poised for retrieval and for immediate use as and when required" ([11], p. 69). Clark tells various stories about various cyborg constructions, such as the Australian cyber-artist Stelarc's electronic 'third' arm strapped to his right wrist and controlled by him via EMG (electromyographic) signals detected by electrodes placed on four strategic muscle sites on his legs and abdomen ([11], p. 115) not normally used for hand control, and thus allowing the third hand to move independently of the two human arms ([11], p. 116). His point is to introduce the notion of an extended mind with the possibility of multiple embodiments in the place of a lonely Cartesian thinking being with limited, or in fact, no certain embodiment.

Here Clark latches onto Dennett's [15] depiction of the mind as a set of processes engaging with its environment in various functional ways, when he writes "[t]here is no self, if by self we mean some central cognitive essence that makes me who and what I am. In its place there is just the 'soft self': a rough-and-tumble, control sharing coalition of processes—some neural, some bodily, some technological—and an ongoing drive to tell a story, to paint a picture in which 'I' am the central player" ([11], p. 138). He challenges us to "face up to our true nature (soft selves, distributed decentralised coalitions) and to recognise the inextricable intimacy of self, mind, and world" ([11], p. 139). Finally, he warns against an image of the human species as a species "of ancient biological minds in colorful young technological clothes", and rather urge turning towards an image of humans as "chameleon minds, factory-primed to merge with what they find and with what they themselves create" ([11], p. 141).

None of the above means that Clark does not acknowledge concerns around the impact of technology on human lives. On the contrary, in his chapter on 'Bad Borgs' he reminds the reader of "the specters that haunt these hybrid dreams" ([11], p. 167) which include concerns about inequality, intrusion, uncontrollability, overload, alienation, narrowing, deceit, degradation and disembodiment. The over-all thrust of his argument, however, is not about trying to "seal the exits, batten down the hatches, and foil the invading digital enemy" ([11], p. 139). In fact he is advocating that our "science, morals, education, law, and social policy... the governing institutions within which we—the soft selves, the palpitating biotechnological hybrids—must solve our problems, build our lives, and cherish our loves" change to adapt to "accelerating cycles of biotechnological interdependence and interpenetration" [11]. The message is that we have to align our notions of what it means to be human with the fact of the "deep intimacy of agents and their cognitive [technological] scaffoldings" and build "laws and social policies that recognise this", guided by the slogan of "[o]ur worlds, ourselves" ([11], pp. 140–141).

In the next section, I suggest a novel approach to effecting this alignment and consequent policy-making in the AI ethics domain, which may also mitigate the practical denialism in current AI ethics regulation contexts. The task Clark ([11], pp. 194–195) sets us is "to merge gracefully, to merge in ways that are virtuous, that bring us closer to one another, make us more tolerant, enhance understanding, celebrate embodiment, and encourage mutual respect". While these are powerful images, the notion of an extended mind merging with technology is not enough to address how to react to moral judgments in a techno-socio world. To give us this depth, to capture not only the interaction between humans and technology, but also human-technology-world inter-activity and its implications for the progression of human moral norms, I suggest we turn to post-phenomenology in the next section.

4 Extended Moral Agency

If minds are extended and multiple embodiments are possible, the self is a "control sharing coalition" of neural, bodily and technological processes ([11], p. 138), and human cognitive architecture is a human-technological hybrid, how does one make sense of human morality? Should traditional notions of the origin of moral values, reasoning and agency be revised? And if so, how? And what kind of impact would this have on technology regulation? Kudina [31] suggests that "how people make sense of technologies can shed light on how moral sensibilities and concerns come to the fore". I will start this section by unraveling her depiction of human-technology-world interaction and the feedback among these three components (or "counterparts") in terms of the notion of a lemniscate that "links people, technologies and the sociocultural world in the joint production of meaning" [31].

In a discussion of how digital voice assistants mediate the interpretations of the world of the user and impact on the user's existing values – e.g., a user of Alexa or Siri learning to be as concise as possible, and reacting to them usually communicating in a female-sounding voice and learning that they do not challenge rude interactions – she argues there is a re-contextualisation of the world of the user that, "in turn, helps to shape them as specific subjects" [31]. In the tradition of mediation approaches in the philosophy of technology (e.g., [27, 52]) she reminds that while technologies "by virtue of their design features" typically emphasise certain aspects of human worlds while ignoring others, "it is upon people in specific embodied sociocultural spaces to interpret that message and act on it" [31]. In this sense, the world humans live in is not a static world they are helplessly thrown into, but a world that they mediate and co-shape via technology that in its turn co-shapes both themselves and their world [40]. And, it is in this process that moral perceptions, values and actions are generated (e.g., [51]) and thus to a certain extent also 'co-shaped' (e.g., [18]).

And here is the core point of this section: "[i]f ethics is about the question of 'how to act' and 'how to live,' and technologies help to shape our actions and the ways we live our lives, then technologies are in fact 'actively' taking part in ethics" ([32], p. 297). Thus, "[b]y helping to shape moral inclinations and decisions, technologies mediate morality" [31]. Think for instance of the presence of CCTV cameras impacting on how people behave, or, more to the point in the context of AI ethics, of the possibility of biased outcomes generated by autonomous algorithms amplifying existing structural identity prejudices and generating "allocation harm" [12] in society. But, how exactly does technology impact on this kind of "moral sense-making" [31]? Where is technology located in the process of interpreting human experience? Kudina turns to the notion of 'appropriation' in response to these questions.

Hans-Georg Gadamer [22] introduces the notion of 'appropriation' as a circular activity of understanding a new phenomenon or event by projecting it onto existing perceptions in the sociocultural environment, and constantly updating "preliminary meanings" [31]. For Kudina, following Gadamer, appropriation is the process of interpreting technology and integrating it "into the existing frameworks of understanding, necessarily updating them" [31]. In terms of moral sense-making, Kudina [31] also builds on Gadamer's [22] placement of moral norms in the 'prejudice' (the "fore-structure of human understanding" [31], where these norms mingle with all other elements that help with interpreting the world, and states that "beyond casting her native normative context onto a new technology, the user would simultaneously be confronted with certain moral ideas and inclinations that technological design and the surrounding world suggest" [31] and which she would need to appropriate and make sense of. She thus goes further than Gadamer, as she ultimately defines appropriation as "an intentional activity of relating to technologies during which moral concerns and perceptions manifest themselves and existing normative ideas can undergo re-articulation and change [my emphasis]" [31].

Right, but how exactly do humans update their (moral and other) beliefs after or during technology mediation? Verbeek's [50] response is that this happens in a process of 'co-shaping' – humans and technology co-shape each other – there are no "pre-given" [31] Cartesian subjects that act upon static objects in the world: "What the world 'is' and what subjects 'are', arise from the interplay between humans and reality" ([14], p. 13). Kudina [31] points out though that

Verbeek still does not capture the full scope and rich nature of the inter-activity (in interlinked feedback loops) of humans, technology and the socio-cultural world. She therefore suggests, as a way of representing "the formative awareness of people, the mediating role of technologies and the productive nature of the sociocultural contexts in the process of interpretation" [31], a technologically mediated hermeneutic lemniscate that "indicates how a sense-making process covers the way people actively appropriate technologies, how the appropriation gets embedded in the world, makes the world meaningful to people in a specific way and reconstitutes the subject of technological appropriation in return" [31]. And, of course, moral norms too, are co-shaped in the lemniscate-like process of mediation as new moral conceptions are formed in the encounters among users, technology, and the social-cultural world in which these encounters are embedded, and appropriated into existing moral frameworks, leading to adjustments and revisions as necessary.

Moving back now to the AI ethics focus of the paper, I want to consider how to navigate the acknowledgement of the impact of such encounters of moral sense-making on broad AI ethics discourses and related regulation. When one considers the values typically mentioned in AI ethics policy-making discourses, values such as protection of human rights and human dignity, diversity and inclusion, solidarity and sustainability, it seems difficult to formulate them other than from a 'neutral' point of view. Diversity and inclusion simply means what it means, whether or not humans and technology are co-shaped by their interaction embedded in the world, surely? I suggest that a first step to considering how moral appropriation in Kudina's sense may impact on AI ethics policy-making is to reflect deeply on the source and the nature of ethical concerns about AI technologies and the context within which these concerns would be impacting on humans in terms of all aspects of inter-linked co-shaping highlighted above. Thus, I suggest reflection on the possibility of ethical concerns being human-technology generated concerns rather than 'pure' or 'objective' human ones. If this is the case, surely the nature of AI ethics discourse as well as policy making should be rethought.

If we turn to Clark for help, notable is that he urges us to "critically embrace" ethical concerns rather than "batten down the hatches" ([11], p. 139), and what he means is that we should consider the nature of the concern and re-interpret it in the context of the extended cognitive architecture of humans as cyborgs that includes the tools they need to navigate their world. Consider his discussion of concerns such as alienation and human control: In terms of alienation and disembodiment, he ([11], p. 194) writes that "[w]here some fear disembodiment and social isolation, I anticipate multiple embodiment and social complexity". In terms of losing human control he writes that we have to be realistic about the level of control we have always had and he concludes that "the kind of control that we, both as individuals and as society, look likely to retain is precisely the kind we always had: no more, no less. ... What matters is not that we be micromanaging every detail of every operation, but that the surrounding systems provide usable, robust support for the kinds of life and projects we value [my emphasis].

But this is all still so abstract – how exactly can we ensure "virtuous mergers" ([11], p. 195) and the "intelligent combination of biological and engineered worlds" ([11], p. 181)? In the AI ethics context, I suggest the key lies in Clark's general point above of ensuring that technologies provide "robust support for the kinds of life and projects we value" ([11], p. 176). Thus, in order to work towards this assurance, and overcome practical denialism and misguided hubris, I build on Clark, Kudina and Verbeek's work. Verbeek [52] asks concrete questions about current conceptualisations of the causal role technology plays in realising or counter-acting human moral goals. The aim of this paper is very much in agreement with Verbeek's call for an "ethical turn" [52] in reflections on the normative aspects (and functions) of technology. In the AI ethics context my suggestion below is to expand traditional depictions of technology's impact on human morality to more than an instrumentalist view, such that technology is acknowledged as a co-creator of human moral norms (see [31,32,52], and in that sense is acknowledged to offer more direct support for the values and lives humans value than Clark may have expected.

Firstly, I suggest a notion of 'extended moral agency' in tandem with Clark's notion of extended human minds. Surely, if we accept that it is a primal biological urge of humans to merge with their non-biological tools and if, in addition, we embrace the notion of moral sense-making via human, technology, and socio-cultural world co-shaping that Kudina suggests, it is not only our cognitive architecture that is 'extended' throughout our lives, but also our moral architecture. I thus suggest that appropriation of feedback on moral norms during technologically mediated co-shaping of humans and their socio-cultural world in fact results in extending human moral agency, as technology is allowed to co-shape our moral norms. Thus, in this sense, the origin of our moral norms is not necessarily 'purely human'.

Secondly, I suggest considering Kudina's notion of moral appropriation against the background of deciphering what I term 'moral scripts' embedded or "inscribed" [52] into technology. In actor-network theory, "scripts" are aspects of technological systems or objects that cause appropriate "programmes of action" [34]. Consider Verbeek's [52] discussion of the example of the Dutch firm, 'Eternally Yours', who inscribed a 'script' into the design of the material of their couches in order for their clients to react to or act on it in a particular way. They covered their couches with material that has a design woven into it that becomes more apparent the more the couch is used. Through embodied perception, the value inscribed in the couch induces humans to react to the couch differently than any other couch, because they see a quality of "affordance" [23] in it, where the notion of 'affordance' refers to qualities in the object that "incline users to see additional use as more attractive than disposability, and to behave in a manner that accords with this feeling" [43].

While Gibson phrased his notion of 'affordance' in the domain of ecological psychology, I suggest we rethink it in the domain of AI ethics. In this sense 'moral affordance' refers to qualities in technology (resulting from co-shaping in the lemniscate pattern incorporating humans, technology and the world) that incline users to see its ethical use as more attractive than its unethical use, and which may contribute to ensuring that AI technology supports the kinds of projects and lives humans value. Such a quality of 'moral affordance', 'co-inscribed' into the technologies that stand in co-shaping relations with humans and their socio-cultural world in Kudina's [31] sense, and forming part of the extended moral agency of humans, could inform the dynamic adjustment to "accelerating cycles of biotechnological interdependence and interpenetration" Clark ([11], p. 139) refers to, and which is clearly also needed to steer AI ethics regulation.

But how could such affordance be inscribed into AI technologies that are mathematical systems rather than concrete tools? We are not talking about couches here, after all. Also, the increasing autonomy of AI systems as well as the increasing complexity of the design of AI systems making any kind of anticipation of the decisions they will generate difficult, makes being concrete even more challenging. To an important extent, value-by-design (an area in which Verbeek is making key post-phenomenological input, see, e.g., [14,52]) is a form of this way of thinking, relating closely to IEEE and other drives for ethically aligned design. The notion of moral affordance is, however, not only focused on the design stage of AI systems, but on all stages of the AI system lifecycle – from research, design, development, deployment to use [47].

Consider the following illustration of what I mean: Recently there has been sharp attention given to suggestions that FAT (fairness, accountability and transparency) concerns in the machine learning (ML) context (e.g., [42,49]) should not only be focused on the design and development stages but also on the deployment and use stages of AI systems (see e.g. [2,28]). In this sense for example, results of post hoc evaluations of ML generated outcomes should not only be fed back into refining the systems at issue, thus should not only be viewed as technical problems demanding technical solutions but should also be considered in collaboration with social scientists to inform concrete redress in cases of harm from generated predictions or decisions (see e.g., [12]). Such discussion may inform subsequent appropriation of relevant moral norms co-shaped in this process of the tech community and end-users engaging with technological systems such that, ultimately, AI systems that afford qualities of retributive justice and non-discrimination throughout the life-cycle of an AI system may come to be more preferred than others.

These are concrete suggestions to illustrate how moral affordance could be 'co-inscribed', via human-technology-socio-cultural world co-shaping and appropriation, into the life cycle of AI systems. Such a perspective on AI technology's role in 'moral-co-making' will influence policy-making discourses in ways that may limit reactions of practical denialism and also may have interesting contributions to make to the kind of social system analysis that Crawford and Calo [13] suggest. It should be clear that humanities and social science scholars should drive the AI ethics discourses enabling reflection on inscribing moral affordances into AI technology as much, if not more, as members of the tech community.

5 Conclusion

I have offered an alternative path (from [24,29,38]) for considering the current impasse in AI ethics policy adherence. I have suggested that ethical concerns about technology seem to be un-actionable when it lacks acknowledgement of the co-shaping role that technology plays in human moral reasoning (see [14,31,32,52]). Firstly, on top of thinking of human minds extending to include the matrixes ([11], p. 190) of technological elements needed to solve cognitive problems, I suggested enriching the nature of this extension with Kudina's [31] view of a continuous lemniscate of feedback among humans, technology, and the socio-cultural world. Secondly, I have suggested that we consider the origin and nature of moral norms in Kudina's context of moral appropriation [31] against Verbeek's critical reflection on the role of technology in human moralizing [52] to come up with a notion of extended moral agency. Thirdly, I have suggested reflecting on the co-creation of moral norms throughout the life-cycle of AI systems by introducing a notion of moral affordance to be co-inscribed into these systems at various stages of their life-cycle, such that technologies contributing to (inscribed with) values such as equality, equity, and beneficence, are more preferred than others.

Right, but humans are still special, no? Yes, humans are indeed special, but here it is highlighted that they are (also) special in an 'extended' or 'stretched' sense, and they are best protected by rethinking what it means to be human, what technology is, and how humans and technology are embedded into the socio-cultural world in a lemniscate-like pattern of co-shaping appropriation, including moral appropriation. Values such as protection of human rights, inclusivity and diversity are still valid and so is human dignity. But, we might have to rethink their formulation, how to ensure their actionability in policy-making (through moral affordance), and take time to reflect on whether humans should be 'in' or 'on' the loop of control of AI systems (both) (see here Mellamphy's [37] excellent article). By adopting the extension of the traditional notion of human moral agency to include the technologies that are co-shaping humans, their world, and their moral norms, members of the tech community also may come to view the technology they create as co-shapers of themselves, their values, future technology, and their worlds. This may introduce a way to overcome alienation from the abstract ideals of AI ethics regulation – in a way that strengthens the constant call for multi, inter- and trans-disciplinary work. Also, there is a sense in which the urgency of acting on regulation becomes more emphasised because of this realisation of an intermingled dynamic world with all three constituents of our extended moral agency (the socio-cultural world, humans, and technology) impacting on each other.

Do we need all these concepts however? The short answer is yes. The scope and nature of the impact of AI technologies on all levels of human lives, all social groups, human culture, communication, information, education and connectedness, as well as the environment and ecosystems, point clearly to the need for a new system of interpretation and sense-making in the era of living with AI technologies. As a philosopher I cannot see how to analyse the linking co-shaping inter-activities of humans, technology and world as drivers of this kind of impact in terms of AI technologies, more appropriately than via the discipline of hermeneutics. There is a rich and respected history of employing hermeneutics in the philosophy and ethics of technology broadly and in post-phenomenology in particular (see e.g., [4,5,9,16,17,26,27,50]) and I suggest we continue on this well-established and fruitful route to come to a philosophy and ethics of AI technologies.

I suggest that we may find that in this rethinking of AI ethics discourses and policy-making humans need the very virtues that Vallor is concerned are threatened by AI technologies: techno-moral values such as "honesty, self-control, empathy, care, courage, justice, humility, flexibility, perspective, and civility" [48]. I further suggest that in addition, humans may need to cultivate 'hermeneutic virtues', such as the ability to update interpretative frameworks, the skill of appropriation, the patience to unravel moral scripts and reflect on how to built moral affordances into AI technologies, as well as and the patience to make sense of and appropriate the moral affordance contained in these technologies in the AI domain, the determination to collaborate and communicate with different expertise; mixed with, or added to, "[c]ore elements of moral practice such as habituation, attention, self-examination, judgment, and moral extension" [48].

Needed urgently is multi-disciplinary research on the nature and practice of moral judgment in the co-shaping human-technology-world spaces of inter-activity humans live in and finding ways not only to use technology to support humans in "promoting and endorsing" already identified ethical values by actively supporting human ethical decision making [48] but to support values that are constantly re- and co-shaped and co-inscribed into technology in the above senses. Apart from policy research, future research linked to the views suggested here is also indicated for example in the contexts of machine ethics and Bostrom's control problem. Moreover, concrete case studies building on and illustrating the initial ideas presented here in terms of inscribing moral affordance into AI technologies are also needed.

These suggestions as well as the main call in this paper for becoming open to the co-shaping of moral norms [52] via Kudina's hermeneutic human-technology-world lemniscate [31] may ultimately assist in heeding Shannon Vallor's call in the AI ethics domain to not only build a "future worth wanting" [9] by actively taking up the centuries old call to make virtue a habit as a matter of urgency and employing our best technologies to assist us in this task, but also to in fact understand both the call and what such employment of technology in fact entails. In this way, a new non-Cartesian framework for AI ethics policy-making practices that are honest enough to overcome practical denialist tendencies becomes a possibility.

References

1. Asaro, P.M.: What should we want from a robot ethic? Int. Rev. Inform. Ethics **6**, 9–16 (2006)
2. Bhatt, U., et al.: Explainable machine learning in deployment. In: Proceedings of the 2020 Conference on Fairness, Accountability, and Transparency, pp. 648–657 (2020)
3. Boddington, P.: AI and moral thinking: how can we live well with machines to enhance? AI Ethics **1**, 109–111 (2021). https://doi.org/10.1007/s43681-020-00017-0
4. Borgmann, A.: Technology and the Character of Contemporary Life: A Philosophical Inquiry. University of Chicago Press, Chicago (1984)
5. Borgmann, A.: Holding on to Reality. The Nature of Information at the Turn of the Millennium. University of Chicago Press, Chicago (1999)
6. Bostrom, N.: Superintelligence Paths, Dangers, Strategies. Oxford University Press, Oxford (2014)
7. Bostrom, N., Yudkowsky, E.: The ethics of artificial intelligence. In: The Cambridge Handbook of Artificial Intelligence, pp. 316–334 (2014)
8. Brundage, M.: Limitations and risks of machine ethics. J. Exp. Theor. Artif. Intell. **26**(3), 355–372 (2014)
9. Capurro, R.: Digital hermeneutics: an outline. AI Soc. **25**(1), 35–42 (2010). https://doi.org/10.1007/s00146-009-0255-9
10. Cassam, Q.: Vices of the Mind: From the Intellectual to the Political. Oxford University Press, Oxford (2019)
11. Clark, A.: Natural-Born Cyborgs: Minds, Technologies, and the Future of Human Intelligence. Oxford University Press, Oxford (2004)
12. Crawford, K.: The Trouble with Bias. NIPS 2017 Keynote. https://www.youtube.com/watch?v=fMym_BKWQzk
13. Crawford, K., Calo, R.: There is a blind spot in AI research. Nat. News **538**(7625), 311–313 (2016)
14. de Boer, B., Te Molder, H., Verbeek, P.-P.: The perspective of the instruments: mediating collectivity. Found. Sci. **23**(4), 739–755 (2018). https://doi.org/10.1007/s10699-018-9545-3
15. Dennett, D.C.: Consciousness Explained. Penguin Books, London (1991)
16. Dreyfus, H.L.: What Computers Can't Do: A Critique of Artificial Reason. Harper & Row, New York (1972)
17. Dreyfus, H.L.: On the Internet. Routledge, New York (2001)
18. Druga, S., Williams, R., Breazeal, C., Resnick, M.: "Hey Google is it OK if i eat you?" Initial explorations in child-agent interaction. In: Proceedings of the 2017 Conference on Interaction Design and Children, pp. 595–600. Association for Computing Machinery, New York (2017)
19. European Union Commission: Ethics Guidelines for Trustworthy AI. https://digital-strategy.ec.europa.eu/en/library/ethics-guidelines-trustworthy-ai
20. Feenberg, A.: What is philosophy of technology? In: Defining Technological Literacy, pp. 5–16. Palgrave Macmillan (2006)
21. Floridi, L., Sanders, J.W.: On the morality of artificial agents. Minds Mach. **14**(3), 349–379 (2004). https://doi.org/10.1023/B:MIND.0000035461.63578.9d
22. Gadamer, H.G.: Philosophical Hermeneutics. University of California Press, Berkeley (1977). (Linge, D.E Trans.)

23. Gibson, J.J.: The Ecological Approach to Visual Perception, Classic Psychology Press Ltd., New York (2014)
24. Hagendorff, T.: The ethics of AI ethics: an evaluation of guidelines. Minds Mach. **30**(1), 99–120 (2020). https://doi.org/10.1007/s11023-020-09517-8
25. Haselager, P., Mecacci, G.: Superethics instead of superintelligence: know thyself, and apply science accordingly. AJOB Neurosci. **11**(2), 113–119 (2014)
26. Ihde, D.: Technics and Praxis: A Philosophy of Technology. D. Reidel Publishing Company, Boston (1979)
27. Ihde, D.: Technology and the Lifeworld: From Garden to Earth. Indiana University Press, Bloomington (1990)
28. Jesus, S., et al.: How can i choose an explainer? An application-grounded evaluation of post-hoc explanations. In: Proceedings of the 2021 ACM Conference on Fairness, Accountability, and Transparency, pp. 805–815 (2021)
29. Jobin, A., Ienca, M., Vayena, E.: The global landscape of AI ethics guidelines. Nat. Mach. Intell. **1**(9), 389–399 (2019). https://doi.org/10.1038/s42256019-0088-2
30. Kruger, J.: Nature, culture, AI and the common good – considering AI's place in Bruno Latour's *politics of nature*. In: Gerber, A. (ed.) SACAIR 2021. CCIS, vol. 1342, pp. 21–33. Springer, Cham (2020). https://doi.org/10.1007/978-3-030-66151-9_2
31. Kudina, O.: "Alexa, who am I?": voice assistants and hermeneutic lemniscate as the technologically mediated sense-making. Hum. Stud. **44**(2), 233–253 (2021). https://doi.org/10.1007/s10746-021-09572-9
32. Kudina, O., Verbeek, P.P.: Ethics from within: Google Glass, the Collingridge dilemma, and the mediated value of privacy. Sci. Technol. Hum. Values **44**(2), 291–314 (2019)
33. Latour, B.: We Have Never Been Modern. Harvard University Press, Cambridge (1993)
34. Latour, B.: On actor-network theory: a few clarifications. Soziale Welt **47**(4), 369–381 (1996)
35. Lidskog, R., Soneryd, L., Uggla, Y.: Transboundary Risk Governance. Earthscan, London (2009)
36. McCarthy, J., Wright, P.: Technology as Experience. MIT Press, Cambridge (2004)
37. Mellamphy, N.B.: Humans in the loop. Human-centrism, Posthumanism, and AI. Nat. Cult. **16**(1), 11–27 (2021). https://www.berghahnjournals.com/view/journals/nature-and-culture/16/1/nc160102.xml
38. Mittelstadt, B.: Principles alone cannot guarantee ethical AI. Nat. Mach. Intell. **1**(11), 501–507 (2019). https://doi.org/10.1038/s42256-019-0114-4
39. Moor, J.: The nature, importance, and difficulty of machine ethics. IEEE Intell. Syst. **21**(4), 18–21 (2006)
40. Rosenberger, R., Verbeek, P.P.: A field guide to postphenomenology. In: Rosenberger, R., Verbeek, P.P. (eds.) Postphenomenological Investigations: Essays on Human-Technology Relations, pp. 7–42. Lexington Books (2015)
41. Russell, S.: Human Compatible - Artificial Intelligence and the Problem of Control. Viking, London (2019)
42. Selbst, A.D., Boyd, D., Friedler, S.A., Venkatasubramanian, S., Vertesi, J.: Fairness and abstraction in sociotechnical systems. In: Proceedings of the Conference on Fairness, Accountability, and Transparency, FAT* 2019, pp. 59–68. Association for Computing Machinery, New York (2019). https://doi.org/10.1145/3287560.3287598

43. Selinger, E.: Confronting the moral dimensions of technology through mediation theory. Philos. Technol. **27**, 287–313 (2014). https://doi.org/10.1007/s13347-011-0054-3

44. Swyngedouw, E.: Impossible 'sustainability' and the postpolitical condition. In: Krüger, R., Gibbs, D. (eds.) The Sustainable Development Paradox, pp. 13–40. Guilford Press (2007)

45. Turkle, S.: The Second Self: Computers and the Human Spirit. Simon & Schuster Inc., New York (1984)

46. Uggla, Y.: What is this thing called 'natural'? The nature-culture divide in climate change and biodiversity policy. J. Polit. Ecol. **17**(1), 79–99 (2010). https://doi.org/10.2458/v17i1/21701

47. UNESCO: Preliminary Report on the First Draft of the Recommendation on the Ethics of Artificial Intelligence. https://unesdoc.unesco.org/ark:/48223/pf0000374266

48. Vallor, S.: Technology and the Virtues: A Philosophical Guide to a Future Worth Wanting. Oxford University Press, Oxford (2016)

49. Veale, M., Binns, R.: Fairer machine learning in the real world: mitigating discrimination without collecting sensitive data. Big Data Soc. **4**(2) (2017). https://doi.org/10.1177/2053951717743530

50. Verbeek, P.P.: What Things Do: Philosophical Reflections on Technology, Agency, and Design. Pennsylvania State University Press, University Park (2005)

51. Verbeek, P.P.: Obstetric ultrasound and the technological mediation of morality: a post-phenomenological analysis. Hum. Stud. **31**(1), 11–26 (2008). https://doi.org/10.1007/s10746-007-9079-0

52. Verbeek, P.P.: Moralizing Technology: Understanding and Designing the Morality of Things. University of Chicago Press, Chicago (2011)

53. Wallach, W., Allen, C.: Moral Machines: Teaching Robots Right from Wrong. Oxford University Press, Oxford (2009)

A Habermasian Approach to Fair Processes in AI Algorithms

Khensani Xivuri[✉] 🆔 and Hossana Twinomurinzi 🆔

University of Johannesburg, Auckland Park, Johannesburg, South Africa
{200911813,hossanat}@uj.ac.za

Abstract. The traditional emphasis of fairness in AI algorithms tends towards developing fair standards, even though the field of AI and its subfields advance rapidly and creatively, meaning that any AI fair standards could similarly become obsolete rapidly. This paper argues rather for an emphasis on fair *processes* that are adaptable to AI's continuous creations and innovations. Specifically, we adapt Jurgen Habermas' critical theory of communication, the lifeworld and *meaning* to develop a process framework for AI algorithmic fairness. The framework engages *logical-semantic*, *procedural* and *performative rules* that can be applied to avoid power imbalances and domination by any entity or individual before, during and after AI algorithm development. The framework is applied to the recent case of the biased Twitter image cropping algorithm, which focused on white faces and women's chests but cropped out black faces.

Keyword: AI machine learning · Active learning algorithms · Fairness · Bias · Ethics · Jürgen Habermas · Theory of communicative action

1 Artificial Intelligence

The creation of Artificial Intelligence (AI) algorithms is often focused on the result without much consideration of the input or bias in the data [1–5]. When not checked before implementation, this tendency has sometimes resulted in embarrassing situations, reputational damage, mistrust, and even financial loss [6–8]. The greatest appeal with AI algorithms is the ability to improve itself as more data is added and the ability to be transferred to other similar contexts [5]. During this transferability, subtle differences in contexts, such as social and cultural differences, are ignored. For example, the recent biased Twitter image cropping algorithm focused on white faces and women's chests but cropped out black faces causing embarrassment and a backlash to Twitter [4]. Such unfairness and bias can be avoided if the process leading to the AI algorithm can be debated or go through a degree of discourse, especially when the AI has a societal implementation.

In this paper, we propose Jürgen Habermas' theory of communicative action as an ideal mechanism to review AI algorithms to improve their fairness before and after implementation. Habermas idealised a better world where social changes occur within

E. Jembere et al. (Eds.): SACAIR 2021, CCIS 1551, pp. 335–343, 2022.
https://doi.org/10.1007/978-3-030-95070-5_22

society in an evolutionary process whereby all those affected by the intended and unintended consequences will accept them [6]. Habermas argued that outside interventions cannot create a better society and would be oppressive if not facilitated through public discourse. Today, AI algorithms are implemented within every society mechanism without any public discourse and, therefore, frequently result in oppressive societal effects that border on intentional social engineering [1, 7, 8].

The remainder of the paper is structured as follows; the next section briefly presents literature on AI algorithmic fairness and Jürgen Habermas' philosophy of communication, mainly focusing on his theory of communicative action. It is followed by a process framework on how fairness could be embedded within AI algorithm development before and after implementation. An example is then followed using the recent Twitter image cropping algorithm, which was found to have bias.

2 Literature Review

2.1 Algorithmic Fairness in AI

One of the first tasks in defining AI algorithmic fairness is deciding what fairness means. Fairness includes the capability to remain impartial and unbiased when making decisions [9–11] and is both a standard and a process [7]. As a standard, fairness defaults to legal principles that govern a society. With this regard, AI has yet to have formalised fairness standards, even though there are ongoing efforts; for example, the international committee for Information Governance ANZ has been struggling with developing standards for responsible and trustworthy AI [8]. IEEE is also in the process of developing standards around AI affecting human beings [11]. As a process, fairness carries the agency to determine one's destiny and access equal treatment and opportunities regardless of demographic profile. A fair process must be consistent in its procedures, transparent, and involve all affected parties [11].

The added complexity with deriving fair standards in AI further stems from the plethora and continuous release of new AI methods, and without any fair standards, the next best thing is to ensure fair processes. For example, if fair processes were followed, the Amazon AI tool for recruitment would not have discriminated against women [12]. Similarly, the US health care algorithm would also not have discriminated against black people despite having worse health conditions and needing more care [12].

The current mechanisms to ensure fairness in AI is through mitigating bias by removing common bias inducing factors such as race, gender and education [13] during testing [14]. Nonetheless, the AI could still have bias if the training data is already biased, for example, when most of the data are from one homogeneous category, such as one race. The existing mechanisms to detect bias mainly focus on already implemented AI. For example, FairML audits the predictive models for bias by quantifying the significance of the model's inputs; Fairness comparison uses an extensive library with bias detection and mitigation methods; AI Fairness 360 [3] uses a library of bias detection metrics and mitigations. The emphasis for all these tools is on completed AI implementations.

In the next section, we present a pre-and post-implementation mechanism that could be adapted to check for bias before, during and after the development of AI algorithms.

2.2 The Habermas Approach to AI Algorithmic Fairness

Social Interactions

Habermas idealised a world where humans create their living circumstances, emancipating themselves from *unwarranted constraints* and moving towards their own most desirable outcomes [15]. This includes the ability to remove obstacles that prevent the ability to achieve *freedom*. Habermas' ideal of a better world centered around the notion that outside interventions cannot create a better society for a single person or group of people, as all these interventions would be oppressive. He argues that the social changes need to occur from within in an evolutionary process whereby all those affected by the intended and unintended consequences will accept them. He refers to these processes as formative with practical intent. A society should be able to facilitate public discourse that would bring out, almost in a psychoanalytic style, some repressed collective memory to deal with it and lead to the collective consciousness that can lead to action. The ideal society consists of a well-functioning public sphere free of domination, particularly political interests and groupthink, allowing public discourse [16]. Societies oscillate towards a shared and common understanding and functioning of *the good life*.

Habermas argued that there are three reasons why individuals seek and apply knowledge in general; to achieve control of nature and other individuals - outer and inner domination respectively; to improve understanding, and; to overcome unwarranted internal and external compulsions. In so doing, he critiques the means-end relationship, as embedded in free economy models and modern economic theory, as the primary motivation for human action. Figure 1 illustrates Habermas' typology of action and social interaction (Fig. 1).

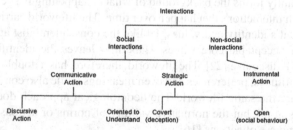

Fig. 1. Typology of social interactions (source: Lyytinen and Klein 1985, p. 210)

There is a distinction between action and interaction; actions that are directed towards achieving success and take into account only the interests of the acting agent, regardless of whether they are oriented towards people (or opponents) or matter (a non-social domain), are *purposive rational actions*. The success of purposive rational actions is measured by a means test to determine how closely they achieve the desired objectives. If it occurs in the physical world and proceeds by applying technical rules, it is instrumental action. The success of instrumental action is measured using engineering-type mean tests. Purposive rational actions are regarded as strategic if they are understood as following rules of rational choice and can be appraised from the efficiency of influencing rational opponents' decisions. The difference between strategic action and instrumental action is that one only needs to know and understand how to apply the technical rules with instrumental action. With strategic action, one also needs to understand the human behaviours necessary to predict the outcome of an action. Instrumental action is passive; strategic action is not passive but is associated with social situations and social values.

Communicative action, on the other hand, takes place through language and aims to achieve mutual understanding. Its focus is on an agreement, a common understanding of norms, meanings and values and maintaining social relationships [20]. In communicative action, individuals and society reach an understanding through having a common pool of values, norms, standards that may be implicit or even taken for granted. At times it is hard to espouse the implicit and taken for granted background assumptions explicitly. When consensus breaks down, cooperation can be broken, or a fight can begin to achieve each one's ends; at this point, communicative action ends, and strategic action begins. Before that, the assumption is that the people try to argue their point to convince others or reach another shared understanding. These arguments are called discourse.

Discourse assumes that it is an open debate and not an attempt to embarrass the opponent. Without such open-ended debate, it is impossible to discover a new shared understanding or reach compromises in good faith. If one party is already decided on the ends, it is only covert strategic action; Habermas refers to this as systematically distorted communication. It becomes manipulation if one side is intentionally misleading the other side. Without systematically distorted communication or manipulation, a new shared understanding can be reached.

The Lifeworld

The concept of a *lifeworld* connects communicative action to society and focuses on the shared values and norms around culture, society, and personality [6]. The lifeworld of individuals constantly forms the background of what is happening in society [21] and is developed through interactions that happen over time. The lifeworld carries assumptions about an individual's identity and values. Unlike the consequentialist approach, which employs a list of acceptable core values, Habermas leaves the identification of core values to the actual discourse [22]. The lifeworld, therefore, has a double role in shaping the individual's attitudes, preferences and even meanings while also conveying meaning to those who share the same lifeworld The deontological approach does not consider value preferences at all, but the normative validity of norms of actions and the moral rightness or wrongness of actions [16].

The notion of the lifeworld is not cast in stone but can be questioned and shifted. Habermas constantly worries about the overpowering of communicative action by instrumental action (and strategic actions) in modern societies, with digital technologies such as AI becoming accessories to engineer social tendencies that undermine existing lifeworlds.

In the next section, we present a mechanism for dealing with AI through a Habermasian lens.

3   A Process Framework for AI Algorithmic Fairness

The Habermasian consensus achieved through communicative action can only claim *generalizability* if it is validated by an informed and voluntary debate that satisfies the conditions of rational discourse. The conditions ensure that all voices are given an equal opportunity to share on the issues for discussion, i.e. an informed, democratic, and publicly open debate – in such a discourse, no force should influence the outcome. [16] formulates discursive requirements as a set of rules organised in three levels; *logical-semantic, procedural* and *performative*.

Logical-semantic rules amount to a clarification of what it means for a discourse to be "domination free". Examples of logical-semantic rules that are free of ethical debate include:

- No speaker may contradict himself
- If predicate F is applied to object A, F should be applied to all objects resembling object A.
- Different speakers may not use the same expression with different meanings

Procedural rules are processes of reaching a thorough understanding by testing validity claims that have become problematic. Examples of procedural rules include;

- Every speaker may assert only what he believes
- A person who disputes a proposition or norm not under discussion must provide reasons for wanting to do so.

Performative rules are processes of communication to reach an agreement while satisfying difficult conditions. Examples of rules to ensure social symmetry (power balance) are;

- All potential participants in a discussion must have an equal opportunity to begin discourse at any time, continue to make speeches and rebuttals.
- There must exist an equal opportunity to interpret, recommend, critique, justify or otherwise, the claims of a discourse. All discourse should be subject to debate.
- All participants must be able to express their attitudes, feelings and intentions
- All participants must equally be able to give and refuse orders and to reciprocate actions from others.

Individuals affected by AI algorithms or the decisions from an AI algorithm should be involved in the planning and development stages of AI algorithms. All stakeholders, developers, and society directly affected by AI should be aware of the discursive requirements set out by [16] and apply them during the development and implementation of AI. The logical-semantic, procedural and performative rules should guide the discussions and debate around input, development, processing and the output of the AI. Figure 2 illustrates the process framework for AI algorithmic fairness.

The process framework highlights the logical-semantic, procedural, and performative rules that should guide the development and implementation of AI.

The process framework can be summarised as follows, a representative of a society that will be affected by the AI, developers, and the stakeholders of the AI should be involved in the development and implementation stages of AI development. All the stakeholders should be domination free and reach a common understanding around

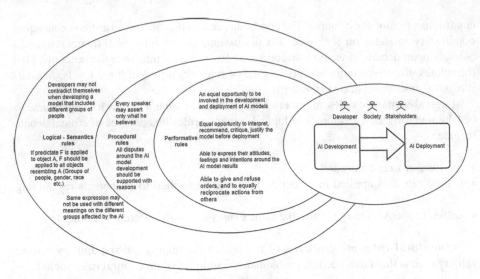

Fig. 2. Process framework for AI algorithmic fairness – A Habermasian approach

problematic validity claims and challenging conditions during the development and implementation of the AI algorithms. All affected parties should freely accept the consequences and effects that might result from the development and implementation of AI algorithms before they can go through implementation. The following section offers an example of the framework applied to the recent case of the biased Twitter image cropping algorithm, which focused on white faces and women's chests but cropped out black faces [4].

3.1   An Example of the Process Framework on the Biased Twitter Algorithm

In *logical-semantic* rules, if predicate F is applied to object A, F should be applied to all objects resembling object A. In the Twitter case, this should have applied to both race and gender. Had the process framework been applied, the representative sub-groups in race and gender would have questioned the input data used and ensured that the training data used was not imbalanced and represented all individuals adequately. The input and training data used would have been noted, discussed, critiqued, debated, and resolved before implementation. The logical-semantic rule requires that all parties to a discussion use the same words to mean the same thing, ensuring no differences in the input data applied to any of the available races or gender. This would have allowed for the output to be the same regardless of race or gender. Speakers are not allowed to contradict themselves and should remain consistent in their use of words. This would have required all involved parties to remain consistent in the rules used for the twitter algorithm for all races and gender.

In terms of the *procedural* rules, every stakeholder group may assert only what they believe and provide sufficient reason. This rule would have allowed respect of poorly represented sub-groups to air their concerns giving due and sufficient reason. The beliefs and concerns of the groups of people taken for granted in this case would have been taken into consideration.

One example of the *performative* rules is for all participants to have an equal opportunity to begin discourse at any time without any contradiction. This rule allows for a deeper discussion around the meanings behind any discourse, which can then be resolved. The process leads to a shared lifeworld where meanings are understood by different audiences and documented. All participants who are capable of contributing to a particular discussion, which in our case would have been the development of the Twitter algorithm, should have been allowed to participate, question any development, input or rules used, introduce their proposal on the algorithm, and express their wishes and desires regarding the output of the Twitter algorithm.

The three rules would have ensured that the Twitter algorithm is approved by at least a sample of all affected parties in their capacity as participants of the planning and development stages of the twitter algorithms. The algorithm would have been developed in conditions free from domination, and these would have assisted in avoiding the issues noted from the Twitter algorithm.

4   Discussion

The rush or focus on implementing AI to achieve higher efficiency is often at the expense of the negative consequences on society. Organisations typically wait until implementation is done and bias is picked up by the users affected by AI decisions before they investigate and try to mitigate bias, and by that time, it is already too late, and society has lost trust. Involving affected parties, stakeholders and developers in the development and implementation stages of AI and incorporating the logical-semantic, procedural, and performative rules during these stages is an important first step.

5   Possible Limitations and Solutions of the Process Framework

- Not all users whom the AI will affect can be involved in the development and implementation of AI - such a function can be crowdsourced.
- The process of involving certain sections of society cannot be automated but may be achieved manually – more time can be allocated to the development and implementation of AI. Sampled affected parties can be used.
- Involving society in the development and implementation can be time-consuming - some solutions involve doing online surveys and getting online inputs from sampled affected parties.

6   Conclusions

Involving society affected by AI algorithms, stakeholders, and developers and ensuring that they consider the logical-semantic, procedural, and performative rules during AI's development and implementation is the first step in avoiding the backlash or unconsidered AI algorithms in practice. The focus on fair processes would promote a domination free environment whereby any opportunity for bias in AI is debated before, during the development and after the implementation. The Habermas allows for the detection, debate, and resolution of bias.

References

1. Završnik, A.: Criminal justice, artificial intelligence systems, and human rights. ERA Forum **20**(4), 567–583 (2020). https://doi.org/10.1007/s12027-020-00602-0
2. Parsheera, S.: A gendered perspective on Artificial Intelligence. Mach. Learn. a 5G Fut. (ITU K). 1689–1699 (2018). https://doi.org/10.1017/CBO9781107415324.004
3. Zhang, Y., Zhou, L.: Fairness assessment for artificial intelligence in financial industry. arXiv preprint arXiv:1912.07211 (2019)
4. Collier, K.: Twitter's racist algorithm is also ageist, ableist and Islamaphobic, researchers find. https://www.nbcnews.com/tech/tech-news/twitters-racist-algorithm-also-ageist-ableist-islamaphobic-researchers-rcna1632. Accessed 24 Aug 2021
5. Michalos, A.C., Simon, H.A.: The Sciences of the Artificial. MIT Press, London (1996). https://doi.org/10.2307/3102825
6. Habermas, J.: The Theory of Communicative Action. Beacon Press, Boston (1984)
7. Limberg, T., Van der Heyden, L.: Why fairness matters. Int. Commer. Rev. **7**, 92–102 (2007). https://doi.org/10.1007/s12146-007-0015-z
8. InfoGovANZ: AI standards: from principles to implementation – InfoGovANZ. https://www.infogovanz.com/ai-ethics/ai-standards/. Accessed 28 Aug 2021
9. Farnadi, G., Babaki, B., Getoor, L.: Fairness in relational domains. In: AIES Proceedings of the 2018 AAAI/ACM Conference on AI, Ethics, and Society, pp. 108–114 (2018). https://doi.org/10.1145/3278721.3278733
10. Neuteleers, S., Mulder, M., Hindriks, F.: Assessing fairness of dynamic grid tariffs. Energy Policy **108**, 111–120 (2017). https://doi.org/10.1016/j.enpol.2017.05.028
11. IEEE: New IEEE Standards for artificial intelligence affecting human well-being. https://transmitter.ieee.org/new-ieee-standards-artificial-intelligence-affecting-human-well/. Accessed 28 Aug 2021
12. Hamilton, I.A.: Amazon built an AI tool to hire people, but reportedly had to shut it down because it was discriminating against women. https://www.businessinsider.co.za/amazon-built-ai-to-hire-people-discriminated-against-women-2018-10?r=US&IR=T. Accessed 27 Aug 2021
13. Murphy, N.: AI bias: Avoiding the bad, the biased and the unethical – Verdict. https://www.verdict.co.uk/ai-bias/. Accessed 27 Aug 2021
14. Larsen, L.: HireVue Assessments and Preventing Algorithmic Bias. https://www.hirevue.com/blog/hiring/hirevue-assessments-and-preventing-algorithmic-bias. Accessed 27 Aug 2021
15. Klein, H.K., Huynh, M.Q.: The critical social theory of Jürgen Habermas and its implications for IS research. In: Mingers, J., Willcocks, L.P. (eds.) Social Theory and Philosophy for Information Systems, pp. 157–237. Wiley, Hoboken (2004)
16. Habermas, J.: Moral Consciousness and Communicative Action: Moral Conciousness and Communicative Action (Studies in Contemporary German Social Thought) (1990)
17. Hanna, R., Kazim, E.: Philosophical foundations for digital ethics and AI ethics: a dignitarian approach. AI Ethics 1–19 (2021). https://doi.org/10.1007/s43681-021-00040-9
18. Beil, M., Proft, I., van Heerden, D., Sviri, S., van Heerden, P.V.: Ethical considerations about artificial intelligence for prognostication in intensive care. Intensive Care Med. Exp. **7**(1), 1–13 (2019). https://doi.org/10.1186/s40635-019-0286-6
19. Twinomurinzi, H., Schofield, A., Hagen, L., Ditsoane-Molefe, S., Tshidzumba, N.A.: Towards a shared worldview on e-skills: a discourse between government, industry and academia on the ICT skills paradox. South Afr. Comput. J. **29**, 215–237 (2017). https://doi.org/10.18489/sacj.v29i3.408
20. Habermas, J.: Communication and the Evolution of Society by Jurgen Habermas. Beacon Press, Boston (1979)

21. Habermas, J.: The Theory of Communicative Action, vol. 2. Beacon Press Books, Boston (1987)
22. Rehg, W.: Discourse ethics for computer ethics: a heuristic for engaged dialogical reflection. Ethics Inf. Technol. **17**(1), 27–39 (2014). https://doi.org/10.1007/s10676-014-9359-0
23. Hagendorff, T.: The ethics of AI ethics: an evaluation of guidelines. Mind. Mach. **30**(1), 99–120 (2020). https://doi.org/10.1007/s11023-020-09517-8

Author Index

Printed in the United States
by Baker & Taylor Publisher Services